CRISIS PREVENTION, CONFIDENCE BUILDING, AND RECONCILIATION IN SOUTH ASIA

CRISIS PREVENTION, CONFIDENCE BUILDING, AND RECONCILIATION IN SOUTH ASIA

Edited by

MICHAEL KREPON

AMIT SEVAK

Under the auspices of

Henry L. Stimson Center

MANOHAR

1996

ISBN 81–7304–144–X

First published 1996

Published by Ajay Kumar Jain for
MANOHAR PUBLISHERS & DISTRIBUTORS
2/6 Ansari Road, Daryaganj, New Delhi 110002
Phone: 3275162, Fax: 3265162

Printed at
Rajkamal Electric Press
G.T. Karnal Road, New Delhi 110033

CONTENTS

ACKNOWLEDGEMENTS

First of all, we are grateful to our chapter authors for their patience and hard work. Stimson Center Research Assistant Matthew C.J. Rudolph deserves special acknowledgement. He was instrumental in launching this book project, suggesting authors and subjects, and providing helpful comments on early drafts. He also assisted with the design of maps of Siachen, Kashmir, and Sir Creek, which were prepared by Philip Schwartzberg.

Jean Newsom and Keir Lieber worked wonders with the manuscript, helping with editing during the final phase of manuscript preparation. Many of our colleagues at the Stimson Center also pitched in. Our thanks go to Sony Devabhaktuni, Jane Dorsey, William Durch, Jill Junnola, Susan Kincade, Maureen Lenihan, Pamela Reed, Nihar Shah, Michael Wilkinson, and Christine Wormuth. Sincere thanks also go to our publishers: Michael Flamini and Alan Bradshaw at St. Martin's Press, Tim Farmiloe at Macmillan, Najam Sethi at Vanguard, and Ramesh Jain at Manohar. Formatting for the book was performed by ACME Art.

Last, but certainly not least, this book would not have been possible without the funders who have made the Stimson Center's work in South Asia possible. Special thanks go to David Hamburg and David C. Speedie III of the Carnegie Corporation of New York, George Perkovich of the W. Alton Jones Foundation, and Peter Goldmark and Thomas W. Graham of the Rockefeller Foundation for their generous support. Hilary Palmer was instrumental in the design and support of the Stimson Center's CBM program while working at the Rockefeller Brothers Fund.

Responsibility for the content of this book rests solely with the authors and editors, not with any of the individuals mentioned above.

PREFACE

Amit Sevak

Although the world has recently witnessed the end of the U.S.-Soviet rivalry, a Cold War continues in South Asia. The nearly fifty-year old rivalry between India and Pakistan has stood at the center of this broken region, like two brothers feuding over a piece of land torn by an earthquake long ago. With Europe, Latin America, and the Middle East now working to end major regional animosities that existed during the Cold War, the Subcontinent continues to lag far behind in the search for a more stable peace.

This book promotes various forms of cooperative measures in South Asia, ranging from conflict avoidance to confidence-building measures (CBMs). Perhaps best known for helping to defuse the Cold War conflict in Europe, CBMs have in recent years been implemented in a variety of other conflict-prone regions, but only to a limited extent in South Asia. The primary challenge in the Subcontinent at this point has become more modest: conflict avoidance and crisis prevention.

Broadly defined, CBMs are measures used to alleviate tensions between states. In the Norwegian statesman Johan Jorgen Holst's famous definition, CBMs are "arrangements designed to enhance . . . assurance of mind and belief in the trustworthiness of states and the facts they create."[1] CBMs are valuable in their own right; they need not be seen as precursors to formal arms control agreements. An initial purpose for these measures is to increase openness or "transparency" into the military activities of rival or potentially rival states.[2]

In recent years, the definition of CBMs has been extended beyond this limited arena. CBMs now include both formal and informal measures that prevent or reduce uncertainties among states. They can be unilateral, bilateral or multilateral in scope. CBMs can also be usefully extended beyond the military arena to include economic, diplomatic, social, and cultural measures that are meant to reduce tensions and build trust between states. For the purposes of this book, CBMs are viewed in this broader context.

Conflict-avoidance measures (CAMs) are essential precursors to CBMs. In South Asia, where enmity between India and Pakistan remains deep, the first order of business is to implement CAMs rather than CBMs. CAMs are useful for decreasing the likelihood of wars occurring as a result of misunderstanding or miscalculation. For instance, a requirement to provide prior notification of military maneuvers, especially along national borders, could serve to alleviate concerns over surprise attack. Failure to provide proper notification could warrant greater defensive preparations. Prior notification measures in no way diminish the need for accurate intelligence assessments, since maneuvers, properly notified, can still be used to mask preparations for war. Properly designed CAMs, however, can help officials distinguish between routine exercises and war preparations—particularly if pre-notified military exercises can be subject to close observation.

CAMs come in many different forms, although they are almost always related to military activities. Perhaps the most well known crisis prevention measure is the "hotline" that was instituted by the United States and the Soviet Union after the 1962 Cuban missile crisis. The hotline is essentially a communications device that allows the heads of state to exchange messages with each other. As a crisis management device, the hotline was intended to reduce the likelihood of accidents or misunderstandings escalating into a full-fledged war.

The hotline is only one of many possible CAMs. Exchanges of information on military equipment and force deployments, cooperative aerial inspections (as in the Open Skies Treaty), and crisis prevention centers can also be useful to prevent crises or unintended escalation.

Once CAMs have taken root and a political process of reconciliation has begun, CBMs can be more easily negotiated. Their form will, of course, vary with the unique circumstances of the region in question. The agreement between Brazil and Argentina to inspect one another's nuclear facilities is currently inconceivable in the Subcontinent. Likewise, CBMs related to economic and trade issues will require a sensitivity to the economic requirements and capabilities of relevant states.

CBMs can create habits of cooperation and patterns of communication between states that can lead, over time, to significant bilateral or multilateral cooperation. In the European context, CBMs in the Helsinki Final Act of 1975 mainly consisted of declarations. The Stockholm Document on Confidence and Security Building Measures of 1986 went further by requiring transparency in military exercises, including mandatory access by foreign observers.

In the East-West context, CBMs facilitated arms control agreements. In the Southern Cone of Latin America, greater transparency has not promoted an arms control process, as states in this region see little need for one. Each region follows its own path. In South Asia, the path to CBMs between India and Pakistan has yet to really begin; crisis prevention remains the first order of business. Relations between India and China are more promising, but the extent of their improvement remains conjectural.

The chapters of this volume cover a number of important areas ranging from crisis prevention to reconciliation in South Asia. Michael Krepon makes the case for more effective CAMs in this crisis-prone region, while seeking to explain why such measures have not taken root as yet. Sumit Ganguly examines the incentives and disincentives for regional CBMs offering specific proposals to strengthen existing measures and to devise new ones. Raja Mohan and Peter Lavoy identify some of the barriers impeding the creation of a nuclear arms control regime in the region and discuss how these barriers might be overcome. Pakistani physicist Pervez Hoodbhoy describes the "myths" and "realities" of the current nuclear confrontation between India and Pakistan, proposing recommendations for Pakistan's nuclear options.

Next, A.G. Noorani proposes suggestions to resolve the difficult Siachen Glacier, Sir Creek, and Wular Barrage disputes. Raju Thomas outlines reconciliation measures that might be adopted to minimize internal dissention and intrastate conflict in India, Pakistan, and Sri Lanka.

Arun Elhance and Moonis Ahmar argue that promoting long-term cooperation between India and Pakistan must entail cooperation in nonmilitary as well as traditional security issues. They offer suggestions for CBMs in areas such as water management and energy-sharing. Poonam Barua argues for the implementation of economic CBMs between India and Pakistan, including joint ventures and increased trade. Navnita Chadha examines how the Indian and Pakistani media have created powerful "enemy images" and what might be done to repair this damage.

The last two chapters address the current and future roles of CBMs between India and China. Kanti Bajpai and Bonnie Coe evaluate the incentives and disincentives for India and China to pursue additional CBMs as well as the role that Pakistan might play in Sino-Indian security discussions. Zhao Weiwen and Giri Deshingkar focus on Sino-Indian CBMs dealing with security, economic, and cultural relations and the thorny issues of Tibet and Pakistan.

The scope of this book is admittedly narrow. Missing are chapters directly addressing the relationship between India and its smaller neighbors. Much more could be said about the important relationship between China and Pakistan. Indeed, this book merely scratches the surface of the CAMs and the CBMs that could help the region address its military and nonmilitary concerns.

In bringing together in a single volume Indian, Pakistani, Chinese, and American authors, we have tried to give the chapters a cross-national perspective. Clearly, the catalyst to negotiate and properly implement CAMs and CBMs must come from within—not outside—the region. We hope this book encourages others in the region to delve more deeply into this field of inquiry, and that it provides further impetus for developing crisis prevention and reconciliation measures in the Subcontinent.

NOTES

1. Johan Jorgen Holst. "Confidence-building Measures: A Conceptual Framework," *Survival* 25, no. 1 (Jan/Feb 1993): 2-15.
2. Cathleen S. Fisher, "The Preconditions of Confidence-building: Lessons from the European Experience." *A Handbook of Confidence-building Measures for Regional Security Second Edition.* A Henry L. Stimson Center Publication, January 1995, 27.

1

A TIME OF TROUBLE, A TIME OF NEED

Michael Krepon

Relations between India and Pakistan are at a low ebb. Formal bilateral discussions on security matters have been stalled since early 1994 with Pakistani Prime Minister Benazir Bhutto's decision to suspend foreign secretary-level discussions on new conflict avoidance or confidence-building measures (CBMs). Government officials in Islamabad cite the need for improvement in India's treatment of Kashmir before discussions are resumed. Both governments are unhappy with the implementation of existing measures to reduce tensions and avoid unintended conflict; but, with bilateral channels of communication closed, the situation is unlikely to improve in the near-term.

Nor is there an agreed regional forum to discuss security concerns; India resists such a framework with a tenacity equal to Pakistan's reluctance to reopen bilateral channels of communication. The existing regional forum that might be employed for discussions of security issues—the South Asian Association for Regional Cooperation (SAARC)—is expressly excluded from doing so by its mandate. Meanwhile, the level of violence in Kashmir remains high, reinforcing hard-line positions in New Delhi and Islamabad.

Domestic politics in Pakistan has assumed a particularly fierce, unforgiving character. The opposition leader and former prime minister, Nawaz Sharif, has found it unacceptable for the incumbent to carry out the same exchanges on CBMs that he endorsed while in office. National politics within Pakistan appears trapped in a bitter contest between arch rivals. The struggle for power supersedes all; effective governance has become an afterthought.

Kashmir has long been the reason for conflict avoidance measures on the Subcontinent. In the current intractable state of Pakistani politics, it is also the reason not to engage in official dialogue on such matters. For Prime Minister Bhutto to acknowledge Indian steps removing New Delhi's heavy hand in Kashmir and to reopen bilateral discussions would be to invite a political firestorm fanned by the opposition. Pakistani media coverage of the Kashmir issue has hardly laid the groundwork for a change in government policy. It will take formidable leadership to engineer such a change, as the city streets of Pakistan, like those in India, have long been mobilized to fan tensions, not to relieve them.

Even with far-sighted and bold political leadership, Pakistan would be hard pressed to initiate gestures of reconciliation with India as long as Kashmir is on the boil. As the weaker party in the dispute, Islamabad has added reason to wait for New Delhi's example. India's Congress (I) Party leaders, however, seem deeply disinclined to initiate change in regional security policies. After all, there is no immediate or pressing reason to chart a new course, unlike the case for economic liberalization.

For New Delhi, the safest position on security matters is one that claims the moral high ground while allowing maximum freedom of maneuver. Thus the ardent embrace of global, nondiscriminatory solutions to security problems places the burden of action on others. Global change, however, is predicated on prior initiative at the personal, local, national, and regional level. By absenting itself until the end of this transformational process, India limits the constructive role it might otherwise play. Gandhi operated under a different philosophy, advising that "An ounce of practice is worth more than tons of preaching." But there are few Gandhis walking the earth today, and fewer still who aspire to high public office.

Indian Prime Minister P.V. Narasimha Rao is clearly cut from different cloth. He has demonstrated a surprising durability in office, but faces resurgent domestic opposition and a restive political base. Rao's natural tendency has been to respond to Pakistani grievances with studious indifference. Since any Congress (I) Party initiatives to soften Indo-Pakistani relations would surely become campaign ammunition for the opposition Bharatiya Janata Party (BJP), Rao's posture is well-grounded in domestic political realities. Provocations within Kashmir, Bombay, and elsewhere, which are universally presumed within India to be inspired by Pakistan's Inter-Services Intelligence Agency (ISI), have been met with armed might and police action. Rao's natural disinclination to take risks for normalized relations has no doubt been reinforced by the unlikely prospect of a favorable response to any such initiative by a besieged counterpart in Islamabad.

Thus, the prospects for small steps to minimize tensions, let alone to promote political reconciliation, are modest at best over the near-term. Indeed, the greater likelihood in the near-term is that Indo-Pakistani relations will continue to worsen, as exemplified by the closing in 1994 of the Indian consulate in Karachi and the Pakistani office in Bombay.

Tensions, Real and Scripted

One of the paradoxes of conflict avoidance and confidence-building measures is that precisely when they are most needed, they are most difficult to negotiate and implement properly. For these measures to be of greatest utility, they must be in place and working properly before tensions mount. Such conditions do not exist on the Subcontinent, where measures have been implemented begrudgingly, at best. Thus, there is no sound and reliable basis for India and Pakistan to defuse a surge in tension, especially when the Indian and Pakistani prime ministers have a poor working relationship or are in a weakened position at home. Under these circumstances, whatever steps to be employed in the event of another crisis will have to be ad hoc and may require third party involvement. India and Pakistan deserve better than this.

One does not need to look far afield for the makings of another ratcheting up of tension. Pakistan's lack of strategic depth and highly vulnerable lines of communication mandate a forward posture and high state of readiness for its ground forces. This in turn mandates prudent defense countermeasures by India. With the fourth and eighth largest land armies in the world facing each other, and with both sides having firepower less than one kilometer apart along the Line of Actual Control (LAC), every large-scale training exercise near the border is necessarily a cause for concern.

The absence of bilateral and regional channels of communication on security matters, the uneven implementation of existing CBMs, the poor personal chemistry between the prime ministers, and the constraints imposed by domestic politics in both countries provide sufficient kindling for new fires on the Subcontinent. The kindling can be lit by sparks from acts of terror and subversion, continued unrest in Kashmir, and the introduction of new missile systems capable of carrying weapons of mass destruction.

It does not take too much imagination to envision how fears, rumors, and provocations can conspire to increase tension significantly between India and Pakistan. Several scripts have already been written and enacted that could form the basis of another dramatic performance gaining international attention.

Act one might begin with an announcement that the Indian army is carrying out military exercises with armored units at the Mahajan training ground adjacent to the Rajasthan/Punjab border. But intelligence officers in Pakistan, notorious for their alarmism and troubled by the lack of proper advance notification, suspect that this may not be a routine training exercise. Some believe that New Delhi wishes to send Islamabad a message about continued interference in Kashmir. Their fears are reinforced by partial evidence suggesting unusual activities involving the use of railroads to support the "exercise."

As a precaution and to signal continued resoluteness in support of the Kashmiri struggle, Pakistani armored units assemble at the training area around Multan, only three hours away from the border. Indian intelligence, notorious for its excitability, believes that Pakistani units are equipped with ammunition and petrol far in excess of that required for a mere exercise.

Then, to be on the safe side or, perhaps, to make for more realistic military exercises, the Indian army commander practices tank crossings of the Indira Gandhi Canal. This, in turn, reinforces fears in Pakistani General Headquarters that the exercise masks hostile intent. To be on the safe side, Pakistani units are placed on a higher state of readiness and, to relieve pressure from the apparent Indian buildup on the border, the ISI or "non-governmental groups" step-up support for those seeking the separation of Kashmir from the Indian Union. Camps conspicuously reappear in Azad Kashmir to train freedom fighters. It is not clear whether the government in Islamabad is aware of, let alone in control of, the reestablishment of these camps.

These activities, in turn, generate formal protests and stern rhetoric from Indian government officials about the risks entailed by heightened support for terrorist activities across the LAC. Opposition leaders demand airstrikes against the camps and, at long last, an end to paramilitary operations against Indian territory.

By this time, our script is well into the third act. In response to hot rhetoric from New Delhi, the Pakistani prime minister travels to Muzaffarabad, declaring Pakistan's unending support for the beleaguered Muslim population of Kashmir. To which government officials in New Delhi join opposition leaders in publicly surmising that it might be time to teach Islamabad a lesson about the dangers of fomenting secessionist movements.

With street demonstrations throughout Pakistan led by opposition leaders now a daily occurrence, the prime minister declares that Pakistan will never cower before Indian threats and that the country is able and willing to respond at whatever level necessary to defend national honor. India responds by moving Prithvi missiles from recessed to overt deployments, actions reported under banner headlines in the Indian press.

At this point, the Pakistani media blares unconfirmed reports, believed to be reliable in some intelligence circles, that India has brandished nuclear weapons against Pakistan. The government responds by deploying Hatf missiles and by moving strike aircraft to forward operating bases. There are also unconfirmed reports that M-11 missiles have been moved from secured storage into the field. In Washington, key members of Congress call for the imposition of sanctions on Pakistan for having violated the Missile Technology Control Regime. The U.S. embassy in Islamabad is stormed and partially damaged by angry mobs.

Pakistani missile deployments and the movement of strike aircraft to satellite bases generate wild reports in the Indian press about hostile preparations for a nuclear attack. Opposition leaders and eminent commentators call for pre-emptive action. The United Nations secretary general offers to play a mediating role, but is rejected by India. The United States offers its services, but is rejected by Pakistan. Acts four and five are left to the imagination of the reader.

Granted, the aforementioned scenario is unduly alarmist, even though it is drawn in part from the 1986-87 Brasstacks exercise and the 1990 crisis. Large-scale military exercises along the Indo-Pakistani border, like those placing both countries on the brink during Brasstacks, hopefully are a thing of the past. Most important, New Delhi and Islamabad do not want to have a fourth war, and leaders in both capitals can be expected to try to avoid one—just as they did during the 1990 crisis.

Nonetheless, this troubling script is worth pondering in a region prone to mishaps. Sometimes the momentum of events during crises controls leaders, rather than the other way around. Simple prudence requires that attention be paid to worst cases. The smoldering resentments of two generations on the Subcontinent have not been doused. Many in both India and Pakistan are eager to pour kerosene on them. The geography of conflict within the region will not change, which places the Indian and Pakistani armies at close quarters, while Kashmir remains an open sore. In these circumstances, no harm can come from taking steps to make highly damaging scenarios increasingly remote. Indeed, there is much to gain for both India and Pakistan in doing so.

The Instability of Nuclear Deterrence

Some strategic analysts and retired senior military officers in India and Pakistan argue that offsetting nuclear capabilities will provide needed stability to South Asia. In this view, it is better to rely on overt nuclear deterrence than on mere shadow play. A few Western analysts have also adopted this view, noting that offsetting nuclear capabilities kept the Cold War from becoming hot and might serve a similar purpose on the Subcontinent.

It is odd that South Asian strategists who have long rejected the imposition of alien Western constructs should warmly embrace the concept of nuclear deterrence developed at the RAND Corporation and other redoubts of U.S. "Cold Warriors." In truth, the Cold War history of nuclear deterrence was far from stable. Instead, it is replete with close calls and near misses. A few of the horror stories or crises that nearly developed have been revealed—especially those surrounding the Cuban missile crisis—and more will come to light as U.S. and Soviet archives are opened. The principal culprits usually have been technical snafus, weak command and control procedures, and faulty intelligence assessments.

The first decade of overt, offsetting nuclear capabilities between the United States and the Soviet Union—and between the Soviet Union and China—were particularly hair-raising. This should come as no surprise, since nuclear equations are most unsettled and tension-producing at the outset of any such pairing. Invariably, tense relations immediately become more tense when the destructive power of nuclear weapons is added to the equation.

Over several decades, offsetting nuclear capabilities can theoretically provide the basis for normalized relations. This did not occur, however, in the U.S.-Soviet case, where new developments related to nuclear weapons repeatedly set back the process of normalization. Long after the point when nuclear deterrence should have helped ameliorate fears, the domestic politics of the United States and the Soviet Union were dominated by paranoia, fueled in part by new variations of overkill.

Even during the 1970s and 1980s, both countries continued to experience brushes with nuclear disaster, despite highly evolved command and control procedures. Far-sighted political leadership, not nuclear deterrence, broke the back of the Cold War. True normalization came with the odd juxtaposition of Mikhail Gorbachev and Ronald Reagan, leaders who utterly rejected traditional Cold War valuations of nuclear weapons. Then, of course, an entirely new set of nuclear dangers emerged, centered on the safe and secure dismantling of bloated stockpiles.

It will take time and considerable research for the full picture of these near-nuclear disasters to be revealed. Such cautionary tales need to be exposed to move discussions about nuclear deterrence away from presumed cultural biases. The message of nuclear danger from Western analysts should not be construed as patronizing; at issue is not whether the "volatile" brown man is more prone to self-immolating behavior than the "rational" white man. White men nearly blew themselves up time and again, despite the "stabilizing" presence of nuclear weapons.

Surely, India and Pakistan will not engage in arms racing of deplorable Cold War proportions. Even engaging in nuclear deployments at a small scale, however, invites multiple dangers. If serious tensions exist between states, they will clearly not be ameliorated by nuclear weapons, regardless of the race, color, or creed of their possessors. The central paradox of offsetting nuclear deployments is that while they may prevent war, they will also increase tensions in any crisis.

The recent history of South Asia—with two nerve-wracking crises during a period when there may have been "offsetting" nuclear weapon capabilities—provides scant testament to the stabilizing role of nuclear deterrence. To be sure, one can take comfort that the crises in 1986-87 and 1990 did not lead to wars and that crisis escalation was contained. Still, no responsible political or military leader in South Asia can be sanguine about this recent track record. To the contrary, recent history cries out for stronger CBMs.

Confidence-building Measures: Barriers and Prospects

The principal reasons why CBMs have not taken root in South Asia relate directly to the hard issues in dispute between India and Pakistan and the ill-will they have engendered—especially Kashmir. There are more subtle reasons, as well, that make such measures even harder to achieve. CBMs, for example, operate on a premise directly contrary to the predominant culture of adversarial politics found between India and Pakistan. In this bitter domain, any step that benefits an adversary must necessarily be bad for the home side. It is remarkable how deeply rooted this "zero-sum" perspective has become for two nations that just two generations ago were united under a central government.

Another reason why CBMs have not been accepted is that they are viewed as a foreign import. CBMs appear to be an outgrowth of the Cold War, as they were most deeply developed and successful in ameliorating conflict in Europe between NATO and the Warsaw Pact. As a result, they are naturally suspect. The India-Pakistan military exercise and airspace agreements were negotiated after the 1990 crisis at the urging of the United States. These conflict avoidance measures appear to have been accepted not so much for their intrinsic merit, but because they would do little harm while satisfying well-meaning outsiders and aid donors.

These "cultural" impediments to proper CBM implementation make difficult problems like the Kashmir dispute even harder to resolve. In Europe, the Middle East, and Latin America, the letter and spirit of agreements are usually honored. In South Asia, there is no cordial spirit to existing agreements, and the letter is often broken, as well. Existing measures have become another means of expression for adversarial politics.

In contrast, U.S. and Soviet military officers took pride in maintaining highly professional and proper implementation of CBMs—even when political relations were abysmal. Once during the Reagan administration, after a U.S. military officer was shot in East Germany by a Soviet sentry, Secretary of Defense Caspar Weinberger wished to cancel a regularly scheduled meeting between U.S. and Soviet naval officers implementing the Incidents at Sea Agreement. He was overruled, much to the satisfaction of military leaders opposed to politicizing their CBM channels of contact. Israeli and Egyptian CBM implementation was similarly correct during their "cold peace."

South Asia follows a far different pattern. Interviews with active-duty military officers in India and Pakistan responsible for the implementation of existing CBMs invariably produce comparable complaints: reasons are found not to provide prior notification of military exercises, and the air space agreement is regularly violated. When asked why he did not raise concerns over compliance, one Director General of Military Operations—the transmission channel for CBM notifications—replied that to do so would only provide more satisfaction to his opposite number than to himself. Demanding proper implementation of CBMs between India and Pakistan is viewed by many military officials as a belittling and fruitless exercise.

Unless there is a greater sense of ownership for existing CBMs and some relief from the culture of adversarial politics, South Asia will continue to lag well behind other regions that have normalized long-adversarial relations. Change is possible with the recognition that, despite all of their heartfelt grievances, India and Pakistan have a strong mutual interest in avoiding war and unintended escalation. The dispute over Kashmir makes such work more difficult to carry out, but more necessary as well.

Creative ways must be found to surmount domestic political constraints in India and Pakistan to re-establishing channels of communication on security issues. For both countries, to do so requires reconsideration of positions that serve short-term political purposes, but at the expense of long-term national security gains. Significant progress in reducing tensions is unlikely unless Islamabad reassesses its firm opposition to the resumption of bilateral discussions with India and unless New Delhi reassesses its steadfast resistance to regional talks.

This is not a time for India and Pakistan to exchange military bands or to conduct joint mountaineering expeditions. It is a time, however, to strengthen measures to avoid unwanted conflict and unintended escalation. Fundamental issues of national security need to be placed above partisan politics. If Pakistan's generals take a renewed interest in conflict avoidance measures, bilateral channels of communication can be reopened. India can help in this process by signaling its intention to propose an agenda for discussion that clearly serves the security interests of both states, while repeating its willingness to discuss the Kashmir issue.

It would be easier to reopen bilateral channels if New Delhi could see the value of regional security discussions. India is concerned that a regional forum will become an unwanted source of outside pressure. In actuality, Pakistan has greater reason than India to fear isolation at this time, given Islamabad's uncertain course and India's much improved ties with China and the United States. A regional forum must therefore operate by consensus to alleviate the concerns of any individual state over outside pressure.

China's economic growth and military potential are not simply India's concern. Consequently, a discussion of regional security issues in which China is constructively engaged can be important for all states in the region, especially when Beijing is undergoing a transition in leadership. Moreover, those in Pakistan who feel estranged from the United States may increase the possibility of erratic behavior in Islamabad. A regional dialogue can therefore be important to engage Pakistan in constructive ties with its neighbors. Far from being a threat to India's security, a regional security forum that engages both of India's neighbors of greatest concern will bring substantial gains. Since the deliberations could clearly advance India's desire to discuss global issues, New Delhi might usefully reconsider its position.

Bilateral and regional channels can obviously be employed to advance conflict avoidance and confidence-building measures. India and Pakistan would be wise to take these measures more seriously—not as a favor to the United States, Germany, or Japan, but as a favor to themselves. The leadership will have to take greater responsibility for existing measures, and ensure their proper implementation in deed and in spirit. Both India and Pakistan might also be well served by considering new measures that serve mutual national security interests, despite lingering grievances. As the essays that follow suggest, there is no shortage of good ideas for CBMs within the region. For progress to be realized, the Subcontinent must be blessed with political leadership equal to the region's promise and problems.

2

MENDING FENCES

Sumit Ganguly

The end of the Cold War has seen both the dampening of certain regional conflicts and the resurgence of violence in other areas. The principal conflict in South Asia, that between India and Pakistan, was not an artifact of the Cold War. Its historical roots are indigenous. They can be traced to competing visions of nationbuilding and to British colonial disengagement policies. Consequently, the end of the Cold War has had a limited impact on the central conflict in the region. Fitful progress, however, has been made toward the resolution of the other major interstate conflict in the region, the Sino-Indian border dispute. The collapse of the Soviet Union, in large part, made this possible: New Delhi could no longer rely on the successor state, Russia, for unequivocal support in the event of a future conflict with China.

The deterioration in Indo-Pakistani relations, on the other hand, stems from the recrudescence of ethnic violence in Kashmir, Punjab, and Sindh. Tensions between India and Pakistan remain high as the two parties continue to exchange accusations about each other's involvement in Kashmir and Sindh. In the mid-1990s the political configurations in both India and Pakistan make it exceedingly difficult to tackle the underlying sources of conflict. Consequently, to prevent possible escalation through a combination of misperception, miscalculation and inadvertence, it is in the interest of both parties to pursue confidence-building measures (CBMs).

Various measures resembling CBMs, both institutionalized and informal, have existed in South Asia since 1946. The very first CBM-like structure was the existence of the Joint Defence Council (JDC). This organization, chaired by the last British Viceroy, Lord Louis Mountbatten, had been created for a variety of purposes in 1946 just prior to partition and the independence of India and Pakistan. Among other matters, the JDC presided over the division of military assets between the two nascent states. The JDC, under Mountbatten's tutelage, continued to function as late as 1948. As the Indian and Pakistani armies were commanded by British military officers, General Sir Rob Lockhart and General Sir Frank Messervy, respectively, Mountbatten was able to communicate with both sides even after the first war over Kashmir broke out in October 1947. In effect, the JDC served as an informal "hotline" between Prime Minister Jawaharlal Nehru and Governor-General Mohammed Ali Jinnah.[1]

The common British legacy of the two armed forces also enabled the pursuit of CBM-like arrangements during the 1965 and 1971 wars. A border dispute and subsequent skirmishes in the Rann of Kutch, in the western Indian state of Gujarat, had preceded the 1965 war in Kashmir. As the hostilities in the Kutch escalated, the chief of the Indian air force, Air-Marshal Arjan Singh, called up his Pakistani counterpart, Air Marshal Asghar Khan, and reached an informal agreement not to use their respective air forces in the open, desert-like area of the Rann of Kutch. They both reasoned that infantry without natural cover and without mechanized armor would be acutely vulnerable to strafing from the air. Both sides honored this arrangement throughout the three-month-long skirmishes.

A similar agreement led to a "city avoidance" strategy once war broke out in September 1965.[2] Both sides carefully refrained from bombing each other's population centers. Also, both sides adhered to a tacit agreement not to bomb dams and irrigation facilities. Although no explicit arrangements were made prior to the 1971 war, they had virtually assumed the stature of informal norms. Despite the significance of the stakes involved in the 1971 war, neither side breached the previous arrangements.[3]

Recent Experience with CBMs in South Asia

In all likelihood, the most recent attempts at formal and institutionalized CBMs stemmed from external prodding. Specifically, it is believed that during a trip to the Subcontinent in June 1990, U.S. Deputy National Security Adviser Robert Gates suggested that India and Pakistan consider measures that would limit the possibility of inadvertent war.[4] Some reports suggest that tensions between India and Pakistan over the Indian suppression of an insurgency in the Indian-held portion of Kashmir had led to a Pakistani nuclear alert.[5] American fears of unintended nuclear escalation prompted Gates' trip to Islamabad and New Delhi.

Even prior to Gates' trip, CBMs were already on the agenda of both states. For example, a hotline had already been instituted between the foreign secretaries of India and Pakistan in 1987. This development followed a similar spiral of misperception and hostility in the wake of India's largest peacetime military exercise, "Brasstacks," in 1987.[6] Later, in December 1988, Prime Minister Benazir Bhutto and Prime Minister Rajiv Gandhi signed an accord that prohibited attacks on each other's nuclear facilities. In 1989, India and Pakistan also signed another accord on border-related problems. Under the terms of this accord, the director-general (DG) of the Pakistan Rangers and the inspector-general (IG) of the Indian Border Security Force (BSF) agreed to meet bi-annually to review such issues as cross-border terrorism, drug-trafficking, smuggling, and illicit border crossings.

The 1990 "war scare," along with U.S. prodding, provided sufficient impetus for both sides to broaden the CBM agenda. Among other matters, it set in motion a series of meetings between India and Pakistan at the foreign secretary level. At the first meeting, held in July 1990, the Indian side suggested the creation of a broad band of CBMs. At the military level, CBMs would include such efforts as information sharing about military exercises, improving communications among military commanders, joint border patrolling, and the exchanges of delegations from the armed forces. The proposals for CBMs also included measures that could be enacted at the political level, such as the ending of hostile propaganda and the avoidance of interference in each other's internal affairs. Later, in the third round of talks in December 1990, it was agreed that the director general of military operations of both sides would converse on a weekly basis over a "hotline." At the fourth round, two key measures were enacted. The first involved providing advance notice of military exercises, maneuvers and troop movements. The other dealt with the violation of air space and permission for overflights and landings of military aircraft. The agreements were ratified in the sixth round. On January 1, 1992, the two sides exchanged the lists of nuclear installations that were safeguarded under the agreement.

Meetings continued at the foreign secretary level until January 1994 when Pakistan suspended further talks, citing India's misbehavior in Kashmir. Prior to the suspension, the two sides had agreed on a code of conduct for diplomatic personnel. The agreement reaffirmed the status of diplomatic personnel in each other's countries and guaranteed freedom from harassment.[7]

Incentives for CBMs

Both India and Pakistan have a number of compelling incentives to pursue CBMs. First, as the episodes of 1987 and 1990 amply demonstrated, the region is fraught with the possibility of misperception and inadvertent conflict. The danger of an escalatory spiral has increased as India and Pakistan have both adopted preemptive military strategies.[8] Although CBMs would not address the underlying sources of conflict between India and Pakistan, they could nevertheless reduce the likelihood of an unintended drift to war.

Second, both sides are engaged in major economic restructuring programs. The pursuit of a CBM regime may well enable them to reduce defense expenditures and divert them toward more productive ends. These economic pressures are not merely internally generated. Bilateral and multilateral aid donors are increasingly willing to put pressure on both sides to curb their defense expenditures.

Third, the region is experiencing a surge of ethno-religious fervor. CBMs may not have any direct effect on curbing such trends, but a CBM regime that limits hostile propaganda, promotes greater people-to-people contacts, and allows freer information flows may help to correct deliberately distorted images of adversaries.

Finally, a CBM regime between India and Pakistan may be a notion whose time has simply come. Academics, bureaucrats, and even military personnel on both sides are in the process of forming an incipient "epistemic community."[9] The formation of such a community facilitates discourse on a subject because the members of such a community share an intersubjective consensus about certain concepts, ideas, and terms. As more individuals in positions of authority understand and accept the concept of CBMs, it may well become possible to give a CBM regime political legitimacy.

Disincentives for CBMs

While compelling reasons for CBMs in South Asia exist, the political and bureaucratic military elites in both countries can inevitably make equally cogent arguments for refusing to pursue them. First, the Indian government finds itself in a virtual state of siege at home. A legion of troubles confronts the Indian polity. Among other matters, the nation's very identity as a secular state is under attack from the rising strength of the Bharatiya Janata Party (BJP), which is riding a tide of Hindu fanaticism. Moreover, an ambitious program of economic restructuring is under way. Finally, India is coping with an insurgency of unparalleled proportions in the critical border state of Kashmir. Under such conditions, no Indian government can muster much energy or imagination to pursue a set of complex negotiations with its principal adversary, Pakistan.

A similar argument can be made for Pakistan. In fact, the Pakistani government has even more compelling reasons to avoid the pursuit of CBMs. Given India's aforementioned troubles, there is no real inducement to alleviate Indian anxieties. Furthermore, the ability of the Pakistani leadership to take strong action is currently limited by the hostile relations between the prime minister, Benazir Bhutto, and Nawaz Sharif, who are locked in a bitter struggle for power.

Second, in addition to myriad problems facing the Indian state, significant constituencies within the government would most likely be hostile to a CBM regime. To begin with, India's intelligence services, particularly the powerful Research and Analysis Wing (RAW), would look askance at CBMs. Greater transparency in military budgets, better knowledge of each other's defense doctrines, and an improved political climate all would help to undermine RAW's shadowy existence. Similarly, Pakistan's Inter-Services Intelligence Agency (ISI) has an equal, if not more urgent, interest in undermining greater contact and openness between the two countries, whether at military, political or cultural levels.

Preconditions for CBMs

What are the preconditions for expanding the existing set of CBMs in South Asia?[10] First, both regimes in India and Pakistan will need to acquire a greater degree of political stability. Any Indian leader must fight fires on several domestic fronts. Under these conditions it is extraordinarily difficult to devote serious attention to an issue that largely concerns India's "attentive public."[11] In Pakistan, the situation is even more fluid, as its leaders struggle with the problems of domestic unrest, democratic consolidation, and civil-military relations. The long periods of military rule in Pakistan have not made its transition to democracy easy. As the fitful process of democratic consolidation takes place, no regime will be willing to expend significant political capital to launch meaningful initiatives on the CBM front with India.

Second, the relevant political and military bureaucracies on both sides have to be convinced of the utility of CBMs. They must come to the realization that such measures are not simply attempts to appease the international community and more particularly the United States. In effect, the bureaucratic players must see that the pursuit of such measures is in their self-interest.

Third, the international community has to learn to rely more on encouragement and incentives than on pressure. Pressure, particularly in the form of sanctions, is likely to have counterproductive effects; both countries, especially India, have self-images of autonomy and hard-won freedom of action in international affairs. Consequently, though sanctions may hurt either country, in the end they will lead only to a hardening of positions.

Prospects for CBMs

Should efforts to promote CBMs in South Asia focus on the bilateral Indo-Pakistani relationship, or should they include China in a trilateral forum? Pakistan and China are likely to see significant advantages to a trilateral forum. They have long had good relations with each other, share border problems with India, and would derive mutual gains from more transparent force structures along India's two fronts. For these very reasons, and the accompanying fear of Sino-Pakistani collusion, India is unlikely to agree to such a trilateral arrangement.[12]

An expansion of the current bilateral CBM regime between India and Pakistan will probably not have much effect on the Sino-Indian negotiating process. The Chinese interest in pursuing a CBM regime with India stems from other sources independent of Indo-Pakistani relations. Three probable sources can be identified. First, the Chinese are interested in creating conditions favorable for the settlement of the long-standing border dispute with India. A robust CBM regime could well contribute toward that end.

Second, the Chinese may have an intrinsic interest in CBMs. As recently as 1986, skirmishes took place between Indian and Chinese forces at Sumdurong Chu near the India-Nepal-Bhutan trijunction. Later in 1987, a substantial Indian military exercise, Checkerboard, held in the border state of Arunachal Pradesh, provoked Chinese misgivings. Subsequently, the two sides agreed to pursue a series of CBMs to prevent inadvertent escalation along the border.[13]

Third, a CBM regime along the Sino-Indian border would reassure the Chinese about India's continued restraint on the Tibetan issue, on which the Chinese have repeatedly sought Indian assurances. During a state visit to China in 1988, Prime Minister Rajiv Gandhi was repeatedly pressed by his hosts to assert publicly India's position on the status of Tibet. Despite reservations within the Indian diplomatic delegation, Rajiv Gandhi openly reassured his hosts that India believed that the status of Tibet was an internal affair of China.[14] Prime Minister Narasimha Rao reiterated the same position when his counterpart, Li Peng, visited New Delhi in December 1991. Furthermore, despite criticism from India's civil libertarians, the Indian government dealt harshly with Tibetans who sought to demonstrate in New Delhi during Li Peng's visit.[15]

Negotiations between India and China do affect Pakistani calculations about negotiations with India. The more India can stabilize the Sino-Indian border, the more it can divert military resources elsewhere as needed. Thus, owing to an agreement to draw down troops along the Himalayan border, India has reportedly been able to move as many as three mountain divisions and deploy them in Kashmir.[16] Furthermore, if the CBMs help contribute to an overall improvement in Sino-Indian relations, at some later moment India may be able to use its influence with China to obtain concessions from Pakistan on bilateral issues. Consequently, the slow but steady improvement in Sino-Indian relations could prompt Pakistan to improve its relations with India.

Expanding the Indo-Pakistani CBM Regime

India and Pakistan can undertake CBMs ranging, for example, across security, political, economic and humanitarian issues. In the security realm, a number of feasible measures might be proposed. Both sides could agree to exchange military data, which has thus far been shrouded in secrecy. The exchange of military data could initially focus on more innocuous matters such as overall force levels and capabilities. Later, they could be made more specific and dwell on the strengths of particular formations.

Taking even these steps would not be easy, however. Two objections would have to be dealt with: both sides would be suspicious of the possibilities of providing incorrect data, and knowledge of force levels could be turned into significant military advantages. Surmounting these objections may necessitate such corollary steps as an agreement to permit mutual or third-party inspections at short notice to verify data. The provision of mutual or third-party inspections, though difficult to negotiate, would go a long way to alleviate the possible objections that the data exchanges might raise.

Both sides could agree to remove their regular forces and leave the Indian border security forces and the Pakistani Rangers to patrol the border. Both sides maintain considerable numbers of regular forces within a short distance of the border for possible operations. This CBM is likely to raise objections in Pakistan because of its lack of geographical depth, which limits the extent to which Pakistani forces can move from the border. To address this problem, India might agree to proportionately move its forces back further.

Both sides could put into effect an existing proposal to exchange military staffs to discuss mutual threat perceptions, strategies, and options. For example, a regular exchange of military personnel could be arranged between the Pakistani Command and Staff College at Quetta and the Indian Command and Staff College at Conoor. Such exchanges would enable the military staffs of both sides to develop a better appreciation of each other's threat perceptions and strategies.

An agreement already exists on the prenotification of military exercises, which might be effectively bolstered. Both sides could agree that all military exercises along the Rajasthan-Punjab border would have military observers from the other side. Such an agreement would significantly allay possible fears of a surprise attack under the guise of a military exercise.

The above list is hardly exhaustive, but it includes some of the more effective measures that can be adopted without enormous expenditure of political capital in either India and Pakistan. They would also contribute in important ways to providing crisis stability.

Another possible CBM might involve a commitment not to engage in the training, arming, and the providing of sanctuaries for secessionist insurgents. There is little question about Pakistan's involvement in Punjab and Kashmir. Similarly, there has been evidence of Indian involvement in Sind and Baluchistan. Despite the obvious temptation to fish in these troubled waters, both sides need to put an end to such support. Actions undertaken by one inevitably invites retaliation and counter-retaliation. One could, in fact, argue that this CBM might well be an effective precursor to the others spelled out above.

Diplomatic CBMs. A number of political-level CBMs could be adopted to reinforce security-related measures. One of the more effective ways of proceeding in this arena might be to expand on and deepen existing agreements. In 1992, in the wake of a series of incidents, the two parties signed an agreement on a code of conduct concerning diplomatic personnel. The code needs to be strengthened and better enforced.

One example will suffice. In the wake of the mob violence that led to the destruction of the Babri Mosque on December 6, 1992, Pakistani mobs attacked the Indian consulate premises in Karachi, ransacking an entire floor and injuring several diplomatic personnel. The Pakistani government appeared to have made little effort to prevent the attack. Shortly after the episode, Pakistan asked India to reduce substantially its diplomatic and consular staff in Karachi. The Indian government promptly retaliated with a similar action in Bombay. Given the ethnically intertwined nature of the two societies, there is little question that Hindu-Muslim tensions within India generate considerable passion within Pakistan. It would have been entirely appropriate for the Pakistani government to have lodged a strong protest with India condemning the destruction of the mosque. The Pakistani government's passive stance during the attack on the Indian consulate further strained relations between the two countries.

Another compelling action needs to be taken. Both sides should restrain their respective intelligence services from pursuing covert and parallel diplomacy. Although difficult to document, it has long been alleged in the region that Pakistan's intelligence agency has been involved in aiding and abetting the insurgents in Punjab and Kashmir. Similar allegations have been leveled at India's intelligence agency about its involvement in Sind and Baluchistan. It appears increasingly unclear whether or not these entities are under the firm control of their respective governments.[17] To the extent possible, both nations need to rein in the activities of these organizations by gradually limiting them to intelligence gathering. Continued failure to do so will undermine diplomatic efforts to improve relations at any level.

Again, this will not be an easy task. Yet some possible means could be identified for signaling mutually benign intentions. India could offer Pakistan assistance in curbing drug smuggling and could even offer to share police and intelligence data. Similarly, Pakistan could agree to tighten the Punjab border and hand over any known Sikh terrorists to Indian authorities. Gestures like these could serve as useful first steps.

Information CBMs. Declaratory joint statements to limit hostile propaganda, dating back to October 23, 1959,[18] need firm enforcement. A substantial body of international relations literature argues that distorted images are an important contributory factor to hostility and conflict.[19] Limiting hostile propaganda from both sides of the border would have salutary effects on popular images. A joint Indo-Pakistani commission of well-known journalists and political commentators could meet at periodic intervals to discuss and exchange views on this subject.

In addition to containing hostile propaganda, both sides could permit and indeed promote scholarly exchanges. It is extraordinarily difficult for Indian and Pakistani scholars to obtain access to each other's countries. Visas and requests for visits are routinely denied. Consequently, much scholarship is heavily slanted because of inadequate access to information, documents, and direct contacts. Furthermore, most Indian scholarship on Pakistan (and vice-versa) remains in the service of the state. It is in the interest of both sides to develop independent and autonomous sources of information about each other's societies. Such a paucity of informed and dispassionate analysis prevents either side from discarding long-held and obsolete images of each other. Moreover, the lack of accurate information stifles useful debate in both societies and limits policy choices.

The availability of dispassionate information is also limited in other ways. Neither India nor Pakistan permit the free exchange of newspapers, magazines, and news programs. Ready access to information from the other side of the border would enable both sides to develop a better appreciation of how issues of common interest are perceived and discussed.

Economic CBMs. Two compelling reasons have hampered economic cooperation between India and Pakistan. First, owing to a relationship of largely unremitting hostility, neither side has been willing to utilize any existing complementarity in their industries. For example, Pakistan's excellent and sizable cotton crop could be used in the Indian cotton mills of Ahmedabad and Bombay. Similarly, Pakistan buys little tea from India despite lower prices, transportation costs, and better quality.[20] Neither side is willing to develop such cooperative arrangements for fear of being exploited in the event of a downturn in relations. Second, protectionist sentiments in Pakistan have also hobbled the growth of Indo-Pakistani trade. Economic cooperation cannot dramatically increase in the absence of significant political initiatives. However small, incremental steps in the economic arena may help develop constituencies on both sides that would pressure their respective governments to make further concessions.

Humanitarian Issues

Humanitarian measures are another area in which CBMs would make an important contribution to improving Indo-Pakistan relations. Despite the deeply conflictual relationship that has characterized these two states, their destinies as well as their peoples remain intertwined. Indians and Pakistanis have substantial numbers of family members in the other state. Despite many other differences, both sides can readily agree that contact between families is far too restricted because of stringent travel regulations. Nonetheless, both governments have been extremely myopic in not facilitating family contacts and easing travel restrictions. When pressed on the subject, officials routinely blame the other side for failing to ease travel restrictions. Ideally, a reciprocal arrangement that would substantially reduce travel barriers could be put into effect. India, as the larger state in the region and with a far better record of democratic processes, could take the initiative in this regard. Although difficult considering the strained political circumstances, New Delhi might consider providing regular, if controlled, access to the most significant Muslim shrines in India.[21] As a demonstration of Indian goodwill, this gesture could be made on a unilateral basis.[22]

The Question of Verification

The vast majority of the CBMs proposed here, with the exception of security-related measures, do not need verification. Their very nature would render them transparent. The security-related measures do call for a degree of verification. It is virtually predictable, however, that at least India would not agree to external sources of verification. India's bitter experience with the United Nations Security Council's handling of the Kashmir question during the early years of the Cold War generated a deep-seated aversion to external involvement in the resolution of bilateral disputes with Pakistan. Indian concerns about third-party involvement notwithstanding, external actors can still play useful, non-intrusive roles.

Which state or third party might be able to play such a role? China would be acceptable to Pakistan, but not to India. Moreover, the Chinese lack adequate technical capabilities or experience for carrying out such activities. Japan would be acceptable to both India and Pakistan, but do not have the technical requirements for the task. Russia may be acceptable to both India and Pakistan. Moscow also possesses the requisite technical means for verification. Russia's severe domestic problems and its apparent lack of interest in South Asia makes it a less than serious candidate. In effect, this leaves the United States as the only meaningful choice. The United States has the requisite capabilities, both material and political, to play such a role. It has played a similar and effective role in the Middle East. Washington might offer to provide satellite or aerial reconnaissance data verifying troop and armor dispositions to both India and Pakistan. Such an offer would reassure both sides about the reliability of commitments undertaken under "thin out" or demilitarized zones. The United States could also provide other forms of technical assistance, including trained observers for verification of exercises. In this way, the considerable experience gathered in the European context during the Cold War years could have some fruitful applications to South Asia.

Conclusion

The prospective benefits from an explicit CBM regime between India and Pakistan far outweigh the disadvantages. Both India and Pakistan can ill-afford to continue their current level of defense expenditures. Quite apart from the opportunity costs that such expenditures represent in two poor countries, external pressures to curb defense spending are mounting. The forging of a CBM regime may be a precursor for conventional arms control in the region. Minimally, it could provide a basis for *de facto* arms control.

Apart from the economic argument, there are sound political and military reasons at this juncture for the pursuit of a CBM regime. Despite the domestic difficulties that both governments face, they have compelling incentives to avoid inadvertent war. Continued tensions in Kashmir or the introduction of new missile systems could plunge the two nations into yet another conflict, which could well have disastrous consequences. Apart from the considerable material losses, a conflict would boost the disintegrative tendencies that plague the entire Subcontinent.

CBMs are not a panacea for the myriad problems that face India and Pakistan. They do offer, however, a politically feasible and effective way to alleviate continued tensions and may provide political space for addressing the underlying issues that have long driven Indo-Pakistani hostility.

NOTES

1. On the functioning of the JDC see Alan-Campbell Johnson, *Mission With Mountbatten.* (London: Robert Hale, 1951). For its limitations in the first Kashmir war, see Lieutenant General Lionel Protip Sen, *Slender Was the Thread* (New Delhi: Orient Longman, 1988).
2. On this point see Air-Marshal Asghar Khan, *The First Round* (New Delhi: Vikas, 1975).
3. Some may object to the use of the term "informal norms." Realists would argue that Pakistan was deterred from bombing Indian cities because India quickly asserted air superiority. India, in turn, it could be argued, was inhibited from attacking West Pakistani cities for fear of a larger war which might bring about U.S. or Chinese involvement. The point nevertheless remains that civilian casualties and collateral damage in this war was small given the enormity of the stakes involved. On battle

figures see Sumit Ganguly, *The Origins of War in South Asia* (Boulder: Westview Press, 1993).

4. The precise objective of Robert Gates' mission is now the subject of some controversy. Seymour Hersh, a former reporter for *The New York Times,* wrote that India and Pakistan had teetered on the edge of a nuclear war in May 1990 and that Gates' mission was instrumental in preventing the outbreak of war. Seymour Hersh, "On The Nuclear Edge," *The New Yorker,* March 29, 1993, 56-73.
5. Seymour M. Hersh, "On the Nuclear Edge." Also see William E. Burrows and Robert Windrem, *Critical Mass: The Dangerous Race for Superweapons in a Fragmenting World* (New York: Simon and Schuster, 1994).
6. On the "Brasstacks" exercise, see Steven P. Cohen's *Beyond Brasstacks: Crisis Management and Perception in South Asia.* Research Report. Urbana, IL: Program in Arms Control, Disarmament, and International Security, February 1995.
7. Special Representative, "Indo-Pak Pacts on Code of Conduct," *The Statesman Overseas Weekly,* August 22, 1992, 1.
8. The shift in doctrines is discussed in Sumit Ganguly, "Avoiding War in Kashmir," *Foreign Affairs,* Vol. 69, No. 5, Winter 1990/91. For a discussion of the dangers of preemptive doctrines see Jack Snyder, *The Ideology of The Offensive and the Disasters of 1914* (Ithaca: Cornell University Press, 1984).
9. The concept of an "epistemic community" is defined and discussed at length by Peter M. Haas in "Knowledge, Power and International Policy Coordination," *International Organization,* 46, no. 1 (Winter 1992).
10. While in New Delhi on a research trip in December 1992, the author interviewed a senior Indian foreign service officer about the prospects of expanding the existing CBM regime between India and Pakistan. His response was the following: "It is extremely difficult to contemplate further CBMs with a regime that is engaged in supporting an insurgency in your country." The question would no doubt have elicited a similar response from a Pakistani counterpart.
11. The term is derived from Gabriel Almond, *The American People and Foreign Policy* (New York: Praeger, 1960), 151.
12. It is pertinent to mention here that the Indian leadership insists on including China in any discussion of nuclear issues in "Southern Asia." The purpose of including China in such discussions serves two purposes. First, it forces Western nonproliferation analysts to take into account the putative Chinese nuclear threat to India. Second, it is also a clever debating tactic. Indian security analysts clearly recognize that the Chinese are not about to limit their nuclear forces to further the prospects of a nonproliferation regime in South Asia. In a discussion involving the expansion of the conventional CBM regime, however, the Indian leadership would perceive no meaningful advantages in including China. Legitimate fears of Sino-Pakistani collusion would be paramount in their minds.
13. For a discussion of the Sumdurong Chu incident and "Checkerboard," see Sumit Ganguly, "The Sino-Indian Border Talks: A View From New Delhi," *Asian Survey,* 24, no. 12, (December 1989), 1123-1135.
14. Ibid., 1133.
15. See Sumit Ganguly, "Joint Beneficiaries," *Far Eastern Economic Review,* February 15, 1992.
16. On this point see Dilip Mukherjee, "Dealing with Beijing: Shared Interests in a New Global Context," *Times Of India,* September 20, 1991.

17. The Pakistani intelligence agency in particular may have greater autonomy because Pakistan has had a fitful history of democratic rule. Consequently, the tradition of democratic oversight and control over intelligence services may not be as firmly established. The agency's powers grew substantially during the Afghan conflict. Similarly, RAW played an important role in India's involvement in Sri Lanka. Its performance in that operation left much to be desired, however.
18. See the Indo-Pakistan Agreement on East Pakistan border disputes, signed in New Delhi on October 23, 1959.
19. The classic statement on this subject is Robert Jervis's *Perception and Misperception in International Politics,* (Princeton: Princeton University Press, 1976).
20. The problems of South Asian trade in general, and Indo-Pakistan economic cooperation in particular, are discussed by Sunil Dasgupta, "Private Initiatives," *India Today,* March 31, 1993, 86-88.
21. Such a gesture has at least one important precedent in the region. In 1979, just prior to the beginning of the first round of border talks between India and China, the Chinese declared that Indian pilgrims would be allowed controlled and guided access to two of the most revered shrines in Hinduism—Mansarovar and Kailash—both within Tibet.
22. On the potential importance of such unilateral gestures in international politics see Robert Axelrod, *The Evolution of Cooperation* (New York: Basic Books, 1984).

3

AVOIDING NUCLEAR WAR

C. Raja Mohan and Peter R. Lavoy

Washington and Moscow regulated the dangers of their global nuclear rivalry through a series of unilateral actions, reciprocal measures, and formally negotiated agreements to establish mutual trust in a stable order of political and military conduct. In contrast, New Delhi and Islamabad have been slow to instill confidence and control their military competition. Although Indian and Pakistani leaders have concluded a handful of mutual confidence-building measures (CBMs), they do not yet accept arms control as a useful means to enhance military security and stabilize strained political relations. With both states engaged in costly defense preparations, fears of surprise attack, military escalation, and even nuclear conflict loom over the Subcontinent. These concerns are exaggerated. This chapter will show that the risk of nuclear conflict in South Asia is significant but controllable.[1]

Arms control was not instinctive for the superpowers. Almost two decades of hazardous cold war elapsed before Moscow and Washington embraced arms control as a vital part of their national security policies. Early in the Cold War, the superpowers espoused lofty and propagandist proposals for general and complete disarmament. Gradually recognizing the futility of efforts to negotiate away the very forces on which they relied for national security, and shocked into action by the Cuban missile crisis, Washington and Moscow finally began to pursue arms control in 1963, agreeing to a communications hotline in June, the Partial Test Ban treaty in August, and a ban on mass destruction weapons in space in September. A subsequent series of strategic arms reduction pacts, a score of mutual confidence-building measures, and some restraint in the development and deployment of military forces helped the superpowers avert the outbreak of global nuclear war.[2]

Although fashioned in unique historical circumstances, nuclear arms control is suitable today for South Asia. Arms control and confidence-building arrangements can help India and Pakistan avoid a war that neither side wants, minimize the costs and risks of their arms competition, and curtail the scope and violence of conflict should it occur again in South Asia.[3] Arms control is possible in South Asia because India and Pakistan each wish to avoid a fourth war. Moreover, arms control is essential because nuclear weapons are available to both states. The prospect of their use compels their careful control.

Although neither India nor Pakistan has openly deployed nuclear forces, both nations have nuclear weapons programs and could on short notice assemble these weapons. According to one recent estimate, by the end of 1991, India possessed an inventory of about 290 kilograms of bomb-grade plutonium available for the manufacture of nuclear weapons, enough for fifty to sixty weapons.[4] Although little is known publicly about the design and development of India's bombs, or even if India has assembled any nuclear weapons, the 1974 "peaceful nuclear experiment" demonstrated that country's ability to manufacture nuclear weapons. It is believed that the Indian Atomic Energy Commission conducts extensive research and development on smaller and more powerful nuclear explosives.[5]

On the other side of the border, Pakistan's enrichment plant at Kahuta is estimated to have produced between 130 and 220 kilograms of bomb-grade uranium by the end of 1991, enough material for six to ten nuclear weapons.[6] Western intelligence agencies have reported Pakistani efforts to acquire, design, and construct the non-nuclear components needed to complete a functional nuclear weapon.[7] Pakistan and India each have aircraft capable of delivering nuclear weapons to targets inside the other's territory; and both states are developing, or have reportedly obtained nuclear-capable ballistic missiles.[8]

India-Pakistan arms control is also necessary because each country engages in coercive strategic behavior—including provocative troop movements and military exercises near tense borders, alleged support for militant groups in unstable regions of the other country, and cross-border firing mainly along the Line of Actual Control (LAC) in Kashmir—and yet both governments understand that they cannot afford escalation to full-scale military combat, much less nuclear warfare.[9]

In principle, arms control can enhance stability among states involved in fierce political disputes, but the stubborn sources of these disputes hinder efforts to control arms. To be successful, an arms control regime must alter at least some of the basic conditions underlying South Asia's cold war. In recent years, a number of intriguing confidence- and security-enhancing measures have been proposed for India and Pakistan: a regional cutoff of fissile material production, a regional nuclear test ban, the placement of new and existing nuclear facilities under safeguards, extension of the nuclear no-attack pledge to cover population centers, strengthened international security assurances, regional risk reduction centers, expanded and upgraded hotlines between military and political officials, and regular exchanges of military personnel.[10] Even the worthiest of these ideas, however, cannot succeed without the prior creation of stable arms control customs and institutions in South Asia.

Nuclear Threats to Regional Security

Six specific concerns arouse consternation about the strategic and military consequences of nuclear proliferation in South Asia. Experts fear that emerging nuclear weapons states, such as India and Pakistan, may be led by internal or external circumstances to engage in preventive or preemptive military attacks, experience nuclear accidents or the unauthorized use of nuclear weapons, threaten or actually use nuclear arms for coercive purposes, or escalate a conventional conflict to the nuclear level.

Military Prevention. The first concern is that India's presumed nuclear superiority over Pakistan may create in New Delhi pressures for preventive war. Indian anxiety about the behavior of a nuclear-armed Pakistan or about the possible loss of strategic superiority could produce calls for decisive military action.[11] This fear became pronounced in the mid-1980s when a flurry of press accounts reported Indian contingency plans for preventive air strikes against Pakistan's Kahuta uranium enrichment plant.[12] Experts have worried that India will try to do to Pakistan's nuclear bomb program what Israel in 1981 and the U.S.-led coalition a decade later did to Iraq's nuclear facilities.

This concern is overdrawn. Fears of preventive war are abating for two reasons. First, India and Pakistan each believe that the other side has acquired the means to produce and employ at least several nuclear weapons. It is thus too late to prevent the development of nuclear options in South Asia; any attack now carries the risk of nuclear retaliation. Second, India and Pakistan have negotiated, signed, and implemented a formal pact essentially outlawing one important form of military prevention. The Agreement on the Prohibition of Attack against Nuclear Installations and Facilities between Pakistan and India was signed by Benazir Bhutto and Rajiv Gandhi on December 31, 1988 and ratified on January 27, 1991. K. Subrahmanyam, then director of the Institute for Defence Studies and Analyses, New Delhi, floated the idea in July 1985 as part of a broad proposal for nuclear confidence-building between India and Pakistan.[13] Meeting in December 1985, the prime ministers of India and Pakistan, Rajiv Gandhi and Mohammed Zia ul-Haq, agreed in principle on the plan, under which:

> Each party shall refrain from undertaking, encouraging or participating in, directly or indirectly, any action aimed at causing the destruction of, or damage to, any nuclear installation or facility in the other country.[14]

Article II of the pact mandates that at the beginning of each year the parties must exchange complete lists of the latitude and longitude of their nuclear facilities. Islamabad and New Delhi exchanged these lists on January 1, 1992 and again on January 4, 1993.

The effectiveness of the nuclear no-attack pact is reduced by the reluctance of Islamabad and New Delhi to accept the legitimacy of the exchanged lists. Although neither government has made its inventory public, a Pakistani newspaper published what it claimed was an authoritative list of Indian nuclear installations but questioned whether New Delhi had provided a complete accounting of its facilities.[15] Mutual concerns that key installations were omitted from the 1992 lists exacerbated regional tensions and may even have heightened fears of military preemption: "The agreement does not protect the facilities not mentioned on the list," warned one Pakistani official.[16]

The mixed record of the nuclear nonaggression pact to enhance confidence and security in Islamabad and New Delhi suggests somewhat paradoxically that a prerequisite for effective confidence building is the existence of considerable mutual trust. The observation supports a point developed by Colin Gray: "Arms control can only till fields already cleared by hard political labor."[17]

Military Preemption. Western experts also worry about the "delicacy" of the Subcontinent's first-generation nuclear forces: a small number of poorly hidden and weakly protected nuclear-weapon sites in a country with limited early-warning capabilities could tempt an adversary to launch a preemptive military attack.[18] Because of Pakistan's limited strategic depth—all of Pakistan's air force bases are within range of India's bombers, and most are within range of India's Prithvi missile[19]—Islamabad may be forced to pursue a doctrine of preemption, as it attempted against India at the outset of the 1971 Bangladesh war.[20] Recognizing Pakistan's strategic vulnerabilities and possibly fearing the proclivity of the Pakistan Army to preempt, India also may be pressured to attack early in a crisis.

India and Pakistan have not formally agreed to any mutual arrangement to reduce the prospect of military preemption, but such an agreement may not be necessary at this time. The measures Washington and Moscow employed to lower the risk of preemption include improving force readiness and dispersing weapon systems, increasing their mobility, and protecting them. The first two options involve loosening central control over nuclear forces and may increase the risk of another problem: unauthorized seizure or use of nuclear weapons. On the other hand, mobility and prevention are prudent and realistic force objectives. Lt. General Hamid Gul, former director of Pakistan's Inter-Services Intelligence Agency (ISI), told a U.S. arms control expert that nuclear force survivability "is not our issue. It is your concern."[21] Nonetheless, Pakistan and India are presumably taking steps to harden the shelters of their nuclear strike aircraft, upgrade air defenses around these installations, and prepare for the introduction of mobile missiles such as the Prithvi and the M-11.

If the superpower experience provides any indication, such unilateral military preparations may help more than any formal arms accord to enhance crisis stability. Again, the primacy of politics must be stressed. As Robert Jervis observes: "If relations remain extremely bad, war can occur even if strategic weapons are not vulnerable; if relations greatly improve, vulnerabilities will not be a major source of danger. Wars are caused predominantly by conflicts of political interests."[22]

Nuclear Accidents. Nuclear weapon systems, like nuclear power plants and many other modern, sophisticated technological systems, are inherently dangerous.[23] All states that posses nuclear weapons must be concerned about accidental nuclear detonation. For less advanced and technologically experienced states, this can be an acute problem.[24] Little is known publicly about the safety and security of nuclear operations in India and Pakistan, and the worst is often feared.[25] Nuclear accidents and operational failures can also have disastrous military repercussions, possibly even triggering a nuclear escalation.[26]

India and Pakistan have not agreed to any formal measures to reduce the risk of accidental nuclear war. Such arrangements are worth pursuing. A possible model is the 1971 U.S.-Soviet Agreement on Measures to Reduce the Risk of Outbreak of Nuclear War. In the "Accidents Measures Agreement," Moscow and Washington recognized that unilateral control procedures might not suffice to prevent the outbreak of a war resulting from technical malfunction, unauthorized acts, or a misinterpreted incident. The pact seeks to limit this possibility by establishing certain procedures to be followed in the event of mishaps. Similar arrangements could be executed in South Asia under bilateral or international auspices.

Unauthorized Nuclear Use. Terrorist violence afflicts both India and Pakistan, generating fears by Western experts about the prospect of nuclear weapons falling into the possession of a violent, separatist group.[27] A separate (although perhaps simultaneous) problem is usurpation of the control of nuclear weapons by a renegade element of the armed forces. Loss of governmental control of nuclear operations is seen as a particular concern for Pakistan, which has a long history of military intervention in domestic politics. This circumstance could also heighten pressures for Indian preemption: possible Indian doubts about the ability of Pakistani political leaders to exercise control and restraint over nuclear decision making could induce New Delhi to act precipitously in the next crisis or conventional war.[28] Several American analysts have suggested "nuclear stability assistance" for emergent nuclear nations as a way of lowering the likelihood of accidents, terrorism, and unauthorized use.[29] Dunn and Giles, for example, suggest several specific aid packages for improving the security of nuclear forces including the provision of permissive action link (PAL) technology, increasing the safety of nuclear weapon systems through better designs that avoid unintended explosions, and improving the reliability of operational procedures.[30] Proponents of such technical assistance recognize that current international agreements and U.S. domestic law proscribe this kind of aid to emerging nuclear weapon states. The provision of technical aid for the security, safety, and survivability of new nuclear forces might help to stabilize a regional deterrence relationship, but it could also enhance the readiness and effectiveness of these forces, thereby making political and military leaders more comfortable with the idea of using nuclear weapons.[31] This may interest India or Pakistan, but probably not the potential assisting powers.

The risk of unauthorized acquisition or use of nuclear weapons in South Asia, even in the absence of technical assistance, is not as high as Western observers fear. First, it is not widely understood that the Indian and Pakistani armed forces are highly centralized and very loyal to the top military leadership.[32] The prospect of unauthorized military action, including the seizure or use of nuclear arms, by either country's armed forces is remote.

Second, the operational requirements of small, minimal deterrent forces can mitigate the dangers of unauthorized use. Unlike the Cold War superpowers, India and Pakistan need not place their nuclear weapons under military control during peacetime; nor need they deploy large arsenals worldwide on land, sea, or underwater. As crises evolve, each country should have ample time to prepare for a nuclear exchange; thus India and Pakistan could keep their nuclear devices stored in a disassembled form at civilian laboratories and separate from their delivery systems—a condition that effectively precludes the theft or unauthorized use of operational nuclear weapons. According to General K. Sundarji, former Indian army chief:

> Very strong centralized negative controls can be exercised, if you are looking at it purely as a deterrent. If you're thinking of first use, on the other hand, then you have to decentralize. But if you see it purely as deterrence, there is no harm done if it is totally centralized, tightly held, because the response time is no longer critical.[33]

Prudent nuclear operations of this sort provide an important source of arms control and do not require time-consuming and politically contentious international negotiations.

Nuclear Coercion. Western analysts worry that a desperate or ambitious ruler of either state might try to use nuclear weapons to coerce or even to attack the other country in order to conquer territory or force political concessions. Even if Islamabad and New Delhi currently exercise caution in their mutual dealings, some fear that a tyrannical figure could come to power during a governmental crisis and recklessly wield nuclear weapons against the foreign enemy. Because leaders of countries like India and Pakistan perceive the stakes of competition to be so high, Western observers fear that they "may be ready to risk nuclear confrontation, if not even to accept a surprisingly high level of nuclear damage, in pursuit of their objectives."[34]

These concerns are overstated. Neither India nor Pakistan developed nuclear weapons with offensive or coercive military action in mind.[35] Moreover, there is no cult of the offensive in South Asia. Neither state has exposed allies or vulnerable foreign possessions whose defense could require immediate aggressive action. Neither country has significant territorial ambitions (except in the case of Kashmir, though the sources of this dispute are more political and ideological than territorial).[36] Finally, neither nation has expansionist political aims.

Despite frequent protestations to the contrary, India and Pakistan accept the political and territorial status quo everywhere in South Asia except, of course, in Kashmir. Even here, there is no evidence that either side has ever considered issuing a nuclear threat to influence the actions of its adversary. South Asia's nuclear bombs are viewed as weapons of last resort. As Subrahmanyam puts it, "The main purpose of a third world nuclear arsenal is deterrence against blackmail," not blackmail itself.[37] The threat of nuclear coercion, therefore, is not a pressing priority for arms control.

Military Escalation. Finally, Western observers fear that the next conventional war between India and Pakistan could quickly escalate into a nuclear conflict. Two general causes of nuclear escalation are the temptation of national leaders to use all weapons at their disposal in a vital political and military contest and the leadership's concern that enemy conventional military operations may jeopardize its ability to use nuclear forces later in a war. Several American analysts observed significant levels of military escalation during the winter 1986-87 and spring 1990 military crises between India and Pakistan. Many also believe that during the 1990 crisis, India and Pakistan came close to a nuclear exchange. According to then-deputy national security adviser Robert Gates, who headed a U.S. crisis management mission to South Asia in May 1990, "Pakistan and India seemed to be caught in a cycle that they couldn't break out of. I was convinced that if a war started, it would be nuclear."[38]

Two Major Crises

1986-87 Brasstacks Crisis. The 1986-87 crisis initially involved a large Indian military exercise, Brasstacks, a corps-level triennial exercise designed and conducted by General Sundarji. In response to the Indian troops' movement and training in the Rajasthan desert, Pakistan apparently deployed its army, including its armored forces, into forward positions. The Indian army responded by occupying its traditional defensive positions. Elements of brinkmanship, crisis manipulation, and escalation were all present; however, Indian and Pakistani leaders managed to de-escalate without violence.

There is one reason to believe that nuclear weapons cast a shadow over the events of 1986-87. The first semi-official unveiling of Pakistan's nuclear weapon capability occurred during this crisis. In a strange series of incidents, Indian journalist Kuldip Nayar was contacted by Pakistani journalist Mushahid Hussain and allowed to meet and interview the renowned nuclear scientist, Abdul Qadir Khan, on January 28, 1987—at the peak of the crisis. Dr. Khan allegedly told Nayar that Pakistan had succeeded in building the bomb and thus had gained a deterrent capability: "Nobody can undo Pakistan or take us for granted. We are here to stay and let it be clear that we shall use the bomb if our existence is threatened."[39] Indian defense analysts viewed this statement as an attempt to convey a nuclear signal to head off the crisis. But for various reasons Dr. Khan's claims about Pakistan's military nuclear capability did not appear in print until March 1, 1987, by which time the crisis had receded.

1990 Kashmir Crisis. The 1990 crisis developed as Kashmiri separatist groups intensified an uprising in Indian-controlled Kashmir and as the Pakistan army conducted its large *Zarb-e-Momin* military exercise. Political leaders on both sides of the border made tough statements about events in Kashmir. Islamabad expected the impending independence of Indian-controlled Kashmir; New Delhi displayed a fierce determination to prevent such a development. The Indian army reportedly moved three divisions into Kashmir and one extra division into Punjab to forestall possible Pakistani military actions. Islamabad apparently inferred aggressive intent in these steps and indicated its alarm to the United States. At this point the U.S. ambassador to India, William Clark, and his military attaches observed the defensive disposition of the Indian forces and reported this to Pakistan, thus defusing the situation substantially.[40]

Several questions remain unanswered concerning the role of nuclear weapons in the 1990 crisis. Did Pakistan alert its nuclear forces? If so, why? What Indian activity was Pakistan's nuclear threat designed to deter? Was the deterrent threat successfully communicated? Did it work? A Pakistani journalist, Shireen Mazari, claims that "one of the major factors in preventing the outbreak of a war over Kashmir in 1990 was Pakistan letting India know its nuclear capability."[41] In contrast, after a discussion with the key Indian officials involved in the 1990 crisis, K. Subrahmanyam writes: "Whatever Mr. Gates may have discussed with Pakistanis no policy maker in India recalls his raising the issue of nuclear confrontation."[42]

Whether nuclear threats were made or not made, and whether they exacerbated or diffused the two recent South Asian crises, it is clear that the most serious consequence of nuclear proliferation in the region—in addition to the prospect of nuclear accidents—is the potential for the escalation of a political crisis, first to conventional military conflict and then to the nuclear level. How likely are these forms of military escalation? The history of

India-Pakistan relations since the 1971 war and since the advent of military nuclear capabilities provides a mixed message.

On the one hand, India and Pakistan regularly engage in mid- to low-intensity warfare and frequently find themselves in tense circumstances. The anguish of partition and the suffering of three wars are not forgotten. Neither country is completely able to control certain elements of its population; as a result, domestic social and political disputes often spill across national borders and become bilateral disputes. Although separatist violence in Indian Punjab and Pakistani Sindh has receded, a military standoff continues along the LAC in Kashmir, where cross-border firings often occur. It is hopelessly naive to believe that crises can be prevented from arising in South Asia.

On the other hand, recent history shows that the region's crises can be contained. The turn of events in 1986-87 and 1990 proved that neither country desired to go to war. With the costly experience of the 1971 conflict still fresh in the minds of Indians and Pakistanis, the political and military leaders of both sides appreciate the very high price a fourth South Asian war would exact. The advent of nuclear weapons sharpens this awareness. Subrahmanyam remarks,

> There is a consciousness in India that in the future Pakistan cannot be driven to a position where it would seriously consider the exercise of [its] nuclear option. That consciousness is already evident in India not repeating the strategy of hot pursuit adopted in 1965 against Pakistan-despatched armed gangs across the line of [actual] control in the state of Jammu and Kashmir.[43]

Pakistan, too, is aware of the immense costs of escalation: several times in the last few years the Pakistan army had to stop, at the risk of firing on its own citizens, the march of Kashmiri supporters across the LAC.

Can arms control help lower the risk of such escalation? Confidence-building measures to establish no first use or no early use of nuclear weapons and to improve crisis communication and decision making deserve investigation. Pledges to abstain from the first or early use of nuclear weapons could help stabilize a relationship of mutual nuclear deterrence in South Asia. Subrahmanyam has proposed such declarations between India and Pakistan, as well as on a wider basis involving all nuclear weapon states.[44] Sundarji argues that a no-first-use pact could help "forswear brinkmanship at the very early stages of a conflict," thus providing crisis stability.[45] The Indian government evidently is convinced: In January 1994 India sent six non-papers (informal proposals) for CBMs with Pakistan, one of which proposed that the two states enter into a no-first-nuclear-use treaty.[46]

Pakistan could fear that under such a regime India's conventional military superiority could undermine Pakistan's ability to deter conventional aggression.[47] As noted above, some Indian defense experts claim that the opportunity for conventional hostilities has passed with the advent of nuclear capabilities.[48] In a dire situation, of course, Islamabad would not be constrained by a no-first-use pledge. So what is the value added? Integrated into a broad regime of military arms control and CBMs, no early use could help foster a climate of reliable expectations about each side's intentions and behavior during peacetime and possibly in crisis situations.

Arrangements for effective signaling and communication during peacetime and crises could further improve mutual understanding. The two sides now employ a hotline between the army director generals of military operations. There are suggestions for a similar mechanism between the chiefs of air operations in the two air forces. Communication hotlines could be extended to key political leaders and others who must be involved in managing a crisis. Establishing risk reduction centers in both countries could provide a way to facilitate communication between complete crisis management teams.

Regional Nuclear Security: A Mixed Picture

Although India and Pakistan are rapidly developing the capabilities to fight a devastating nuclear war, and remain far from working out a stable order based on mutual and minimal deterrence, the present strategic situation does appear to be manageable. Ever conscious since 1971 of the enormous costs of another regional war, whether conventional or nuclear, Islamabad and New Delhi successfully negotiated their way through several hazardous crises in recent years. Still, regional crisis management skills—particularly in the area of escalation control—could be further improved.

With the mutual acceptance of arms control as a practical means to enhance military security and stabilize strained bilateral relations, Islamabad and New Delhi may be able to establish mutual confidence in a peaceful order of political and military conduct, even in the absence of a complete resolution of the region's outstanding political and territorial disputes. In order to accomplish this, however, the governments of India, Pakistan, and even the United States will have to alter the way they think about and make policy for nuclear security in South Asia.

An Arms Control Regime in the Subcontinent: Obstacles and Requirements

Even the most deserving proposals for nuclear arms control or military confidence building in the Subcontinent are likely to flounder unless India, Pakistan, and the United States can develop the institutions and attitudes required to facilitate and sustain effective force management arrangements. Today, five stubborn obstacles impede efforts to establish a viable arms control climate in South Asia: (1) the diplomatic preoccupation with nuclear disarmament to the detriment of more modest but also more feasible measures for nuclear restraint; (2) a reluctance to acknowledge the military purposes of Indian and Pakistani nuclear programs in order to develop a realistic debate about reasonable limits on regional nuclear forces and strategies; (3) an unwillingness by India and Pakistan to accept and implement arms control as a vital element of national security policy; (4) an inability to transform the India-Pakistan strategic dialogue from tacit to explicit bargaining; and (5) a persistence of insensitivity, resentment, and defiance among the three powers rather than strategic understanding and reciprocity.

Inertia of Disarmament Diplomacy. A major obstacle to new thinking about nuclear deterrence and arms control in the Subcontinent is the persistence of long-espoused ideas of disarmament and denuclearization among the three key actors involved: India, Pakistan, and the United States. Traditional diplomatic postures on regional nuclear weapons issues are so firmly entrenched in the foreign policy bureaucracies of all three states that it is difficult for anyone to consider altering them. Continued calls for the elimination of nuclear weapons at the global level by India—and within the region by Pakistan and the United States—inhibit creative thinking about arms control. Winds of change are blowing today in South Asia. Prominent individuals in all three countries now argue the value of regional arms control over disarmament, but this new thinking remains hesitant and is yet to enjoy widespread support among policy elites.

India: Global Disarmament. India has long been an outspoken opponent of nuclear deterrence and arms control. Even before the country's 1947 independence, Jawaharlal Nehru campaigned to outlaw nuclear weapons. Like Mahatma Gandhi, Nehru argued that nuclear violence could not be countered by the threat of nuclear retaliation; such a condition eventually would spell suicide for mankind.[49] Every Indian prime minister since has characterized the doctrine of deterrence as immoral and forming an irrational basis for national security in the nuclear age. This view was expressed most clearly in the Delhi Declaration issued by Rajiv Gandhi and Mikhail Gorbachev in November 1986 and in India's Action Plan on nuclear disarmament presented to the United Nations in June 1988.[50] Welcoming the START II Treaty signed by Washington and Moscow in January 1993, the Indian government urged the "nuclear weapon states to re-examine doctrines of nuclear deterrence which have been used by them in (the) past to justify expansion of their nuclear arsenals."[51]

India also has rejected nuclear arms control and confidence-building agreements as inadequate responses to the nuclear threat. Even during the peak of the East-West detente, Indian officials characterized superpower arms control agreements as incomplete and diversionary. New Delhi regarded the Soviet-American arms limitation treaties of the 1970s essentially as truces in the war against the nuclear arms race and it dismissed the confidence-building arrangements promoted in Europe under the Helsinki process as cosmetic measures designed to distract from the real issues of ending the nuclear arms race and scaling down military forces in Europe.[52]

India makes a sharp distinction between "disarmament" and "arms control," consistently championing the former over the latter. Although largely ritualistic from the late 1940s through the 1970s,[53] Indian arguments in favor of nuclear disarmament became far more central and explicit in the 1980s.[54] New Delhi continues to advocate global nuclear disarmament, despite the accumulation of evidence about Pakistan's acquisition of military nuclear capabilities, the string of political advantages Islamabad gained through its espousal of regional denuclearization, the mounting international pressures on India to move toward regional arms limitations, and the increased domestic pressures for India openly to declare itself as a nuclear weapons power.

This policy remains intact even as the world nuclear order has changed and the international diplomatic focus has shifted from East-West arms control to regional nonproliferation. Having long identified *horizontal proliferation* (an increase in the number of nuclear-armed states) and *vertical proliferation* (expansion and modernization of existing nuclear arsenals) as two sides of the same coin, India is more outspoken about the later and insists that both problems must be solved simultaneously.[55] Stressing the importance of equity and justice in international non-proliferation efforts, most Indian policy makers and opinion shapers still see the global elimination of nuclear weapons as the only fair and effective way to curb the spread of military nuclear capabilities.[56] Popular support for this policy line, the bureaucracy's resistance to rethink it, and the reluctance of the political leadership to revise it are three factors that sustain India's disarmament diplomacy.

Pakistan: Regional Disarmament. If India is tethered to the goal of global denuclearization, the idea of regional disarmament preoccupies Pakistan. Pakistan did not participate as actively as its rival in international debates on nuclear weapons during the 1950s. When Pakistani officials became alarmed about India's military nuclear potential in the early 1960s, however, Islamabad initiated a campaign to draw international attention to the military implications of India's civil nuclear program and to raise the diplomatic costs to India of developing nuclear weapons. Although the policy means have changed over time, these objectives continue to guide Pakistan's arms control diplomacy.

From the early 1960s through the mid-1970s Pakistan sought to prevent India from going nuclear by encouraging international support for measures to stop the spread of military nuclear capabilities to all non-nuclear-weapon states. Pakistan was a hopeful proponent of the Nuclear Nonproliferation Treaty (NPT). Indeed, as early as 1962, President Ayub Khan urged the international community to conclude "a treaty to outlaw the further spread of nuclear weapons."[57] While acknowledging the need to control vertical proliferation, Pakistan's NPT negotiator, Agha Shahi, stressed that curbing horizontal proliferation (a problem that he said posed the greater threat to the security of non-nuclear-weapon states) was the "top priority,"[58] and insisted that "to tie the question of non-proliferation of nuclear weapons to other measures restricting the nuclear arms race could only result in an impasse."[59] In the end, Pakistan refused to sign the NPT because it was not binding on India, which refused to sign, and because it contained no mechanism for assuring the security of Pakistan and other non-nuclear-weapon states.[60]

Shortly after Pakistan's decision not to join the NPT—and after Pakistan's loss to India in the 1971 war—Islamabad launched a two-track policy to match and contain India's growing nuclear capabilities. First, Prime Minister Zulfikar Ali Bhutto assembled the nation's top scientists and bureaucrats at a secret January 1972 meeting in Multan and instructed them to develop a nuclear bomb for Pakistan.[61] Several months later Bhutto set in motion the second track—a diplomatic bid to elicit Indian denuclearization through a public campaign to rid South Asia of nuclear weapons. Originally announced at the unveiling of Pakistan's KANUPP reactor in November 1972, a South Asia Nuclear Weapon Free Zone (SANWFZ) plan was submitted by Pakistan to the U.N. General Assembly in November 1974, six months after India's nuclear test.[62]

Pakistan continued to pursue each policy track in the 1980s. As part of his diplomatic offensive against India, General Zia ul-Haq proposed six specific measures for regional disarmament: joint India-Pakistan renunciation of the acquisition or manufacture of nuclear weapons (1978); mutual inspection of each side's nuclear facilities (1979); simultaneous acceptance of International Atomic Energy Agency (IAEA) "full-scope safeguards" (1979); simultaneous accession to the NPT (1979); a bilateral nuclear test ban treaty (1987); and a multilateral conference under U.N. auspices on nuclear non-proliferation in South Asia (1987).[63] Prime Minister Nawaz Sharif added another proposition to this list in June 1991 when he called for the meeting of five powers—China, India, Pakistan, Russia, and the United States—to discuss the nuclear issue in South Asia. Owing to its global orientation, India has rejected all of these regional nuclear disarmament proposals.

Pakistan's nuclear diplomacy provided two important benefits during the 1970s and 1980s. First, it put India on the defensive and made New Delhi appear intransigent: India could be counted on to reject any regional approach to nuclear arms limitation. Islamabad's disarmament posture also provided a convenient cover for Pakistan's own pursuit of a military nuclear capability. Its calls for regional denuclearization helped mute growing U.S. apprehension during the 1980s about the progress of Pakistan's nuclear bomb program. Although Pakistan continues to put some pressure on India to negotiate regional disarmament, Islamabad has not been able to persuade the United States to resume the military assistance relationship it terminated in October 1990. Pakistan's nuclear diplomacy has lost its effectiveness.

United States: Nuclear Nonproliferation. As part of its global nonproliferation policy, the United States has long advocated nuclear disarmament for South Asia. U.S. efforts to curb the bomb's spread rest on the premise that danger and instability inhere to new nuclear weapon systems; more is always seen as worse. Although Washington has shifted its strategies and tactics for controlling the bomb's spread globally and in South Asia, preventing the emergence of new nuclear states has been a steady goal.[64] In the aftermath of the Cold War, the dissolution of the Soviet Union, the Gulf War, the activities of the IAEA and the U.N. Special Commission in Iraq, and the North Korean crisis, nuclear nonproliferation has emerged as a pre-eminent U.S. security concern.

The Clinton administration's nonproliferation policy toward South Asia is clear. The administration's April 1993 "Report to Congress on Progress Toward Regional Nonproliferation in South Asia" specifies that the U.S. objective "is first to cap, then over time reduce, and finally eliminate the possession of weapons of mass destruction and their means of delivery."[65] In pursuit of this goal, Washington stresses nonproliferation in special bilateral discussions with New Delhi and Islamabad, encourages both states to sign the NPT, urges them to cease the production of fissile material for weapons purposes on a unilateral or regional basis, withholds economic and military assistance from its erstwhile ally, Pakistan, until nonproliferation progress can be verified, supports direct high-level Indo-Pakistani discussions on regional security and nonproliferation, and engages other states—such as Britain, France, Germany, Japan, and Russia—to undertake bilateral nonproliferation discussions with India and Pakistan.

The United States has little to show for all of this effort. Washington and New Delhi seem today to be placing far more emphasis on improving trade and economic concerns, placing the nuclear question largely on the back burner. Islamabad reportedly accepted some unilateral nuclear restraints under heavy U.S. pressure, but Pakistan strongly resents U.S. bullying.[66] U.S.-Pakistan relations remain deeply troubled, though Prime Minister Bhutto's U.S. visit in April 1995 may lead to some improvement.

New Signs of Nuclear Realism

Emerging today in New Delhi, Islamabad, and Washington are new arguments for "nuclear realism." Conceding that nuclear disarmament is beyond reach both globally and in South Asia, and convinced that current diplomatic approaches have become counter-productive, the new nuclear realists have set their sights on arms control and CBMs to avoid a nuclear war in the region.

There are increasing appeals to recast India's nuclear policy from its present emphasis on global and normative considerations to a new focus on national security requirements.[67] Strategic analysts Subrahmanyam and Sundarji accept the permanence of military nuclear capabilities in the region and stress the need for India and Pakistan to learn to live peacefully in such an environment.[68] Although the Indian government continues to argue for global nuclear disarmament, and is not now prepared to accept—much less act on—the nuclear realist perspective, it is beginning to show signs of greater flexibility and pragmatism.

Since the summer of 1990 (shortly after the denouement of the military crisis over Kashmir), New Delhi has embraced the concept of confidence building with Pakistan. Several concrete measures have been negotiated and implemented by the two sides, and a high-ranking advisory group (including serving and retired officials of the Atomic Energy Commission, General Sundarji, and defense expert Air Commodore Jasjit Singh) recently stressed the importance of confidence-building and risk-reduction measures to prevent conflict with Pakistan and China.[69] The gradual recognition of the utility of confidence-building and arms control measures thus could stimulate new Indian thinking about regional nuclear restraint in the Subcontinent.

In Pakistan, too, there are isolated indications of a willingness to move beyond the traditional posture of regional denuclearization in order to stabilize the region's nuclear reality. The former vice chief of army staff, General K. M. Arif, has urged the Indian and Pakistani governments to consider turning the region into a "nuclear safe zone" since Islamabad's current nuclear diplomacy has lost its effectiveness. In a similar vein, General Mirza Aslam Beg, former army chief of staff, writes:

> Our proposal that both India and Pakistan sign the NPT and that South Asia be declared a nuclear-weapon free zone has not worked because the concept of a nuclear-weapon free zone does not provide for the denuclearization of nations which have already gone nuclear. Nor have any foolproof verification measures been devised so far which could divest a country of weapon-grade fissile material or weapons which it is known to possess or has produced. The same argument applies if both Pakistan and India were to enter the NPT fold as non-nuclear weapon states.[70]

In the United States there also is an emerging sense that complete nuclear disarmament in South Asia may no longer be a feasible policy objective. In his congressional testimony, John Malott indicated that while the United States continues to advocate Indian and Pakistani adherence to the NPT, "our efforts also focus on trying to achieve more immediate goals," including the adoption of regional confidence-building measures "such as ending all firing across the line of control and notifying each other of troop movements."[71]

These governmental efforts do not go far enough for some policy analysts who argue that regional nuclear security should replace nonproliferation as a U.S. policy priority. Richard Haass was one of the first observers to articulate this perspective in regard to South Asia.[72] Stephen Cohen and a group of colleagues conducted a comprehensive study of nuclear arms management issues for India and Pakistan.[73] Many others have made the case for "managing" nuclear proliferation in more general terms.[74] And still other experts propose arms control arrangements to manage nuclear arsenals and stabilize mutual deterrence in other regions of the world.[75]

Although its proponents include talented and highly respected scholars and policy analysts, the management perspective has had only a superficial impact on the general debate over nuclear proliferation (except in the case of the former Soviet Union). The reluctance of influential U.S. governmental officials to countenance a radical departure from present practices flows from four formidable constraints. First, because only a handful of threshold nuclear weapons states currently exist, the United States and its principal nonproliferation allies are loathe to jeopardize what they consider to be a largely successful global nonproliferation approach in order perhaps to respond more effectively to a few problematic cases. Second, a large corpus of international legislation—especially the NPT—and nontreaty commitments prohibit many of the arms control measures favored by nuclear management enthusiasts. Third, domestic U.S. legislation dating from the Atomic Energy Act of 1946 to the Nuclear Non-Proliferation Act (NNPA) of 1978 and subsequent amendments to foreign aid bills are even more restrictive concerning proliferation management. And finally, military self-interest dissuades the defense planners of the world's great powers from seeking to affirm foreign nuclear forces that may at some later date either be targeted against their territory or impair their ability to intervene effectively in a regional security dispute.

Nuclear Opacity and Strategic Stability

The common reluctance of the de facto nuclear weapon states to discuss openly their force capabilities and intentions—combined with the insistence of foreign powers for them not to do so—pose two potential problems for efforts to ensure regional nuclear security. The first complication concerns the strategic instabilities arising out of covert nuclear forces, the source of considerable intellectual debate. The second is that nuclear opacity impedes Indian and Pakistani efforts to openly propose, negotiate, and accept nuclear arms control agreements. Opacity, however, could also enable policymakers to work out in private measures that would be politically unpopular if publicized in either country.

Many experts believe that secrecy concerning military nuclear capabilities, weapon employment doctrines, targeting plans, and escalation thresholds weakens deterrence and creates other political and military problems.

Shai Feldman argues that covert nuclear weapons programs entail closed decision making without wider scrutiny, dominance of the military in the formulation of doctrine, biases toward offense and preemption, and strained crisis management and nuclear signaling.[76] Sundarji sees two strategic problems of nuclear opacity for India and Pakistan. The first is the possibility of a war between India and Pakistan being triggered through miscalculation of each other's nuclear status, as well as ignorance of the nuclear doctrines to which the two countries are likely to adhere. This could culminate in a tragic nuclear exchange. The second problem concerns the difficulties of ensuring the safety of nuclear warheads and the prevention of unauthorized use in a clandestine state.[77]

On the other hand, nuclear opacity probably is required to preserve the current condition of "non-weaponized deterrence" between India and Pakistan. George Perkovich and several South Asian analysts cited above contend that a condition of mutual deterrence deriving from the power of India and Pakistan to construct nuclear weapons quickly can be a steady source of regional security.[78] As Perkovich and others recognize, however, the stability of nonweaponized deterrence requires Islamabad and New Delhi to undertake a "rather demanding set of confidence-building measures to assure each other and the international community that they have not built weapons" and that they seek a situation of mutual security.[79]

Nuclear Opacity and Arms Control. In India and Pakistan, nuclear weapons have acquired a significance that extends well beyond their value as military and strategic bargaining instruments. A large portion of the Subcontinent's population sees both civilian and military nuclear programs as components of, and indeed symbols for, national sovereignty and security. Therefore, it is difficult for Indian and Pakistani politicians to make public concessions on nuclear matters. As Neil Joeck writes, "managed proliferation benefits from secrecy insofar as the symbolism and popularity that may attach to nuclear weapons are thereby contained."[80]

Opaque nuclear proliferation in South Asia may have constrained a regional arms race and provided policymakers flexibility in negotiations, but it has probably done so at the cost of preventing Indian and Pakistani political leaders from cultivating domestic constituencies for nuclear arms control and from identifying the precise nuclear security problems that are in the most need of control. Without a clear understanding of the role nuclear weapons played in exacerbating or defusing the 1986-87 Brasstacks and the 1990 Kashmir crises—an understanding that can best emerge from an open strategic dialogue—nuclear arms control could remain an ill-defined and elusive objective.

Arms Control and National Security. New Delhi and Islamabad have devoted considerable manpower, time, and paper to bilateral arms control, but neither side has accepted limits on military activities that it realistically might wish to pursue at some point in the future. Past and existing Indo-Pakistani treaties and CBMs have helped to reduce tensions and resolve troublesome disputes, but have not significantly altered the sources of military rivalry, stabilized nuclear security, or seriously constrained the strategic behavior of either country. Because neither Islamabad nor New Delhi sees arms control as a valuable source of national security, arms control does not yet play a central role in South Asian military and nuclear affairs.

Tacit to Explicit Bargaining

Writing in 1990, Joeck argued that

> tacit bargaining [between India and Pakistan] has been an important factor for a decade or more. It is possible to identify a pattern of cooperative action that stands in contrast to what on the surface has appeared to be a competitive arms race. There is a false impression that India and Pakistan are hurtling, uncontrolled, toward a nuclear armed confrontation . . . the leaders of both India and Pakistan are quite consciously and continuously attempting to prevent that from happening. Such efforts have persisted for a number of years and despite leadership changes in both countries.[81]

The changed political and military conditions of the region require more explicit bargaining—especially on the issue of nuclear security.

In the 1980s India and Pakistan enjoyed strong political leaders who had sufficient maneuvering room at home and the confidence needed to engage the other side and de-escalate crises. It is not clear if the tacit bargaining that worked well in the 1980s can be managed as effectively in the current era. The destruction of the Babri Masjid at Ayodhya, communal rioting and bombings in Bombay, and low-intensity conflict in Kashmir have disrupted the political dialogue. The transformation of domestic politics in each country, marked by the rise of the religious right and the erosion of national leadership, makes it necessary to open up and institutionalize arms control negotiations.

The effectiveness of tacit bargaining depends largely on the immediate state of relations between India and Pakistan and on the strength (especially the perceived strength) of the political leadership of each country. Unfortunately, India and Pakistan have had weak and unstable governments for several years; and there are no signs that political conditions are improving in either country. In response to a July 1993 call for bilateral tension-reducing talks by Pakistan's interim president, Wasim Sajjad, for example, India's junior foreign minister, Salman Khursheed, stated: "India wants to ease these tensions, but there is a period of uncertainty in Pakistan. For the present let us wait and watch."[82] Even today there are few indications that India is finished waiting and is prepared to sit down with Pakistan at the negotiating table.

Unilateral restraint and tacit confidence-building measures are important in any adversarial relationship, especially when the threat of nuclear war is involved. But arms control arrangements must be formally negotiated and ratified if they are to garner widespread domestic support and survive sudden changes in political leadership, popular sentiment, and international events.

Strategic Understanding and Reciprocity

The final obstacle that impedes efforts to establish a viable climate for arms control in South Asia is the prevalence of insensitivity, resentment, and defiance among India, Pakistan, and the United States. Specific conflicts often confound amicable relations between each of these countries, but more important, each state often acts with moralism and sometimes hypocrisy.[83] The lack of trust and understanding between India and Pakistan is well known: at present neither side is willing to make an effort to initiate a relationship of reciprocated good gestures. The growing animosity that differences over the nuclear issue produce between the United States, on the one hand, and India and Pakistan, on the other, has perhaps as much destructive potential.

American pressure for strict nuclear nonproliferation in South Asia probably prevents a more open discussion between India and Pakistan on regional nuclear security. In Pakistan there is strong resentment over the imposition of the Pressler amendment,[84] which Pakistanis view as discriminatory. Indians object as strenuously to U.S. efforts to force New Delhi to join the NPT, participate in a five-power conference on regional nonproliferation, and accept strict limitations on its space and missile programs. As a result, much of Indian and Pakistani diplomatic energies go to stalling or diverting American pressure rather than thinking about and proposing innovative measures to promote regional nuclear security.

At a deeper psychological level, the sense of U.S. and collective Western pressure on nonproliferation is creating the basis for deep and enduring anti-Western feelings in both countries. Such sentiments could produce a situation far more serious than that created by the "nuclear nationalism" that presently exists in India and Pakistan. Despite fragmentation of the domestic fabric in both nations, the defense of national sovereignty—which the nuclear programs symbolize—is an evocative rallying cry. The Islamic extremists of Pakistan and Hindu nationalists of India have become the most vocal advocates of defiance against the West. A signal of deteriorating conditions is the propagation throughout Indian and Pakistani societies of the religious and racial metaphors that long existed in the Subcontinent's nuclear establishments.

One of the unfortunate consequences of the current U.S. nonproliferation strategy toward South Asia is the formulation of the nuclear issue as a political conflict between India and the United States, on the one hand, and Pakistan and the United States, on the other. Officials in Islamabad and New Delhi find it politically difficult to address such problems as nuclear safety and crisis stability, which are growing along with the military nuclear capabilities in each country. Instead, defiance of the United States and defense of national sovereignty are the central elements of domestic nuclear debates in both South Asian countries. Rather than encouraging a regional debate on preventing a nuclear arms race and avoiding the dangers of war in the Subcontinent, heavy-handed external pressure may have made this more difficult than ever.

Conclusion

The advent of nuclear weapon capabilities in South Asia poses new risks for India and Pakistan. The United States and the Soviet Union were able to manage similar risks during the Cold War, but not easily. After several dangerous episodes, the Cuban missile crisis in particular, Washington and Moscow eventually learned to bring their foreign policy practices, defense programs, and military behavior in line with the requirement of avoiding nuclear war. India and Pakistan are now on the verge of undergoing a similar learning process. The outcome remains to be seen, but the evidence assembled in this essay suggests that the risks of nuclear war in South Asia can be controlled if India and Pakistan effectively apply arms control and confidence-building measures to their emerging nuclear relationship.

NOTES

1. Director of Central Intelligence James Woolsey told the Senate Governmental Affairs Committee on February 24, 1993: "The arms race between India and Pakistan poses perhaps the most probable prospect for future use of weapons of mass destruction, including nuclear weapons." Woolsey's opinion is typical in the U.S. government; it was repeated in the April 28 congressional testimony of John R. Malott, deputy assistant secretary of state for South Asian affairs, and in the Clinton administration's "Report to Congress on Progress Toward Regional Nonproliferation in South Asia," April 1993. Outside the government, a *Washington Post* editorial remarked that South Asia is "the likeliest place in the world for a nuclear war" ("The Next Nuclear War," October 13, 1989, 13). See also Leonard S. Spector, "India-Pakistan War: It Could Be Nuclear," *New York Times*, June 7, 1990, 23.
2. See McGeorge Bundy, *Danger and Survival: Choices About the Bomb in the First Fifty Years* (New York: Random House, 1988); George Bunn, *Arms Control by Committee: Managing Negotiations with the Soviets* (Stanford, Calif.: Stanford University Press, 1992); and Coit D. Blacker, *Reluctant Warriors: the United States, the Soviet Union and Arms Control* (New York: W. H. Freeman, 1987).
3. These are the three objectives of arms control that Thomas C. Schelling and Morton H. Halperin identified in *Strategy and Arms Control* (New York: Twentieth Century Fund, 1961), 1.
4. This estimate is based on the operating histories of India's Cirus, Dhruva, and unsafeguarded power reactors, less the amount of plutonium used for nonweapon ends. David Albright, Frans Berkhout and William Walker, *World Inventory of Plutonium and Highly Enriched Uranium, 1992* (New York: Oxford University Press, 1993), 157-62.
5. Albright and Mark Hibbs, "India's Silent Bomb," *Bulletin of the Atomic Scientists* 48, no. 7 (September 1992): 27-31.
6. Albright, Berkhout, and Walker, *World Inventory*, 162-67.
7. Albright and Hibbs, "Pakistan's Bomb: Out of the Closet," *Bulletin of the Atomic Scientists* 48, no. 6 (July/August 1992): 38-43.
8. Most notably, India is developing the Agni, an intermediate-range ballistic missile, and the Prithvi, a battlefield ballistic missile. Pakistan has produced the HATF I and II (copies of French Dauphin and Eridan sounding rockets) and is reported to have received components for China's M-11 medium-range missile. See Timothy V. McCarthy, "India: Emergent Missile Power," and Cameron Binkley, "Pakistani Ballistic Missile Development: The Sword of Islam?" both in William Potter and Harlan Jenks, eds., *The International Missile Bazaar: The New Suppliers' Network* (Boulder, Colorado: Westview, 1994).
9. For an estimate of the catastrophic physical effects of a few nuclear explosions in South Asia, see S. Rashid Naim, "*Aadhi Raat Ke Baad* (After Midnight)," in Stephen Philip Cohen, ed., *Nuclear Proliferation in South Asia: The Prospects for Arms Control* (Boulder, Colorado: Westview, 1991), 23-61.
10. A more comprehensive list is included in Malott's "Report to Congress on Progress Toward Regional Nonproliferation in South Asia," U.S. Department of State, April 1993.

11. Robert Glasser, "Avoiding Strategic Instability in South Asia: Some Insights from the Cold War," unpublished paper, November 14, 1990, 16-21. Some defense experts now claim that India's armed forces are losing their edge against Pakistan as the result of five years of resource cuts, disrupted supplies from the former Soviet Union, and deepened army involvement in internal peacekeeping. See Shekhar Gupta with W. P. S. Sidhu and Kanwar Sandhu, "A Middle-Aged Military Machine," *India Today* (New Delhi), April 30, 1993, 22-30.
12. "Report on Kahuta Denied," Karachi Domestic Service, September 30, 1985, reprinted in *Joint Publications Research Service (JPRS)/Nuclear Development and Proliferation*, October 21, 1985, 37; "Plans to Attack Pakistan Nuclear Complex Denied," Delhi Domestic Service, November 6, 1985, reprinted in *Foreign Broadcast Information Service (FBIS)/South Asia*, November 6, 1985, E-1.
13. K. Subrahmanyam, "Building Trust on the Bomb: What India and Pakistan Can Do," *Times of India* (Bombay), July 30, 1985, 8.
14. The text of Article I is printed in Sreedhar and John Kaniyalil, eds., *Indo-Pak Relations: A Documentary Study* (New Delhi: ABC Publishing House, 1993), 234-35.
15. The News (Rawalpindi), January 5, 1992, 1. This dispute may stem from the fact that the treaty language is ambiguous as to what constitutes a nuclear facility (e.g., inoperative facilities or installations under construction).
16. "Pakistani Sources Charge India Failed to Adhere to Nuclear Pact," United Press International (UPI), January 8, 1992.
17. Colin S. Gray, "Arms Control Does Not Control Arms," *Orbis* (Summer 1993): 343.
18. For U.S.-Soviet nuclear deterrence, see Albert Wohlstetter, "The Delicate Balance of Terror," *Foreign Affairs* 37, no. 2 (January 1959): 211-34. For South Asia, see Susan M. Burns, "Preventing Nuclear War: Arms Management," in Cohen's *Nuclear Proliferation in South Asia*, 89-126.
19. The *Hindustan Times* reported in May 1993 that the Indian Army's 11th Corps was armed with the Prithvi, a medium-range ballistic missile capable of carrying a one-ton warhead. The report evidently was false, but Prithvi deployment may begin within the next few years. Three versions of the Prithvi reportedly have been produced with ranges of 218, 155 and 93 miles. See Brahma Chellaney, "India Carries Out Surprise Test of An Extended Prithvi Missile," UPI, June 12, 1993.
20. See Richard Sisson and Leo E. Rose, *War and Secession: Pakistan, India, and the Creation of Bangladesh* (Berkeley and Los Angeles: University of California Press, 1990); Siddiq Salik, *Witness to Surrender* (Karachi: Oxford University Press, 1977); and Robert Jackson, *South Asian Crisis: India, Pakistan and Bangladesh* (New York: Praeger, 1975).
21. George Perkovich, "A Nuclear Third Way in South Asia," *Foreign Policy* 91 (Summer 1993): 89.
22. Robert Jervis, "Arms Control, Stability, and the Causes of War," *Daedalus* 120, no. 1 (Winter 1991): 178.
23. Scott D. Sagan, *The Limits of Safety: Organizations, Accidents, and Nuclear Weapons* (Princeton: Princeton University Press, 1993); and Charles Perrow, *Normal Accidents: Living With High-Risk Technologies* (New York: Basic Books, 1984).
24. Sagan, "The Perils of Proliferation: Organization Theory, Deterrence Theory, and the Spread of Nuclear Weapons," *International Security* 18, no. 4 (Spring 1994): 66-107.
25. Gregory F. Giles, "Safeguarding the Undeclared Nuclear Arsenals," *Washington Quarterly* 16, no. 2 (Spring 1993): 173-86; Peter D. Feaver, "Command and Control

in Emerging Nuclear Nations," *International Security* 17, no. 3 (Winter 1992/93): 160-87; and Burns, "Preventing Nuclear War," 116-18.

26. Lewis Dunn, "*Containing Nuclear Proliferation*," *Adelphi Paper* (Summer, 1993), 47.
27. Paul Leventhal and Brahma Chellaney, "Nuclear Terrorism: Threat, Perception, and Response in South Asia," *Terrorism* 11 (1988): 447-70.
28. Giles, "Safeguarding the Undeclared Nuclear Arsenals," 178.
29. Considerations of technical aid to new nuclear states go far back. The Kennedy administration is said to have considered such assistance to the Soviet Union in the early 1960s. Washington provided this aid to Britain and France. See Joel Larus, *Nuclear Weapons Safety and the Common Defense* (Columbus: Ohio State University Press, 1967); Colin S. Gray, "Arms Control in a Nuclear Armed World," *Annals of the American Academy of Political Science* no. 430 (March 1977): 110-21; Daniel Caldwell, "Permissive Action Links: A Description and Proposal," *Survival* 29, no. 3 (May/June 1987): 224-38.
30. Dunn, "*Containing Nuclear Proliferation*," 47-51; Giles, "Safeguarding the Undeclared Nuclear Arsenals," 184-86.
31. For this reason, Dunn suggests helping new nuclear powers solve doctrinal rather than technological problems. See Dunn, *Containing Nuclear Proliferation*, 49-53. Also, Peter R. Lavoy, "Nuclear Myths and the Causes of Nuclear Proliferation," *Security Studies* 2, nos. 3/4 (Spring/Summer 1993).
32. Journalistic reports suggest that in India the prime minister, the civilian defense minister, and the Cabinet Committee on Political Affairs dominate nuclear decision-making; the armed services are not intimately involved. Although Pakistan has a long history of direct and indirect intervention by the military in governmental affairs, and military leaders (especially the chief of army staff) probably are key players in nuclear decision-making, military loyalty appears to be strong. It is not likely that a renegade service faction would emerge, much less attempt to usurp control over nuclear weapons. An excellent discussion of Pakistan's armed forces is Stephen P. Cohen, *The Pakistan Army* (Berkeley and Los Angeles: University of California Press, 1984).
33. Michael O'Rourke, "Nuclear Stand-off: Interview with General K. Sundarji," *Far Eastern Economic Review*, September 13, 1990, 26.
34. Dunn, *Controlling the Bomb* (New Haven: Yale University Press, 1982), 70. See also Kathleen C. Bailey, *Doomsday Weapons in the Hands of Many: The Arms Control Challenge of the '90s* (Urbana: University of Illinois Press, 1991), 2.
35. Stephen P. Cohen, "Perception, Influence and Weapons Proliferation in South Asia," report prepared for the U.S. Department of State, Bureau of Intelligence and Research (#1722-920184, August 1978), 24.
36. *Perspectives on Kashmir: The Roots of Conflict in South Asia*, ed., Raju G. C. Thomas (Boulder, Colorado: Westview, 1992).
37. K. Subrahmanyam, "Nuclear Policy, Arms Control and Military Cooperation," paper presented at the conference on India and the United States after the Cold War, sponsored by the Carnegie Endowment for International Peace and the India International Center, New Delhi, March 7-9, 1993, 7.
38. Quoted by Seymour M. Hersh, "On the Nuclear Edge," *The New Yorker*, March 29, 1993, 57. While Hersh's account suggests that a nuclear exchange could have occurred in 1990, other accounts paint a far less catastrophic picture. See *Conflict Prevention and Confidence-building Measures in South Asia: The 1990 Crisis*, eds., Michael

Krepon and Mishi Faruqee, Occasional Paper No. 17, The Henry L. Stimson Center, April 1994.

39. Kuldip Nayar, "We Have the A-Bomb, Says Pakistan's Dr. Strangelove," *Observer* (London), March 1, 1987.
40. In the Hersh interview, Gates suggests that his visit to New Delhi and Islamabad helped to defuse the nuclear crisis and prevent a war. General V. N. Sharma, then chief of the Indian army, disagrees, however, stating that India did not fear a Pakistani nuclear threat and that U.S. embassy officials in India and Pakistan assisted these countries in averting a war well before Gates arrived in the region. Sharma, "It's All Bluff and Bluster," *Economic Times* (New Delhi), May 18, 1993, 13.
41. Shireen M. Mazari, "Nuclear Weapons and Structures of Conflict in the Developing World," in W. Thomas Wander and Eric H. Arnett, *The Proliferation of Advanced Weaponry: Technology, Motivations, and Responses* (Washington, D.C.: American Association for the Advancement of Science, 1992), 48.
42. K. Subrahmanyam, "Down Memory Lane," *Economic Times*, March 24, 1993, 15.
43. Subrahmanyam, "Nuclear Policy, Arms Control and Military Cooperation," 15.
44. Subrahmanyam, "Building Trust on the Bomb," 8.
45. General K. Sundarji, "Nuclear Deterrence: Doctrine for India, Part 2," *Trishul* (professional journal of the Defence Services Staff College, Wellington, India) 5, no. 3 (July 1993).
46. Raj Chengappa, "Nuclear Dilemma," *India Today*, April 30, 1994, 53.
47. Chengappa, "Nuclear Dilemma," 53.
48. Shekhar Gupta and W. P. S. Sidhu, "The End Game Option," *India Today*, April 30, 1993, 28.
49. Several major statements by Gandhi and Nehru are contained in the Indian government's official anthology of writings and speeches on the nuclear issue, *India and Disarmament* (New Delhi: Ministry of External Affairs, 1988). See also J. P. Jain, *India and Disarmament: Nehru Era*, Vol. 1 (New Delhi: Radiant Publishers, 1974).
50. See *Disarmament: India's Initiatives* (New Delhi: Indian Ministry of External Affairs, 1988), 81-86.
51. Indian press statement on START II, January 12, 1993; reprinted in *FBIS*-NES-93-008, January 13, 1993, 44.
52. See Charles C. Flowerree, "CBMs in the U.N. Setting," in John Borawski, ed., *Avoiding War in the Nuclear Age: Confidence-building Measures for Crisis Stability* (Boulder, Colorado: Westview, 1986), 107-108.
53. India opposed the Baruch Plan because of reservations about the ability of an international nuclear control authority to operate impartially and promote the peaceful application of atomic energy in the developing world. See Jain, *India and Disarmament: Nehru Era*, 15-19.
54. At the 1983 summit of nonaligned nations in New Delhi, India called for a test ban, production freeze, and number reduction in the nuclear weapons of the United States and the Soviet Union. When Soviet-American nuclear negotiations broke down at the end of 1983 on the issue of Euromissiles, Prime Minister Indira Gandhi and Swedish Prime Minister Olaf Palme launched a six-nation, five-continent peace and disarmament campaign. Rajiv Gandhi also made nuclear disarmament a top priority in India's international diplomacy. The 1986 Delhi Declaration, the 1988 Action Plan, and related diplomatic activities generated international publicity for New Delhi and also

helped to establish a strong domestic consensus in India for its positions on nuclear disarmament.

55. For an early Indian perspective, see V.C. Trivedi, "Statement to the Eighteen Nation Disarmament Committee," September 28, 1967, in *U.S. Arms Control and Disarmament Agency, Documents on Disarmament, 1967* (Washington, D.C.: U.S. Government Printing Office, 1968), 436.
56. For instance, a senior Indian diplomat observes: "The adoption of an 'arms control' approach, as distinct from the 'disarmament' framework, has failed to arrest proliferation and is unlikely to provide a viable paradigm for the future." Prakash Shah, "Nuclear Non-Proliferation Implications and the NPT Review," *Strategic Analysis* (New Delhi) (May 1993): 145.
57. President Ayub Khan, Statement to the 17th session of the U.N. General Assembly, in Hameed A. K. Rai, *Pakistan in the United Nations* (Lahore: Aziz Publishers, 1979), 241.
58. Statement to the First Committee of the General Assembly, December 13, 1967, in *Documents on Disarmament,* 1967, 671.
59. Statement to the First Committee of the General Assembly, May 13, 1968, in *Documents on Disarmament,* 1968, 318.
60. See "Statement by the Pakistani Representative to the First Committee of the General Assembly," November 4, 1966, in *Documents on Disarmament,* 1966, 689-90.
61. Steve Weissman and Herbert Krosney, *The Islamic Bomb: The Nuclear Threat to Israel and the Middle East* (New York: Times Books, 1981), 42-46.
62. Ashok Kapur, *Pakistan's Nuclear Development* (London: Croom Helm, 1987), 155, 165; Ziba Moshaver, *Nuclear Weapons Proliferation in the Indian Subcontinent* (New York: St. Martin's, 1991), 130-32.
63. Ali Sarwar Naqvi, "Pakistan: Seeking Regional Peace and Progress in Non-Nuclear South Asia," *Arms Control Today* 23, no. 5 (June 1993): 11.
64. Peter R. Lavoy, "Learning and the Evolution of Cooperation in U.S. and Soviet Nonproliferation Activities" in George W. Breslauer and Philip E. Tetlock, eds., *Learning in U.S. and Soviet Foreign Policy* (Boulder, Colorado: Westview, 1991), 735-83.
65. See also the April 28, 1993 congressional testimony of John R. Malott, deputy assistant secretary of state for South Asian affairs.
66. Mushahid Hussain asserts that "under pressure from the Bush administration, the government of Prime Minister Benazir Bhutto had stopped production of highly enriched uranium before the former Prime Minister arrived in Washington for her official visit in June 1989." "Nuclear Issue: Ball is Now in Pakistan's Court," *Nation* (Lahore), November 29, 1990.
67. C. Raja Mohan, "Nuclear Fundamentalism Must Go," *Hindu,* November 21, 1991.
68. For examples, see K. Subrahmanyam, "An Indo-Pak Nuclear Restraint Regime," in two parts, *Economic Times,* September 30, 1992 and October 1, 1992. Also see General K. Sundarji, "The Nuclear Threat," *India Today,* November 30, 1990, 90, and Sundarji, "Nuclear Realpolitik," *India Today,* August 31, 1991, 81.
69. See K. K. Katyal, "Signing NPT Not in Indian Interest," *Hindu,* July 8, 1993.
70. General Mirza Aslam Beg, "Pakistan's Nuclear Program: A National Security Perspective," unpublished paper, 20.
71. Malott, "Report to Congress on Progress Toward Regional Nonproliferation in South Asia," April 28, 1993.

72. Richard N. Haass, "South Asia: Too Late to Remove the Bomb?" *Orbis* (Winter 1988): 107-118. See also Haass, *Conflicts Unending: The United States and Regional Disputes* (New Haven: Yale University Press, 1990), 91.
73. Cohen, *Nuclear Proliferation in South Asia.*
74. Dunn, *Controlling the Bomb,* 149-75; Giles, "Safeguarding the Undeclared Nuclear Arsenals," Colin Gray, "Arms Control in a Nuclear Armed World?" *Annals of the American Academy of Political Science Studies,* no. 430 (March 1977); Michael T. Klare, "Can Third World Arms Control Work?" *Arms Control Today* 20, no. 3 (April 1990).
75. On Israel and the Middle East, see Shai Feldman, "Managing Nuclear Proliferation," in Jed C. Snyder and Samuel F. Wells, Jr., eds., *Limiting Nuclear Proliferation* (Cambridge, Mass., Ballinger, 1985).
76. Feldman, "Managing Nuclear Proliferation."
77. K. Sundarji, "Former Military Chief Discusses Nuclear Options," *India Express* (Delhi), December 20, 1992.
78. Perkovich, "A Nuclear Third Way in South Asia."
79. Ibid., p. 86.
80. Neil Joeck, "Tacit Bargaining and Stable Proliferation in South Asia," *Journal of Strategic Studies* 13, no. 3 (September 1990): 79.
81. Ibid., 89.
82. "No Talks Until Stable Government in Pakistan," *Nation,* July 28, 1993.
83. Peter R. Lavoy, "Introduction," in Leo E. Rose and Eric Gonsalves, eds., *Toward a New World Order: Adjusting India-U.S. Relations* (Berkeley: Institute of East Asian Studies, University of California, Berkeley, 1993), 16.
84. Introduced in 1985 by Senator Larry Pressler (R-SD) as an amendment to the Foreign Assistance Act, the Pressler amendment prohibits U.S. assistance to Pakistan, including military equipment and technology, unless the President certifies that Pakistan does not possess a nuclear explosive device. When President Bush could not make this certification in 1990, U.S. aid was terminated.

4

NUCLEAR ISSUES: MYTHS AND REALITIES

Pervez Hoodbhoy

The renowned eighteenth-century physicist, Blaise Pascal, offered an argument for why one should believe in God. If God exists, he argued, the penalty for not believing in Him is eternal damnation. Supposing, however, that He does not actually exist, then the believer will have suffered but a light penalty: some restrictions on food and drink, abstinence in conduct, and perhaps a few other relatively minor inconveniences. Therefore, on balance, it is far better to believe than not.

This kind of logic has often been applied to the issue of nuclear deterrence. Today, a widely shared premise in India and Pakistan is that possession of nuclear weapons provides the ultimate guarantee of national security and stability. Not maintaining a nuclear capability, it is argued, amounts to dropping one's defenses and inviting annihilation. Therefore, since survival is apparently at stake, financial and other costs become insignificant.

The strong emotions generated by the nuclear issue have precluded a genuine debate—at the public level or within the higher echelons of government—on a matter that is both complex and of vital importance. Instead, nuclear hawks, both in India and Pakistan, have long held center stage with their quixotic belief that a "balance of terror" is in the best interest of both countries. Consequently, a plethora of myths and false perceptions abound, none of which is seriously challenged. This chapter examines a number of critical issues that the nuclearized Subcontinent must face squarely.

First, how much security does a nuclear capability really buy? Some in Pakistan believe that it has already proved its worth in May 1990 during the Subcontinent's "Cuban Missile Crisis." Given the significance of the event, however, the lack of commentary on it is astonishing; little attempt has been made to understand its wide-ranging implications.

Second, what accounts for the linkage of national pride with the bomb? In the international arena, big boxers must be able to pack big punches—kilotons and megatons worth. Power, prestige, and politics have thus become intertwined in the consciousness of many. How reasonable is such a linkage and how much pride should rightly be associated with the strictly technical achievement of nuclear capability?

Third, one is often confronted with the argument that nuclear weapons on the Subcontinent are a reality. Therefore, goes this argument, it is better for both nations to accept this fact and expose their capabilities rather than leave them shrouded with uncertainty. The benefits of the position are frequently extolled, but what are the costs?

Fourth, if South Asia is indeed irreversibly nuclearized, then one must deal with the possibility that nuclear war can occur not only by the will of one or both parties but also through chance and accident. What are the possible mechanisms by which this could happen? In this context, one must also ask how South Asian nuclear deterrence might be different from nuclear deterrence between the United States and the Soviet Union.

Fifth is the all-important question: What can be done to avoid nuclear conflagration in South Asia, whether by design or by accident? This is no longer an issue for the future and cannot await resolution of the fundamental disputes between the two countries. Therefore, what is needed is an India-Pakistan dialogue on nuclear issues and a set of possibly workable measures that could alleviate the dangers. What are these measures?

Finally, what are Pakistan's nuclear choices? Pakistan will soon have to make agonizingly difficult decisions regarding its nuclear program. As global pressure mounts for Islamabad to denuclearize, Pakistan's policy of deliberate ambiguity—which had served it so well politically and diplomatically in the past—is coming under greater stress. Therefore, Pakistan must explore new options.

Understanding the May 1990 Crisis

Many Pakistani believers in nuclearization cite May 1990 as the nation's first exercise of its nuclear muscle and offer it as proof of its power to deter. The truth of the matter is of secondary importance; perceptions are more important here, and the facts may never really become known. Enshrined as an article of faith is that Pakistan's threat of nuclear devastation stopped Indian aggression dead in its tracks.

How exactly the nuclear threat was communicated to India is not clear. Local and foreign commentators offer versions which differ. But the lore in Pakistan is the following.

Troops had been massed on both sides of the border following heightened tension over Kashmir. Robert Gates, the national security advisor to President George Bush, rushed to Islamabad to defuse the crisis. He met President Ghulam Ishaq Khan and General Mirza Aslam Beg, one of whom said that "we are desperate enough to blow India to smithereens." Subsequently, U.S. satellites picked up a heavily armed convoy of trucks moving out of Kahuta toward Chaklala airport, where F-16s with nuclear capable bomb-racks stood ready on the tarmac.[1] The information was conveyed to the Indians, and they backed off.

General Beg, now retired, has staunchly denied this version of the May 1990 events.[2] In an interview almost three years after the crisis, he claimed that Pakistan did not possess a usable nuclear device at that time. Therefore his country could not have been poised to use such a weapon against India. Moreover, in his opinion, such readiness was unnecessary because Pakistan had not faced a critical or desperate situation. Furthermore, "There was a solid fear of massive retaliation from India," he recalled, "as they [the Indians] have a stockpile of more than a dozen warheads."[3]

General Beg could well be telling the truth, and May 1990 could have been a nuclear nonevent. Indeed, some senior officials in Pakistan and India believe that the crisis was exaggerated and that there was, in fact, no imminent danger of nuclear conflict. In that case, the only losers are the Pakistani journalists and political commentators who had cheered a false victory.

What if Pakistan, however, sensing an Indian attack had indeed communicated a nuclear threat in May 1990? What if the Gates and trucks-out-of-Kahuta story were actually true? If correct, there are at least four profound implications.

First, the Kahuta crisis would have revealed weaponization. The official line taken by both India and Pakistan is that they have developed the technical capability of producing nuclear weapons. Such capability means that enough fissile material, other components, and technical know-how exist. However, both countries claim that, by choice, they have refrained from constructing actual weapons. But if weaponization had indeed been disclosed to the U.S.

intelligence community, then Pakistan surely laid itself open to application of the Pressler amendment against it. This amendment specifically refers to the possession of a nuclear weapon and was already in effect at the time of the crisis. By convincing Washington that it possessed a workable nuclear weapon, Pakistan would also have prompted the United States to apply the amendment strictly. In having choked off the major source of its weapon supplies, it is far from clear whether Pakistan's alleged action was to its security benefit.

Second, and much more ominous, some possibility now exists that the next Indo-Pakistani war will not go through the phase of conventional warfare. Hitherto, the general assumption has been that if hostilities commence, they shall do so in a controlled way and conventional weapons will be used. Unsheathing the nuclear sword would then either cause the war to stop or to escalate gradually into a nuclear one. If Pakistani nuclear hawks are correct in saying that Pakistan suddenly brandished the bomb in May 1990 before a single shot had been fired, however, then the next war may begin and end with a horrific nuclear exchange that would destroy tens of millions of lives in both countries. In such a war, India could suffer major damage to some of its population centers and key installations like dams and nuclear power stations. Pakistan, being geographically much smaller and facing a much larger nuclear adversary, would be entirely devastated.

Third, published accounts of the "nuclear threat" in May 1990, if true, reveal the appalling possibility that Third World leaders may play with the nuclear button even when their countries' existence is not mortally threatened. This would serve to reinforce existing fears and prejudices against Third World nuclear powers in the international community. A trigger-happy nuclear nation, as General Beg correctly pointed out in his interview, is certain to be viewed as irresponsible. This situation is certainly not made any better by the statements of certain zealots in Pakistani politics who have invoked concepts of *jehad* and *shahadat* in the context of nuclear weapons.

Fourth, Pakistan's future security could be seriously compromised if indeed it did choose to exercise a nuclear threat. The nuclear sword is double edged. On the one hand, the terror it inspires can deter a potential attack. On the other hand, this very fear can inspire a preemptive attack aimed at destroying the opponent, or at least its nuclear weapons, before they can be used. In a situation of extreme tension, uncertainty and mistrust of the adversary's intentions are rampant. In all probability, quick decisions based upon incomplete information will have to be taken. Past behavior of the adversary is likely to play an important role.

Given that Pakistan is the smaller and weaker of the two nations, it is unlikely that it would initiate a conventional attack on India. The Indians certainly understand this. They know that Pakistan would keep open a nuclear option as a last resort against a situation in which Pakistan's armed forces were being overrun by Indian military might. But, the Indians also understand that Pakistan, because it feels insecure and threatened, may resort to desperate acts. To preempt such an act, a first strike would then become a distinct possiblity. Therefore, the Indian government could use the alleged May 1990 crisis as an argument to justify an attack.

Does Nuclear Deterrence Work?

The most frequently cited example of successful deterrence is that of Europe after World War II. For example, defense analyst Edward Luttwak argues that "We have lived since 1945 without another world war precisely because rational minds extracted a durable peace from the terror of nuclear weapons."[4] It is impossible to verify or disprove such claims. There are other possible explanations for the nonoccurrence of war: the memory of the immense destruction in World War II, the absence of a territorial conflict between the United States and the Soviet Union, and the relative timidity of Soviet ideology. Although nuclear deterrence may have contributed to stability, the case is not ironclad.

Nonetheless, nuclear rivals are less likely to go to war against each other. Assuming that both sides make rational decisions, the onset of hostilities is likely to be delayed or may not take place at all. The "balance of terror" argument does have a certain amount of validity, even in a situation of nuclear asymmetry such as exists between India and Pakistan.

There is no guarantee, however, that, even in the presence of a nuclear deterrent, conventional war will not take place. Emotional responses of leaders cannot be predicted with any degree of certainty should a major crisis occur. If war does commence, in all likelihood the course of events will soon cause it to escalate into a nuclear exchange.

The Iran-Iraq war provides one example where nuclear deterrence may have failed had it become available to the adversaries during the course of a conflict. This war was a no-holds-barred conflict. Every type of weapon in the opponents' arsenals was used. Each side knew it would receive a response in kind but was undeterred. In the War of Cities, population centers were devastated by long-range missiles. A missile arriving on Tehran led to a missile departing for Baghdad. Both populations experienced the horror of chemical warfare. Would they have been spared the horror of nuclear warfare?

The ability of rivals to deter each other presupposes rational behavior. Again, there is an available example where this assumption was not fulfilled: Saddam's Scud attacks on Israel were launched with the full knowledge that Israel could make Iraq a radioactive wasteland in a matter of hours. There was no military or strategic logic to these attacks; these were potentially suicidal acts motivated by desperation and fury. For the people of Iraq it was extremely fortunate that Saddam's missiles missed their mark or were intercepted before they could inflict real damage on Israel.

Bombs for Prestige?

Why do some nation-states seek nuclear weapons? The standard reply is that they feel their security is at risk, but this is obviously not the whole answer. The quest for power and prestige may be important, perhaps even paramount. France and India provide two clear examples where nuclear weapons have been pursued primarily out of hunger for political power rather than for national security. Other countries too, including Pakistan, yearn for these instruments of mass destruction because they supposedly endow their possessors with true power.

Nuclear weapons, in a sense, are viewed by several Third World countries as a sequel to modernization; they come with "growing up," so to speak. The Indian case is perhaps the clearest demonstration of this. Nuclear weapons, with their surrounding mystique and awesome power to destroy, symbolize the mastery of advanced technology. National chauvinism finds a rallying point: Build the bomb! The bomb means power.

The United Nations has done little to dispel this perverse view—all five permanent members of the Security Council are nuclear weapon powers. This constitutes a tacit admission that nations that command the power of mass annihilation are more important than those that do not. But the UN is behind the times. Fortunately, the values of past decades are rapidly changing. The end of the U.S.-Soviet confrontation has created the dramatic new possibility of a world with far fewer nuclear weapons. Today, bomb worship is no longer the rage. There are excellent reasons for this.

One reason is that designing nuclear weapons has become old hat. Unquestionably, the first atomic bomb was an exceedingly brilliant, if terrible, achievement by the world's finest physicists. It required the creation of wholly new physical concepts, based on a then newly acquired understanding of the atomic nucleus. The ensuing technological effort, the Manhattan Project, was unparalleled in the history of mankind for its complexity and difficulty. Thereafter, the ability of a country to make nuclear bombs became synonymous with its technical prowess and, hence, its strength.

Today, the design of atomic weapons, while still nontrivial, is vastly simpler than it was. Basic information is freely available in technical libraries throughout the world. The theory of chain-reacting systems, data on critical masses, equations for neutron transport, the assembly-disassembly phase of an exploding device, and so on, are published. Also available are technical treatments of compression, achievement of "criticality," initiation of chain reactions, buildup of kinetic energy, and the final phases of the explosion as the pieces start to move apart. Advanced textbooks and monographs contain a staggering amount of detail that can enable reasonably competent scientists and engineers to come up with "quick and dirty" designs for nuclear explosives. Benefitting from various declassified documents in the United States, the general reader, as well as the nuclear weapon specialist, can now see cut-away drawings of weapons, photographs, and even once-classified test data. The Iraqis, it is now known, made direct use of the Manhattan Project data in their program.

Nevertheless, not everyone or any nation can build its own bombs so easily. The biggest technical obstacle is the difficulty of obtaining high-grade fissile materials, uranium-235 or plutonium. Plutonium is available only as a reactor by-product, and uranium-235 occurs naturally only in a heavily diluted form. These bomb materials are presently unavailable in the international market, even though covert sales of former Soviet-made, weapons-grade materials have been alleged. A nation that wants bombs almost certainly has to produce the materials itself. But the march of time has made this immensely simpler.

Today, a variety of techniques is available for the production of fissile materials for bombs. India has chosen the reprocessing route because it has a large number of civilian reactors whose spent fuel can be used for extracting plutonium. Pakistan has opted for centrifuge technology. Iraq had an extensive calutron program based on an electromagnetic separation method, which is still in the process of being destroyed under international supervision. Still more modern and effective methods are now available, and isotope separation by lasers is just around the corner.

None of these processes is trivially acquired or developed. Even today, substantial amounts of resources and engineering ingenuity are required to make any of these methods actually work. It would be folly and ignorance, however, to think of nuclear weapon development as being at the cutting edge of science or technology. Nuclear weapon designers are no longer considered to be among the giants of science today.

More than a dozen Third World countries with quite marginal technological infrastructures and no standing in the world of high science can develop the rudiments of a nuclear weapons program. No scientific genius is needed; good engineering competence, dedication, and hard work will suffice. The principal requirements are a sufficient degree of motivation and adequate funds. Pakistan has proved this point extremely well.

Threatened by the Indian nuclear explosion of 1974, and fearing attack from a much stronger and aggressive neighbor, Pakistan set about establishing its own program. By heavily concentrating its limited scientific energies, Pakistan was able to build up a fairly sophisticated nuclear establishment that is disproportionately large relative to other areas of scientific endeavor in the country. This is not a minor achievement for a country with a per capita gross national product of $400 per year, a 74 percent illiteracy rate, and an educational system among the poorest in quality anywhere in the world.

Whatever security benefits or liabilities they may bring to Pakistan or other countries, however, in today's world nuclear weapons have irretrievably lost their old political clout and have been stripped of much of their mystique. With further passage of time, they will inevitably come to be viewed much as chemical and biological weapons are seen today—as a brutish means of mass annihilation, not as technical marvels.

Proof of the impending delinkage of international prestige from nuclear capability becomes evident upon examining the pecking order of nations today. Compare nonnuclear Japan with its giant neighbor, nuclear China. Which of the two exercises greater power in world affairs? Which is respected and courted more by other nations? Finally, which offers a higher quality of life and opportunities to its citizens? Within Europe, one can similarly compare nuclear Britain with non-nuclear Germany.

No one doubts the ability of Japan, or other non-nuclear industrialized countries, to develop a full-fledged nuclear arsenal in a very short period of time if they should so desire. Unlike the crude, unreliable, and bulky weapons that countries like India and Pakistan are capable of developing, these would be slick, high-tech, state-of-the-art marvels. But such weapons would not add one iota to the well-being of these countries. On the contrary, they would exchange some degree of their prosperity for a whole range of dilemmas that would render them much less secure.

Nevertheless, old ways of thinking die hard. Many on the Subcontinent continue to rely upon the bomb to endow respectability and status. In India, the message of the dawn of a new age has been lost, and it is pursuing nuclearization for prestige with unabated vigor. Indian militarism is on the rise and is being fueled by the emergence of a new political culture in New Delhi based on an alliance between the Congress elites, the bureaucracy, the military establishment, and a rising national bourgeoisie. The rise of Hindu chauvinism, most recently demonstrated in Ayodhya, has led to a preoccupation with achieving great-power status. Following rapid military expansion after 1978, India now looks to nuclear weapons to project its military might far beyond its borders.

Although India may succeed in setting itself up as a fearsome regional power, this success will not make it the great power it aspires to be. Great powers, after all, are not so easily made. The masses of India, whose ignorance the Indian elite would like to ignore, are drowning in a sea of poverty. Religious, ethnic, and tribal conflicts exact their dreadful toll, and the blackest forms of human misery stalk this land. No hope exists for the abandoned pavement dwellers of Indian cities, whose number runs into tens of millions, or for their generations to come. Bombs are indeed a curious way to seek greatness.

The pride factor exists in Pakistan, too, although to a somewhat lesser extent. There is a strong belief that the bomb would elevate Pakistan's image among Muslim countries. Some cherish the fond hope that oil money will pour into the country once Pakistan explicitly demonstrates its nuclear capability through a test explosion. There is, however, not the slightest reason to believe that with or without nuclear capability Pakistan will thereby become less disadvantaged in its relations to Arab countries. Pakistani workers in Saudi Arabia and the Gulf states will continue to receive shoddy treatment. Pakistan's political leaders will continue to make humble pilgrimages, as they do now, and supplicate Arab sheikhs for aid.

The Overt-Covert Debate

Let India and Pakistan both become nuclear weapon states openly and without reservations. They are both mature nations which need no counseling on their international responsibilities and conduct.[5] —General K.M. Arif

This statement by retired Pakistani general K.M. Arif could just as well have been written by his Indian counterpart, retired general K.S. Sundarji, or by numerous other Indians and Pakistanis. There is indeed a curious meeting of minds, quite independent of the side to which they belong, between nuclear hawks committed to the "balance of terror" argument.

General Arif's argument requires that the Pakistani government shed its position of "calculated ambiguity" and, instead, openly declare possession of nuclear weapons. In part, General Arif's position comes from alarm at the aggressive pace of Indian militarization, particularly the continuing development of the Agni missile. But, this view also results from anger that the United States has chosen to severely penalize Pakistan while effectively acquiescing to a much bigger Indian nuclear weapons program.

Pressure from nuclear hawks like Generals Arif and Beg to overtly nuclearize must be resisted, as it has been in the past, even though Pakistan's anxiety and anger have genuine cause. Rational conduct requires that the consequences of going overt be clearly thought out. This is critically important because such a decision may be essentially irreversible. Once a country goes nuclear, pulling back may be impossible.

Of the damages that Pakistan could suffer, the certain loss of economic and military aid from the West and Japan is a relatively small matter, even though it has received the most attention. Much more serious, but never openly discussed, are the consequences for Pakistan's national security.

It is therefore crucial to examine the five main arguments offered by advocates of Pakistan's nuclearization. First, they argue, declaring the bomb is unlikely to have any major effect because the Indians are likely to have cheated and most probably already possess nuclear weapons. Second, a declaration of nuclearization will lead to a freezing of the status quo through the existence of a credible and stable mutual deterrent. Third, even a few Pakistani bombs can constitute "minimal deterrence," which will cause military competition to vanish. Fourth, the cost of a credible nuclear deterrent is affordable. Fifth, a nuclear deterrent will allow Pakistan to make up for the superiority of Indian conventional forces.

The arguments are apparently logical and carry force. But they must be weighed against even stronger counterarguments. First, the current need to keep nuclear activities covert imposes severe constraints on weapon development, the size of arsenals, and means of delivery. Such constraints have meant that the pace of nuclearization, both Indian and Pakistani, has been slower than it would otherwise be. This factor should not be dismissed, particularly insofar as it rules out full-scale atomic testing. Keeping bomb development covert means that only "zero yield" and non-nuclear testing is possible. These tests, while crucial, are not sufficient if one wishes to develop fission weapons, which are physically small, have high yield, and are reliable.

A nuclear testing ban is a far more important issue for India than for Pakistan, as is evident from the doublespeak adopted by Indian hawks complaining about the nuclear issue. On the one hand, a test ban makes the mating of nuclear warheads to the Prithvi and Agni ballistic missiles difficult and perhaps impossible, because missiles require a somewhat miniaturized warhead capable of sustaining huge accelerations. In addition, it makes very difficult India's development of the far more complicated hydrogen fusion bomb or the miniaturized tritium-boosted bomb.

There is little doubt that India's huge nuclear establishment is awaiting a Pakistani move. *The Bulletin of the Atomic Scientists*, quoting a 1985 German intelligence document, writes that the Bhabha Atomic Research Agency's job was to ensure that "within two months of a Pakistani nuclear test, the second Indian nuclear test should be carried out. Such an Indian test should simultaneously be used for the development of a fusion explosion."[6]

Second, the declaration of overt nuclear status by one country is likely to have consequences that nuclear hawks have religiously avoided discussing. Although a plausible argument can be made that mutual nuclearization will serve as a deterrent, such arrangements are mere statements of belief and do not preclude instantaneous response, nor do they guarantee that such a deterrent would be stable.

To make the discussion more precise, one could define a deterrent system as stable if it incorporates sufficient checks and balances to prevent a nuclear war on the basis of false or inadequate information, accident, or unauthorized command. Stability is crucial because nuclear deterrence cannot tolerate a single failure or mistake. The issue of false information is an exceptionally serious one. In the U.S.-Soviet deterrence system, extensive early warning networks, both space- and ground-based, were needed to detect missile launches. Despite relatively long flight times of twenty to thirty minutes, the networks remained severely stressed and generated false attack messages. The existence of redundant and multiple safeguards prevented accidental war, but the margin was not comfortable.

Indian-Pakistani deterrence will not enjoy the luxuries of the U.S.-Soviet case. With contiguous borders, a flight time of five to eight minutes, and no space-based, early warning systems available, much less data will be available to make reasoned judgments. Hence the temptation would be to adopt a Launch On Warning (LOW) strategy.

In this scenario, the mere assumption that a nuclear attack is imminent would precipitate a preemptive attack. Pakistan would probably be forced to opt for this hair-trigger strategy, as it has no capacity to absorb an Indian first-strike and then respond. But this knowledge would in turn make the

Indians nervous since crisis misperceptions have a way of feeding and enlarging themselves, and mutual nervousness might cause one or the other adversary to strike first for no good reason.

Third, the assumption underlying "minimal deterrence"—that the game ends once a country has made a few fission bombs and declared them—is highly suspect. With security assured, one can then go on vacation. Consequently, "minimal deterrence" assumes there is no constant drive toward larger or more effective weapon systems, or any need to talk about second-strike capability—the ability to strike the enemy after absorbing the damage sustained in the initial nuclear attack.

The superpower experience, however, provides the antithesis to this argument. From the day that the United States tested the first fission bomb in 1945, the story has been one of constant escalation. In rapid succession there followed the jet bomber, fusion bomb, nuclear artillery, intercontinental ballistic missile, submarine-launched ballistic missile, supersonic bomber, multiple independently targeted re-entry vehicle (MIRV) warhead, and so on. Each new development, almost invariably pioneered by the United States, was followed a few years later by the Soviets until, in 1991, the Soviet Union collapsed from sheer exhaustion.

This example is not enough to discourage hardened hawks like General Sundarji or like-minded Pakistanis. In the course of a lengthy thesis, Sundarji approvingly quotes Bernard Brodie as saying that "Weapons that do not have to fight their like do not become useless because of the advent of newer and superior types."[7]

This pronouncement makes little sense in the nuclear context. Even a nuclear deterrent comprising a handful of bombs will require continuously dealing with the enemy's new countermeasures, upgrading the means of delivery, developing ever more sophisticated surveillance systems, and modernizing the nuclear command and control system. Whereas initially there may be a fair chance of penetrating enemy defenses, in later stages the nuclear arsenal will have to be greatly increased in size and made more sophisticated to compensate for diminishing penetration factors. Therefore, what may start out as "minimal" is likely to become anything but that with the passage of a few years.

A curious line of argument ought to be mentioned here: Nuclear escalation will not, as it did with the United States and the Soviet Union, occur on the Subcontinent because South Asians have a special psyche—they are less greedy and would be satisfied once they achieve a simple deterrent. This hopelessly naive belief, which defies military logic, is based on an inverted form of racism: we are somehow different and better than the rest of the world.

Fourth is the issue of costs. Some argue that if India or Pakistan go overtly nuclear, then they would be able to cut defense spending and concentrate on social priorities. This logic relies on the fact that atomic weapons give "more bang for the buck." In the 1960s, the U.S. Atomic Energy Commission estimated the cost of a 100 kiloton bomb at only $460,000, only one quarter of one cent per pound, whereas chemical explosives cost more than 25 cents per pound.

The catch, of course, is that this figure comprises just the manufacturing cost and ignores the billions put into setting up the huge infrastructure needed for research and development of nuclear weapons. No figures are available for Pakistan, but Iraq has reportedly spent $5 to 10 billion in its efforts to produce nuclear weapons. India, because of its large civilian nuclear program, is able to hide a good fraction of its weapon development costs. Nonetheless, some rough estimates have been made by certain Indian defense analysts.

Bhabhani Sen Gupta, for example, writes, "If the first-generation nuclear deterrent we talked about would cost less than 4% (Rs 5000 crores) of a year's GNP in 1981 terms, the second generation of improved deterrent would cost a little under 8% of the 1991 GNP. This is affordable."[8] What constitutes "affordable" can be endlessly debated, but the Indian government apparently cannot provide the most minimal needs to the street dwellers of Bombay and Calcutta, a quarter of the cities' total population. Resources diverted away from the social sector feed an increasingly voracious military-industrial complex.

Finally, to expect that nuclear weapons can credibly substitute for conventional weapons once their existence has been openly declared is unwarranted. It is difficult to imagine that there would be any reduction of spending on conventional arms or a reduction of the size of the Pakistani military. Like the Indian military, the Pakistani armed forces are heavily involved in matters of internal security and in border skirmishes, which require visible demonstrations of military might.

As in Europe, Pakistan and India will be unable to substitute their conventional force for a nuclear one. The European experience provides a clear example of a massive nuclear force possessed by both sides that had to be backed up with a huge amount of airpower, seapower, armor, and infantry. In this case, conventional arms were considered credible and thus indispensable because there was a much smaller area of destruction involved.

If India and Pakistan should convert the currently vague and existentialist nuclear threat into something palpable and poised for use, the two rival countries would be irreversibly driven by the force of logic and circumstances into a situation whose gravity nuclear hawks either do not realize, or do not wish to discuss.

To conclude, if Pakistan were to lead India in declaring the bomb, its security would be damaged and it would be rendered vulnerable to any and every kind of attack. But Pakistan's subsequent insecurity will not work to India's advantage; a nuclear Pakistan will surely pose a grave threat to India.

On the other hand, if India declares nuclearization first, Pakistan would be inevitably dragged into responding to the extent that it can. It would have to make the best out of a bad situation. But whichever government takes the first step, it will be justly reviled by the world for having put a billion people under the nuclear sword and, in the process, making both its adversary and itself more insecure than ever before.

Nuclear War by Accident

Neither India nor Pakistan wanted to go to war, but we could have easily gone to war.

—General Zia ul-Haq

General Zia-ul-Haq's remark, made soon after the crisis precipitated by India's Brasstacks exercises along the Pakistani border in 1986, shows that an unwanted or accidental war between the two countries is not outside the realm of possibility. That such a war could perhaps lead to a catastrophic nuclear exchange is a fearsome thought.

Fortunately, this may be fairly improbable today. Although India and Pakistan have repeatedly stated that they have the capability to build nuclear weapons, both countries also insist that they have refrained from weaponization. Except for a small but vociferous lobby calling for bombs to be immediately deployed, most people appear to be satisfied that their country's capability is sufficient to deter the other side without an explicit demonstration. Therefore, if indeed neither country has readily operational weapons, then these may be relatively safe times.

But it is also possible that one or both countries have already secretly stockpiled nuclear weapons, or that at some time in the future a declaration of weaponization by one state will be made, followed by a similar declaration by the other. An unwanted nuclear war then becomes a possibility.

How could accidental war occur? The most likely setting for a nuclear holocaust arises out of an existing crisis, such as the Kashmir dispute. Assuming that Pakistan and India are both nuclear armed states, they will be constantly watching and monitoring each other's activities. At a time when tensions are particularly high, each side will live in fear of a decapitating nuclear strike that could wipe out military or governmental centers of power. Thus, to attack before being attacked becomes dangerously tempting. In such a situation, fear and misperceptions about the adversary's intentions could precipitate an unwanted confrontation.

Clearly, this is a situation that has been encountered before. The United States and the Soviet Union had an eye-to-eye confrontation for the major part of the Cold War. In this nuclear competition, billions of dollars were spent on acquiring the most sophisticated forms of intelligence gathering by satellites, aircraft, ships, and submarines. The data was then analyzed, using computers equipped with artificial intelligence programs. The information enabled both sides to know each other's level of readiness for combat. If such an elaborate command and control system had not existed, a doomsday nuclear confrontation might well have occurred out of fear or suspicion.

For India and Pakistan this possibility has clear implications. It would be folly to weaponize without developing an adequate command and control system. Moreover, this system should be protected so as to survive even a nuclear blast in the vicinity: i.e., be protected against the electromagnetic pulse that accompanies a nuclear blast and destroys all normal telecommunications. Without this safeguard, either country would be like a blind and deaf giant twirling a nuclear truncheon, a threat to one's own self as much as to the other.

But then many worrisome and nagging questions arise: Would India or Pakistan be willing, or able, to invest massively in command and control? Although a simple comparison of weapon platforms would imply that the command and control requirements for India or Pakistan are less demanding than they were for the United States and the former Soviet Union, they are in some ways more challenging. For example, missile flight times for Subcontinental trajectories are only five to eight minutes as compared to twenty to thirty minutes for intercontinental ones. In this time, a decision will have to be made as to whether the alarm is genuine and whether the missiles are nuclear-armed. In the absence of accurate information, the only alternative is the dangerously unstable Launch On Warning (LOW) policy.

A second kind of danger arises from the possibility of unauthorized use of nuclear weapons by a single individual (a pilot or field commander) or by a small, fringe group whose ideology does not represent that of the mainstream "enemy." Regardless, any such misunderstanding could initiate nuclear war, and the chances for this would be much higher in a preexisting state of tensions such as during military exercises or a conventional war.

There are other possibilities that could initiate an accidental Indo-Pakistani nuclear war: Disenfranchised subnational groups within either country could somehow acquire access to a nuclear device; or, a nuclear detonation could occur in the crash of an aircraft on one's own soil, and so on. Explosive dumps have often blown up for unexplained causes; one such explosion rained death and devastation on the cities of Rawalpindi and Islamabad a few years ago. The explosion of a nuclear device would be immeasurably more serious. The natural assumption would be that the device belonged to the other side. Even if the device actually belonged to one's own side, a government fearful of public reaction may not want to admit it. In some circumstances, retaliation might be more likely than investigation.

It is mathematically impossible to reduce the probability of accidental war to zero. The real question is: What can be done to decrease the risk?

The Second-Best Option: Confidence Building

It is a canonical truth that peace can only come about if the cause of conflict is removed. In the Indo-Pakistani context, a resolution to the Kashmir dispute is needed that takes into account the wishes of the people of Kashmir as well as the legitimate security interests of India and Pakistan. Today this seems a distant prospect. The chance of yet another confrontation more disastrous than the last two appears closer. The urgency of the situation demands that one ask what partial measures, as opposed to a comprehensive peace settlement, might serve to inhibit war.

At a minimum, preventing a crisis in Pakistani-Indian relations from possibly escalating into a nuclear war requires that both countries soberly consider establishment of regular contacts at the highest level to deal with nuclear issues. What is needed is an institutionalized basis for exchanging and communicating information with the intent to reassure each other that a military attack is not about to begin, or that an ongoing conflict is not about to be escalated to a higher dimension. Since the need for this would be greatest in times of crisis, such contacts should not be made conditional on whatever state of relations exist. Pakistan and India don't have to be friends to talk. But to talk may be critically important for mutual survival. The United States and the Soviet Union recognized this when they signed the "Agreement on Measures to Reduce the Risk of Outbreak of Nuclear War" at a time of continuous confrontation and competition.

Much needs to be discussed in such high-level meetings. First, routine military activities—such as troop or aircraft movements during exercises or missile testing—could be misinterpreted by the other side as a preparation for attack. For example, the requisition of a large number of rail cars in 1986 by the Indian army to support military exercises set off alarm bells in Pakistan because a similar mobilization had occured in 1971. Meetings between the militaries could allay false suspicions.

Second, such meetings would be vitally important for establishing a truly operational "nuclear hotline" between Islamabad and New Delhi, perhaps on the pattern of the White House–Kremlin hotline, but it should be exclusively reserved for use in times of a potential nuclear crisis. Although the basic idea would probably be acceptable to both sides, an enormous number of details would need to be worked out. How, for example, should the identity of individuals using the hotline be authenticated? What technical means should be adopted to ensure that the hotline never fails to function? What protocols need to be established so that the line is used only for forestalling nuclear action and not to transmit threats? How may the psychological impediments to use of the hotline—such as the fear of appearing fearful or nervous—be dealt with?

Third, procedures for dealing with nuclear accidents, an unexplained nuclear explosion, or thefts of nuclear materials should be discussed. For example, the reported theft of some kilograms of highly enriched uranium from the Bhabha Atomic Research Center, if correct, is of grave concern to both countries.

Perhaps the greatest obstacle to bilateral nuclear contacts is the myth that nuclear secrecy enhances security. In actual fact, nuclear transparency is the key to survival. The reason is clear: Unreasonable secrecy leads to suspicion, and suspicion can lead to unpredictable or paranoid reactions by the adversary. Both countries benefit by permitting the other a "peek" into its secrets. Thus, the recent exchange between India and Pakistan of updated lists of nuclear installations should be welcomed. But this does not go far enough. Much more is needed.

Safer Bombs

An unsafeguarded nuclear weapon can, in principle, be detonated by an unauthorized individual or by several kinds of accident. Given the drastic implications of such scenarios, the tremendous amount of energy and effort that have gone into constructing Permissive Action Links (PALs)—the elaborate electronic and mechanical safety catches installed on U.S. and Soviet nuclear weapons—cannot be overemphasized. While no weapon can ever be totally safeguarded against misuse or sabotage, PALs certainly have made them safer.

Before 1958, U.S. nuclear weapons were reportedly unprotected against unauthorized use. Only two special keys had to be inserted into a bomb to ready it for use. Soon it was realized that this system was extremely unsafe and, in the 1960s, a massive effort was launched to ensure that a bomb would never explode without authentic instructions from the highest authority.

Modern PALs installed on nuclear devices are impressive. The most recent can detect if the device has been stolen and moved to an unauthorized place and can even sense efforts at sabotage. They feature combination locks that monitor attempted access and make the device permanently inoperable if attempts exceed a predetermined limit. In a similar vein, some PALs are "environmentally sensitive" and will not permit a bomb to explode unless it attains a certain acceleration.

An additional benefit of PALs is that they can increase the degree of civilian control over nuclear weapons. Presuming that the ultimate launch authority in India or Pakistan is the elected government and not the military, no nuclear weapon can be activated unless a secret code has been received from the president or prime minister. This veto power may be vitally important in preventing a holocaust.

One can therefore argue that the United States should make the general principle underlying PALs avaliable to India and Pakistan once the existence of assembled nuclear weapons has been determined. Because the mechanisms are weapon-specific, however, these principles should be sufficiently general so that they make existing weapons safer but do not reveal how to make them better.

Safer bombs will also require new kinds of high explosives. In recent years, there has been much discussion of the so-called One Point Safety, a strategy that attempts to forestall a nuclear bomb from being ignited even if the surrounding explosive is detonated. During the last decade, scientists concluded that there is a fair chance that a nuclear weapon could detonate in the event of fire or ordinary explosion even if it had not been readied for use. Detonation could happen, for example, if a bomber were to crash in one's own territory.

To prevent this kind of catastrophe, new types of conventional explosives called Insensitive High Explosives (IHEs) have been created. Again, such explosives are the result of intensive research and development, and one could again argue that the technology be made available to both countries.

The best PAL and the best guarantee of One Point Safety is, of course, a disassembled nuclear weapon. If India and Pakistan refrain from assembling bombs, these complicated measures will not be necessary. But if bombs are assembled, then several critical questions will arise. Would either country be willing, or able, to invest in the tremendous amount of research needed to make its bombs safe for itself? Or, since there would be total secrecy in such matters, would there be a strong temptation to cut corners?

Taming Ballistic Missiles

With flight times of a few minutes, and with virtually no prospect of an effective defense against them, intermediate-range ballistic missiles (IRBMs) are the single most destabilizing element in the India-Pakistan confrontation. Carried on mobile launchers, and with little preparation time needed by solid-fueled boosters, missiles can carry out a sneak attack much more easily than manned aircraft. India has a sophisticated IRBM program that includes the Agni, with a range of 1500 to 2500 kilometers, and the Prithvi, with a range of 150 to 350 kilometers. The latter has been repeatedly tested and plans are reportedly under way for its deployment by the end of 1993. Pakistan has sought to counter this development principally through import of the Chinese M-11 missile, which corresponds roughly to the Prithvi. Pakistan's indigenously developed missiles are as yet in a relatively primitive stage.

Although the accuracy of the guidance systems of the Prithvi and the M-11 is a secret, in all probability these missiles are inaccurate to at least several hundred yards. Their utility, when armed with conventional warheads, would not be for precise attacks on military targets but, instead, for attacks on cities and population centers. They are, therefore, weapons of terror.

A still more ominous possibility is the use of IRBMs as delivery vehicles for nuclear warheads, for which accuracy is not critical. India or Pakistan have presumably not yet developed the technology of mating warheads to missiles, but this next development could be just a matter of time. Because a nuclear armed missile cannot be distinguished externally from a conventionally armed one, the deployment of any missile could be viewed with great alarm by the other side.

Nor can the highly destabilizing effect of IRBMs be offset by their having moved out of range of an adversary's cities. The problem here is that they could be quietly moved back for a sneak attack. Further, with the Agni, every point in Pakistan—and far beyond—falls within its range. The conclusion is obvious: There must be a regional accord involving China, India, and Pakistan that serves to cap IRBM deployments and, hopefully, reverse them.

Options for Pakistan

Pakistan's nuclearization continues to be driven by the need to match the relentless pace of India's conventional and nuclear militarization and derives support from the domestic political environment. But stronger brakes are being applied by an international community increasingly more hostile to nuclear weapons in general and fearful of a South Asian conflagration. Furthermore, it is becoming increasingly clear that Pakistan's fairly limited technological capability sets a limit to how far it can match India's. A rational assessment of Pakistan's nuclear choices must be based on a consideration of four factors.

The speed of Indian militarization has been repeatedly underscored by tests of the Prithvi missile and the announcement of India's intent to deploy the missile in 1993. In 1989, with the successful launch of the Agni missile, India joined an exclusive club hitherto dominated by the world's five technological and military giants—the United States, the Soviet Union, France, China, and Israel. India's armaments industry is the largest in the Third World in terms of product diversity, research and development, and value and volume of production. It has matured since 1970 into a producer of diverse equipment and weapons, especially aircraft and ships, and now intermediate-range ballistic missiles.

India's ability to produce nuclear weapons rapidly in large numbers is not doubted by anyone. But India seems to be awaiting an opportune time and has maintained a yes-and-no nuclear posture. Articulating India's desire for big power status, Bhabhani Sen Gupta states that "If India goes nuclear—it may be in the 1990s—it will do so as a credible nuclear power befitting its self-image and its international and regional power. That will be only when India has developed a respectable satellite launching capability, acquired the capability of launching IRBMs and of building sophisticated warheads and carriers as well as surveillance systems."[9] He concludes that India will not join the "junior club of small nuclear powers," but will wait to crash directly into the big time.[10]

Domestic politics in Pakistan also pushes that nation toward nuclearization. Since 1988, the nuclear issue has been used by both incumbent governments and the opposition as a stick with which to beat one other. Each has sought to establish its patriotic credentials by accusing the other of damaging Pakistan's security shield through accommodation on the nuclear issue. Although India's growing military might is a genuine source of worry, the heavy military expenditure (36 percent of the current budget) deemed necessary to counter this threat has led Pakistan to neglect important social priorities.

Both the challenge of Indian militarization and popular domestic sentiment for the bomb drive Pakistan along the nuclear road. But formidable obstacles lie ahead. Global pressures to denuclearize, particularly from the United States, continue to mount. No longer a frontline proxy warrior against communism, Pakistan has been virtually abandoned by its decades-old ally. For all the brave talk about self-reliance, the fact remains that the cutoff of military supplies authorized by the Pressler amendment has gravely weakened Pakistan's ability to defend itself. A good fraction of the navy will be lost as ships leased from the United States are returned. In spite of having paid for them, Pakistan will not receive additional units of its most advanced fighter, the F-16.

It is not, however, the United States alone that has taken a firm stand on proliferation, but also Japan and Western Europe. Proliferation has become a bad word almost everywhere. Since the fall of the Soviet Union, there has been a major global move toward denuclearization. U.S. and Russian nuclear arsenals will soon be one-eighth the size they were at the peak of the Cold War. Further, three proliferant states—Argentina, Brazil, and South Africa—have formally renounced nuclear arms and have agreed to full safeguards.

But in diametric opposition to these global trends, three states stand out as veritable bastions of nuclear proliferation—Israel, India, and Pakistan. The penalties, however, have less impact on the strongest than on the weakest. In the context of the Subcontinent, Pakistan, being far more susceptible to external pressure because of its economic and military dependencies, has suffered much more than India.

Limited technological capability also sets fundamental constraints on Pakistan's efforts to match Indian advances in high-tech weaponry. Although Pakistan, like India, is capable of making nuclear weapons, these would probably be few in number, crude in design and manufacture, rather large in size, and not altogether reliable. Explosive-yield boosting, miniaturization, PALs, and other sophisticated measures are possible for Pakistan.

More important, Pakistan is not in a position to match India's development of IRBM technology or contest it in the field of satellite surveillance. These elements will be decisive for all future military strategies, including those relying on nuclear weapons as a last resort. Thus, while a full-fledged nuclear race would be bad for both countries, Pakistan would stand to lose far more. It is therefore in Pakistan's interest to go out of its way to prevent such a race from occurring.

Given this fairly grim situation, what course of action would maximize Pakistan's security? Go overtly nuclear? Maintain nuclear ambiguity as far as possible? Or follow the path of Argentina and Brazil?

The first course—overt deployment of a nuclear deterrent—would be the ultimate folly. It would be like manna from heaven for the Indian defense establishment, because a Pakistani declaration of nuclearization would sanction a no-holds-barred game where India would enjoy all the advantages. Released from constraints, India could immediately weaponize and develop thermonuclear and artillery bombs, accelerate its IRBM and space satellite programs, start work on submarine-launched missiles, develop nuclear command centers, and aim for second-strike capability. Meanwhile its rival, while still a threat because of the few crude weapons in its possession, would be screwed to the wall by an angry world and threatened by internal collapse as it seeks to raise defense expenditure.

The third route—which amounts to unilateral nuclear disarmament by Pakistan—is both impractical and unwise at a stage when India shows no signs that it would reciprocate the action. Although it would be in the interests of both India and Pakistan to renounce instruments of mass annihilation, it is also true that Pakistani proposals for a nuclear-free zone and a five nation conference have been met with scornful rejection by India, which has accused Pakistan of "propaganda ploys" and playing to the world gallery.

This leaves only the second option: continuation of Pakistan's policy of deliberate nuclear ambiguity in the form of "Yes, we have it, no we don't." But what worked in the 1980s is not working in the 1990s. The real question is: What will? To answer this question, it is important to recognize that, in diplomatic terms, Pakistan has played the nuclear game with great astuteness. But it must learn to play still better. Its proposals for a regional solution have put India on the spot. New Delhi has been unable to dispel the impression that it is merely stone-walling and resisting every reasonable Pakistani move.

Pakistan must once again seize the diplomatic initiative. But it can do so only if it is perceived by the international community as being sincere in working towards nuclear accommodation with India. Therefore, it will be necessary for Pakistan to take some form of meaningful unilateral action. This action could, for example, be a declaration that it will freeze the production of enriched uranium for a period of eighteen months and will not conduct a nuclear test during this period. If India responds positively, the freeze would be extended. Otherwise it would reserve the right to revert to its former position.

Together with this initiative, Pakistan could work to assuage concerns that it seeks to export nuclear weapon technology to other countries in the region. By agreeing to the inspection of all nuclear exports, and pledging not to transfer nuclear weapons related information, it would show itself as a responsible country, genuinely concerned with limiting the spread of nuclear weapons. Pakistan's security interests would not be harmed by these declarations.

What could the possible outcomes of such a move be? If India responds by stopping plutonium production, then this would be an important victory for peace in South Asia. This step could lead toward more effective measures for denuclearization. But more likely than not, this will not happen. India's imperatives for nuclearization go beyond the need to match Pakistan; it dreams of grander things. Some slowing down of its nuclear program may be all that might occur.

The real bonus, however, would be reaped in diplomatic and political terms. On the one hand, Pakistan's initiative would have clearly demonstrated its desire to halt a nuclear race on the Subcontinent, even at some cost to itself. The economic, political, and military pressures on it would be substantially lessened. India, on the other hand, would stand out as rejectionist, or be forced to the bargaining table.

What are the costs, military and diplomatic, inveighing against the proposed initiative? The obvious objection is that freezing enriched uranium production for as long as eighteen months would affect Pakistan's nuclear defense capability in relation to India's, especially since India has a much larger stock of fissile materials. But, in fact, given existing stockpiles, the nuclear asymmetry would not be greatly enhanced beyond what it is at present. Further, at least at the present time, both nations use the veiled threat of nuclear weapons to deter each other. This relies on some diffuse meaning of "nuclear capability"; real numbers are not now the major issue.

Another objection could be that any unilateral initiative by Pakistan would give the impression of weakness. One might ask, however, is sticking to one's old position really a sign of strength? Or is it just a reaction to being cornered? The cards are now stacked against Pakistan; it is up to the shrewdness of its policy planners to make the best of a bad situation.

NOTES

1. In his essay, "On the Nuclear Edge," (*The New Yorker*, March 29, 1993, 56-73) Seymour Hersh makes the claim that U.S. intelligence had picked up news that General Beg had authorized technicians at Kahuta to put together nuclear weapons.

Subsequently, U.S. satellites picked up a convoy of trucks coming out of a remote nuclear storage site in Baluchistan and moving toward a nearby airforce base.

2. *Critical Mass* (New York: Simon and Schuster, 1944) by William Burrows and Robert Windrem, contains a dramatized account of the May 1990 confrontation. The authors identify the remote nuclear storage site in Baluchistan as Chagai and claim that Pakistan possessed an implosion design for its nuclear weapons, which the Chinese tested in the mid-1960s.
3. General Mirza Aslam Beg, interviewed by Ikramullah, *The News,* Islamabad, December 3, 1992.
4. Edward N. Luttwak, "Of Bombs and Men," *Commentary,* August 1983, 82.
5. General K.M. Arif, *The Globe* (Islambad: 1990), 13.
6. *Bulletin of the Atomic Scientists*, June 1989, 20.
7. Bernard Brodie, *War and Politics,* (New York: Macmillan Publishers) quoted in K.S. Sundarji, "Strategy in the Age of Nuclear Deterrence and its Application to Developing Countries," June 21, 1984. (unpublished work)
8. Bhabani Sen Gupta, quoted in *Dawn,* July 2, 1991, 11.
9. Ibid.
10. Ibid.

5

CBMS FOR THE SIACHEN GLACIER, SIR CREEK, AND WULAR BARRAGE

A.G. Noorani

Anyone who follows the course of events on the Subcontinent will be struck by its utter immunity to the winds of change that have recently blown over the globe. The former Soviet Union withdrew its troops from Afghanistan, and the regime it had installed collapsed. The two Germanies reunited; the Soviet empire in Eastern Europe collapsed, and the Soviet Union itself fell apart. The Israeli-Palestinian accord and the adoption of a constitution for a multiracial democracy in South Africa followed the trend.

Estrangement between India and Pakistan is a disturbing exception to that trend, particularly so because both states possess nuclear weapon capabilities, official denials notwithstanding. Since the end of British rule in 1947, nothing like a sustained period of détente has ever come about on the Subcontinent. Rather, adversarial relations have been the abiding norm. In these countries, where very large sections of people live in dire poverty, the enormous expenditure on arms and the tragedy of three wars is a testimony to the failure of leadership.

It was against this backdrop that, having gone to war for the third time the previous year, India and Pakistan negotiated the 1972 Simla agreement. A major issue on the negotiation agenda was Kashmir: specifically, agreement on a redefining of the cease-fire line (CFL) that had been delineated in

Kashmir in 1949 under the auspices of the United Nations Commission for India and Pakistan and agreed to by both countries.[1]

The agreement signed on July 3, 1972, by Prime Minister Indira Gandhi of India and President Zulfikar Ali Bhutto of Pakistan was intended to serve as a compass for better relations in the future. It pledged both sides "to settle their differences by peaceful means through bilateral negotiations or by any other peaceful means mutually agreed upon between them." Further, "Pending the final settlement of any of the problems between the two countries, neither side shall unilaterally alter the situation."[2]

With respect to Kashmir, the Simla agreement resulted in a redefining of the CFL, from that time forth known as the Line of Actual Control (LAC). The CFL agreed to by India and Pakistan at Karachi in 1949 was identified as beginning in South Kashmir, from the border with Pakistan, and from there proceeding north, turning east in an arc, and then proceeding north again. (See Figure 5.1.)[3] However, according to the Simla agreement:

> In Jammu and Kashmir, the line of [actual] control resulting from the cease-fire of December 17, 1971 shall be respected by both sides without prejudice to the recognized position of either side. Neither side shall seek to alter it unilaterally, irrespective of mutual differences and legal interpretations. Both sides further undertake to refrain from the threat or the use of force in violation of this Line.

Shortly after the 1972 Simla agreement was signed, India's minister for external affairs, Swaran Singh, speaking before the Indian parliament, linked the issues of troop withdrawals and the LAC: "Action regarding the withdrawals [of troops] and delineation of the line of [actual] control in Jammu and Kashmir will have to be taken simultaneously." A new LAC was drawn up. The change of terminology—from "cease-fire line" to "line of actual control" still signified a degree of tentativeness.

On December 12, 1972, Swaran Singh revealed details of the LAC agreement in a formal statement to parliament. "The broad description," commencing south and "ending in Turtok—Partapur sector in the north," was laid on the table. Paragraph C of that document ended thus: "Up to Chorbat La [La is the Tibetan word for a mountain pass] in Turtok sector." Paragraph D added: "From there the Line of Control runs northeastward to Thang (inclusive to India) thence eastward joining the glaciers."[4]

Nineteen mosaic maps and an appended written description of the LAC were signed by Major General M.R. Rajwade of India and Brigadier S.M. Abbasi of Pakistan. These documents, however, actually repeated the discrepancies of the Karachi agreement, its maps, and their detailed description, defining the northern extremity as "thence along the boundary line to NJ9842," exactly as the description of the 1949 maps had done. The LAC stopped at NJ9842 and did not extend north to the glaciers.

Since the signing of the Simla agreement, little progress has been made toward a final settlement on Kashmir and its boundaries. This is true despite a commitment by the heads of government, recorded in that agreement, to "meet again at a mutually convenient time in the future" to discuss further "the modalities and arrangements for the establishment of durable peace and normalization of relations, including the question of repatriation of prisoners of war and civilian internees, *a final settlement of Jammu and Kashmir and the resumption of diplomatic relations*" (emphasis added).[5] The text clearly implied early negotiations on Kashmir as part of the process of normalization of relations and resumption of diplomatic relations. Not until May 1976 were diplomatic relations resumed. It would be January 1, 1994, before the foreign secretaries of India and Pakistan met in Islamabad "in accordance with the Simla Agreement" for "a comprehensive discussion on bilateral issues" to include all aspects of the Kashmir issue.[6]

On the Kashmir issue, however, the position of both sides remained far apart. Furthermore, by 1994, the self-assertion of the people of Kashmir had emerged as a key factor. This development can be traced back more than twenty years, to the time of the Simla agreement, when the popular leader of Kashmir, Sheikh Mohammed Abdullah, upon his release from internment, remarked that the leaders of India and Pakistan were going to decide the future of Kashmir "behind our back as if we are a forgotten factor. That is wrong. We register our strong protest against it."[7] Later, in February 1975, Abdullah entered into an accord with Prime Minister Indira Gandhi endorsing the state's membership in the Indian Union under special terms stipulated by Article 370 of the Indian Constitution.

The current situation in Kashmir can best be summarized thus: First, among the population living in the most significant part of the Indian state of Jammu and Kashmir—that is, the Kashmir Valley—there is a deep sense of alienation from the Indian Union. Second, since 1988 Pakistan has mounted a covert military operation to exploit this alienation and instigated and aided acts of terrorism.[8] Third, Indian security forces have systematically, and with impunity, perpetrated outrageous violations of human rights in the valley.[9]

It is reasonable to conclude that relations between India and Pakistan will never be normal until the Kashmir dispute is settled. It is no less obvious that the two sides will be unable to tackle this old and vexing issue unless a basic level of normalization has already been achieved. In other words, a measure of confidence needs to be developed through accords on other issues. Such agreements would serve to convince each side of the other's bona fides without in any way compromising its stand on Kashmir. Three pending issues on the Indo-Pakistani agenda are preeminently susceptible to a solution in the near future: demilitarization of the Siachen Glacier in northern Kashmir, the barrage to be constructed by the state government of Jammu and Kashmir on the Jhelum River below Wular Lake, and a demarcation of the Indo-Pakistani territorial and maritime boundaries in the Sir Creek area between Gujarat (India) and Sind (Pakistan).

Each issue lends itself to an approach that blends legal and political considerations. Although each issue is of limited proportions, the impact of a solution to all three points would be significant for Indo-Pakistani relations, imparting momentum to discussions on other confidence-building measures and on the dispute over Kashmir. The only obstacle to such an accord is a lack of political will.

Siachen Glacier

On September 17, 1993, U.S. Assistant Secretary of State Robin Raphel stated: "Kashmir remains a major source of Indo-Pakistani tensions which could lead to war. There has been little follow-up to the 1972 Simla Agreement, when India and Pakistan committed to deal seriously with this issue. They should work on near-term steps such as demilitarization of the Siachen Glacier and more support for ongoing monitoring efforts along the line of control." Briefing the news media on Raphel's visit to Pakistan, a senior U.S. official in Islamabad said, on November 9, 1993, "India and Pakistan are crossing the T's and dotting the I's of their agreement on demilitarizing Siachen which was almost complete in 1989."

The next day, however, Foreign Secretary Shaharyar Khan of Pakistan told the media that the Kashmir and Siachen disputes were linked and could not be discussed and negotiated separately. He also stated that both sides had come very close to an agreement on Siachen. His remarks probably represented nothing more than a bargaining ploy. It was, in fact, around that time that Prime Minister Benazir Bhutto of Pakistan, in an interview with an Indian correspondent appeared to show strong interest in a Siachen accord. She claimed that in 1989 defense secretaries of both countries had "reached an agreement with exact locations on the map on where everybody was supposed to go but Prime Minister Rajiv Gandhi delayed it because he had decided to go in for an early election. Thus India publicly withdrew from that agreement saying that it had not been concluded."[10] She went on to say that, "after 1989 the Indian position changed on Siachen and further demands were made on Pakistan."[11] As stated in this interview, it is her belief that a return to the 1989 agreement, and its implementation, would give Pakistan greater confidence that bilateral agreements can take off.[12] Bhutto's version of why the 1989 agreement collapsed is arguable, but her emphasis on its implementation and on the confidence it could engender is sound.

Hostilities Commence. The genesis of the Siachen dispute has been described honestly and objectively by Indian Lieutenant General M.L. Chibber (ret.). As army commander (Northern Command), Chibber was responsible for directing the April 1984 Indian military initiative in the vicinity of the Siachen Glacier. The operation, code-named *Meghdoot*[13], triggered armed clashes between Indian and Pakistani forces in the area and eventually led to the current phase of this dispute. The details Chibber cites, however, reveal the earlier origins of the conflict.[14]

As noted earlier, the LAC that was drawn up following the Simla agreement defined the line's northern extremity exactly as the 1949 CFL maps had. The 1949 description reads: "Thence northwards along the boundary line going through point 18402 up to NJ9842." The line stopped at NJ9842 and did not extend further to the glaciers. Therein lay a discrepancy. The 1949 agreement had left the delimitation of the northern extremity vague, in the vain hope that the glaciers would keep the peace. The descriptions to the 1972 maps similarly referred to the glaciers in establishing the LAC. Clearly, however, there was no LAC in the area of the Siachen Glacier that lay *beyond* NJ9842. Further, the commitment of both sides under Paragraph 1 (ii) of the Simla agreement, which stipulates that "neither side shall unilaterally alter the situation" in regard to "any of the problems between the two countries," unquestionably applied in this case.

Nevertheless, the lack of clarity over territorial rights in the glacier area was a sufficient catalyst for a new round of armed rivalry between India and Pakistan. Regarding the outbreak of hostilities, Robert G. Wirsing, a long-time student of the Siachen case, writes,

> What is publicly known about events leading up to the outbreak of hostilities in the vicinity of the Siachen Glacier in the winter of 1983-84 does not supply unambiguous evidence that either India or Pakistan was the aggressor. Precisely who shot first is probably impossible to determine. Which of the two armed forces had the "right" to be on the glacier—since the question of the legitimacy of the two sides' territorial claims has never been submitted to impartial adjudication—is a matter obviously

Figure I

Figure II

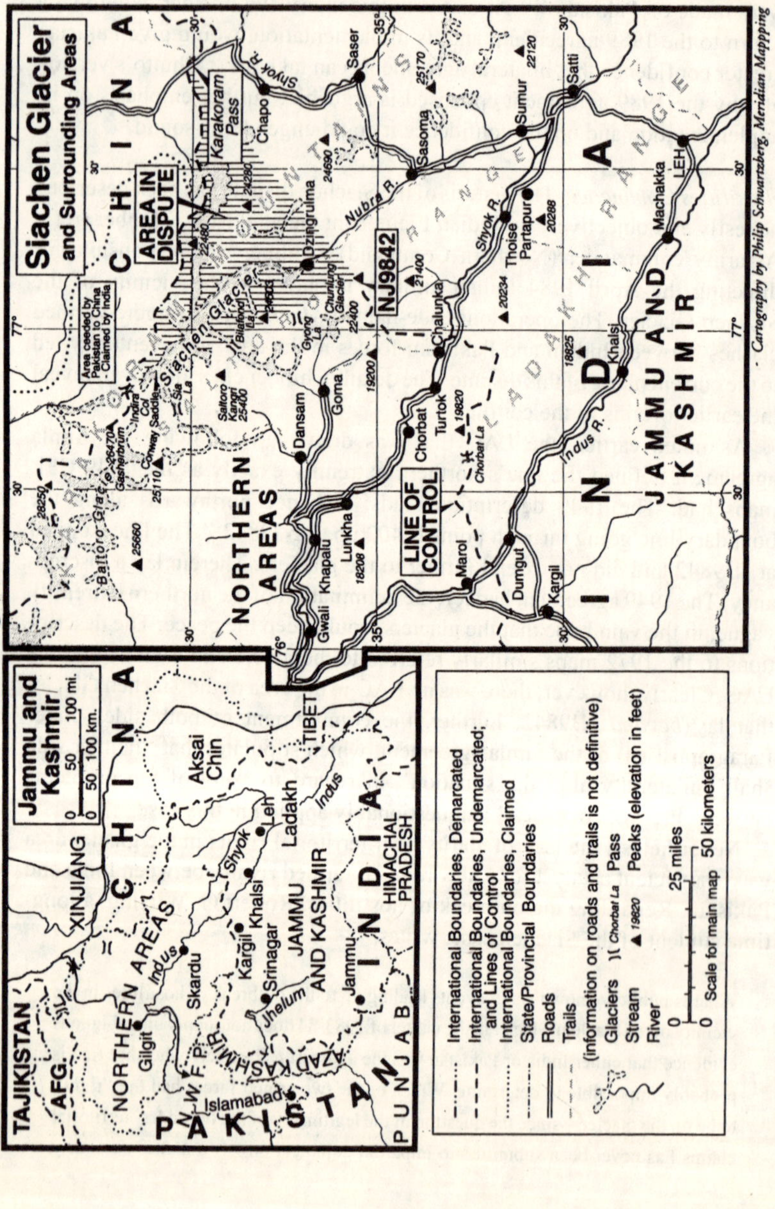

The external boundaries of India depicted in both the above maps are neither correct nor authentic

Figure III

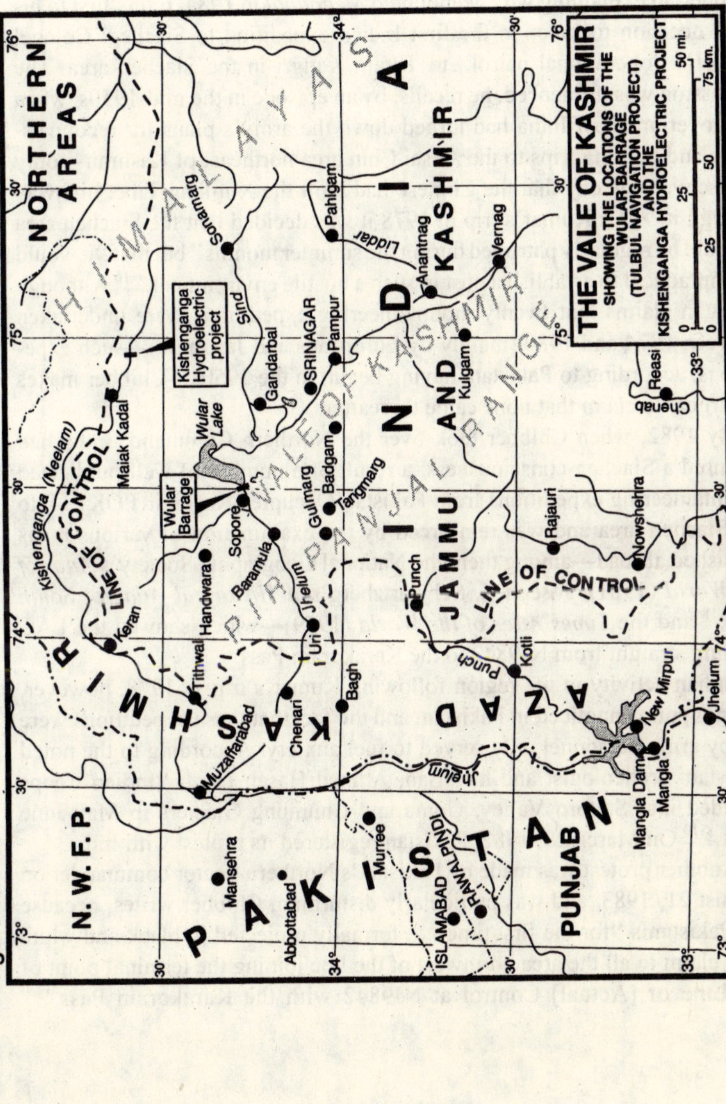

The external boundaries of India depicted in this map are neither correct nor authentic

> open to disagreement. There is ample evidence, however, that Indian armed forces were the first to establish permanent posts on the glacier and that they had prepared themselves long and well for the task. Published Indian accounts of Operation *Meghdoot* leave little room for doubt, in fact, that the Pakistanis were caught napping and that their principal strategy for fortifying Pakistan's claim to the glacier—sponsoring foreign mountaineering expeditions to the area—had failed.[15]

Chibber, in explaining why he mounted *Meghdoot* in 1984, refers first to his 1978 decision to sanction the first Indian expedition to Siachen: Colonel Kumar's "operational patrol" to Teram Kangri in the Siachen area. The discussion was influenced, he recalls, by an episode in the mid-1950s, when the government of India had turned down the army's plans for reconnaissance and hunting trips to the Aksai Chin area northeast of Kashmir—only to discover one day that the Chinese had built the Xinjiang-Tibet highway through it. After Kumar's trip in 1978 it was decided that the Siachen area "should be regularly patrolled during the summer months" but that "it would be impractical to establish a post in such a hostile environment."[16] Although Pakistan claims that twenty mountaineering expeditions were undertaken between 1974 and 1980 (mainly by Europeans and Japanese)—such expeditions, according to Pakistan, having begun in the 1950s—Chibber makes the arguable claim that none came thereafter.

By 1982, when Chibber took over the Northern Command, India had acquired a Siachen-consciousness, a result of a number of well-publicized mountaineering expeditions from Pakistan-Occupied Kashmir(POK)[17] into the Siachen area and was reinforced by the examination of various maps published abroad—among them the National Geographic Society's *Atlas of the World* (1981), Joseph E. Schwartzberg's *A Historical Atlas of South Asia,*[18] and the *Times Atlas of the World* (1959)—which showed the LAC running straight from NJ9842 to the Karakoram Pass.

Indian activity in the region following Kumar's trip in 1978, however, had not gone unnoticed in Pakistan, and the fact that these expeditions were led by army personnel only served to fuel anxiety. According to the noted Pakistani archeologist and historian, Ahmed Hasan Dani: "Indian troops intruded into Saltoro Valley, Goma and Chunlung Glaciers in May-June 1981."[19] On March 29, 1982, Pakistan registered its protest with India.

Another protest was made by Pakistan's Northern Sector commander on August 21, 1983, and was particularly disturbing, Chibber writes, because the Pakistanis "for the first time . . . formally projected in black and white their claim to all the area northwest of the line joining the terminal point of the Line of [Actual] Control at NJ9842 with the Karakoram Pass."[20]

Language in a subsequent protest on August 29, 1983, referred to the "LAC *NORTH* OF POINT NJ. 980420—KARAKORAM PASS," with the Pakistanis asserting that the Siachen Glacier was "INSIDE OUR TERRITORY" (capital letters from the official cable cited by Chibber; emphasis added).[21]

In September-October 1983, Indian intelligence detected a column of Pakistani troops moving toward the Saltoro ridge, presumably with the intention of occupying the passes. The Saltoro range—an off-shoot of the Karakoram range—is topped by a high ridge punctuated by several passes that offer the only viable route to the Siachen Glacier from POK. Inclement weather, however, prevented the Pakistani troops from reaching their destination that season.

Pakistani writer Zulfikar Ali Khan describes what happened next: "Pakistan decided to establish a permanent picket at Siachen. To *preempt* this move, the Indians airlifted a Kumaon battalion by helicopters" (emphasis added).[22] On April 13, 1984, at least two months before the beginning of the regular mountaineering season in the area, a platoon each was placed at the Sia La and Bilafond La—two key passes along the Saltoro ridge (see Figure 5.1).

As a result, an extremely costly, futile, and wholly avoidable conflict had begun in the world's principal mid-latitude mountain glaciation. It could have been averted had Indian and Pakistani leaders acted in 1983 to freeze the status quo as it then existed. The establishment of a permanent picket in the area—contemplated by Pakistan, on the one hand, and accomplished by India, on the other hand, constitutes a breach of the Simla agreement. No LAC was violated, to be sure, but both sides had sought to unilaterally alter the situation. In the tense atmosphere of late 1983, a political decision at the highest level of leadership in both countries was needed in order to divert the course of events from the use of force and toward a diplomatic solution.

Any number of confidence-building measures could have been considered to stave off an imminent military confrontation. Confidence-building measures, however, imply the existence of a willingness, if not to compromise, at least to forswear the use of force in a given context. But confidence has always been in short supply in Indo-Pakistani relations.

Few now attempt to justify the 1983-84 decision on the grounds that the region is of strategic value. The logic of the decision was preemptive; its military, diplomatic, and human consequences have been considerable.

A minority view, however, does argue for the area's strategic significance. To Major General P.M. Pasricha, former deputy director of the Institute for Defence Studies and Analyses in New Delhi, "Geo-militarily, the most significant feature of the Siachen Glacier is that it adjoins the 4,500 square kilometers of Kashmir ceded by Pakistan to China unauthorizedly in 1963."[23] Was the objective of the Indian military effort to nullify the Sino-Pakistani boundary pact by forcibly edging Pakistan out of territory contiguous with Xinjiang? Pasricha also raises another concern: the possibility for a military threat to Ladakh. "The northern approach from the Siachen Glacier to its snout and thence along the Nubra Valley towards Leh is one aspect of it."[24] Lieutenant General P.N. Hoon (ret.) led the 1984 Indian operation as corps commander and, as director general of military operations in 1986, attended the first two rounds of talks on Siachen. Hoon argues that without control of Siachen and the Saltoro ridge, "Pakistan would have soon been able to threaten the Nubra Valley and even Leh."[25]

Notwithstanding these arguments, most observers, including some prominent Indian security specialists, disagree and discount the glacier's military value. Wirsing contends: "The glacier itself . . . has no obvious military value."[26] Captain S.S. Ahlawat poured cold water on India's fears of threat to Ladakh and Pakistan's fears of threat to the Sino-Pakistani Karakoram Highway west of the glacier: "These widely believed perceptions are far from the truth. . . . Siachen represents a glaring example of political expediency in sacrifice of human lives." The region "has no significance for the security of either country." He counseled "a political solution for immediate de-escalation."[27]

An equally strong reaction came from Lieutenant General P.N. Kathpalia, former director general, military intelligence, whose explanation of the troop presence in Siachen dismissed strategic considerations. "When you start putting troops [in the area], the other side also does the same and now even if you want to you can't pull out. . . . a soldier always overassesses. . . . If you know this character of the army, it is for the civilian government to make a correct judgment and put the actions right."[28]

Indian correspondent Arun Chacko wrote in 1989 that, strategically, Siachen was of "little importance."[29] He noted: "Contrary to initial Indian wisdom, the Pakistanis cannot get into Ladakh along the Siachen Glacier route, and neither can the Chinese. Nowhere has a road been built on a glacier."[30] Moreover, Chacko pointed out that, "according to several senior Indian army officials in key positions during the period, the Indians were to blame for upping the ante; the Pakistanis only reacted when Indian troops were put there. In reality, the Indians created an emergency when there wasn't any."[31]

Arguing from another Indian viewpoint, Pravin Sawhney, the defense correspondent for a leading Indian daily, commented in 1992 that the 1984 deployment was "a panic reaction" to Pakistan's moves.[32] He questioned why the Pakistanis would have bothered crossing the Saltoro ridge and the Siachen Glacier to approach Leh when they could easily have used the Shyok and Indus River approaches. It is interesting to note the disclosure made in Sawhney's article. The Indian and Pakistani representatives asked to draw the LAC in 1972 "had never visited NJ9842 and had defined it only from the map"; rather, "It was in 1985 that an Indian survey team identified NJ9842 with an approach from Urdolep Glacier."[33]

Ahmed Hasan Dani has outlined certain Pakistani concerns. According to Dani, India's plan, was "to advance gradually from Nubra into Khapalu and Skardu and thus cut away Baltistan from Northern Areas of Pakistan"; another objective was "to cut off Pakistan from direct link with China."[34] The same issue was raised by a respected Pakistani journalist, Ghanie Eirabie: "India has sought to block three Pakistan-China passes; one northeast of the glacier, the Karakoram Pass, and the other two to the northwest, the Indira Col and Turkestan La. That leaves only the Khunjerab Pass to Pakistan."[35] This statement, however, is not quite accurate insofar as there are (as Dani pointed out) other common passes from Kilik and Mintaka to Saltoro, including the Khunjerab and Shimshal Passes. (See Figure 5.1.)

The record shows that the fears of both Eirabie and Dani were exaggerated. India's venture into the area was inspired by distrust of Pakistan's intentions, not by any malevolent or deliberate desire to achieve the objectives alluded to by these individuals. That the success of India's operation took the Indian military presence as far as it eventually did is another matter.

Predictably, Pakistan reacted to *Meghdoot* by launching its own Operation *Ababeel* (the swallow), with one platoon dispatched to each of the key passes atop the Saltoro ridge, Sia La and Bilafond La. In spring 1984, Pakistani forces launched two unsuccessful attacks on the Indian picket at Bilafond La.

In June 1987, Indian troops attacked and captured the Qaid post, which Pakistan had established in the winter of 1986-87 and which dominated the Bilafond La. Pakistan countered the attack with 150 soldiers, preceded by heavy artillery fire, and self-propelled munitions. Benazir Bhutto seized upon the debacle to criticize the Zia regime in Pakistan, and a full report on the incident was published in *The Muslim* under the editor's by-line.[36]

As of the end of 1993, Indian troops held Indira Col and controlled both Sia La and Bilafond La. Pakistani forces controlled Gyong La overlooking the Nubra River valley, the Indian access route to the Siachen Glacier from Leh. Pakistan also held Conway Saddle (see Figure 5.1) at the junction of the Karakoram and the Saltoro ranges, thus controlling ingress to the Siachen

Glacier. The three southern passes under Pakistan's control are barely twenty kilometers from the road head at Dzingrulma and consequently pose a threat to the Indian supply route. An unstable status quo has persisted.

Estimates of troop strength vary. According to one correspondent, Pakistan deployed two brigades—the 323d Infantry Brigade and much of the 86th Infantry Brigade, whereas India deployed a brigade on what it calls the Actual Ground Position Line (the frontline of Indian forces along the Saltoro ridge).[37] Another correspondent reported that Pakistan had brigade-strength garrisons at Dansam, Khapalu, Siari, Skardu, with the corps head quarters (Force Command Northern Area) at Gilgit.[38]

Defense Secretary and Foreign Secretary Talks. When Prime Minister Rajiv Gandhi of India and President Zia ul-Haq of Pakistan met in New Delhi in December 1985, they agreed to hold talks on the Siachen dispute at the level of defense secretaries. By early 1993 six such rounds of talks had taken place.[39] At the fifth round in June 1989, a breakthrough was achieved. The joint statement issued at Islamabad on June 17, 1989, recorded some kind of "agreement." According to the statement,

> There was *agreement* by both sides to work towards comprehensive settlement, *based on redeployment of forces* to reduce the chances of conflict, avoidance of the use of force and the determination of future positions on the ground so as to conform with the Simla Agreement and to ensure durable peace in the Siachen area. The Army authorities of both sides will determine these positions (emphasis added).[40]

The existence of the agreement was denied by India the very next day.

To appreciate the controversy that ensued—which is crucial to the settlement of the dispute—it is necessary to analyze the terms of settlement proposed by each side since the dispute arose. Broadly, India tried to freeze the situation brought about by Operation *Meghdoot.* As early as March 5, 1985, General A.S. Vaidya, chief of army staff, said that India was ready for proper demarcation of the Siachen Glacier zone, which had escaped "strict" demarcation, and that it was awaiting Pakistan's response to the offer.[41] Chibber, however, revealed on June 3, 1985, that during a flag meeting at Kargil in February 1985 between sector commanders of both sides, Pakistan had asked India to leave. "Since the Indian army has been occupying the glacier for the last so many years it could not agree to what the Pak authorities are demanding."[42]

Pakistan, for its part, sought withdrawal of troops by both sides. Three rounds of talks (at the level of field commanders) had failed to yield results, the parliamentary secretary of defense, Lt. Col. W. Herbert, told the National Assembly on August 17, 1985. According to Herbert, India insisted that the present positions be regarded as the LAC, whereas Pakistan sought India's withdrawal from the territory—which, he added, was neither theirs nor Pakistan's.[43] President Zia ul-Haq explained his stand in detail in an interview to an Indian journal: "Let us go back to the de facto [*sic*] position. What was before you occupied, you go back and we will go back. Let us sit at a table and we will talk. . . . We have earmarked every inch right up to the Karakoram Pass."[44]

The record belies claims to control by both sides. To begin with, Chibber was manifestly wrong in asserting Indian occupation of the glacier in the recent past. The first Indian expedition to Siachen, as noted earlier, was led by Colonel Kumar, when he ascended Teram Kangri on October 13, 1978; the second was by Brigadier Thadani to Apsaras, approximately two years later, on September 18, 1980. Kumar's expedition as far west as Indira Col and Turkestan La in 1981 and his ascent of Sia Kangri refute Zia's prior claim to the territory.

Clearly, confidence between the two countries and their leaders was sparse. But the absence of a *permanent military* presence by *either* before April 13, 1984, is an incontestable fact. India might have asked for demarcation of the line and demanded maintenance of the status quo as of 1983, with a clear hint that any effort by Pakistan to acquire such a presence in the interim would invite military response. Instead, it chose a different course.

The first round of defense secretaries' talks in January 1986 was spent in sparring. Each side accused the other of violating the Simla pact. Furthermore, Pakistan cited the statements of Indian Prime Minister Jawaharlal Nehru of India and India's protests in 1962-63 over Sino-Pakistani negotiations, which resulted in the boundary agreement of 1963 (described further in note 1 of this paper)—and from these attempted to infer the Indian recognition of Pakistan's possession of areas to the west of the Karakoram Pass. Specifically, Pakistan cited India's protest note of May 10, 1962, which referred to "that portion of the boundary between India and China west of the Karakoram Pass *which is presently under Pakistan's unlawful occupation*" (emphasis added), and Nehru's statement in parliament on March 5, 1963 which said that "Pakistan's line of actual control . . . reached the Karakoram Pass."[45] India rejoined that these statements were made on the basis of Pakistan's claims and did not express India's acceptance of those claims.

The second round of talks, in June 1986, saw a repeat of familiar assertions. India hinted at a cease-fire in all but name and proposed accord on nonescalation of the situation. Pakistan rejected anything approximating a cease-fire.[46]

In September 1988, India pressed for a cease-fire and for demarcation of LAC in places where the troops of both sides confronted each other; the rest of the demarcation could be postponed. Pakistan's rejection of the proposal prompted another Indian offer: a cease-fire and partial withdrawal of troops, with a token military presence left by each side in existing positions. Pakistan rejected the offer. In its view this put a seal of approval on the Indian presence in Siachen. Nor would Pakistan accept an accord on mutual restraint, lest it be misconstrued as a cease-fire. The Pakistanis were prepared, though, to make concessions to Indian concerns about its domestic constraints by introducing the concept of "redeployment" under an agreed schedule and with a view to the eventual total withdrawal of forces.

On February 8, 1989, Prime Minister Benazir Bhutto had expected India to withdraw its forces to pre-Simla positions.[47] Her assumption of power in late 1988 as the first democratically elected head of government since 1971 had vastly improved the climate on the Subcontinent. The two sides' initial positions in the fifth round in June 1989 was revealed to Robert G. Wirsing later, on June 12, 1990, by the Indian army headquarters in New Delhi and subsequently by members of the Pakistani delegation.

The Indian terms were:

1. Cessation of "cartographic aggression" by Pakistan (that is, of its unilateral attempts in recent years to extend the LAC from its agreed terminus at map reference point NJ9842 to the Karakoram Pass of the border with China).
2. Establishment of a demilitarized zone (DMZ) at the Siachen Glacier.
3. Exchange between India and Pakistan of authenticated maps showing present military dispositions on the ground.
4. Delimitation by India and Pakistan of a line from map reference point NJ9842 northward to the border with China "based on ground realities."
5. Formulation of ground rules to govern future military operations in the area, and, definitely "the last step" to be taken.
6. Redeployment of Indian and Pakistani forces to mutually agreed positions.

Pakistan's formal terms by the opening of the fifth round of talks, in contrast, were fewer in number. As identified for the author by members of the Pakistani delegation to the fifth round, they contained only two essential points:

1. Deployment of Indian and Pakistani forces to mutually agreed positions held at the time the cease-fire was declared in 1971 (i.e., pre-Simla positions); and only then—
2. Delimitation of an extension of the LAC beyond map reference point NJ9842.[48]

Against this background, the use of the word "agreement" in the joint statement at the end of the fifth round, on June 17, 1989, was highly significant. This was in striking contrast with all previous joint statements. The next day separate talks between the foreign secretaries of the two countries concluded. At a joint press conference, Foreign Secretary Humayun Khan of Pakistan, referring to the defense secretaries' meeting, called it "a significant advance" and spoke of a joint commitment to relocate "forces to positions occupied at the time of the Simla Agreement." He went on to say: "The exact location of these positions will be worked out in detail by military authorities of the two countries."[49] Foreign Secretary, S.K. Singh of India said: "I would like to thank the Foreign Secretary, Dr. Humayun Khan, and endorse everything he has said."[50]

The next morning the press was summoned by Aftab Seth, the joint secretary and official spokesman of the Ministry of External Affairs in New Delhi, to be told that *no* agreement had been reached on troop withdrawals. "There was no indication of any such agreement in the joint press statement issued at the end of the talks."[51]

Bhutto's view of the reasons for India's veto was confirmed three years later by a journalist who was close to Rajiv Gandhi and who was also a member of his Congress Party: "S.K. Singh had his knuckles rapped sharply on his return to Delhi because it was felt that photographs of Indian troops withdrawing from Siachen would not look too good for the government in an election year."[52] At the time, on July 2, 1989, Pakistan's minister of state for defense, Ghulam Sarwar Cheema, urged the press not to speculate, saying that a Siachen agreement would be signed when Rajiv Gandhi visited Pakistan. The Indian prime minister's visit to Islamabad on July 16-17, 1989—the first bilateral visit by an Indian prime minister since 1960—yielded no result on this issue, however.

Nor was there any progress at the two meetings of military representatives on July 11-13 and on August 17-18, 1989. According to a member of the Pakistani team, India both insisted on Pakistan's withdrawal from all military positions in the vicinity of the glacier that it had taken since 1972, including those at Conway Saddle, and suggested that Indian forces redeploy only so far as Dzingrulma near the glacier's snout and that a "civilian" camp be placed at this center.[53] The report was confirmed in 1992 by a prominent Indian defense correspondent.[54]

The sixth round was held three years later, in New Delhi, on November 2-6, 1992. In Islamabad's view the task was simply one of implementing the agreement of June 1989. It should not take "more than a day" for the two teams to work out the details, Foreign Secretary Shaharyar Khan said at New Delhi when the sixth round was announced in August 1992. As he put it: "Some elements in the disengagement require detailed wrapping up. Some loose ends need to be tied." (For instance, how far the troops would be pulled back and where the observation posts would be located to monitor the demilitarized zone to ensure that neither side rushed back in.) "We are talking of civilian observation posts, not military observation posts."[55] The defense secretaries were to be assisted by military officers.

In response, India promptly denied the existence of any agreement to withdraw troops from the glacier. Evidently, the new Indian policy was not to implement the "agreement" of 1989. Instead, the Indians hoped to have the foreign secretaries meet "to carry forward the process of discussions on the Siachen Glacier which had remained suspended since June 1989."[56] On the day the talks were due to begin, the Indian press reported that India was unlikely to pull back its troops from the Siachen Glacier area "in view of Pakistan's 'proxy war' in the Kashmir Valley and Punjab," and that "any breakthrough is unlikely."[57]

India's proposal at this round of talks suggested the following: (1) the demarcation of the LAC in the area as a matter of priority; (2) redeployment of troops on both sides to agreed positions, but only after the recording of existing positions; (3) definition of a Zone of Disengagement (ZOD) that would come into being in consequence of the redeployment; and (4) undertakings by both sides not to reoccupy vacated positions, occupy new positions "across the alignment determined by the vacated positions," or undertake any military or mountaineering activity in the zone.

The ZOD and the alignment of existing positions suggested a hardening of India's position since the 1989 agreement. Monitoring would have been along the existing positions. The ZOD itself was defined to accord with the existing Actual Ground Position Line.

Pakistan's riposte was to propose a triangle whose points were Indira Col in the west and the Karakoram Pass in the east, with both joined to NJ9842. Troops of both countries would be withdrawn from the area within this triangle. The status quo would be maintained pending demarcation of the LAC by a joint commission.

Both proposals were ostensibly nonstarters. Vexed by the Indian proposal, Pakistan made one that India could not possibly have accepted. Confronted with deadlock, Pakistan sought to revive the 1989 agreement by formally making a simple proposal, including a major—and unpublicized—concession to India: Existing positions would be recorded, albeit in an annex and on the understanding that it would not constitute a basis for a claim to the area legally, morally, or politically. The annex would also mention the points to which the troops were to "redeploy" (read: retreat). Demarcation of the LAC would follow thereafter. India did not respond to the proposal, and the talks ended.

Nevertheless, interestingly, the blanks in the 1989 agreement had been filled in. After that accord the parties were to discuss two major topics: the positions to which the troops were to withdraw and the mode of surveillance (whether by posts, joint patrolling, or other means). During the technical talks in November 1992, it was agreed that: (1) India would withdraw to Dzingrulma and Pakistan would withdraw to Goma, at the base of the Bilafond Glacier, and (2) surveillance was to be accomplished by helicopter.

Each side gave its version to the public after the talks ended. On November 6, a spokesman of the Indian Ministry of External Affairs acknowledged that "there was a certain progress made in terms of technical details of the disengagement." He claimed that the 1989 talks had floundered on this point but that this was not the case this time.[58] Soon thereafter, reports appeared in the press that India's concessions would not go beyond "minor adjustments" on the Saltoro ridge.[59] On November 11, Pakistan confirmed progress on the positions to which the forces would withdraw. It also alleged that India had imposed "certain preconditions."[60]

Solving the Siachen Dispute. The solution to the tangle of the Siachen dispute lies in a return to the 1989 agreement. There is no longer any disagreement on the mode of monitoring or on the positions to which forces would withdraw. Indian fears arising from the closer proximity to POK of the salient points in the Saltoro ridge as well as the Siachen Glacier itself suggest simply the need to firm up the monitoring arrangements.[61]

With respect to such arrangements, there is no role for the United Nations Military Observer Group in India and Pakistan (UNMOGIP),[62] emplaced to monitor observance of the 1949 agreement, defining the cease-fire line.[63] There are now approximately forty observers, mostly in Pakistan-Occupied Kashmir.[64] Those in India are not allowed to monitor the LAC, although they are permitted to cross it to reach POK. Siachen, UN observer sources said on June 15, 1985, was outside their operational area. A team of three UN observers was barred by India from going to the glaciers, according to an Agence France Press report on October 6, 1987.

Apart from operational impediments, India's stress on bilateralism rules out any role for the UNMOGIP, and without Indian consent, the UNMOGIP cannot function. It should be noted, however, that in extreme situations India has sought or accepted foreign diplomatic assistance, as demonstrated in early 1990, when "India invited U.S. observers to monitor troop and equipment deployments (related to Indian exercises) as an assurance of non-hostile intent."[65] Thus it is conceivable that India might find acceptable an alternative type of monitoring arrangement, such as that contained in the Open Skies Treaty.

The 1992 Open Skies Treaty, signed by more than twenty-five countries, provides for cooperative aerial overflight procedures that can be useful in confidence building and crisis management. Such procedures, for example, might be emulated to advantage in a defined zone, such as the Siachen area. It was reported that Indian delegates to the 1992 talks argued that "given the weather in the Siachen area, it would be easy to predict when a helicopter patrol would take place, and any troops on the ground could then conceal themselves."[66] A leading Indian defense analyst, K. Subrahmanyam urged India to propose a treaty to Pakistan and China that would allow for cooperative aerial overflights. That step would be a sound diplomatic initiative to take; the advantages of having "open skies" over a precisely defined area on the glacier region are obvious.[67]

The only issue that divides India and Pakistan on the Siachen dispute is the implementation of the agreement of June 1989. India and Pakistan should undertake a full withdrawal of troops of both sides to the agreed points, in the spirit of the Simla agreement, *without* any attempt to legitimize post-1972 military advances by either side, whether by recording the existing Actual Ground Position Line as the sole area of inspection or otherwise. Agreement on "open skies" in the Siachen Glacier region would help enormously in generating the mutual trust needed to put this issue to rest.

The Wular Barrage

India and Pakistan disagree even on the name of the controversy referred to here as the Wular barrage dispute. To India, it is the Tulbul Navigation Project; Pakistan calls it the Wular barrage. At issue is a barrage that is to be constructed by the government of the Indian state of Jammu and Kashmir on the Jhelum River just below Wular Lake. The rationale behind the project is as follows: From late October to mid-February the flow in the Jhelum is about 2,000 cubic feet per second (cusecs), perhaps less; the water is 2.5 feet deep. A depth of four feet with a flow of 4,000 cusecs is necessary for navigability. During these lean months, the obvious remedy is to control and regulate the depletion from Wular Lake so as to provide the requisite flow in the Jhelum.

The barrage is located just below Wular Lake, at its mouth, in the town of Ningli, near Sopore, fourty kilometers north of Srinagar. (See Figure 5.3). The object of the barrage is to solve the problem of navigation over a distance of approximately twenty kilometers between Wular Lake and Baramula allowing easier movement between Sopore and Baramula.

The lake, at its highest level, has a natural water storage capacity of about 300,000 acre feet. The Tulbul Navigation Project is not intended to add storage capacity as such, but to regulate water depletion in order to ensure year-round navigability on the Jhelum. The project would attempt to accomplish this by constructing a barrage about 440 feet long, with a navigation lock, on the Jhelum at the mouth of Wular Lake.

Some Pakistanis have argued that this is a work not of navigation control but of storage and is a breach of the 1960 Indus Waters Treaty, which assigns the Jehlum River waters to Pakistan. The Indus Waters Treaty divided between the two countries the six great rivers of Punjab: the eastern rivers including the Beas, the Ravi, and the Sutlej; and the western rivers including the Chenab, the Indus, and the Jhelum. All the waters of the three eastern rivers are for the unrestricted use of India. Pakistan received for unrestricted use all the waters of the three western rivers, and India is under treaty obligation to let them flow into Pakistan without any "interference."[68]

This basic division is qualified with precise exceptions. India is allowed four distinct kinds of uses of the western rivers: domestic use (drinking, washing, and so on), agricultural use for irrigation, a restricted use for generation of hydroelectric power through a "run-of-river" plant, and what is called "nonconsumptive use."[69] The nonconsumptive use is key to the present dispute.

The treaty defines nonconsumptive use to mean "any control or use of water for navigation," and other specified purposes, provided, however, that "the water (undiminished in volume within the practical range of measurement) remains in, or is returned to, the same river."[70] This is the dominant concern written all over the treaty. The expression "interference with the waters" is also defined to mean any act of withdrawal therefrom or "any man-made

Figure IV

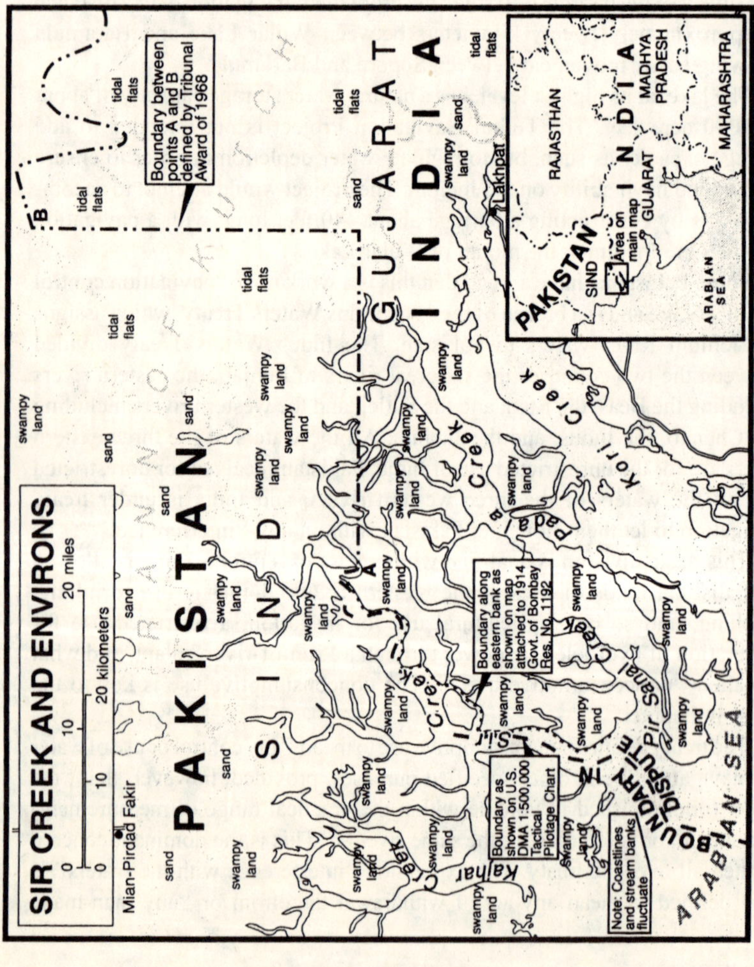

Cartography by Philip Schwartzberg, Meridian Mapping

The external boundaries of India depicted in both the above maps are neither correct nor authentic

obstruction to their flow which causes a change in the volume . . . of the daily flow of waters'' unless it is of an insignificant degree.[71]

According to Article IV (2):

> Each party agrees that any Non-consumptive Use made by it shall be so made as not to materially change, on account of such use, the flow in any channel to the prejudice of the uses on that channel by the other party under the provisions of this Treaty. In executing any scheme of flood protection or flood control each party shall avoid, as far as practicable, any material damage to the other party, and any such scheme carried out by India on the Western Rivers shall not involve any use of water or any storage in addition to that provided under Article III.

India's permitted nonconsumptive use of the western rivers includes the Jhelum and its ''connecting lake,'' Wular. The central issue of the present dispute arises from the treaty's forbidding India, except within certain defined limits, to ''store any water of, or construct any storage works on, the Western Rivers.''[72] Thus, the controversy: Is the Wular barrage essentially a project for the ''control or use of water for navigation,'' or is it a ''storage work''?

There are two exceptions to the ban on India's storing waters of the western rivers. One concerns certain hydroelectric projects. The other, which is pertinent to the dispute, is a limited permission for India to store waters of the western rivers as spelled out in Annex E of the treaty. India is allowed ''any natural storage in a connecting Lake,'' such as Wular, but this must be ''storage not resulting from any man-made works.''[73] India may construct on the Jhelum works for flood control of the river. Storage incidental to a barrage on the Jhelum must not exceed 10,000 acre ft. Storage work is defined as a work constructed ''for the purpose of impounding the waters of a stream.''[74]

This narrows the issue still further. Is it the ''purpose'' of the Wular barrage to ''impound,'' that is, collect or confine, the waters of the Jhelum or to ''control'' them for navigation? Since the waters will, indeed, be confined for some time in order to raise the level of the lake, there is some storage, albeit temporary. But how far does the treaty permit control of the waters for navigation? Can such control be exercised without some element of storage as defined in the treaty?

The treaty lays down three procedures for resolving disputes. First, it establishes a Permanent Indus Commission consisting of two commissioners for the Indus waters appointed from each country. Questions of ''interpretation or application'' of the treaty are to be submitted to the commission, which serves as a regular channel of communication on all matters relating to the treaty's implementation. If the commissioners do not reach agreement, the dispute is then to be referred to a neutral expert for resolution, at the request of either side, if it concerns any of the twenty-odd questions that fall within the expert's jurisdiction; otherwise, either side may request that the matter be referred to a seven-member court of arbitration.

The dispute between India and Pakistan falls neatly within the scope of the neutral expert's competence: "Whether or not any use of water or storage in addition to that provided in Article III is involved in any of the schemes referred to in Article IV (2) or in Article IV (3)(b) and carried on by India on the Western Rivers" (Question 3).[75] The treaty, however, enables either government to take up any particular issue directly with the other government, leaving the commission high and dry. In its zeal to settle the matter directly, India did precisely that in 1987, thereby disabling its commissioner from referring the problem to the neutral expert and leaving open only two alternatives for resolving the dispute—an accord or an expensive, time-consuming reference to a court of arbitration.

With respect to an accord on this matter, there is indeed a basis for compromise. India has provided two assurances, *both of which are substantially capable of objective verification.* The volume of water that flows into the Jhelum as it enters Pakistan would not be diminished, and there would no material change in the flow in any channel, to the prejudice of the uses by Pakistan of any such channel. These precautions observed, the project would be in the interests of Pakistan as well. Pakistan's argument on storage proper may be conceded. But if fully assured that there will be no diminution in the flow of the Jhelum, and if full appropriate safeguards are established, Pakistan must concede "control" over the Jhelum waters to India for navigation. There is ample room for compromise between "storage" and "control" in light of technical studies and on the basis of trust—to the benefit of both countries.

Progress toward such an accord was reported by the Pakistani newspaper *Dawn* on September 22, 1989: "India has agreed to surrender 0.30 million acre [ft.] . . . of the total general storage capacity at the Jhelum tributaries, allowed to it under the Indus Waters Treaty, if Pakistan gives it the go-ahead for the construction of the Wular dam. The total storage capacity of the dam is equivalent to the storage capacity India is prepared to forgo." It revealed that India had sent a draft agreement comprising twelve articles and that Pakistan had prepared its own six-article draft.

On November 12, 1989, a furor ensued when the *Pakistan Observer* published the full text of Pakistan's draft according consent to India's project on certain terms. The draft was later revised. The basic disagreement was now gone. It was only a matter of stipulations.

On October 16, 1991, India's minister for water resources, V.C. Shukla, claimed that agreement on this dispute was expected shortly. However, *The Nation,* a Lahore daily, reported on March 25, 1992, that Pakistan had rejected the Indian draft given in November 1991. Earlier on February 9, 1992, another daily, *The News,* published the following report:

> The Pakistan Government has decided to arrive at a negotiated settlement on the Wular Project with India, allowing it to build the disputed barrage if India agrees to keep 6.2 m. of the structure as ungated with crest level at EL 1,574.90 m., forgo general storage capacity of 0.30 million acre [ft.] . . . out of the provision of 75 maf. permitted to it on the Jhelum, and does not construct the Kishenganga (390 mw) hydro-power generating unit, highly placed sources disclosed.
>
> India has agreed to surrender on the first two points but consensus on the Kishenganga project is still to be reached, the sources said, adding: "This is the only disputed issue left for the amicable settlement of the Wular barrage melodrama. Pakistan is of the view that if India constructed Kishenganga Project, it would affect the construction of Pakistan's Neelam-Jhelum power generating project. If we compromise on other points, then India would compromise here, and construction on Neelam-Jhelum, held up due to this dispute, could begin, as it was in Pakistan's interest."
>
> Prime Minister Nawaz Sharif has given the green signal to the Ministry for Water and Power to go ahead for the negotiated settlement of the issue and a high-powered delegation of the ministry would soon be visiting Delhi to reach an agreement acceptable to both the countries, the sources said.

The Indian Ministry of External Affairs 1992-1993 annual report claims that a meeting of representatives of both countries was held on August 6-9, 1992, and that "all legal and technical aspects were discussed." It indicates that "Pakistan's clearance on the joint draft [worked out in October 1991] is awaited."[76]

As on Siachen, the dispute on Wular Lake centers now on the implementation of the basic accord, which, it seems, has already been agreed upon. The state government of Jammu and Kashmir will be able to build the barrage on the Jhelum River just below the lake on certain conditions that are designed to assure free flow of the waters into Pakistan. The legal and technical points have been sorted out. The sticking point now is India's Kishenganga hydroelectric power generating project which bears on the Neelam-Jhelum power project that Pakistan has planned with great enthusiasm. The problem here is part technical and part political. Adjustment or trade-off is possible, but the issue arouses strong emotions in Pakistan's Punjab province.

Sir Creek

Sir Creek is a sixty-mile-long estuary in the marshes of the Rann of Kutch, which lies on the border between the Indian state of Gujarat and the Pakistani province of Sind.[77] In 1965, armed clashes followed Pakistan's claiming that half of the Rann along the 24th parallel was Pakistani territory and India's claiming that the boundary ran roughly along the northern edge of Rann. The matter was referred to arbitration, and the Indo-Pakistan Western Boundary Case Tribunal's Award on February 19, 1968, upheld 90 percent of India's claim to the entire Rann, conceding small sectors to Pakistan.

The dispute arises from the parties' agreement before the tribunal to limit their dispute only to the boundary in the north. Well to the south lay an agreed boundary that began at the head of Sir Creek and ran a short distance eastward roughly along the 24th parallel. India, however, contended that this line moved up sharply at a right angle to meet the northern boundary of the Rann. Pakistan sought to extend the line further eastward and claim half of the Rann along the 24th parallel. The sole issue, therefore, was whether the short agreed boundary from the head of Sir Creek went all the way east or rose at a right angle at its western end to reach the northern limit of the Rann. The tribunal accepted India's case that it did turn north and that the entire Rann was Indian. (See Figure 5.4.)

That the short agreed border from the head of Sir Creek eastward was excluded from the tribunal's consideration was understandable. *Unfortunately, the parties agreed also to exclude the boundary from the head of Sir Creek downward to the west, right up to the mouth of the creek on the Arabian Sea; in short, the Indo-Pakistani boundary along Sir Creek.* The Tribunal noted, "In view of the aforesaid agreement, the question concerning the Sir Creek part of the boundary is left out of consideration."[78]

The Sir Creek part of the boundary has now become a bone of contention. According to the 1992-93 Ministry of External Affairs annual report, even the sixth round of talks, on November 2-6, 1992, made no progress on this issue. India asserts that the boundary lies in the middle of the creek. Pakistan claims that the line lies on the creek's eastern bank, the Indian side, and, therefore, that the entire creek is Pakistani. The delineation of the Indo-Pakistani maritime boundary is linked to this determination. Pakistan insists that the boundary in the creek first be delimited in order to establish the point on the land from which a sea boundary may be defined. India's concerns center on the maritime boundary.

Pakistan, in its arguments, refers to the map on which India had relied prior to the tribunal and which does show the boundary on the eastern bank, on the Kutch side. (See Figure 5.4.)[79] It is authoritative, and India's earlier reliance on it constitutes an admission in law. Pakistan itself, however, had contended in a May 19, 1958, note that "this map was intended to be no more than an annexure to the Bombay Government Resolution" of February 24, 1914. Pakistan was right. It is the resolution, not the attached map, that is decisive.[80]

This resolution refers to the Indian government's "sanction" on November 11, 1913, of the Kutch-Sind compromise over Kori Creek, which the government of Bombay had spelled out in its letter of September 20, 1913. This letter refers to the line on the accompanying map "from the mouth of the Sir Creek to the top of the Sir Creek," which ran on the Kutch side. It also contained a proviso by the commissioner in Sind that supports India's stand. It reads: "He observed, however, that the Sir Creek changes its course from time to time and the western boundary of the area, which it is proposed to surrender to the Rao [of Kutch], should therefore be described as 'the center of the navigable channel of the Sir Creek.'"[81] On this, the secretary to the Bombay government commented in that very letter: "I am to explain that the term 'navigable' is really inappropriate in the larger sense. The creek is, of course, tidal, and it is only at certain conditions of the tide that the channel is navigable and then only to the country craft as far as the point from which the proposed boundary turns due east from the creek."[82] This is not a rejection of the Sind commissioner's condition but essentially an acceptance of it.

It is not difficult to see that a compromise could be worked out in light of the conditions of navigation today. Such a compromise might be reached by itself or, better still, as part of a wider accord on the maritime boundary. As a confidence-building measure, a resolution to the Sir Creek dispute would thus have both a technical and a political basis.

International arbitration will be an expensive and lengthy process. A boundary along "the center of the navigable channel" would be in accord with the internationally recognized principle of *thalweg*—the middle of the river channel. The ideal course of action would be to consider this issue while negotiating the Indo-Pakistani maritime boundary. Both should be undertaken soon and in a spirit of give-and-take.

Conclusion

The Siachen, Wular, and Sir Creek issues are ripe for a settlement. The mechanics are all but agreed. Only a political decision to execute the plans remains to be taken. Decisive leadership now to end these disputes is of the greatest importance. Not only would agreement on these issues have a considerable impact on relations between India and Pakistan, but it would also impart momentum to consideration of other confidence-building measures—most notably, mutual balanced force reductions and reduction of defense budgets in both countries. Finally, resolution of these smaller disputes holds the promise that talks on the larger question of Kashmir could be held in a more relaxed, and more cooperative, atmosphere.

Postscript

Following the talks between the foreign secretaries of India and Pakistan in Islamabad on January 1 and 3, 1994, India sent, as promised, six "non-papers" on confidence-building measures to Pakistan. Three of these dealt with Siachen, Wular, and Sir Creek. On January 26th, *The Hindu* reported: "As regards Siachen, India has veered to the view taken by Pakistan towards the end of 1992. There is an element of frankness in New Delhi's explanation that the domestic political environment of that period came in the way of acceptance. In doing so, India may have exposed itself to criticism that decisions on crucial issues were allowed to be influenced by narrow domestic considerations. But could Pakistan now refuse to agree to what it wanted India to accept not very long ago?" This was an allusion to recent Pakistani statements linking Siachen with the Kashmir problem.[83] The report confirms the view expressed earlier in this chapter that a settlement was very much possible in 1992, if not in 1989.

NOTES

1. An interesting episode that took place in the interim between 1949 an 1971 and that demonstrated continuing tensions over the boundaries of Kashmir occurred in 1963, when on March 2 Pakistan and China signed an agreement defining the boundary between China's Xinjiang province "and the contiguous areas" in northern Kashmir, "the defense of which," the agreement states, "is under the actual control of Pakistan." As illustrated in Figure I, the boundary's broad

alignment (Article 2) commenced in the northwest at the trijunction of China, Afghanistan, and Pakistan-Occupied Kashmir (POK) and continued eastward, ending "at the Karakoram Pass." Article 6 provided that "after the settlement of the Kashmir dispute between Pakistan and India, the sovereign authority will re-open negotiations" with China on the boundary to sign a formal treaty replacing the agreement. (For text of this agreement, see Dorothy Woodman, *Himalayan Frontiers: A Political Review of British, Chinese, Indian, and Russian Rivalries* [New York: Praeger, 1969].)

India protested the agreement on the grounds that legally the whole of Kashmir was Indian territory and that Pakistan had unlawfully ceded 4,500 sq. km. to China. In fact, Pakistani concessions to China were only on maps; actually, China had ceded 1,250 sq. km. of Chinese-administered land on which there is no known permanent habitation.

2. The Simla agreement, 1972, Paragraph 1(ii). The official name of this agreement is the "Agreement on Bilateral Relations Between the Government of Pakistan and the Government of India."
3. According to Paragraph B2 of the Karachi agreement, "The cease-fire line runs from Manawar in the south, north to Keran and from Keran east to the glacier area." Paragraph B2 (d) defined the extremity thus:

   "From Dalunang eastward the CFL will follow the gen [sic] line Pt 15495, Ishman Manus, Gangan, Gunderman, Pt. 13620, Junkar (Pt. 17628), Marmak, Natsara, Shangruthi (Pt. 17531), Chorbat La (Pt. 15700), Chalunka, Khor, *thence north to the glaciers.* This portion of the CFL shall be demarcated in detail on the basis of the factual position as of 27 July 1949 by the local Commanders, assisted by United Nations Military Observers" (emphasis added).
4. Air Commodore Jasjit Singh, director of the Institute for Defense Studies and Analyses, has been misleading in his assertion that Swaran Singh's statement described the LAC as "going westward joining the glaciers," and not *eastward* (emphasis added). (See Jasjit Singh, *Times of India*, May 19, 1988. *The Hindu*, July 10, 1987, also uses the word *eastward*, as do Syed Rifaat Hussain, *The Muslim*, June 15, 1986, Lahore edition, and Ahmed Dani, *The Muslim*, September 16, 1988.) This author has verified that the official text, as distributed by agencies of the government of India, indeed reads eastward.

   Jasjit Singh, however, made an important but often neglected point: in this mountainous region a straight line of the kind drawn from the Karakoram Pass is notable. Although there are precedents for straight boundary lines in mountainous terrain, they are usually associated with agreements delineating them as such. Singh remarked that the straight line started appearing on maps in the United States and Europe sometime around 1963 "when US Air Force Aeronautical maps started indicating this as the limit of the Indian ADIZ (Air Information Defense Zone)," which does not necessarily represent a national frontier. "Even within a country a number of ADIZs may exist."

   By contrast, a map published in 1963 by the Information Department of the Embassy of Pakistan in Washington, D.C., showed the CFL as ending at NJ9842—constituting an authoritative admission of the terminus of the line, providing no conclusive information about Pakistani possession of the territory north and east of the terminus point. (See Figure II).
5. Simla agreement, 1972, Paragraph 6.

6. *Hindustan Times*, November 25, 1993.
7. *Indian Express*, June 21, 1972.
8. For evidence, see A.G. Noorani, "Pakistan's Complicity in Terrorism in J & K: The Evidence and the Law," *Indian Defense Review* (January 1992).
9. See the author's article, "The tortured and the damned: Human rights in Kashmir," based on reports of Indian and international human rights organizations, in *Frontline*, January 28, 1994.
10. *The Hindu*, November 12, 1993.
11. Ibid.
12. Ibid.
13. *Meghdoot* is the name of a divine cloud messenger from classic Sanskrit texts. The operation's title may have been inspired by its lofty venue.
14. M.L. Chibber, "Siachen—The Untold Story (A Personal Account)," *Indian Defense Review* (January 1990): 89-95.
15. Robert G. Wirsing, *Strategic Studies* Autumn 1988: 41 (Islamabad, Pakistan, The Institute of Strategic Studies). See also Robert G. Wirsing, *Pakistan's Security Under Zia 1977-1988: The Policy Imperatives of a Peripheral Asian State* (New York: St. Martin's Press, 1991), 143-94.
16. Chibber, "Siachen," 91-92.
17. These areas are referred to in Pakistan as Azad (Free) Kashmir and the Northern Areas.
18. Schwartzberg distinguished two sectors of the line, 'AB' of which he wrote, "Cease-fire line as of January 1, 1949; delimited on July 27, and demarcated by October 1949," and 'BC' of which he wrote, "Undelimited extension of cease-fire line as shown on many maps." Map (h), plate IX.C.2, Joseph E. Schwartzberg, ed. *A Historical Atlas of South Asia* (Chicago, University of Chicago Press, 1978).
19. Ahmed Hasan Dani, *The Muslim*, September 16, 1988.
20. Chibber, 89-95.
21. Ibid.
22. Zulfikar Ali Khan, "Geopolitics of the Siachen Glacier," *Asian Defense Journal* (November 1985).
23. P.M. Pasricha, *Strategic Analysis* (December 1985): 855 and 858.
24. Ibid.
25. P.N. Hoon, *Indian Express*, November 14, 1992.
26. Wirsing, *Strategic Studies* (Autumn 1988): 38.
27. S.S. Ahlawat, *Indian Defense Review* (July 1988).
28. Sunday Observer, November 13, 1988.
29. Arun Chacko, *Indian Express*, July 2, 1989.
30. Ibid.
31. Ibid.
32. Pravin Sawhney, *Indian Express*, August 25, 1992.
33. Ibid.
34. Dani, *The Muslim*, September 16, 1988.
35. Ghanie Eirabie, *The Muslim*, September 6, 1988.
36. Maleeha Lodhi, *The Muslim*, October 22, 1987.
37. *The Hindustan Times*, August 23, 1992.
38. *Indian Express*, August 26, 1992.
39. January 10-12, 1986; June 11-13, 1986; May 18-20, 1988; September 22-24, 1988; June 15-17, 1989; and November 2-6, 1992.

40. Richard M. Weintraub, "Pakistan and India Take Steps to Defuse Long Confrontation Over Siachen Glacier," *Washington Post*, June 20, 1989.
41. *Indian Express*, March 6, 1985.
42. *The Hindustan Times*, June 4, 1985.
43. *The Muslim*, August 18, 1985.
44. *The Week*, October 20, 1985.
45. *Sino-Pakistani Agreement*, 1963, pamphlet, 33, India, Ministry of External Affairs.
46. Accounts in this chapter of the talks from 1986-1992 are based on interviews with diplomats and journalists—Indian, Pakistani, and others.
47. Robert G. Wirsing, "The Siachen Glacier Dispute: Can Diplomacy Untangle It?" *Indian Defense Review* (July 1991): 99.
48. Ibid.
49. *The Statesman*, June 22, 1989; *The Muslim*, June 1989. (Humayun Khan was quoted on The Voice of America, and the BBC and *Deutsche Welle* reported the same thing.)
50. Ibid.
51. *The Telegraph*, June 20, 1993. See also Wirsing, "The Siachen Glacier Dispute," 99.
52. M.J. Akbar, *The Telegraph*, August 20, 1992.
53. Wirsing, "The Siachen Glacier Dispute," 102.
54. Pravin Sawhney, *Indian Express*, August 25. 1992.
55. *Pioneer*, August 22, 1992.
56. *Hindustan Times*, August 25, 1992.
57. *Hindustan Times*, November 2, 1992.
58. *Hindustan Times*, November 7, 1992.
59. *Indian Express*, November 8, 1992; *Sunday Mail*, November 15, 1992.
60. *Times of India*, November 12, 1992.
61. Opinion seemed to be shifting in this direction in late 1993 and early 1994. For example, Vinod Sharma wrote, "India and Pakistan were very close to an agreement in 1989. It seems perfectly sensible that they now take that off the shelf, dust it off, and look at it again." "Pakistan Almost Off the Hook Again," *Hindustan Times*, November 10, 1993.
62. Rosalyn Higgins, *United Nations Peacekeeping 1946-1967* vol. 2 (Asia) (London: Oxford University Press, 1970). See also, Karl Th. Birgisson, "UNMOGIP," in William J. Durch, ed. *The Evolution of UN Peacekeeping*, ed. (New York: St. Martin's Press, 1993), Chapter 16.
63. A nucleus of the UNMOGIP existed before the July 27, 1949, cease-fire agreement, having arrived in Kashmir on January 24, 1949. Approximately two years after the UNMOGIP was emplaced, the United Nations (UN) Security Council passed Resolution S/2017 on March 30, 1951, which authorized the Military Observer Group to continue supervising the cease-fire in the state. Foreign Minister Swaran Singh of India later said that a new cease-fire had come into force as of December 17, 1971, and there was "no subsisting agreement" for the UNMOGIP. (Government of India, Press Information Bureau, May 17, 1972).
64. Unofficial United Nations documents estimated 1993 UNMOGIP troop strength to be thirty-eight or thirty-nine observers. See, Barry M. Blechman, and J. Matthew Vaccaro, *Training for Peacekeeping: The United Nations' Role* (Washington, D.C.: The Henry L. Stimson Center, 1994), Appendix C.
65. Michael Krepon et al., eds., *A Handbook of Confidence-Building Measures for Regional Security* (Washington, D.C.: The Henry L. Stimson Center, 1993), 47.

66. Joydeep Gupta, *Sunday Mail,* November 15, 1992.
67. K. Subrahmanyam, review of Michael Krepon and Amy E. Smithson, Open Skies, Arms Control, and Cooperative Security, in *Book Review* (July 1993).
68. Aloys Arthur Michel, *The Indus River: A Study of the Effect of Partition* (New Haven, Conn.: Yale University Press, 1967); Niranjan D. Gulhati, *Indus Waters Treaty* (New Delhi: Allied Publishers, 1973).
69. *Indus Waters Treaty*, 1960, Article III (1).
70. Ibid., Article I (11).
71. Ibid., Article I (15).
72. Ibid., Article III (4).
73. Ibid.
74. Ibid.
75. Ibid.
76. *Annual Report* 1992-1993, Ministry of External Affairs, India.
77. Sir Creek is actually a fluctuating tidal channel, not a true flowing "creek."
78. Indo-Pakistani Western Boundary Case Tribunal, February 19, 1968.
79. Sind had claimed in 1905 that its boundary lay on Kori Creek, which is well to the south of the Sir Creek. A compromise was arrived at in 1913, approved by the government of India, and recorded in the Resolution of the government of Bombay, to which the map was attached. This map (see Figure IV) which had been annexed to the Resolution of the Government of Bombay dated February 24, 1914, recorded a compromise of the dispute between Kutch and Sind which was then part of the Bombay Presidency.
80. *The Kutch-Sind Border* (New Delhi: Indian Society of International Law, 1965).
81. Ibid.
82. Ibid.
83. K.K. Katyal, "Pak May Not Take Proposal Seriously," *The Hindu,* January 26, 1994.

6

MANAGING INTERNAL SECURITY PROBLEMS

Raju Thomas

With the rise of ethnic nationalism and the resort to violent insurgencies and terrorism in India, Pakistan, and Sri Lanka, the greater threat to these countries now originates not so much from external aggression, but from the possibility of internal conflict aided by external enemies. Proxy wars, as in the case of reported Pakistani assistance to the Kashmiri and Sikh separatist movements, may slide into full-scale Indo-Pakistani wars. This chapter will explore whether various confidence-building measures (CBMs) can be devised and adopted to minimize the problems of ongoing internal conflict and proxy wars and reduce the likelihood of full-scale wars in South Asia.

Confidence-building measures in South Asia should serve three basic purposes: to prevent war among states, or to reduce the level of destruction if war does occur; to stop the conduct of proxy wars; and to minimize or eliminate internal conflict. In the 1990s and beyond, the third objective may be the most important to address. Future interstate wars and proxy wars in South Asia may be seen essentially as the higher stages of escalation of internal conflict. As such, controlling internal conflict is essential to controlling proxy wars, which, in turn, should lead to the prevention of interstate conflict. Therefore, the key to the avoidance of war in South Asia is increasingly the management of internal conflict. The international community may have limited influence in affecting the outcome of domestic conflict but greater influence in restricting the conduct of proxy wars or in preventing the outbreak of regional wars.

Under these circumstances, CBMs must attempt to address all three types of conflict separately. Thus, for example, if no resolution appears in sight for the insurgency in Kashmir, or if little can be done to minimize the proxy war reportedly being conducted in that state by Pakistan, then CBMs must be directed and intensified to prevent the outbreak of a full-scale war between India and Pakistan. But the interrelatedness among the three types of conflict must also be recognized, especially the root causes of wars arising from domestic violence and political instability.

Except for the Indo-Pakistani war, which was triggered by the insurgency in East Pakistan that led to an independent state of Bangladesh, other earlier secessionist movements and internal conflicts did not threaten to escalate into interstate wars. The earlier danger of war between India and Pakistan arose from their dispute over Kashmir. Until 1989, there was no major internal conflict in Kashmir. The 1965 war may have had its immediate origins in a riot in the Kashmir Valley over the theft of the Prophet's hair. Pakistani expectations that a military invasion at this point would trigger a mass uprising among the Kashmiri Muslims, did not occur. After the breakup of Pakistan in 1971, the threat of war over Kashmir receded largely because of Pakistan's inability to resolve the issue in its favor through military force. The credibility of Pakistan as the representative of Muslim interests on the Subcontinent also appeared discredited when Bangladesh broke away.

Before the breakup of Pakistan in 1971, India had also alleged that Pakistan had aided the guerrilla warfare conducted by Nagas and Mizos to achieve independence from India. These unsuccessful separatist movements posed no serious threat of war between India and Pakistan. Nor was there any danger of war over the Baluchistan and Pushtunistan secessionist movements in Pakistan before 1980, which Pakistan alleged was supported by India. Similarly, India's assistance to Tamil guerrillas seeking an independent state did not threaten to explode into a war between India and Sri Lanka because the latter could not match India's military capabilities had India chosen to intervene with military force.

The exception was the struggle for Bangladesh in 1971. The 1971 Indo-Pakistani war clearly arose from the civil war in East Pakistan. India first resorted to a proxy war in East Pakistan and then embarked on direct military intervention to accelerate the creation of Bangladesh. This experience of more than two decades ago may serve as the model of future wars in South Asia.

The Nexus between External and Internal Security Threats

CBMs have been proposed and tried in South Asia to alleviate Indo-Pakistani tensions and the prospect of war. Some of the CBMs conducted through intellectual and cultural exchanges were at the nonofficial level, sponsored by overseas organizations (mainly U.S.), as well as by some South Asian nongovernmental organizations. Although these nonofficial discourses emphasize an exchange of views across national boundaries, ultimately it is government-to-government exchanges and agreements that will prove decisive in lowering tensions in South Asia. For example, the Indo-Pakistani agreement, formalized in 1990, not to attack each other's nuclear facilities may be considered a significant CBM between the two countries at a time of mounting tensions in the region. Such official and unofficial CBMs may have been responsible—at least in part—for the avoidance of war between India and Pakistan over the ongoing Kashmiri revolt that erupted in 1989. Of course, Pakistan's relative conventional military weakness and the prospect of escalation to a nuclear war may have also played a part in the avoidance of war over Kashmir.

Unregulated insurgencies and proxy wars complicate conventional and nuclear deterrence and defense strategies. CBMs to mitigate external security pressures among states become difficult or ineffective, unless CBMs are also introduced concurrently to alleviate internal security pressures. India has complained repeatedly that various Kashmiri "mujahadeen" operating on the Indian side are being trained and equipped in Pakistan. Insurgency in Indian Punjab by Sikh militants demanding an independent state of "Khalistan," and sporadic violence by Sindhi militants in Pakistan calling for an independent "Sindhudesh," have led to allegations of material support to these separatists from across international frontiers. The rise of Hindu nationalism and continued Hindu-Muslim strife within India has produced protests and demonstrations in Pakistan, Afghanistan, and Bangladesh, adding to the tensions within the greater South Asian region. Although the prospect of an Indo-Pakistani war over these issues had receded by the mid-1990s, both countries have not settled their explosive internal security problems. Meanwhile, Indo-Pakistani conventional arms acquisitions, and the covert or "latent" nuclear weapons technological buildup, continue as before.

India's involvement in the struggle for an independent "Tamil Ealam" in Sri Lanka has been somewhat different from Indo-Pakistani issues. In the mid-1980s, India armed the Sri Lankan Tamil separatists and even provided some of the guerrillas training within India for operations in Sri Lanka. War between India and Sri Lanka was most unlikely, however, during the prolonged Tamil crisis; Sri Lanka could not challenge India's military might on its own. Instead, an Indo-Sri Lankan pact was signed by Prime Minister Rajiv Gandhi and President J.R. Jayawardene in 1987. In accordance with this agreement, about 50,000 "Indian Peace-Keeping Forces" (IPKF) were sent to Sri Lanka to protect the Tamils, separate the warring sides, and end the fighting. The IPKF produced no political solution and no peace. Instead, it ended up fighting the main Tamil guerrilla faction, the Liberation Tigers of Tamil Ealam (LTTE). At the same time, the IPKF was perceived by the Sinhalese as violating Sri Lanka's territorial sovereignty, and was eventually withdrawn in 1990 after a mainly fruitless and costly "foreign" campaign. That Indian experience subsequently produced considerable cooperation between India and Sri Lanka to suppress the LTTE's drive for an independent Tamil state. Indeed, the experience of failure or disaster of military objectives, rather than the introduction of formal CBMs, may sometimes contribute more toward confidence among antagonistic countries.

If the root cause of tensions and the threat of war in South Asia are found mainly in the potential spillover effects of domestic ethnic conflict, then various CBMs must be developed and applied to alleviate the struggle between governments and secessionists within the state. If the governments of India, Pakistan and Sri Lanka cannot adequately address their internal security problems, then their efforts at promoting cross-border CBMs will not make much headway. Promoting CBMs at the domestic level is usually a more difficult proposition since the secessionists may consist of several factions, may be scattered and disorganized, or may be involved in an armed power struggle among themselves. With whom should the government negotiate? Moreover, the government may refuse to negotiate with any of the secessionists as that may acknowledge the legitimacy of these groups and increase the prospect of state disintegration.

Meanwhile, a new global dimension has been added to the problems of violent secessionist demands in South Asia since the late 1980s. The breakup of the Soviet Union, Yugoslavia, and Czechoslovakia, the secession of Eritrea from Ethiopia, as well as the continuation or rise of other ethnic conflicts and separatist demands elsewhere in the world, have exacerbated tensions within the multi-ethnic states of South Asia.

Sikh and Kashmiri separatists in South Asia have specifically pointed to conditions in the former Yugoslavia and the Soviet Union to justify their own demands. The Sikh Council of Khalistan—a dissident Sikh representative group in exile, based in Washington D.C.—moved swiftly to recognize Slovenia and Croatia when they declared their independence in July 1991, long before any state in the world had done so. Similarly, Kashmiri "Councils" based in London and Washington have pointed to the newly found independence of the Baltic states. They have justified their own call for independence on the grounds that the Indian absorption of Kashmir in 1947 following partition had not been recognized by the United Nations. This status of nonrecognition was declared to be similar to, if not the same as, the Soviet annexation of the Baltic states in 1939.

The promotion of CBMs between the government and the secessionists may prove futile if the secessionists will settle for no less than independence. If Slovenians, Croatians, Bosnian Muslims, Lithuanians, Ukrainians and others are entitled to secede from the former Yugoslavia and the Soviet Union, are not Kashmiris, Sikhs, Assamese, Sindhis, Baluchis, and Tamils entitled to secede from India, Pakistan, and Sri Lanka? Are there measures that can be adopted to isolate the secessionist movements of South Asia from those taking place elsewhere in the world? Indeed, is there any point in initiating CBMs if global conditions and trends constantly negate or neutralize positive advances that may be gained through CBMs in South Asia? Thus, to achieve effective results, CBMs must address the linkages among domestic, regional, and global conditions in resolving violent internal secessionist movements. International policies adopted to address violent secessionist demands in one part of the world may adversely affect conditions in other parts.

Confidence-building measures to diffuse political crises and reduce violence within the state may have to be specially designed to meet the specific exigencies of each problem and situation. Thereafter, CBMs may have to follow a strategy of improvisations as negotiations proceed with various groups and leaders. Nevertheless, a set of general guidelines and methods (some basic "do's and don't's") may be drawn up to deal with the problems of internal security.

An ethnic group usually passes through various stages of communal expectations and demands: from living in communal harmony within the state or province, then moving toward conditions of ethnic disaffection, confrontational politics, peaceful autonomy demands, violent autonomy demands, and, finally, insurgent separatist demands. The last step invariably provokes state counter-violence to prevent secession. Underlying the various stages of ethnic violence is the crucial dividing line between the group's self-perception as part of the state and then as part of a distinct ethnic identity; between their nonsecessionist demands to address grievances and then to secessionist demands for an independent state.

Domestic CBMs must be designed and introduced to fit the problems found at the various stages of political disaffection and deterioration described in the sequence above. Perhaps CBMs intended to deal with nonsecessionist ethnic violence (e.g., spontaneous Hindu-Muslim communal strife or demands for statehood within India such as Gurkhland and Jharkhand state) should be more conciliatory and accommodating than secessionist-based violence (e.g., Kashmir, Khalistan, Tamil Ealam, or Sindhudesh). Domestic CBMs could include the offer of amnesty to the insurgents, an effort to negotiate with the moderates within the alienated ethnic group, attention to their genuine grievances, and the granting of autonomy short of independence to the insurgents. Such moves could be supplemented with economic subsidies to the populations affected by the strife. Above all, efforts should be made to reduce the human rights violations committed by security forces. At the more general level, the central government could adopt new constitutional clauses that would bring about a greater devolution of political and economic power to the provinces, districts, and villages. The more self-governing the disaffected group, the less likely their resort to violence to achieve a separate independent state.

The confidence-building measures suggested are nothing new. They reflect old-fashioned common sense policies of negotiations in good faith and a desire by governments to settle issues fairly and peacefully. These measures may serve at times as a substitute for military policies, or they may have to be conducted concurrently to military steps in a "carrot-and-stick" approach.

The Dynamics of Ethnic Disaffection, Nationalism, and Violence

As in the case of Europe, religion and language can breed diverse ethnic nationalisms in South Asia. Punjabis, Sindhis and Bengalis (linguistic groups that are found across borders in India, Pakistan, and Bangladesh) are united by language, race, and culture, but separated by religion. The United Bengal movement before partition in 1947 emphasized language and culture over religion. Today, Sindh Muslims talk about recovering the old Sindh where Sindhi-speaking Muslims and Hindus would live together in an independent Sindhudesh.

An examination of the dynamics of the two successful independence movements in South Asia will show the nature of overlapping identities and the changing emphasis among these identities. When Muslims ruled Hindus in India, there was a great deal of social and political interaction, of communal intermingling through intermarriages or through Hindu conversions to the Islamic faith. Cultural and linguistic differences became more regional rather than religious, although religion still dictated major differences in social practices within the same regions.

For example, while religion may have divided Muslim and Hindu Punjabis or Bengalis, race, language, and culture also united them. It was only toward the end of the nineteenth century that Indian Muslim political elites began to perceive themselves distinctly as a separate nation of Muslim Indians who could find salvation only in the creation of an Islamic Pakistan. The founding of the Anglo-Mohammedan College in 1875 (later Aligarh Muslim University) by Sir Sayyid Ahmad Khan, and then the All-India Muslim League in 1906, gave impetus to the development of a separate Muslim identity. These Muslim elites, primarily from the Hindi-speaking Hindu heartland of the United and Central Provinces of British India, then began to emphasize Muslim religious symbols and identity in order to mobilize support in the 1930s for the "Two-Nation" theory of Mohammed Ali Jinnah.

The shifting nature of ethnic or national identity may be seen in the variations of Bengali nationalism in the twentieth century. At what point did "Muslim Bengalis" who had identified with Pakistan become "Bengali Muslims" who would accept nothing less than an independent Bangladesh?[1] During the "Pakistan" movement that paralleled the Indian nationalist movement, some Bengali leaders toyed with the idea of a united Hindu-Muslim Bengal state, separate from the proposed independent states of India and Pakistan. Such a demand had been made before partition in 1947 mainly by Bengali Muslim leaders such as H.S. Suhrawardy and A.K. Fazlul Haq.

A united Bengal concept may have briefly crossed the minds of some Bengali nationalists on either side in West and East Pakistan during the struggle for Bangladesh in 1971. Although Indian military intervention helped create Bangladesh, the possibility that Hindu Bengali nationalists in West Bengal might also want to join this "Bengal Nation" must surely have worried Indian policymakers. Underlying this outlook for a greater Bengal state was the belief that language and culture superseded religious differences. India's West Bengal has a population of sixty million, of whom about ten million are Muslims. The total Bengali-speaking population of both Bangladesh and West Bengal in India in 1995 numbered almost 180 million and would have constituted a powerful state if a united independent Bengal had been forged in 1947. Reunification schemes for a "Greater Bengal" have not been heard since the creation of Bangladesh in December 1971, perhaps because Bengali Hindus do not wish to be a minority, albeit a significant one, in a larger Muslim majority Greater Bengal. They would rather be part of a much larger Hindu majority India. Similarly, while Bengali Muslims may want a united Greater Bengal where they are a majority, they did not wish to be part of the Indian Muslim minority in a Greater India with a Hindu majority.

When looking at the Kashmiri problem, it is important to recognize that the self-perceptions of Kashmiri Muslims have fluctuated among three identities over the last half century. The first identity may be found in the ideology of the "Kashmiriyat," which incorporates Valley Muslims, Hindu Pandits, Hindu Dogras, and Ladakhi Buddhists into a regional whole.[2] This perception of a distinct Kashmiri identity generates demands for separate nationhood. At one time or another, Pandits, Dogras, and Muslims have all sought an independent state of Kashmir. The second identity is marked by perceptions of the broader Indian secular heritage that prevailed among many Kashmiris. This outlook was best enunciated and exemplified by the Kashmiri Pandit, Prime Minister Jawaharlal Nehru, but also shared by other Valley Kashmiri Muslim leaders such as Shaikh Abdullah. The third identity may be found in the rise of Muslim nationalism in Kashmir and the spread of transnational Islamic fundamentalist values into the state that make Kashmiri Muslims feel more a part of Islamic Pakistan and of the Islamic world.

Another transition in group identity may also be seen in the Sikh resistance to being classified as a subdivision of Hinduism. This eventually turned into a clear-cut rejection of Hindu absorption, and then to the identification of being a separate religious group needing to live within an independent state. Indeed, the dramatic turnaround in the mid 1980s from Sikh perceptions as staunch Indian nationalists (together with Hindu perceptions of Sikhs as the "sword arm" of Hinduism) into a troubled state of Hindu-Sikh conflict in Indian Punjab, is revealing in the transforming nature of ethnicity and conflict in South Asia. It is important to recall that relations among Punjabi Muslims, Sikhs, and Hindus were cooperative and cordial under the British Raj. Indeed, the Punjabis of all three religious persuasions constituted the bulk and the backbone of the British Indian army. They fought shoulder-to-shoulder in two world wars. Even during the mass slaughter and migration of Hindus, Muslims, and Sikhs in Punjab after the province was partitioned in 1947, members of the three religious communities in the British Indian army remained disciplined despite the emotional stress produced by the human havoc in Punjab. Since partition, Indo-Pakistani wars have tended to resemble a civil war among Punjabis since the Pakistani armed forces are about 80 percent Muslim Punjabi, and the Indian armed forces are almost one-third Hindu and Sikh Punjabi.

The above examples indicate that religious antagonism may override cultural and linguistic ties. The past record of cooperation and goodwill among Hindus, Muslims, and Sikhs in Bengal, Kashmir, and Punjab suggests, however, that these positive ties may be restored, given the right attitudes and conditions.

Disintegrative Tendencies in South Asia

Separatist demands based on religion, language, or race have risen and fallen in the Subcontinent. They need not always lead to territorial partitions and disintegration. The South Asian experience indicates that the emphasis on a particular identity provoking separatism can be reshaped, that the stages of armed escalation can be de-escalated, and that the separatist group can be reabsorbed into the larger concept of a multi-ethnic nation.

The Tamils' demand in India for an independent Dravidastan (or Dravida Nadu) ended when the separatist party, the Dravida Munnetra Kazhagham, gained power in Tamil Nadu through the electoral process in 1967. After years of guerrilla warfare, India largely (but not entirely) resolved the Naga, Mizo, and Gharo separatist movements by granting greater autonomy and internal statehood to the Christian tribals who were converted by Western missionaries. The fluctuating Pashtunistan separatist sentiment in Pakistan's Northwest Frontier Province ended abruptly with the Soviet invasion of Afghanistan in December 1979. Greater Pashtun participation and prosperity within Pakistan also helped dissipate separatist demands in the Frontier. Although the Pakistani government used military force to quell the Baluchistan separatist movement in 1974, the government has since pacified the separatists by redressing some of their grievances.

Meanwhile, new independence movements have replaced old ones. In the early 1990s, five significant independence movements were taking place in South Asia: among the Sikhs, Kashmiris, and Assamese in India; among the Tamils in Sri Lanka; and among the Sindhis in Pakistan. The intensity of violence in these separatist movements varies considerably. The Kashmiri, Sikh, and Assamese insurgencies in India, and the Tamil insurgency in Sri Lanka, have been prolonged, intense, and bloody. The ethnic violence in Sindh between Sindhis and Mohajirs, despite its lower intensity (there is no insurgency), appears, however, to threaten the disintegration of the country if only because Pakistan cannot afford another partition. On the other hand, if any part of India such as Kashmir, Punjab, or Assam were to gain independence, India may unravel faster than Pakistan. As in the case of the Soviet Union and Yugoslavia, the independence of one Indian state may generate a chain effect in other Indian states that had hitherto not considered independence. This prospect explains India's paranoia and determination not to concede independence to any separatist group irrespective of the justification of the cause and the intensity of the violence. The implicit internal security doctrine followed by successive governments of India is that all ethnic grievances must be resolved within the boundaries of the Indian union.

Pakistan. The factors leading to Pakistan's disintegration arise from three sources.[3] First, independence movements in Pakistan have tended to encompass ethnic groups that constitute a significant proportion of the total population and/or the land mass. The Bangladesh independence movement involved more than one-half the population of pre-1971 Pakistan and one-fourth the land mass. Although Baluchis constitute only 2.5 percent of the total population, the province constitutes almost half of Pakistan's land area so that the earlier separatist movement in Baluchistan threatened to reduce Pakistan into a state with even less strategic depth. The sporadic Pashtunistan separatist movement that prevailed before the Soviet invasion of Afghanistan was destabilizing because the Pashtuns constitute a powerful political and military force within Pakistan. With three million more Afghan Pashtun refugees in the Northwest Frontier Province, the revival of the separatist movement here could again threaten the disintegration of Pakistan. Awami National Party chief Khan Abdul Wali Khan declared that all Pashtuns on either side of the Pakistan-Afghanistan border were one people and no one could separate them from each other.[4] Wali Khan claimed that Pashtuns would never accept the Durand Line, which the British had drawn in 1894, dividing the Pashtuns. In the early 1990s, Pashtun nationalism had spilled over into Baluchistan with cases of sporadic ethnic violence between Baluchis and Pashtuns.[5]

The separatist movement among significant segments of Sindhis tends to rise and dissipate periodically depending on the nature of the regime in power in Pakistan. Sindhi grievances and nationalism have risen when the Punjabi/Pashtun-dominated military controlled the reins of government and have dissipated when the Bhuttos—Zulfikar and his daughter, Benazir—gained power of the central government. Rising Sindhi nationalism threatens to undermine Pakistan's unity for a variety of reasons. Sindhis constitute only 13 percent of the total population, but they are the second largest ethnic community of Pakistan. (Punjabis form 66 percent of the population,

Pashtuns 9.5 percent, Mohajirs [immigrant Muslims from India] 7.6 percent, and Baluchis 2.5 percent.)[6] Sindh is also a large province through which the Indus river flows and where the largest city, Karachi, is located. Sindhi violence is also directed against the economically powerful Mohajir community, which was primarily responsible for the creation of Pakistan. In response, the Mohajir Qaumi Movement of the Altaf Hussain faction want a separate province for the Mohajirs to be carved out of Sindh within Pakistan. Since Mohajirs control the main cities of Karachi, Hyderabad, and Sukkur, dispersed through Sindh (which presumably would be linked by Mohajir-controlled corridors or, as demanded by the MQM, much of Sindh south of the 26th parallel), the remnant Sindh province for the Sindhis would be reduced to an uneconomic unit.[7] On the other hand, an independent Sindh, locked in a civil war between Sindhis and Mohajirs, would probably end the rationale for the existence of Pakistan since it would essentially become a Punjabi Muslim state.

Second, as Indian analysts have argued for decades (unconvincingly, no doubt, to Pakistanis and others), the initial *raison d'être* for the creation and existence of Pakistan was weak. Jinnah's "Two-Nation Theory" of two separate Hindu and Muslim nations in India took little account of linguistic and cultural diversity among the Muslims in various parts of the Subcontinent who often had more in common with their Hindu counterparts. The "Two-Nation Theory"—Hindustan and Pakistan—was extremely difficult to implement because the Muslims who demanded Pakistan the most were in regions with Hindu majorities. Although many of the elites migrated to Pakistan (the Mohajirs), masses of Muslims were left behind in India after partition.

The concept of Pakistan also produced the need to enforce often artificial domestic policies that exaggerated Pakistan's separate characteristics and identity from India. The need for a separate national identity has also led to a search for support and union with other Muslim states west of Pakistan on the premise that Pakistan was more a part of this region than South Asia. On the other hand, both India and Sri Lanka emerged from British imperial rule with no special identity that needed to be demonstrated. They simply existed as political entities before independence under the British, and they have sought to consolidate their new identities after independence on the basis of the British parliamentary system of democracy.

The democratic system and process did not develop readily in Pakistan, but endured in both India and Sri Lanka despite some occasional setbacks. Democracies allow for periodic elections and freedom of expression which, in turn, provide an outlet for political frustrations. Indeed, ethnic separatism in India and Sri Lanka have occurred largely in areas where the democratic process has broken down. At least one of the reasons for the breakdown of the democratic process in Punjab and Kashmir has been the centralization of economic and political powers in New Delhi and the manipulation of electoral politics in these two states by Congress Party governments, especially under Prime Minister Indira Gandhi. In Sri Lanka, the existence of a Sinhalese-controlled unitary system of government during the first few decades after independence contributed to the separatist sentiments in the Tamil-dominated areas of the northeast and east-central regions. With these exceptions, democracy has prevailed in India and Sri Lanka. In contrast, Pakistan has been under the rule of the military—from 1958 to 1971 and then from 1977 to 1988. The military was more than 80 percent Punjabi in composition, but it also included powerful groups of Pashtuns. The first two military leaders, Ayub Khan and Yahya Khan, were both Pashtuns; the third, Zia ul-Haq, was a Punjabi. This perception of Punjabi-Pashtun domination of the Bengalis, Sindhis, and Baluchis—whether real or imagined—has been one of the major sources of ethnic grievances and demands for independence.

Despite the greater proclivity of Pakistan to disintegrate, as it did in 1971, there are factors to suggest that this is less likely to happen again. After the separation of East Pakistan, more than a thousand miles away across hostile Indian territory, Pakistan is territorially a more integrated and defensible unit. Its old national ethos as the "homeland" and voice of the Muslims of the Subcontinent is no longer mentioned nor found acceptable to much of its population to the disadvantage of the Mohajirs whose future status appears uncertain. Pakistan is now a "territorial" state encompassing four distinct provinces and seven significant ethnic groups. (Siraiki-speaking people in Punjab and the Hazaras of the Frontier may be added to Punjabis, Sindhis, Pashtuns, Baluchis, and Mohajirs.) Pakistan has also been a democratic state since 1988 and may be able to channel and negotiate its ethnic grievances through the democratic process. Compared to India, Pakistan would have less difficulty in integrating these various communities, given the right policies of economic and political accommodation. The major problem is Sindh, where a very difficult situation prevails.

India. The extensive ethnic diversity and frequent separatist movements in India could give the impression that the country is perennially falling apart. The dangers of separatism and territorial disintegration, however, have not yet reached critical proportions. Nationalism and violence have emerged only among a small percentage of the total number of ethnic divisions that exist in India and, at its worst phase, affect less than 10 percent of the total

Indian population. Size is an advantage that India possesses over the other smaller states of South Asia, and, ironically, diversity has proved to be a positive rather than a negative characteristic. Apart from Hinduism, broadly defined to include the variety of upper and lower castes including the Harijans, there is no single majority group in India. The Hindi-speaking Hindus of North India constitute only 30 percent of the total population.[8] No other linguistic group exceeds 9 percent of the total population. Therefore, domination and exploitation by one group over another could become difficult. Even the high-caste Brahmins of Tamil Nadu and the Brahmin Pandits of Kashmir, both of whom have experienced exile from their own states, consider themselves to be persecuted minorities.

Thus, when separatist or nonseparatist territorial violence surfaces in one or more regions, the Indian government is able to cope with the problem while maintaining normal conditions elsewhere in the country. The economies of Punjab and Assam continued to prosper despite the residual violence and counter-violence among armed separatists and government security forces. Punjab's agricultural economy continues to feed much of India, and Assam's tea, timber, and oil industries continue to boost the economies of the state and the nation. Indeed, the economy of Punjab grew by 7.5 percent in 1990-91 compared to the national average of 5.5 percent. Even in Kashmir, only the state's tourism industry has ground to a halt. The Central government continued to assist Kashmir in finding markets and outlets in India for its timber, horticulture, and handicrafts industries in the hope of restoring some semblance of normalcy amidst the violence and social chaos. Meanwhile, it's business as usual (by Indian standards, of course) in the rest of India.

The situation in the northeast sector of India has been perpetually more volatile compared with the rest of the country. Because the region is a complex patchwork of several tribal and linguistic groups divided further by religion, there have been extensive demands for independence or statehood within India. Violent insurgencies have accompanied these demands, occasionally spilling over into the neighboring states of Bangladesh and Myanmar where similar insurgencies prevail among Chakmas, Shans, and Kachins. Insurgents in all of these countries are able to find sanctuaries for their operations across international boundaries. Out of the old state of Assam, three mini Indian states called Nagaland, Mizoram, and Meghalaya have already emerged. There are further demands for the creation of separate Bodoland and Gurkhaland states out of Assam. Separatist insurgencies have appeared in the other northeast Indian states of Tripura and Manipur, bordering Bangladesh and Burma. For over a decade since the early 1980s, a major violent movement for a separate independent state of Assam was conducted by the United Liberation Front of Assam. The Assamese separatist movement arose from grievances that were similar to the Sindhi separatist movement in Pakistan—the denial of benefits from the State's economic resources and grievances over legal or illegal immigration.

The most serious potential internal security problem that India faces is Hindu-Muslim violence. The problem dates back to pre-independence India and the movement for the creation of Pakistan. The partition of India in 1947 resolved very little because the Muslims of central and northern India who had most vociferously demanded a separate state were mainly left behind in India. Although sporadic Hindu-Muslim violence continued with increasing frequency, and growing numbers of lives were lost after independence, the problem took on a new dimension in the 1980s with the rise of militant Hindu nationalism. Hindu nationalism has been a response to increasing Muslim assertiveness throughout India, in contrast to three decades of relative Muslim submissiveness following the creation of Pakistan. The growing Hindu-Muslim confrontation and the decline in India's secular commitment is reflected in the mosque-temple dispute in Ayodha, Uttar Pradesh.

The campaign by Hindu nationalists to construct a temple to the Hindu god, Ram, at the site of an existing mosque built by the first Moghul emperor, Babar, aroused passions among both Hindus and Muslims. Hindu zealots claim that Ram, a hero of the Hindu epic mythology, Ramayana, was born on the exact spot where the Emperor Babar had built the mosque around 1530. A Hindu temple built here centuries earlier had been torn down by the first Moghul for the construction of the mosque. The mosque itself, of no aesthetic value compared to later Moghul architectural wonders, has not been used by Muslims for decades. But some Muslims depicted the preservation of the mosque as symbolic of the security of Muslims and the future of Islam in India. The Ram Janmabhoomi-Babri Masjid (the Birthplace of Ram versus the Mosque of Babar) controversy provoked widespread Hindu-Muslim communal conflict in early 1993 when Hindu extremists demolished the mosque. The violence that followed threatened to drag in Pakistan, Bangladesh, and Afghanistan as well as develop into a wider Muslim-Hindu imbroglio.

Sri Lanka. The experience in Sri Lanka shows that the fewer number of ethnic groups in a state does not necessarily mean more stable ethnic relations or more manageable national security policies. The Sinhalese and the Tamils have been engaged in a savage civil war since 1984.

The separatist movement among the three million Tamils in Sri Lanka is closely linked to the politics and perhaps aspirations of the sixty million Tamils of the Indian state of Tamil Nadu which lies across the narrow Palk Strait. Aggressive ethnic Tamil nationalism in one country can affect the politics and nationalist demands in the other. The Indian experience with the Tamil problem in Sri Lanka has long-term implications for the management of Tamil politics in India since Tamil problems are likely to spill across the Palk Strait in both directions. The intra-ethnic Tamil battles of Sri Lanka have been fought sometimes in Tamil Nadu, and Tamil support for the cause of their co-linguists in Sri Lanka can affect the outcome of the Tamil Ealam separatist movement on the island.

The direction of Tamil politics in India has always been viewed with sensitivity by the central government in New Delhi. The Tamils were one of the first major ethnic groups to demand a separate independent state called Dravidastan (or Dravida Nadu) soon after the partition and independence of India in 1947. Underlying this demand was the contention that the people of the southern peninsula speaking the Dravidian languages (mainly Tamil, Telugu, Kannada, and Malayalam) constituted a separate nation from the Indo-Aryan north. The movement for independence was led by the Tamil nationalist party, the Dravida Munnetra Kazagham (DMK). Although supposedly representing all the Dravidian speaking peoples, the Dravidastan movement found little support outside Tamil Nadu in the other Dravidian states of Andhra Pradesh, Karnataka, and Kerala.

The Aryan-Dravidian north-south linguistic divide in India is paralleled in Sri Lanka between the Sinhalese, who constitute 74 percent of the population, and Tamils who constitute 18 percent.[9] About 7 percent of the population are Muslim Moors. The Moors are mainly Tamil-speaking, but traditionally have been classified separately from the Tamils by the government. They do not support the separatist movement. The Tamil separatists count them as Tamils, however, in order to claim that the Eastern province has a Tamil majority. The Sinhalese language belongs to the Indo-Aryan group of languages, although it is written basically in a Dravidian script. Unlike India, where northern Aryans and southern Dravidians are all mainly Hindu, the Aryan-Dravidian divide in Sri Lanka is aggravated by the fact that 95 percent of the Sinhalese are Buddhist and 85 percent of Tamils are Hindus. Among the Tamils, however, religion is not the issue; the remaining Tamils, who are mainly Roman Catholic, are just as much involved in the independence struggle as are the Hindu Tamils.

The Sinhalese, however, see Sri Lanka as the sanctuary for Buddhism, a religion founded in India in the sixth century B.C. and then spread throughout the Subcontinent and Asia by the Emperor Ashoka in the fourth century B.C. By the first century A.D., Buddhism had disappeared in India through Hindu revivalism. The Sinhalese, therefore, believe that they have a special duty to protect Buddhism in Sri Lanka. The intensity of this commitment has increased with the current Sinhalese-Tamil civil war. The Sinhalese also argue that the Tamils have their own state in India, a predominantly Hindu country, but the Sinhalese have only Sri Lanka. The Tamils of the Jaffna peninsula reject this view, claiming that they arrived in Sri Lanka from southern India about the same time as the Sinhalese did from northern India more than 2,500 years ago. A second group of Tamils known as Indian or "Plantation" Tamils were brought in by the British to work the tea plantations in the late nineteenth century. They are not engaged in the Tamil separatist movement.[10]

The Sri Lankan war brought about prolonged Indian military intervention and eventual Indian military failure to establish peace. The legacy of Indian intervention led to the assassination of Prime Minister Rajiv Gandhi by a Sri Lankan Tamil suicide killer in June 1991. In April 1993, the main opposition Tamil leader, Lalith Athulathmudali, was assassinated. A few weeks later, in May, the killing of the President of Sri Lanka, Ranasinghe Premadasa, by a suicide Tamil assassin generated new uncertainties about the future of the island state. Some hopes were raised in August 1994 when Chandrika Kumaratunga's Sri Lankan Freedom Party (SLFP) won the national elections, ousting the United National Party (UNP). Kumaratunga campaigned on a platform that indicated a willingness to negotiate a just settlement with the LTTE; subsequently it did so in October 1994.[11] But the assassination of the UNP presidential candidate, Gamini Dissanayake, in late November by an alleged Tamil terrorist, threw the negotiations into a tailspin. By spring 1995, the war between the Tamil separatists and Sinhalese government forces was once again in full swing. Sri Lankan instability, therefore, can produce destabilizing effects in India.

India and South Asia

The problem in Sri Lanka arising from the ties between Indian and Sri Lankan Tamils carries a particular significance for the rest of South Asia. Common ethnic populations also exist between India and its other neighbors. There are Punjabis, Sindhis, and Bengalis on both sides of the Indo-Pakistani and Indo-Bangladeshi borders. These cultural and linguistic ethnic links are offset, however, by varying degrees of Hindu-Muslim religious antagonism, more among the Punjabis than among the Bengalis. In 1971, the secessionist Bangladesh movement in East Pakistan aroused Bengali nationalism among Hindu Bengalis in West Bengal, causing some concern in India as well.

The Urdu-speaking Mohajirs of Pakistan, who settled in Pakistan from the various states of central and west India, may only be a small part of the various ethnic Muslim groups in India (less than 10 percent), but they are yet another community commonly found in both India and Pakistan. Indo-Pakistani tensions and wars produce considerable tension and stress on the loyalty of Indian Muslims and Hindu attitudes toward this group. Similarly, large numbers of Gurkhas live in both India and Nepal. In the districts surrounding Darjeeling in West Bengal, there was a violent demand for a state of Gurkhaland within the Indian Union. The movement appears to have dissipated in 1993 with partial concessions to their demands.

As a consequence of these common ethnic populations, India tends to treat the problems of Tamils, Bengalis, Gurkhas, Sindhis, or Urdu-speaking Muslims across the international borders almost as though they were an Indian domestic problem. After all, these groups were all at one time part of British India, and they are not much different from the scores of other ethnic groups that remained in India. The instinctive political reaction in India to ethnic problems across its borders, and the record of Indian military interventions in Sri Lanka and Bangladesh in the past, raise apprehensions among India's neighbors of potential Indian political and military interference in their domestic affairs.

Domestic Reconciliation Measures in the Subcontinent

The following CBMs may serve to alleviate domestic strife and internal security problems:

1. Negotiate with moderates to undercut extremists.
2. Be willing to consider all options short of secession.
3. Train special security forces to be sensitive to the issues.
4. Compensate all innocent victims of violence.
5. Set up an agency to promote national integration.
6. Create an independent tribunal to examine grievances.
7. Create a national human rights commission.
8. Amend the constitution to create a decentralized federal state.

No single CBM may be appropriate or effective in all cases of secessionist movements. Taken together, however, they are likely to minimize internal conflict and, thereby, also external conflict. Even if the respective governments feel that an internal military campaign is essential to weaken the power of armed secessionists, negotiations need to be kept open, though not necessarily on an agenda dictated only by the government.

The governments of the region need special security forces to deal with domestic communal violence, insurgency, and terrorism. The perennial use of the armed forces to combat insurgency and terrorism within the state can lead to the corruption of the military. In a democracy, military involvement in domestic matters compromises the principle of military subordination to the civilian authorities. If external threats exist at the same time, defense preparations to conduct war may be undermined while aggravating the internal security problem.

The continued use of the armed forces for the maintenance of internal security will also alienate the military from its own people. Civilians will increasingly see the military as their enemy rather than their protector. These observations provide an increasing dilemma for the states of South Asia, all of which are now civilian democracies. To what extent should the regular military be used for the maintenance of internal security? The answer becomes more difficult when a proxy war is also being waged through the training and arming of insurgents across international frontiers. The lines between internal and external wars become blurred.

The experience and policies of India, Pakistan, and Sri Lanka have all been different in dealing with the internal enemy. In the case of India, with rising communal violence and several armed separatist movements, the use of the Indian army within the country became more frequent and widespread in the 1970s and 1980s.[12] But this trend has also produced demands from the Indian military that their deployment for internal security purposes should be undertaken sparingly, if at all. The demands took on an added urgency following the Indian army assault on the Sikh Golden Temple in Amritsar (Operation Blue Star) in June 1984. The attack produced a brief mutiny among some Sikh regiments in the Indian army. Far from ending Sikh terrorism, which was then confined to a small section of the population, it contributed to a massive Sikh insurgency and widespread terrorism in Punjab thereafter.

The Indian government's handling of a similar situation in Kashmir proved more successful, when about thirty-three armed militants occupied the Hazratbal mosque in Kashmir on October 15, 1993.[13] After a siege lasting a month, the militants surrendered to the Indian army. During this time, not a single shot was fired by the security forces and none of the thirty hostages held within the mosque was hurt. While the peaceful end to the siege of Hazratbal mosque was in sharp contrast to that of the Indian army's assault on the Golden Temple that led to the deaths of hundreds of people (Sikh militants, Indian army personnel and Sikh pilgrims), the basic problem underlying the armed insurgency in Kashmir has not been resolved. Indeed, amid the ongoing insurgency in 1995, the Charar-i-Sharief mosque was destroyed in exchange of fire between militants and Indian security forces. India claimed that the mosque was deliberately set on fire by the militants in order to blame the security forces and scuttle the central government's proposed elections in Kashmir.

Given the linkages between Pakistan and the Kashmiri insurgents, together with the threat of war between India and Pakistan, the role of the Indian army in the maintenance of internal security in Kashmir has been overwhelming. It is also considered by Indian policymakers to be inevitable. In contrast, the Indian army was used extensively to crush the separatist insurgency being conducted by the United Liberation Front of Assam, despite the fact that no direct or deliberate external intervention existed.[14] At its peak in late 1991, the military operation involved at least four Indian army divisions and 270 paramilitary companies.[15] The devastating military blows that these military operations inflicted have brought the ULFA leaders to the negotiating table with the promise of government amnesty if the ULFA were to end the separatist movement. The success of these negotiations is by no means assured, however. It will depend on the extent to which the central government of Narasimha Rao and the state government of Chief Minister Hiteswar Saikia are able to redress the grievances of the Assamese people. After all, the ability of ULFA to conduct their operations over the last decade was made possible through the shelter and support given by sympathetic Assamese villagers and townspeople.

The Indian government's response to the demands of the armed services to be used sparingly for internal security duties has been to increase the size of existing paramilitary forces, or to raise new ones.[16] This has satisfied the Indian military, but other problems associated with the policy of deploying paramilitary forces have arisen. First, the paramilitary forces, especially the Provincial Armed Constabulary (PAC), have proved to be often undisciplined, reckless, and destructive. Instead of solving the problems of Hindu-Muslim killings and ethnic insurgencies, they have added to the problem or become part of the problem itself. The PAC has taken sides with the Hindus and massacred Muslims indiscriminately in Moradabad and Meerut in Uttar Pradesh. Similarly, allegations of human rights violations including torture and rape have been leveled at other paramilitary forces, especially those in Kashmir, by both Indian and foreign groups. There have been some allegations against units of the Indian army as well in Kashmir, but not to the same extent as those alleged against the Border Security Force and the Central Reserve Police Force. The Indian army claims that it has quietly dealt with the atrocities that its forces have committed, wherever proven, through court martials and punishments.

Indeed, one of the major aggravating factors in the struggle between government forces and armed secessionists is the widespread violations of human rights, especially on the part of the security forces. The military campaigns by government forces against Tamil insurgents, and against Sindhi insurgents in Pakistan, are further complicated by the ethnic composition of security forces. In Sri Lanka, government forces deployed against Tamils are almost exclusively Sinhalese, thereby intensifying Tamil perceptions of Sinhalese oppression. Similarly, in Pakistan, the security forces are exclusively non-Sindhi—Punjabi, Pashtun and Mohajir—adding to Sindhi perceptions of isolation and persecution.

In the long term, the central government needs to devise an appropriate constitutional framework that provides maximum autonomy to the ethnic group. Since the government cannot provide such arrangements exclusively for special groups and regions without raising cries of favoritism and pampering, it needs to establish a decentralized and loose autonomous political system. Clearly, the deeper sources of internal conflict lie in the perceptions of various segments of national society that they are ruled by others and do not control their own destiny. A more decentralized state would be more democratic and more pragmatic and efficient. This would be true even for a state composed of a single ethnic group. It becomes a necessity for a multi-ethnic state.

Maintaining International Frontiers

If the ultimate purpose of domestic CBMs is to address ethnic minority grievances, to minimize the potential for conflict, and to prevent the disintegration of the state, then there must be an understanding among the states of South Asia that prevailing international frontiers need be maintained as much as possible. The main lesson from the former Soviet Union and Yugoslavia is that in volatile regions with past conflicts, promoting the right of national self-determination proves to be more disastrous than maintaining the territorial integrity and sovereignty of existing states.

No doubt, disintegration has already taken place twice in the Subcontinent: the breakup of India into India and Pakistan; and the breakup of Pakistan into Pakistan and Bangladesh. Both were wrenching experiences, although their supporters would argue that they resolved what appeared to be irreconcilable domestic situations. The immediate aftermath of the partition of British India in August 1947 produced Hindu, Sikh, and Muslim migrations and communal bloodshed on an unprecedented scale. Almost a million civilians lost their lives in the communal carnage, and more than fifteen million were uprooted. The breakup of India was followed by war between the two newly independent states of India and Pakistan. As in the division of India in 1947, the breakup of Pakistan was preceded by a violent internal civil war from March to December 1971 and the flight of millions of Bengali refugees to India. The civil war culminated in the third Indo-Pakistani war of December 1971. This brief record of state disintegration in South Asia since the British departed in 1947 has been tragic and dismal.

Recognizing the independence of Kashmir or transferring it to Pakistan poses similar dangers. The demand by Kashmiris for self-determination may be legitimate, given the controversial nature of the accession of Kashmir to India in 1947. Conceding the right to self-determination, however, must be judged against the potential consequences of granting this right. At a time when Hindu nationalists are demanding a Hindu state, and with Hindu-Muslim violence on the increase in recent years, an attempt to separate Kashmir from India could be disastrous. More extreme Hindu zealots are talking about driving all Muslims from India if Kashmir is lost, especially since nearly all Hindus and Sikhs were driven out from the new state of Pakistan in 1947. Self-determination for the Kashmiri Muslims may be at the price of a Hindu-Muslim communal holocaust and yet another Indo-Pakistani war with nuclear weapon capabilities on either side. The secession of Kashmir from India would also make it difficult to prevent the secessions of "Khalistan," Assam, Nagaland, Mizoram, and indeed, the entire northeast sector of India. Once Hindu Assam is lost, it would be difficult to prevent the secessions of the Hindu Dravidian states, and then perhaps, Maharashtra, Gujerat, and Orissa, leaving only the Hindu Hindi heartland as part of India. If this happens, it would be difficult to prevent the secessions of Tamil Ealam from Sri Lanka, and then "Sindhudesh," Baluchistan, and "Pashtunistan" from Pakistan. The experience in the breakup of the former Yugoslavia is illustrative. Thus, the cure demanded by Kashmiri Muslims may imply catastrophe for the Subcontinent. Given this potential, the territorial *status quo* appears preferable.

Perhaps the countries of South Asia could agree on two fundamental principles: that existing international borders are inviolable, whether good or bad, legal or illegal; and that none of the states in the region will aid and abet each other's separatist movements. Instead, states could seek to resolve the problems of ethnic grievances and separatist movements through policies of "decentralization" and "confederalization" within the existing borders of the state. Confederal arrangements could be expanded externally to include all of the countries of the South Asian Association for Regional Cooperation (SAARC). Pakistan, however, prefers such confederal arrangements with the ECO bloc of Muslim countries rather than with the multi-religious countries of SAARC.

India would find proposals for maintaining the territorial status quo in South Asia more to its liking. Pakistan would surely insist on making an exception for Kashmir, especially since it feels that it had a moral right to Muslim majority Kashmir at the time of independence. In reality, India can enforce the *status quo* in Kashmir by the sheer weight of its military power. It did so in the past and continues to do so during the Kashmiri crisis of the 1990s. In any case, most Kashmiris want an independent state that would include Azad Kashmir now under Pakistani control. This arrangement would hardly be acceptable to Pakistan. Readjusting the complex ethnic distribution of South Asia through territorial changes could unravel all the countries in this region into several smaller states at a very high human cost, a consequence that should be avoided in the interests of maintaining stability in the region.

NOTES

1. Urmila Phadnis, *Ethnicity and Nation-Building in South Asia* (New Delhi: Sage Publications, 1989), 15. For an in-depth analysis of conditions and events leading to the creation of Bangladesh, see Richard Sisson and Leo E. Rose, *War and Secession: India, Pakistan and the Creation of Bangladesh* (Berkeley: University of California Press, 1990).
2. Riyaz Punjabi, "Kashmir's Bruised Identity," in Raju G. C. Thomas, ed., *Perspectives on Kashmir: The Roots of Conflict in South Asia* (Boulder, Colo.: Westview Press, 1992), 45.
3. For an assessment of the ethnic crisis in Pakistan, see Ikram Seghal, "There is a Fuse Burning," *The Nation* (Lahore), October 22, 1992.
4. See report entitled, "We will Never Accept Durand Line: Wali," *The Nation* (Lahore), February 13, 1992. Although the old cry for an independent Pashtunistan was not

made, implicit in the search for Pashtun unity is the demand for an independent state or a greater Afghanistan to include the Pashtuns of Pakistan.

5. For a discussion of the Baluchi problem, see B.H. Poswal, "Let Us Do Some Soul Searching on Baluchistan," *Pakistan Times Overseas Weekly,* June 19, 1992.
6. Figures from *The World Almanac and Book of Facts, 1992* (New York: Pharos Books [St. Martin's Press, distributor], 1992), 790.
7. For a discussion of the situation in Sindh, see "Road To Anarchy," *Pakistan Illustrated,* October 1994.
8. Craig Baxter, Yogendra K. Malik, Charles H. Kennedy, and Robert C. Oberst, *Government and Politics in South Asia* (Boulder: Westview Press, 1991), 48.
9. *Background Notes: Sri Lanka, 1989* (Washington, D.C.: U.S. Department of State).
10. For a discussion, see K.M. de Silva, "Separatism in Sri Lanka: The 'Traditional Homelands' of the Tamils"; and S.W.R. de A. Samarasinghe, "The Dynamics of Separatism: The Case of Sri Lanka," in Ralph R. Premdas, S.W.R. de A. Samarasinghe, and Alan B. Anderson, eds., *Secessionist Movements in Comparative Perspective* (International Centre for Ethnic Studies, Sri Lanka) (London: Pinter Publishers, 1990), 32-70.
11. Reports of developments in Sri Lanka may be found in *Daily News* (Colombo) during these months. See also, *India Abroad,* October 21 and November 4, 1995.
12. For a study of internal security from an Indian military standpoint, see Lieutenant General V.K.Nayar, *Threat from Within: India's Internal Security Environment* (New Delhi: Lancer Publishers, 1992). For a study of Hindu-Muslim violence as seen by a former director-general of the Central Reserve Police Force, see P.R. Rajagopal, *Communal Violence in India* (New Delhi: Uppal Publishing House, 1987).
13. See *India News* (Embassy of India, Washington D.C.), November 15, 1993; and *India Abroad,* November 26, 1993.
14. See Raju G. C. Thomas, *South Asian Security in the 1990s,* Adelphi Paper No. 278 (London: Brasseys and the International Institute for Strategic Studies, 1993).
15. See reports by Subir Bhaumik, "Is Assam Going the Kashmir Way?" in *India Abroad,* October 11, 1991; and by Farzand Ahmed, "Assam: A Critical Crackdown," *India Today,* October 15, 1991.
16. See Lieutenant General A.M. Vohra (retd.), "More Paramilitary Forces Are Needed," *Times of India,* July 14, 1992.

7

NONMILITARY CBMS

Arun P. Elhance and Moonis Ahmar

Military confidence-building measures (CBMs) established in Europe in the mid-1970s engendered and sustained an atmosphere of trust that made it easier for the superpowers to agree on dramatic cuts in their nuclear and conventional arsenals as well as to keep lines of communication open during times of East-West crises. Similar measures need to be more rigorously pursued in other parts of the world where the danger of an unintended escalation of armed hostilities or inadvertent armed conflict is ever present and where deep-rooted suspicions and mistrust continue to frustrate the quest for peaceful coexistence among nations. South Asia is one region where the adoption of military CBMs—especially by the two hostile neighbors, India and Pakistan—may be particularly helpful in avoiding the future possibility of an inadvertent escalation of armed hostilities and of undeclared and undesired wars.[1]

The fact that India and Pakistan have engaged in three *undeclared* wars since gaining independence in 1947 and that both may now possess substantial ballistic missile and nuclear weapons capabilities has prompted some security analysts to suggest that an incremental establishment of military CBMs between them may help to allay profound tensions and suspicions. In 1986-87, a major crisis ensued when the Indian army conducted a large-scale military exercise, code-named "Brasstacks," very close to the India-Pakistan border.[2] A few years later, in the spring of 1990, the mutual distrust between these two countries almost led to an inadvertent war, perhaps with nuclear weapons.

Proponents of establishing military CBMs between India and Pakistan have pointed to some additional factors that make it imperative to develop and implement such measures. According to Raja Mohan, among these factors are the tragic deterioration in Indo-Pakistan bilateral relations during 1993-94, probably to the lowest level in their independent history of the last four decades; the nonamenability of the Kashmir question to a mutually acceptable solution; the escalation in military expenditure in both countries for advanced weapons, such as ballistic missiles; the rising fluidity and instability of domestic politics in both countries; and the disorientation in the foreign policy of both countries, engendered by the end of the Cold War.[3] It can be argued that current India-Pakistan relations cannot possibly be much worse than they were before and during the three wars they have already fought and that in recent years there have been some cutbacks in military expenditure in both countries.[4] Nonetheless, these disturbing developments point to the urgent need for finding ways and means for moderating and hopefully eliminating the possibility of any large-scale military engagement between the two potential nuclear powers in South Asia.

Although the establishment of military CBMs may help prevent an inadvertent war between India and Pakistan in the short run, substantial progress also needs to be made in establishing nonmilitary CBMs in the environmental, economic, technical, cultural, and social arenas to moderate and perhaps eliminate the possibility of an undesired and unintended war in the long run. Mark A. Heller argues convincingly that "CBMs can play a potentially constructive role, provided that 'confidence building' is better understood to mean *both* enhanced trust in the other side's intentions . . . *and* sustained faith in one's own capacity to cope with the consequences of trust which may turn out to have been misplaced"[5] Confidence-building measures, especially of the nonmilitary variety, are just what the term implies. These measures tend to develop confidence in one's own capabilities and to build trust in the mind of a potential adversary.

In this context it is heartening to note that, despite all the gloomy scenarios for current and future Indo-Pakistan relations, discussions on the nature and feasibility of establishing CBMs between India and Pakistan are going on. Nonetheless, much remains to be done before mutual trust and enlightened cooperation between India and Pakistan become a reality. This chapter on nonmilitary CBMs is intended to contribute to the ultimate aim of bringing peace, security, and prosperity to two developing nations and to nearly a billion people, who are blessed with a tremendous but largely unexplored potential for great achievements regionally and globally.

The South Asian Context

In the post–World War II era, South Asia has not only witnessed the emergence, after much bloodshed, of three sovereign nations—Bangladesh, India, and Pakistan—but also the forcible inclusion (assimilation) of Tibet by China and absorption of Sikkim by India.[6] China's occupation of India's northern neighbor has resulted in two of the most populous nations on earth, one with a huge arsenal of nuclear weapons and the other with a proven nuclear capability, sharing a long and contested border.[7] Furthermore, the breakup of Pakistan, leading to the emergence of Bangladesh as a sovereign nation in December 1971, has substantially altered the structure and dynamics of the regional security complex in South Asia.[8] From all recent indications it seems certain that Pakistan has also now acquired nuclear weapons capability.[9]

A border war between China and India and the three wars between India and Pakistan, following the bloodiest partition of a country in modern history, have left behind acrimonious legacies that overshadow all attempts at military and nonmilitary cooperation in the region. The eruption of armed insurgencies in Kashmir and Punjab have made the already tension-ridden relationship between India and Pakistan more contentious. In particular the contested and unresolved status of Kashmir, at least from the Pakistani perspective as well as the perspective of a growing number of Kashmiris, continues to undermine the quest for peace, security, and prosperity in South Asia.

The past two decades have been filled with momentous events that have shaped relations between India and Pakistan. They include India's explosion of a nuclear device; large-scale military exercises on the border separating the two countries; the rise of Islamic and Hindu "fundamentalism" in the Subcontinent, allegedly stoking "ancient hatreds";[10] two military operations by the Indian army outside India's borders, in Sri Lanka and the Maldives; the buildup of conventional, nuclear, and ballistic weapons capabilities in both India and Pakistan; the Islamic revolution in Iran; Soviet occupation of and subsequent withdrawal from Afghanistan; and the end of the Cold War and the breakup of the Soviet Union.

It can be argued that in the post–Cold War world the security environment of Pakistan may have deteriorated while India's alleged dream of being recognized as a regional power may be closer to realization.[11] These changes have profoundly affected security perceptions and military preparedness in both countries. Post–Cold War attempts at a Russia-China, China-India, and Pakistan-Russia rapprochement have also left their imprint on the India-Pakistan relationship.[12] Central to the contentious interactions between India and Pakistan, however, are the conflicting claims relating to Kashmir, which have not been settled despite three wars.

Although external security threats continue to be enunciated by Indian and Pakistani leaders, domestic threats may actually be more profound in both countries. In India, political fissures and secessionist movements have reinforced communal, ethnic, and socioeconomic sources of violence to create a situation in which internal unrest now seriously threatens India's territorial integrity as well as its identity as a secular and democratic nation. A growing dissatisfaction with the political system combined with growing weaknesses of the central government now raise serious questions about India's survival as a political entity. In this troubling situation there is the added danger that rather than undertaking substantial political and economic reforms the ruling elite in India may continue to blame external sources, especially Pakistan, for many of its societal ills.

In Pakistan, the dismissal, reinstatement, and subsequent resignation of the Nawaz Sharif government, following on the heels of the earlier dismissal of Benazir Bhutto's government, clearly points to the turmoil that the country is still experiencing on the way to establishing a representative democracy after forty-six years of independence. Although the victory of Bhutto's party in the November 1993 elections points to the progress Pakistan has made toward democratization, the elections were held under close military supervision. In the post-election period, the country has witnessed sharp opposition and confrontation toward the government. As with India, relations between provinces and the center in Pakistan can at best be described as problematic. Many Pakistani leaders and opinion makers are also prone to blame outsiders, particularly the government of India, for internal problems.

Major problems threaten South Asia as a whole: population explosion, accompanied by high rates of urbanization and unemployment; severe environmental degradation, leading to acute domestic conflict;[13] growing scarcities of water and energy;[14] increased migration across international borders; mushrooming trade in narcotics, leading to widespread drug addiction and the spread of AIDS; flourishing and unregulated trade in small but lethal weapons; and growing terrorism and sectarian violence.[15] A large portion of the region's population is uneducated, underemployed, and continues to live in abject poverty. While significant economic reforms and liberalization are currently under way in the region, there is a real danger that the vagaries of domestic politics or costly external adventures may further marginalize South Asia in the increasingly competitive and rapidly globalizing international economy. In the long run, a prosperous South Asia, with an equitable distribution of the fruits of economic development in all the countries and in the region as a whole, may be the best guarantee for sustained peace.

As a result, there is a growing convergence of Indian and Pakistani interests in pursuing nonmilitary CBMs. From a long-term perspective, India and Pakistan have no choice but to interact with each other; their common history and geography make interactions inevitable, whether or not the two countries are able to resolve the contesting claims to Kashmir. Geographical factors, such as common borders and natural resource and environmental dependencies, compel them to interact. The Indus River system is the most obvious example of such interdependency.[16] The two antagonists thus have a choice either to continue draining each other's resources and potential for long-term economic growth and societal well-being or to turn away conflict and get on with building the peaceful and prosperous South Asia of which many visionaries in both countries dream.

If the two countries can avoid a war for another few years, the period of peace (1972 to 1997) in South Asia will have lasted longer than the period of wars since independence (1948 to 1972). It is imperative for both countries to take steps to ensure that their new leaders have the shared experience of a long peace as well as the foresight and courage to ensure that the lessons of history are well learned and that the follies of the past are never repeated.

The two countries can benefit substantially from the incremental establishment of nonmilitary CBMs that may, in turn, lead to a gradual reduction of antagonism in their contentious military relationship. What then is the rationale for adopting nonmilitary CBMs and what are the needed conditions to encourage otherwise hostile nations to establish such measures?

Rationale for Nonmilitary CBMs

It is increasingly apparent that national security is more than military security. Definitions of national security need to be expanded to include environmental security, natural resource security, food security, and economic security, all of which have the potential to seriously undermine military security, both in the short and long run. This is especially true for developing countries where national insecurity and acute conflict may increasingly arise more from environmental degradation and economic stagnation (or decline) than from military insecurity.[17]

The functionalist and neofunctionalist theories of international relations provide further rationale for the adoption of nonmilitary CBMs between otherwise hostile countries. These theories posit that cooperation between adversary nations on "low politics" issues, such as environmental and economic issues, may facilitate cooperation in the contentious issues of "high politics," such as war and diplomacy.[18] Despite some criticism of these theories, evidence suggests that establishing nonmilitary CBMs between two states engaged in a protracted conflict can and does help to create an environment of diminishing mistrust in the military arena.

Although the "core" conflicts between two adversaries may remain unresolved, progress can be made in resolving peripheral conflicts and in exploring all avenues for nonmilitary cooperation in order to engender and maintain trust. Furthermore, while ecology and geography necessarily tie up neighboring nations in a web of interdependency,[19] countries need to consciously and carefully promote economic, political, social, and cultural interactions to raise the cost of any military confrontation between them beyond acceptable thresholds. Finally, improving the quality of the bilateral political environment between hostile nations and changing the opinions of those on both sides who are deeply distrustful are the main aims of nonmilitary CBMs.

Military CBMs, especially in the initial stages, are mostly passive instruments in that their principal aim is to avoid an unwanted outcome, such as an accidental war or a surprise attack. In contrast, nonmilitary CBMs are necessarily pro-active since their main aim is to expand areas for cooperation. Nonmilitary CBMs immediately lead to building cooperative institutions and arrangements, both formal and informal, incrementally and over time. The goal is to accumulate long-term institutional and personal memories of communications and interactions among different strata of the civic societies in the adversary nations. What are the conditions and circumstances that may facilitate adoption of a range of nonmilitary CBMs between potentially hostile nations in general and between India and Pakistan in particular?

Conditions and Circumstances for CBMs

According to Kanti Bajpai, "In general, states have an incentive to pursue (military) CBMs under the following conditions:

1. when they are involved in an enduring dispute in which the stakes are high;
2. when there is a substantial probability or expectation that the dispute will lead to hostilities;

3. when military technologies and strategy favor the offense over the defense, i.e., when there are incentives to strike first;
4. when conventional and nuclear weaponry, which may be used offensively or defensively, make the costs of war disproportionate to any reasonable goals in the dispute;
5. when there is a fear that miscommunication, misperception, and misinterpretation arising from various technical problems or cognitive failures could lead to inadvertent war; and
6. when neither war nor peace seem plausible or sufficient to regulate a relationship.[20]

Bajpai argues that conditions now seem ripe for establishing such CBMs between India and Pakistan during the ongoing "liminal period" between war and peace.[21] If this is indeed the case, it would seem that the need and opportunity for establishing nonmilitary CBMs between India and Pakistan should also be greatly enhanced. Indeed, it may be more timely and perhaps easier to adopt and implement nonmilitary CBMs in this liminal period.

To the above list of conditions for adopting CBMs, the following additions are suggested:

7. favorable external (international) response to any attempt at establishing CBMs including financial, organizational, and technical support; and
8. domestic support from the influential circles within the two countries, especially from industrialists, traders and other business leaders, academicians, media and other opinion makers, and last but not least from a range of nongovernmental organizations.

In the 1990s, attempts at military confidence building in South Asia have received a favorable response from the international community, but encountered considerable domestic opposition in both countries. In such a climate the incremental adoption of well-thought-out nonmilitary CBMs may be the most effective way of overcoming domestic hurdles. What is needed is to build support and constituency for peace between the two countries, a constituency that will make it easier for the national leaders to proceed with confidence building.

Unfortunately, although the conditions for establishing nonmilitary CBMs may seem ripe from a purely analytical point of view, the political will has been lacking at the highest levels of authority in India and Pakistan. Some would argue that as long as the conflict between India and Pakistan over Kashmir remains unresolved it would be naive to assume that the leadership in either country would be willing or able to pay more than lip-service to the idea of establishing military and nonmilitary CBMs. Despite all the hurdles to be overcome on the way and despite ongoing tensions over Kashmir, India, and Pakistan have managed to cooperate on a variety of issues and to put in place military CBMs dealing with information exchanges, prior notification, observation, and stabilization. While many of the existing bilateral and multilateral agreements are not recognized as CBMs, many of these measures contain elements of nonmilitary CBMs.

Nonmilitary CBMs in Place

Since independence, India and Pakistan have managed to resolve many highly contentious bilateral issues in a peaceful manner. In the aftermath of the bloody partition, the two sides resolved such complex and thorny issues as the transfer of official assets (1948), prevention of an even larger exodus of refugees (1948), protection of the rights of minorities (1950), property compensation for refugees (1950), maintenance of places of religious worship (1953, 1955), and resolution of some lingering territorial claims (1958, 1959, 1960, and 1963).[22] In the wake of the 1965 war, India and Pakistan signed the Tashkent Agreement (1966) and an agreement relating to the territorial dispute in the Rann of Kutch (1968). And since the signing of the Simla agreement in 1972,[23] South Asia has generally witnessed a period of peace despite ongoing internal turmoil and occasional bloodletting over the control of the Siachen Glacier.[24]

The Indus Treaty. The Indus Waters Treaty of 1960 is the most important of the nonmilitary CBMs already in place. The Indus system comprises six rivers and some tributaries that India and Pakistan now share. In 1947, when the Indian Subcontinent was partitioned, the unified Indus Basin Irrigation System irrigated about thirty-seven million acres of land, the largest irrigation system in the world at that time. The partition of British India was carried out without any regard for the physical and economic integrity of the basin, with the result that the headwaters of the rivers as well as some regulating works were awarded to India (and Kashmir), whereas a large part of the irrigation system (about thirty-one million acres) was allocated to Pakistan. A dispute over the two riparians and the sharing of river waters arose as early as in 1948, and was not resolved until 1960, with the aid of the World Bank and key donor countries.[25]

Among its other provisions, the Indus treaty established the Permanent Joint Indus Commission, which is required to meet at least once every year to resolve all issues relating to the shared waters and to establish and maintain cooperative arrangements for the implementation of the treaty. While emphasizing bilateral resolution of all disputes relating to the basin's waters, the treaty also makes provision for mediation by a neutral expert and by a court of arbitration, if agreed to by the two parties.

Although not recognized as such at the time, many provisions of the Indus treaty can be best characterized as nonmilitary CBMs. For example, the two countries agreed, in principle and in practice, to treat each other as equals, to separate the issue of water-sharing from all other contentious bilateral issues, to share hydrological and other data, to provide prior notification for any project in the basin, and to seek mediation and arbitration by a third party if any water dispute can not be resolved bilaterally. The two national commissions comprising the Joint Commission were also given a large amount of discretionary power as well as substantial autonomy from the vagaries of domestic politics in their respective countries.

Critics of the Indus Waters Treaty have argued that the water-sharing solution it imposed in the basin was far from optimal. It can also be argued that many special and unique circumstances of the time (e.g., the newly independent status of the two countries, the active role played by the World Bank, and so forth) facilitated such an accord and that perhaps the experience cannot be repeated. The treaty also did not lead to a prevention of future wars between the two nations nor to a substantial improvement in their bilateral relationship. Nonetheless, despite two subsequent wars in the Indus Basin, in 1965 and 1971, and despite the ongoing hostilities in Kashmir, neither country has contemplated abrogating the Indus treaty nor dared to attack each other's water projects in the basin.

Other Nonmilitary CBMs. On March 10, 1983, India and Pakistan signed an agreement establishing a joint commission to strengthen good neighborly relations and to promote cooperation in a range of areas, with the exception of political and military matters. Four subcommissions were established to promote cooperation in the areas of economics, health, science and technology, sports, travel, tourism, and consular matters.[26]

In May 1984, India and Pakistan decided to establish through bookings on their respective railways, to issue double-entry transit visas, and to lay down a co-axial cable between Amritsar and Lahore. They also signed an agreement to permit group tourism and ease visa difficulties and police reporting in either country. To improve communication links, India and

Pakistan signed an agreement in 1986 to open telephone circuits between Lucknow and Lahore, New Delhi and Islamabad, and New Delhi and Lahore. They also agreed to resume negotiations for the reopening of the Khokhrapar-Munabao route (Sind-Rajasthan). In December 1988, India and Pakistan signed an accord to end double taxation of each other's airlines operating in or through the other's territory and to increase cultural cooperation and exchange.

In the third meeting of the Indo-Pakistan Joint Commission, in July 1989, discussions were held for extending the facilities for travel and tourism. In addition, a three-year (1989 to 1991) cultural exchange program was approved that envisaged cooperation in education; art and culture; sports; exchange of newspapers and periodicals; participation in each other's film festivals; exchange of film delegations and radio and TV professionals; and translation and exchange of books, periodicals, and other educational, cultural, and sports publications. They also agreed to strive to ensure that there was no misrepresentation of facts about each other's country in their respective text books.[27] This agreement was to be automatically ratified after the expiration of its original duration unless one of the signatories notified the other in writing of their desire to cancel it. In August 1992, India and Pakistan signed an agreement regarding a code of conduct on the proper treatment of diplomats in the two countries.

Unfortunately, despite this impressive array of nonmilitary CBMs, full implementation has fared badly due to ongoing political tensions. Thus, while there are regular telephone circuits and communication lines between the major cities of India and Pakistan, direct dialing is virtually nonexistent. Telephone connections have still to be made through operators, resulting in substantial delays and frustration. Travel between the two countries is even more difficult. For example, there is no direct airline connection between the two capital cities. Although the agreement on avoiding double taxation for airlines is working, air travel has suffered because of hidden restrictions imposed by each government. The governments issue some visas for official travel and for visiting relatives, but it is extremely difficult for ordinary citizens to obtain tourist visas to visit the other country. Furthermore, the cultural agreement has also become a victim of a political tug-of-war between the two central governments. In recent years, treatment of each other's diplomats has also reached an all-time low.

Thus, despite all the proclamations on the part of the two governments to build confidence and despite all the agreements signed, so far both sides have continued to undermine the implementation as well as the proper functioning of existing agreements. The first task for confidence building between India and Pakistan, therefore, is fully and properly to implement existing accords.

Permanent joint commissions can be established to implement each one of these accords and to protect CBMs from the vagaries of domestic politics.

Proposing Additional Nonmilitary CBMs

While discouraged by the lack of progress in implementing earlier CBMs, additional areas of confidence building and cooperation in South Asia are possible. If established, these nonmilitary measures will help promote cooperation and stability between India and Pakistan.

Sister Cities. The central and provincial governments in India and Pakistan could allow and encourage the pairing of sister cities across borders.[28] Natural pairs for such declarations are Lahore and Amritsar and Karachi and Bombay. The process of confidence building could begin with the exchange of visits by the administrators and opinion-makers (e.g., journalists and religious leaders) of the sister cities, by teachers and students, and by all those interested in knowing and learning about their sister city. Given the fact that today there are still many people in India and Pakistan who have once lived in a city in the other country and who share its history and culture, such an arrangement could help the post-independence generation in India and Pakistan develop an appreciation of their shared history. At the very least, such visitors may come to realize how much they have in common with the people of their sister city. Exchange visits by school children and college students who will inherit the legacies of friendly or acrimonious relations between the two countries could be especially useful. It would, of course, be the responsibility of the host city, and country, to ensure the safety and well-being of visitors. Perhaps such exchanges will set into motion a friendly competition between the pairings of sister cities to outdo one another in showing traditional Asian hospitality to their visitors. Going further, sister-city games, cultural festivals, and art exhibitions can be organized to build trust between the two countries from the bottom up.

Energy Sector. In the energy sector, India and Pakistan share common problems. Both countries suffer from severe shortages of oil and electric power for use in the household, agricultural, industrial, and service sectors. Both face the serious problem of dealing with accumulated, and growing, piles of nuclear waste. Both will need more and more oil and electric power as their populations continue to rise and as their economies expand and diversify. The rising demand for fertilizers and chemical pesticides in the agriculture sector, most of which can only be satisfied from petrochemical resources, and most of which are processed and refined with the help of electricity, will put increasing pressures on food production in both countries. This situation has special relevance for the divided Punjab region that continues to outpace all others in agricultural production.

As a result, substantial opportunities exist for India and Pakistan to collaborate in jointly exploring, developing, and sharing their energy resources. For example, the hydroelectric potential of the many Himalayan rivers that flow through Nepal, India, and Pakistan has been estimated to be one of the largest in the world. If properly developed and shared, these rivers could easily satisfy for a long time to come the accelerating demands for electricity in Nepal, northern India, and Pakistan as well as help generate income and employment for millions of impoverished citizens of the three countries.[29] It is conceivable that a future integration of the power grids in Nepal, Pakistan, and initially, in the northwestern part of India, may lead to a thriving international trade in electricity among the three countries. Similarly, India and Pakistan could collaborate in exploring and developing the oil and gas resources of the areas close to their borders as well as in the Arabian Sea, where India already has sizable operations.

India has signed a contract with Oman for constructing an undersea pipeline to supply oil to the western shores of India. There is also the possibility of another undersea pipeline bringing oil and gas from Iran to India. At the same time, Pakistan is making similar arrangements with newly independent countries in Central Asia that are rich in oil and gas. As long as the situation in Afghanistan remains unstable, however, Pakistan will have to continue relying on oil and gas supplies shipped by sea from the Middle East or to develop alternative access to the Iranian and Central Asian resources through Iran. Once again, if conditions are ripe, it should not be difficult to design an integrated system of oil and gas pipelines from the Middle East and Central Asia that could supply both India and Pakistan as well as other countries in South Asia. A thriving intraregional trade in Indian coal and iron ore, the latter currently being sold to Iran, could further benefit the two countries.

In a changed political and security climate, it is possible to imagine an integrated, efficient, economical, and environmentally sound development, and sharing, of the vast energy resources of South Asia for the good of all countries and peoples. As a start, India could begin selling small amounts of electricity to Pakistan after the two countries have partially integrated their power grids at some chosen points across the common border, perhaps in Punjab. At the same time the possibility of jointly exploring the energy potential of the Arabian Sea could be pursued in a gradual manner. Such a venture may require considerable technological and financial assistance from outside the region, but this would be easier to obtain within a climate of cooperation between the two countries. In September 1994, the U.S. energy secretary, Hazel O'Leary, paid a visit to India and Pakistan and discussed with concerned officials matters concerning cooperation with the two countries in the field of energy.

A Nuclear Waste Facility. Both countries face the serious problem of disposing accumulated nuclear waste produced by their nuclear power stations and research reactors. Both are struggling to find safe and economical ways of storing or processing this waste. Perhaps a solution for the problem lies in jointly exploring the storage potential of shared and relatively uninhabited desert regions. If India and Pakistan opted to reprocess nuclear waste, this alternative, too, could be carried out more economically in a larger, jointly operated plant. The project would have the added benefit of serving as a transparency measure, keeping each country informed of the level of nuclear activity in the other. If both countries were to implement this proposal, it would be an excellent example of the intersection of military and nonmilitary CBMs.

Many serious problems and hurdles would need to be surmounted to implement this proposal, especially given the politics of nuclearization in South Asia. But, given the requisite political will and with help and guidance from the international community, the problems relating to nuclear waste storage and processing can be resolved.

Water Sharing and Management. Large areas in both countries periodically suffer from flooding and severe water shortages, even though India and Pakistan share the Indus Basin with its tremendous multiple-use potential for integrated development. All analysts agree that while the 1960 Indus Waters Treaty helped to resolve the immediate problem of water sharing between India and Pakistan, the treaty is not an optimal arrangement for developing and sharing the full potential of the river waters. It is possible to design a much better integrated system of water works and water management for the Indus.

Indeed, the countries of the region will have to overcome formidable difficulties to share equitably the waters and the hydroelectric potential of South Asia. Given the political will at the highest levels, these difficulties can gradually be overcome.[30] As a start India and Pakistan could try out some joint pilot projects in the Indus Basin, again perhaps in Punjab, that do not alter the present allocation of water between the two countries, but that can lead to a more efficient use of the existing allocations, especially in the agricultural sector where a large portion of irrigation water is typically wasted.[31]

Other Areas for Infrastructure Development. In addition to collaboration over energy, nuclear waste, and water resources, both countries can benefit substantially from integrating and upgrading highway and railway networks to facilitate speedier and more economical movement of goods and people across their borders, perhaps to other adjoining countries in South and Central Asia. As a first step, direct airline links could be developed between New Delhi and Islamabad and among other pairs of cities. Going further, region-wide airlines could be developed, as is happening in Europe, to introduce upgraded service and compete with other international airlines. Similar collaboration could also be brought about in the shipping industry.

The upgrading of infrastructure in one country, especially for moving large amounts of goods and people, can be perceived as a security threat by the other country. Such fears can be assuaged in the kind of cooperative and confidence-building scenario visualized for the two nations. It is also possible that, to begin with, the benefits from such cooperation may not be equitably distributed between the two nations. This problem, however, can also be handled in an amicable and incremental manner when the time arrives. Here the example of integrated infrastructure in Western Europe—especially the Channel Tunnel between France and the United Kingdom—could serve as the guiding light. Attempts in Southeast Asia to develop a region-wide infrastructure may also need to be studied, both for their successes and failures.

Technology Sharing. Neither country should be expected to give away any strategic technology—indigenously developed or purchased from the outside—but India and Pakistan could begin a process of identifying civilian or dual-use technologies that can later be used for arms control monitoring and verification. The two countries could jointly develop and deploy technologies such as remote sensing systems not only for verification of arms control agreements but also for multiple civilian uses. Both countries have proven scientific and technological capabilities, and both need new technologies to further their economic development and social welfare. For too long, India and Pakistan have looked outside the region for technology at a high cost to both. Joint development and sharing of technologies and proven practices for improving irrigation efficiency and for preventing deforestation and decertification can substantially benefit both countries, as can efficient and economical techniques for desalination of sea water along their coasts. These are only a few areas where technical collaboration can pay handsome dividends for India and Pakistan.

Framework for Future Nonmilitary CBMs

The larger framework for establishing nonmilitary CBMs between India and Pakistan has already been established by their membership in the United Nations and other international organizations, by the various bilateral and multilateral agreements the two countries have entered into since 1947, and by the mandate of the South Asian Association for Regional Cooperation (SAARC). Inspired by the successes of the European Union (EU) and the neighboring Association of South East Asian Nations (ASEAN) in fostering economic cooperation and peaceful coexistence among their respective members,[32] SAARC was set up in 1985 at Dhaka during a summit meeting of seven South Asian states: Bangladesh, Bhutan, India, the Maldives, Nepal, Pakistan, and Sri Lanka. According to its mandate this multilateral organization has the primary aim of achieving an accelerated rate of economic growth, with social justice, in each member country by promoting regional cooperation, collective self-reliance, and peaceful coexistence.[33]

The initially envisaged areas of cooperation within the SAARC framework included agriculture, meteorology, rural development, telecommunications, postal services, transportation services, scientific and technological development, sports, arts, and culture. Three new areas of cooperation were subsequently added to this list—women and development, education, and prevention of drug trafficking. The list was further extended at the Bangalore Summit in 1986 to include access to broadcasting in the electronics media; establishment of a documentation center for SAARC; promotion of intraregional tourism; establishment of SAARC chairs, fellowships, and scholarships at academic institutions; and promotion of youth programs, especially in agriculture and forestry extension work.

In August 1988, the SAARC countries agreed to establish the regional Food Security Reserve,[34] and in December 1988, in Islamabad, a Pakistani proposal entitled, "SAARC 2000: A Basic Needs Perspective," was adopted by all the countries. The idea behind SAARC 2000 is to establish specific targets to be fulfilled by the year 2000 for each country that relate to the basic needs for food, clothing, shelter, education, primary health, population planning, and environmental protection.[35] Furthermore, the SAARC summit of 1990 held at Male, recognizing the common environmental problems

South Asia faces, approved the formation of a Committee on Environment, and it declared 1992 as the SAARC Year of the Environment to coincide with the Earth Summit at Rio de Janeiro. In April 1993 at the seventh SAARC summit in Colombo, an understanding was reached among the members to establish a South Asian Free Trade Zone to augment the pace of economic cooperation in the region.[36]

Despite this broad framework (or perhaps because of it) and despite the expressed desire by all the member countries to move ahead with regional cooperation, two provisions of the SAARC mandate have stood in the way of substantial progress. First, mainly on the insistence of India and to some extent Pakistan, the SAARC mandate requires unanimity of all decisions. Second, all contentious bilateral issues are excluded from the deliberations of the only truly regional organization in South Asia. Furthermore, until very recently, the organization was prohibited from seeking and obtaining funding for any of its programs and projects from sources other than the member governments because of the fear of "foreign influence" on SAARC's deliberations.

Even though SAARC provides the larger framework for establishing a variety of nonmilitary CBMs between India and Pakistan, the two countries would need to agree upon and implement such measures themselves with perhaps some help from other SAARC countries and from the international community. Can the two adversaries agree on a common strategy that might allow them to put such measures in place? In the following discussion, a strategy that, given the requisite political will, promises the best results is outlined.

Strategy for Implementing Nonmilitary CBMs

The Graduated Reciprocation in Tension Reduction (GRIT) strategy offers the best hope of successful incremental implementation of nonmilitary CBMs between India and Pakistan. Alexander L. George describes the purpose of the strategy in the following way:

> GRIT is not a strategy for resocializing and reforming outlaw states. Rather, it has the much more limited aim of removing distrust between states and thereby paving the way for a relaxation of tensions. GRIT attempts to do so by taking a series of meaningful conciliatory actions, which may include concessions, carefully chosen to impress on the adversary that one genuinely desires to bring about an improvement in the relationship. These conciliatory actions are intended to encourage the adver-

> sary to replace his distrust with a more trusting, open attitude that will result in a relaxation of tensions, thereby creating an opportunity for dealing with some of the underlying disagreements that divide the two sides. Unlike conditional reciprocity, GRIT means initiating conciliatory actions without demanding that the adversary respond to the first conciliatory action with one of his own. And in contrast to the strategy of behavior modification, which rewards the subject only after he makes the desired changes in behavior, GRIT offers its conciliatory actions beforehand, to induce a change in the adversary's perceptions and attitudes.[37]

As much as India and Pakistan would like to see, or bring about, radical changes in each other's behavior in the short run, it is not feasible for either party to seek to modify drastically its adversary's behavior through the use of bribes or coercion. Consequently, given the deep mistrust between the two countries and the danger of any *major* unilateral conciliatory action being misinterpreted and possibly being exploited as a weakness by the other state, both countries would do well to pursue GRIT as a flexible, conditional, reciprocal strategy that "can encompass initiating a positive action in order to elicit an appropriate reciprocating move from the adversary."[38]

What is important to remember in implementing the GRIT strategy is that a state does not have to respond immediately or in an exactly equal measure to every conciliatory action or concession that its adversary makes. As long as a party conveys a positive response to a unilateral conciliatory action within a reasonable time period, then either party can initiate a series of such moves to create an interactive environment. Consequently, either or both sides can make major concessions without the risk that such moves are misinterpreted by the adversary as weaknesses or exploited by domestic opposition as "sell-outs" of the "national interests." It is hoped that this approach may lead to what can loosely be termed "the strategy of embarrassing the adversary" by undertaking a series of well-thought-out unilateral conciliatory gestures and actions.[39]

Nonetheless, the question does arise as to *what* is an acceptable reciprocal response to a unilateral, conciliatory action, and when is it to be accepted as sufficient to warrant another conciliatory action. Here, the available literature does not provide any formal guidelines. Indeed, given the uniqueness and complexity of each contentious bilateral relationship and each regional context, universally applicable guidelines may be impossible to develop. Policymakers in India and Pakistan would thus have no choice but to play it by ear, as it were, as they engage constructively in the process of confidence building. Thus, a mutual and genuine desire (or imperative) to build confidence at different levels of authority on a range of contentious bilateral issues is a necessary and perhaps sufficient prerequisite for implementing the GRIT strategy.

Conclusion

For far too long, more than a billion people in South Asia have been denied the fruits of economic development and social justice due to the vagaries of domestic politics, contentious external relations, and the unwillingness or inability of the ruling elite to resolve intraregional problems in a peaceful and cooperative manner. Confidence building is essential if South Asia is to advance in the interdependent and increasingly more competitive global economy. The leaders and peoples of India and Pakistan must learn not only to live and let live, but also to forge ahead and build trust and confidence between themselves. The preferred future of peace, security, and affluence for these two countries requires both to follow a road that necessarily passes through a series of CBMs, not only in the military arena but also in the environmental, economic, cultural, and social arenas.

The needed framework for bilateral and multilateral confidence building and cooperation already exists in South Asia and full implementation of current nonmilitary CBMs as well as some new measures will go a long way in building trust and confidence between India and Pakistan. To argue that until the Kashmir problem is fully resolved no progress can or should be made in this direction is to abdicate responsibility for the survival and well-being of hundreds of millions of their citizens. Even if the Kashmir problem is unresolved, India and Pakistan will not be able to avoid interacting indefinitely; they will not be able to undo the web that geography and history have woven around them. Consequently, the leaders and the peoples of the two nations have a choice to make: continue with the confrontational rhetoric and bloody skirmishes that may lead to a nuclear war or move away from the brink of disaster and toward the preferred future of peace and prosperity.

Leaving aside Kashmir and other security issues, the "core" problem in South Asia is how to restore the earlier ecological and economic integrity of the Subcontinent without trampling on the sovereignty or jeopardizing the interests of any country. South Asian countries could study the examples of Western Europe, Southeast Asia, and North America, with all the difficulties these regions have encountered and are still encountering on the way to regional cooperation and confidence building. If erstwhile enemies in other regions can sort out their affairs in a peaceful and constructive manner, there need be no insurmountable hurdles to regional cooperation and peace in

South Asia. Establishment of both military and nonmilitary CBMs between India and Pakistan is essential if peace and affluence rather than war and poverty are to be the fate of the people of South Asia.

NOTES

1. United Nations, *Confidence- and Security-building Measures in Asia* (New York: UN Department for Disarmament Affairs, 1990). Also see, Michael Krepon, Dominique McCoy and Matthew C. J. Rudolph, *A Handbook of Confidence-building Measures for Regional Security* (Washington DC: The Henry L. Stimson Center, September 1993).
2. C. Raja Mohan, "Crisis Management and Confidence Building in South Asia," paper presented at the Conference on Confidence-building Measures in South Asia, New Delhi and Islamabad, May 24-28, 1993, 1. Cited with the author's permission.
3. Ibid, 1-2.
4. Pakistan currently faces an arms embargo by the United States, and India is facing difficulty in procuring arms and spare parts from Russia. Also see, Shekhar Gupta, W. P. S. Sidhu and Kanwar Sandhu, "A Middle-Aged Military Machine," *India Today,* April 30, 1993.
5. Mark A. Heller, "Arab-Israeli Confidence-Building Measures: Implications for South Asia," paper presented at the Conference on Confidence-building Measures in South Asia, New Delhi and Islamabad, May 24-28, 1993, 10.
6. The generally accepted boundaries of South Asia include the territories of Afghanistan, Bangladesh, Bhutan, India, the Maldives, Nepal, Pakistan, and Sri Lanka. However, both Maldives and Sri Lanka are island nations, and Afghanistan is not a member of the South Asian Association for Regional Cooperation (SAARC).
7. Based on the purchasing power parity (PPP) measure of gross domestic product (GDP), these two nations may also now be the third and the seventh largest economies in the world. See "Economic Giants," *The Economist,* June 10, 1993, 67.
8. See, Barry Buzan, *People, State and Fear,* 2nd ed. (Boulder: Lynne Rienner, 1991) and Barry Buzan, Gower Rizvi, Rosemary Foot, and Nancy Jetly, *South Asian Insecurity and the Great Powers* (London: Macmillan, 1986).
9. Selig S. Harrison and Geoffrey Kemp, *India and America: After the Cold War* (Washington DC: The Carnegie Endowment for International Peace, 1993). Also see Seymour Hersh, "On the Nuclear Edge," *The New Yorker,* March 29, 1993, 56-73.
10. For an interesting and critical view on "ancient hatreds" see Suzanne Hoeber Rudolph and Lloyd I. Rudolph, "Modern Hatred," *The New Republic,* March 22, 1993, 24-29.
11. Shaheen Akhtar, "India in South Asia: An Analysis of Hegemonical Relationships," *Regional Studies,* XI (3) (Summer 1993): 60-89.
12. See, for example, Shekhar Gupta and Sudeep Chakravarti, "Sino-Indian Relations: Vital Breakthrough", *India Today,* September 30, 1993, 22-26.
13. Nural Islam, "Management of Environmental Disaster in South Asia: A Regional Approach," *BIISS Journal,* 9 (3) (1988): 341-342. Also, Shaukat Hassan, "Environmental Issues and Security in South Asia" *Adelphi Paper* 262, London, 1991.

14. Mohammad Iqbal, "SAARC: Problems and Prospects," *Regional Studies.* XI (1) (Winter 1992-93): 35-68.
15. Mianur Rahman, "Terrorism and the Legal Challenge," *BIISS Journal,* 9 (3) (1988): 271.
16. See the later discussion of the Indus Treaty 1960, 14-16.
17. For an interesting debate on the issue of environmental changes leading to problems of national security, see T. F. Homer-Dixon, "On the Threshold: Environmental Changes as Causes of Acute Conflict," *International Security,* 16 (2) (1991): 76-116; and Daniel Duedney, "The Case Against Linking Environmental Degradation and National Security," *Millennium: Journal of International Studies,* 19 (3) (1990): 461-476.
18. See David Mitrany, *A Working Peace System* (Chicago: Quadrangle Books, 1986), first published in 1943; J. P. Sewell, *Functionalism and World Politics* (Princeton: Princeton University Press, 1966); A. J. R. Groom and Paul Taylor eds., *Functionalism: Theory and Practice in International Relations* (London: University of London Press, 1975); Ernst Haas, *The Obsolescence of Regional Integration Theory* (Berkeley: Institute of International Studies, 1976) and "Turbulent Fields and the Theory of Regional Integration," *International Organization,* (Spring 1976).
19. See, for example, Arun P. Elhance, "Geography and Hydropolitics," *Swords and Ploughshares,* Bulletin of the Program in Arms Control, Disarmament, and International Security, University of Illinois at Urbana-Champaign, VII (2) (Winter 1992-1993): 3-6.
20. Kanti Bajpai, "Brother Enemies: The India-Pakistan and India-China Conflicts as Seen from New Delhi," paper presented at the Conference on Confidence- and Security-building Measures In South Asia, New Delhi and Islamabad, May 24-30, 1994, 40-41. Cited with the author's permission.
21. Ibid, 41.
22. Charles Heimsath and Surjit Mansingh, *A Diplomatic History of Modern India* (New Delhi: Allied Publishers, 1971), 121-183. For a comprehensive account of all the bilateral accords and agreements between India and Pakistan since independence, see Sreedhar and John Kaniyalil, *Indo-Pak Relations: A Documentary Study* (New Delhi: ABC Publishing House, 1993).
23. Gulab Mishra Prahar, *Indo-Pakistan Relations: From the Tashkent Agreement to the Simla Agreement* (New Delhi: Sheetal Printing Press, 1987).
24. Lt. Gen. M. L. Chibber, "Siachen:The Untold Story (A Personal Account)," *Indian Defense Review* (January 1990): 146-152.
25. M. Yunus Khan, "Boundary Water Conflict Between India and Pakistan," *Water International,* 15 (1990): 195-199. Also see Aloys Arthur Michel, *The Indus River: A Study of the Effect of Partition* (New Haven: Yale University Press, 1967).
26. *Kessing's Record of World Events,* XXXII (March 1988): 34240.
27. *Spotlight on Regional Affairs* (Islamabad), June 1990, 12-23. Also see *Dawn* (Karachi) July 20, 1989. Indo-Pakistan trade, which was suspended from 1966 to 1974, was resumed when a protocol was signed in New Delhi on November 30, 1974. Protocol on resumption of shipping services was signed on January 15, 1975. For further information see Ranjit Singh Ghuman, *Indo-Pakistan Trade Relations* (New Delhi: Deep & Deep Publications, 1986), 50-51. The Indo-Pakistan trade is currently restricted to 521 items. However, the trade turnover registered an increase between 1988 and 1992 from 40 to 157 crore rupees. Although official trade between New

Delhi and Islamabad is still quite low, a lot of trade is going on illegally, e.g., through smuggling in border areas. Also see "Pakistan-India Relations in the Eighties," *Spotlight on Regional Affairs* (Islamabad), IX (6) (June 1990): 22-24.

28. As an example, Lahore and Dushanbe were declared sister cities at a time when relations between Pakistan and former the Soviet Union could at best be characterized as semi-normal.
29. India and Nepal do have some joint projects in the Ganges Basin. They also trade some electricity. There are also some proposals for the private sector in India setting up energy-intensive industries in Nepal once the water disputes between the two countries are resolved.
30. See Arun P. Elhance, *Hydropolitics in the Third World,* (Washington DC: United States Institute of Peace Press), 1995.
31. See Sandra Postel, *Conserving Water: The Untapped Alternative,* (Washington DC: Worldwatch Paper 67, September 1985).
32. There were other reasons for the smaller countries in South Asia to want to establish a multilateral regional organization; however, the examples of the EU and ASEAN were among the primary motivations. See , for example, M.D. Nuruzzaman, "Global Change & Regional Cooperation in South Asia," *Regional Studies,* XI (3) (Summer 1993): 48-52.
33. For text of the SAARC Charter, see Mohammed Iqbal, "SAARC-Problems and Prospects," *Regional Studies,* XI (3) (Winter 1992-93): 63-67.
34. The food reserve was to be established with an initial 125,000 metric tons contributed by the member countries.
35. Samina Ahmed, "SAARC: Regional Security and National Development," *Regional Studies,* VIII (2) (Spring 1990): 35-45. For an account of SAARC's achievements see V. Kanesalingam, "General Overview of SAARC's Achievements," *Marga,* 2 (1) (1991).
36. See Umashankar Phadnis, "Bright future for Indo-Pak trade foreseen," *Dawn,* September 8, 1993.
37. Alexander L. George, *Bridging the Gap: Theory & Practice in Foreign Policy,* (Washington, DC: United States Institute of Peace Press, 1993), 52. Also see A. L. George, P. J. Farley, and A. Dallin, eds., *U.S.-Soviet Security Cooperation* (New York: Oxford University Press, 1988), 702-707; and Charles E. Osgood, *Graduated Reciprocation in Tension Reduction* (Urbana IL: University of Illinois Press, 1960).
38. A.L. George, *Bridging the Gap,* 52.
39. For example, the unilateral gestures and actions that Mikhail Gorbachev undertook to bring about substantial reductions in the arsenal of the two superpowers meet this test.

8

ECONOMIC CBMS BETWEEN INDIA AND PAKISTAN

Poonam Barua

Most of the unofficial dialogues between India and Pakistan have focused primarily on security issues.[1] Few of these unofficial dialogues engage private businessmen and young professionals in the confidence-building exercise, perhaps because many assume that the national chambers of commerce, which are responsible for promoting economic and commercial activities, will take such initiatives. It is also assumed that discussions within the South Asian Association for Regional Cooperation (SAARC) and the SAARC Preferential Trading Arrangement (SAPTA) already provide the basis for bringing together representatives of the private sector on both sides.[2] SAARC's proposals include setting up a special trade zone in the region, offering preferential tariff and nontariff treatment to member states, giving "Most Favored Nation" status to each other, creating a payments union, and setting up the Regional Fund for Development.

Little or no progress, however, has been made in carrying out SAARC's recommendations. Intra-SAARC trade still accounts for less than 3 percent of the total trade of these countries, and this figure has shown a downward trend in the last few years, as seen in Table 8.1. Trade between India and Pakistan fares even worse. Trade figures indicate no substantial increase in trade volume between the two countries during the last decade. In 1980-81, for example, only 3.29 percent of Pakistan's total exports went to India, which declined to 0.51 percent in 1985-86, and recovered to only 1.23

Table 8.1:
Intra-SAARC Trade in Relation to the World.

Year	Intra-SAARC Trade (millions of US$)	World Trade of SAARC (millions of US$)	Percent (%)
1980	1210.0	37885.3	3.2
1981	1176.8	36616.2	3.2
1982	1015.3	39875.3	2.5
1983	969.0	40410.1	2.4
1984	1119.0	44055.1	2.5
1985	1088.7	43759.5	2.5
1986	1054.5	44041.8	2.4
1987	1145.9	49480.3	2.3
1988	1731.5	52669.4	3.3
1989	1722.8	58595.1	2.9
1990	1584.7	65042.6	2.4
1991	2136.8	68462.4	3.1

Source: "Economic Cooperation in the SAARC Region," *Research and Information System for the Non-Aligned and Other Developing Countries*, New Delhi, 1992.

percent in 1992-93. From 1980 to 1986, Pakistan's imports from India accounted for as little as 0.04 percent of its total imports, edging up only slightly to 0.68 percent in 1992-93. Pakistan's trade with India accounts for less than one percent of India's total trade since 1982-83, and there has been no significant change in this percentage despite India's substantial increase in trade with the rest of the world (see Table 8.2).

Despite their geographical proximity, India and Pakistan are treating each other as "residual" trading partners. On an official level, these countries are failing to exploit the full potential for trade in a range of products that could be bought at lower costs and with shorter delivery time. With formal trading channels blocked, "unofficial trade" between the two countries has flourished—currently estimated to be in "several billions of dollars" by the Independent Planning Commission of Pakistan. "Smuggled" Indian goods (such as textiles, spices, coffee and tea, spare parts, small engineering goods, and audiovisual cassettes) can be bought with ease in Pakistani markets. Pakistani products, such as edible oils, dried fruits, and textiles, have also made their way across the Indian border.[3]

Table 8.2:
Pakistan's Total Trade with India.

Year	Exports*	Exports as % of total exports	Imports*	Imports as % of total imports
1979-80	479	2.05	130	0.28
1980-81	962	3.29	22	0.04
1981-82	602	2.29	79	0.13
1982-83	340	0.99	60	0.09
1983-84	343	0.92	148	0.19
1984-85	498	1.31	261	0.29
1985-86	465	0.94	197	0.22
1986-87	324	0.51	166	0.18
1987-88	483	0.62	341	0.30
1988-89	940	1.04	614	0.45
1989-90	757	0.71	816	0.55
1990-91	933	0.67	1026	0.60
1991-92	2814	1.64	1213	0.53
1992-93	2175	1.23	1748	0.68

* In millions of Pakistani Rupees.

Source: *Pakistan Economic Survey:* 1987-88/1993-94.

Recent programs of liberalization and economic reform in India and Pakistan have led to the emergence of a growing class of young professionals, private entrepreneurs, business consultants, and technical experts in both countries. The burgeoning class of energetic and forward-looking business professionals in India and Pakistan needs to be recruited into the confidence-building process. The enormous potential of this constituency for influencing public opinion and political leaders, as well as for mobilizing business resources, still remains to be tapped.

Dismal Trade Relations

At the time of independence in 1947, Pakistan's foreign trade was closely linked to India and the United Kingdom. Pakistan exported foodstuffs and primary commodities, such as cotton and jute, in return for imported manufactured goods. In 1948-49, India's share of Pakistan's exports was almost 56 percent. India was also the largest source of imports in Pakistan, accounting for 31.8 percent of that country's total imports.

Formal trade between the two countries was suspended following the Indo-Pakistani wars of 1965 and 1971, remaining suspended for seven years. In the years following the Simla accord of 1972, a separate trade protocol was signed to regulate trade. In 1975, a list of potential items to be traded between the two countries was finalized. India and Pakistan agreed to restart formal trade soon thereafter, although only through governmental trading agencies without any participation from the private sector. This restriction was removed two years after a trade protocol between India and Pakistan was signed.

In December 1981, Pakistan for the first time rented a pavilion at the Delhi International Trade Exhibition. A delegation of the Federation of Pakistan Chambers of Commerce and Industry also visited India, which reciprocated with a visit by the Punjab, Haryana and Delhi Chamber of Commerce and Industry to Pakistan.

Due to these exchanges, Pakistan announced a list of fourty-two items that could be traded between the two countries. In 1986, as a result of the Indian commerce minister's visit to Pakistan, the method of routing imports from India through the Trade Commission of Pakistan was abolished. In April 1988, the government of Pakistan substantially increased the number of importable items from India—from 42 to 247. Shortly thereafter, in July 1989, the list was further expanded to 571 items. The New Trade Policy of Pakistan, announced on July 25, 1994, permits the import of three new items from India, in addition to the specified 571 items. These include import of raw materials and intermediate products required for the manufacture of dyes which hitherto were banned, leather ball bladders, and parts of drilling rigs.

The composition of bilateral trade has mainly been confined to primary and intermediate goods and raw materials. Pakistan's exports to India are primarily fruit and fruit products, rock-salt, raw cotton, petroleum products, cotton fabrics, cotton yarn, leather, and miscellaneous manufactured articles. India's principal exports to Pakistan include tea, spices, iron ore and its concentrates, crude vegetable materials, synthetic organic dyestuff, vegetable oil, and bide leaves. Yet, this considerable expansion in the list of tradable commodities did not lead to any significant jump in bilateral trade.[4]

Potential Areas for Economic Cooperation

The basis for mutually beneficial economic collaboration was laid during the June 1983 India-Pakistan Joint Economic Commission meeting in Islamabad, when eight Indian industries were permitted to extend technical cooperation to Pakistan: automotive components, agricultural machinery and implements, chemicals and dyes for tanning and textile industries, the drug and pharmaceutical industry, dairy products and equipment, medium and heavy electrical equipment, material testing and process control equipment, and compressors. Recent studies have identified several additional areas for economic and trade cooperation between India and Pakistan, including potential areas for joint ventures and regional economic cooperation projects.[5] The following areas of potential economic and trade expansion would be especially beneficial.

Iron Ore. Pakistan lacks iron ore for its steel mills, importing from countries as far away as Australia, Canada, Brazil, and Liberia. But India is a major producer and exporter of this vital raw material, accounting for approximately 15 percent of world production. Pakistan's imports of iron ore from India, however, constitute less than 10 percent of its total, despite the savings that would accrue from the geographical proximity and shorter delivery time from Goa.

Tea and Coffee. Pakistan imports 70 to 90 thousand tons of tea every year, of which India's maximum contribution was only about 5,000 tons in 1985. The bulk of Pakistan's imports of tea come from Kenya, China, Bangladesh, Indonesia, and Sri Lanka, despite the lower average unit price of Indian tea exported to Pakistan of about $2.42 per kilogram, compared to Kenya's $3.25, Indonesia's $2.98, Sri Lanka's $2.90, and Bangladesh's $2.46; and the cost of transporting Indian tea to Pakistan would be much lower than tea imports from Kenya or China. Furthermore, Indian tea is commonly believed to be of better quality than that of Kenya, Argentina and China.[6] Similarly, India is a large exporter of coffee to the rest of the world. Pakistan curently imports coffee from Brazil and the Middle East. In the absence of official trade, it is well known that Indian coffee is being smuggled into Pakistan.

Cotton and Related Fibers. Both India and Pakistan are major producers of raw cotton, which accounts for a large percentage of their total exports. The production of cotton in India is subject to wild fluctuations, however, requiring India to import cotton for domestic use during certain periods, such as in 1986-87. Pakistan can be an excellent source of raw cotton during shortfalls in Indian production, to ensure a steady supply to mills at stable prices. While possessing a surplus in short and medium staple cotton, Pakistan needs long and extra-long staple varieties. An occasional shortage of cotton yarn in Pakistan also adversely affects production and exports to upstream textile industries. Duty-free imports of cotton yarn have recently been allowed into Pakistan, providing considerable scope for Indian exports to Pakistan of long staple cotton, cotton yarn mixed with higher counts of polyester staple fiber, polyester filament yarn, and textile machinery.

There is also considerable scope for India to export viscose filament yarn and viscose fiber to Pakistan. The curent Indian policy treats these items as "limited permissible items," however, thereby unnecessarily discouraging potential exports of these items to Pakistan.[7] The cotton textile industries in both India and Pakistan can be significantly strengthened by exploiting these complementarities and the cost savings from transportation via land routes.

Pig and Scrap Iron. India has imported considerable quantities of pig iron from Pakistan in the past; imports are likely to grow as India has decided not to set up large blast furnace mills that can produce pig iron as a by-product. Instead, Indian industry has favored small arc furnaces for manufacturing alloy and steel. Scrap iron accounts for more than two-thirds of the input cost of small electric arc furnaces. Because of India's short supply of scrap iron, imports have risen from 9,800 tons in 1979-80 to 2 million tons in 1986-87. Despite the fact that Pakistan is the fifth largest producer of scrap iron in the world, India has not taken advantage of the low transportation costs of obtaining Pakistani pig and scrap iron, especially for electric arc furnaces located in Western India.

Aluminum. Aluminum is imported by all South Asian countries, except India. For example, Pakistan imported 15,269 tons of aluminum and its alloys in 1986, valued at $26 million. There is considerable scope for Pakistan to fulfill its requirement of aluminum from India, particularly as the price per ton of Indian aluminum is much cheaper than the international price, even after basic and special duties are added.

Transport Equipment. India produces a wide range of commercial vehicles (both heavy and light), passenger cars, two-and three-wheel scooters, diesel railway locomotives, and other railway equipment that is exported to South and Southeast Asia, Africa and Europe. Indian transport equipment is designed to withstand the adverse local road conditions in developing countries. Pakistan, however, has to meet a large part of its requirement for automotive equipment through imports, a part of which can be supplied by India on a competitive basis. Indian companies can also provide after-sales service and spare parts to Pakistan more conveniently because of geographical proximity.

India and Pakistan have both set up plants for assembling "Suzuki" design cars and "Yamaha" two-wheelers. A division of labor between the automobile industries of the two countries can increase domestic production and help the two countries reap economies of scale in manufacturing components. The automobile industries of the two countries could set up a joint task force to establish production requirements of different components and spare parts and allocate production between the two industries efficiently on the basis of existing capability.

Industrial and Household Equipment. Trade and industry circles in Pakistan appear to be interested in importing industrial machinery from India. For instance, the Faisalabad Chamber of Commerce and Industry urged the government of Pakistan to include textile machinery in the list of items permitted to be traded between the two countries. They have found Indian machinery to be about 30 percent cheaper than European supplies. Further, European and Japanese manufacturers are quoting delivery periods in excess of two years, while the delivery of Indian supplies could be much shorter due to surplus capacity. India also produces at competitive prices a wide range of quality household electrical equipment including air conditioners, refrigerators, and washing machines, which Pakistan can import from India instead of from other countries.

Broad Areas for Joint Ventures and Regional Projects

Joint ventures and technology transfers are valuable for expediting the process of industrialization in developing countries. Indian enterprises have accumulated enormous experience in setting-up, managing, and successfully running a wide range of industrial projects locally as well as in other countries in the Middle East and Asia. Indian enterprises have developed expertise in intermediate technology, which is especially appropriate in South Asia. The similarity of language, culture, environment, and administrative structures in India and Pakistan make these two countries natural partners in joint ventures.

Indian enterprises have developed technological capability and expertise in processing, canning, preservation, and packaging of a variety of food items as well as manufactures of intermediate goods such as sugar. Joint ventures can be established for the processing and packaging of fruits and vegetables, breakfast foods, dairy products, skimmed milk powder, starch and glucose, malt, instant tea and tea blends. There is also potential for joint venture partnerships in the manufacturing of vital drugs and pharmaceuticals and for chemical, fertilizer, and petrochemical plant operations.

South Asian countries have a very low per capita energy consumption. The availability of electricity is likely to be a major constraint to expediting industrial development. To increase power generation for local industrial requirements, Pakistan has opened up its energy sector to investment from foreign companies. India possesses the manufacturing and design capability for large steam turbines and generators required for power generation with a unit size of up to 500 megawatts. Indian companies have already supplied and erected several power projects all over the developing world on a turn-key basis. Indian technology has also been adapted to coal with a high ash content, a process that is especially suitable for countries like Pakistan.

Indo-Pakistani joint ventures can help in balancing trade between SAARC countries. Indian enterprises have already set up such joint ventures in Southeast Asian countries like Thailand and Malaysia for the production of carbon black, paper, and palm oil, which is then refined for repurchase in India.[8]

An example of regional cooperative projects between India and Pakistan is in the area of phosphate fertilizers, in which all SAARC countries have a deficit. In Pakistan, large deposits of rock phosphates have been discovered at Hazara that can be used to meet the regional demand. India has developed technologies that can be used to exploit Hazara phosphates in joint ventures set up in Pakistan and/or India.

The promotion of tourism is perhaps one of the areas with the maximum potential for earning foreign exchange, but also one which requires broad changes in the existing visa regulations for businessmen and tourists. Centers for booking railway passengers between important cities of the two countries could be established. Easing of policies with respect to police reporting procedures on short visits, and greater liberalization of travel facilities, as envisaged in the 1974 agreements, can greatly facilitate business enterprise between the two countries.

New Opportunities

With the introduction of significant market-oriented economic reforms intended to make the country more competitive, Pakistan has become a more attractive partner for private sector activity. Reforms include substantial elimination of exchange controls, removal of barriers to foreign investment, reduction of tariff and other trade barriers, and elimination of much of the system of investment licenses and permits.[9]

Pakistan has sold to the public more than half of the approximately 100 industrial units initially slated for privatization in 1991 and is moving ahead with plans to privatize the remainder. Some regulatory changes have also been made to prepare for privatization of the Pakistan Telecommunications Corporation (PTC) and for increasing private sector participation in the energy industry.[10]

With increased incentives for foreign investment, the State Bank of Pakistan currently estimates total foreign direct investment as approximately $850 million, with U.S. investment accounting for approximately 400 million, or 47 percent. The Pakistani government is providing foreign investors rights regarding repatriation of funds and security against expropriation. Tax and other incentives are available for investments in key industries, including biotechnology, electronics, fertilizers, fiber optics, solar energy, engineering goods, cement manufacturing, dairy production, and mining. There is also no restriction on the share of foreign equity in investment projects.

In July 1991, the Indian government launched a concerted drive to modernize its economy which has attracted the attention of the international investment community. With its 200 million-strong middle class, its vast pool of skilled labor, and its relatively well-developed financial system, India offers both a rich market and a tremendous productive capacity. For investors, the crux of the 1991 economic reforms consisted of the deregulation of most domestic industries, the removal of licensing requirements, the reduction of sectors reserved for government enterprises, and an increase in the equity ceiling on foreign investment. Regulatory reform has been accompanied by a far more positive attitude toward private enterprise and foreign investment by the Indian government.

Previously closed sectors, such as power, telecommunications, mining, ports, roads, river transportation, air transportation and banking, are now open to private investors. In industrial and manufacturing areas, the government has eliminated much of the existing investment licensing regime. Similar measures have been taken with regard to foreign investment, which has risen from less than $200 million in the early 1990s to $600 million in 1992-93 and to $4.7 billion in 1993-4.

Several rounds of tariff cuts have reduced maximum tariffs from 400 percent in 1990-91 to 65 percent. The Indian government has also indicated that over the next few years remaining licensing restrictions on imports of consumer goods will be eliminated. It has also liberalized foreign exchange markets. The Indian rupee was floated in March 1992, and full current account convertibility was established in August 1994.

Financial institutions have been allowed more discretion over their portfolio compositions, with increased incentives for efficient use of funds. In April 1992, the Reserve Bank of India issued new guidelines for income recognition, asset classification, and relaxed controls on interest rates and access to capital markets. Since September 1992, foreign multinational investors have been allowed to invest in all nongovernment securities traded in India's primary and secondary markets. The most significant aspect of these reforms is the move to make nationalized banks more autonomous by allowing them to mobilize resources from the stock market.[11]

Prospects for Cooperation under SAARC

The value of intra-SAARC trade ranged from $1.2 billion to $1.7 billion between 1980-1987. During the same period, the global trade of SAARC countries increased from $37.9 billion to $58.6 billion. Consequently, intra-SAARC trade declined steadily as a percentage of world trade for these countries from 3.2 percent in 1980 to 2.9 percent in 1989. Trade policies have tended to discourage intra-regional trade while encouraging trade with the developed world.

The signing of the SAPTA agreement, which will come into force after all contracting states have completed the formalities of ratification, promises expanded trade in the region. The first round of trade negotiations under SAPTA will result in only a modest increase in intraregional trade flows because the number of products covered under SAPTA tariff concessions are not large enough to dramatically affect existing trade patterns. A significant impact on the intra-regional trade flows will result if subsequent rounds of trade negotiations under SAPTA cover a larger number of products and deeper preferences.

SAPTA envisages a gradual and controlled process whereby each country has the full discretion and sovereign authority to choose a product or set of products to be imported. Any apprehension about the products from one country swamping the market of another country, and thereby causing serious injury to domestic industry, has been minimized through SAPTA's Article 14, in which the agreement's safeguard measures provide for remedial action to the affected party, including temporary suspension of preference granted. Similarly, a provision is made for temporary suspension of trade concessions to meet serious economic problems, including balance of payments problems.[12]

The major responsibility for expanding trade within the region obviously lies with India. India accounts for 76.5 percent of the gross domestic product of the region, 80 percent of the region's total exports, and 60 percent of South Asian imports. However, India and Pakistan, the two largest economies of the region, account respectively for only 1.1 percent and 1.7 percent of imports from SAARC trade. It is sometimes argued that prospects for expanding this share are limited due to the similarity in the production structure of the two economies which leads to a considerable degree of overlapping or competitiveness.[13] Although this may be the case, one must not overlook the complementarities that exist among the SAARC countries. As demonstrated earlier, India is a net exporter of tea, while Pakistan is a net importer of tea. Likewise, the manufacturing sector, while India is an exporter of engineering goods, Pakistan's engineering sector is not so advanced.[14]

The development of regional trading blocs, such as the European Union (EU), the North American Free Trade Agreement (NAFTA) and the Association of Southeast Asian Nations (ASEAN), along with preferential treatment for members trading within these regional blocs, has heightened awareness among business groups in South Asia of the need to accelerate the process of regional economic integration. Created after World War II, the European Union has been successful in fostering peaceful coexistence and in supporting economic development in Europe. The European experience demonstrates that regional cooperation is a necessary step for reaching peace and prosperity among member states. However, there are several limitations in applying the EU model to the South Asian region. The institutions of the EU were primarily built around a common objective to foster integration of the European states, which involved a transfer of some sovereign rights to the EU. This is a very sensitive task which can work only when existing conflicts between the states are successfully reduced or resolved.[15]

Initiating a Framework for Economic Confidence-building Measures

To take maximum advantage of the opportunities that have been opened up by the economic liberalization process in both India and Pakistan, and by the establishment of SAPTA, economic confidence-building measures are critical. Despite political constraints, overwhelming evidence indicates a growing pool of bright and dynamic young professionals, private consultants, and entrepreneurs who are looking for ways to initiate contacts with each other. This is also reflected by the substantial level of "unofficial trade" between the two countries and by discussions with professional business groups in India and Pakistan.[16]

The creation of an India-Pakistan business roundtable to harness the entrepreneurial spirit of the new class of young professionals in the region would be a useful step. The elite business community in Lahore has already taken the lead in the matter, working for the approval of the Pakistani business community for starting such a dialogue.[17] Another step has been taken by a group of women from South Asia, who have joined together to form an association of businesswomen. The first meeting of this forum took place in Jakarta in September 1994, which has formalized the process of informal business meetings among group members.[18] The ongoing India-Pakistan Neemrana initiative has recently sought to expand its dialogue on security-related CBMs to include an exchange of views by prominent businessmen and industrialists of both countries. For such an exchange to be meaningful, however, those participants should be committed to following up their meetings with sophisticated lobbying to encourage greater commerce across borders.[19]

In spite of efforts by the Indian and Pakistani chambers of commerce and industry to keep their members informed of the new economic reforms and liberalization policies, private businessmen in both countries still suffer from a severe information gap. If poor diplomatic relations constrain information flows, perhaps detailed industrial information could be compiled by private business consultants, which can then be made available "on-line" to businessmen in both countries.

The Punjab, Haryana and Delhi (PHD) Chamber of Commerce has set up a "Pakistan Desk" in New Delhi to look into potential trade areas and to solicit trade inquiries from their business counterparts in Pakistan. A recent report of the PHD Chamber of Commerce listed eleven trade inquiries from businesses in India and thirty-four from Pakistan.[20] There is an urgent need to set up a companion "India Desk" at the Chamber of Commerce in Karachi and Lahore to facilitate the follow-up on trade inquiries. The Confederation of Indian Industries has also set up a "Pakistan Committee" with a similar objective, although, at this writing, the committee has yet to establish an agenda for action and has reported no interaction with Pakistani business forums.

One of the most promising areas for confidence building lies in the exchange of scholars, economic analysts, and management experts between

Indian and Pakistani academic and business centers. A series of conferences and seminars dealing with international trade and global competitiveness, top-quality management, and training in managerial skills, could be initiated. Experts from the Lahore University of Management Sciences and the Institutes of Management in Bombay, Ahmedabad, and Lucknow, could exchange ideas toward a common goal of increased commerce.

A major constraint on expanded trade relations is that Indian exports to Pakistan are governed by periodic lists issued by the government of Pakistan. In contrast, India gives all the countries in the region a "Most Favored Nation" status. Although the list of items that can be imported into Pakistan has undergone significant expansion since 1988-89, it still does not cover a large number of items imported from other countries that can be supplied by India at lower costs. As a result, Pakistani businessmen acquire Indian goods such as textile machinery, dyes, and spices through Singapore, Dubai and elsewhere. It has been alleged that items such as cardamom, goat meat, zari for thread embroidery, and stainless steel are smuggled across the border because of trade restrictions.

Conservative Pakistani business circles express strong reservations about allowing Indian goods free access into the country. There is good reason for such a view. Indian goods flooded some markets in the brief period in 1975 when Pakistan allowed relaxation in imports. India maintains a tight import policy, particularly in the consumer goods areas, as compared to the liberal import policy of Pakistan, further substantiating a dubious Pakistani view about increased trade. India must relax its import policy or come forward with proposals for special trading arrangements to address Pakistani concerns.

Liberal business circles in Pakistan, eager to excel in the global marketplace, argue that the national economy is now mature enough to withstand competition from outside, including that of Indian goods. They also argue that protection of local industry would only delay its entry into global competition. If it is possible for Pakistan to import from India items at a cheaper price than from other sources, they would like to do so. In the case of exports, Pakistan may have to provide tax concessions and other relief so that its products could be exported to India competitively. Pakistan's trade deficit could be reduced because Indian goods would be cheaper than those from alternative sources, due to low transportation costs and geographical proximity.

In June 1983, India's external affairs minister, Narasimha Rao, led a delegation to a four-day session of the India-Pakistan Joint Economic Commission in Karachi. The parties agreed to cooperate on long-term planning in areas that included technology, industry, and agriculture, joint ventures in third countries, telecommunications, implementation of the 1975 protocol on resumption of shipping, avoidance of double taxation, and measures to facilitate the travel of businessmen. In view of the economic liberalization policies that have recently been undertaken, the joint economic commission needs to be activated, and a new agreement that will provide for a more liberal flow of trade between the two countries needs to be proposed.

The existing ban on using each other's shipping lines should be removed, and lengthy bureaucratic procedures need to be altered to facilitate overseas trade. The requirement to obtain a coastal license for foreign vessels loading cargo from Bombay to Karachi should be eliminated. The current India-Pakistan Shipping Protocol prohibits ships of either country from carrying cargoes to and from third countries for the benefit of third country shopping, further discouraging bilateral trade.

The land route between India and Pakistan needs to be opened to allow freer movement of goods and inter-border trade. Businessmen in both countries believe that trade cannot increase substantially unless goods can pass through the land routes at Wagah and Jodhpur instead of being rerouted via Karachi and Bombay, as at present. Sea-borne exports increase the costs of the goods to consumers in both countries.

International financial institutions, such as the International Monetary Fund (IMF) and the World Bank, have a role to play in promoting regional economic projects in South Asia. Because India and Pakistan have historically relied heavily on international financial assistance and borrowing, there is scope for promoting collaborative ventures.[21] Some regional co-operative projects proposed among other members of the SAARC countries—such as the Asian Highway Transport Project between Nepal, Bhutan and India, and the establishment of a gas grid for the North Eastern states of India, Banglādesh, and Myanmar which is being proposed by the Asian Development Bank—represent a basis for greater regional ventures in South Asia.[22]

Conclusion

Consumers and producers in both India and Pakistan can benefit from trade expansion and economic collaboration. Private businessmen on both sides are willing to explore possibilities for lucrative trade nearby, rather than pay high transport and overhead costs with distant countries. In some industries and commodities, increased trade will reduce profits and market share, or worse; in other areas, mutual trade benefits will accrue. Severe dislocations, however, can be settled through negotiations within SAPTA.

Influential professional and business lobbies in both countries should be mobilized to initiate a process whereby confidence building can take place to encourage expansion of bilateral trade and joint ventures. There is also a significant role for "third party" involvement—such as the World Bank, Asian Development Bank and the United States Agency for International Development (USAID)—for initiating regional economic projects in non-military areas in which India and Pakistan can become cooperative partners.

It is important to look at the future with a view toward demolishing prejudices that have held back the region and already resulted in enormous economic losses for the past four decades. Economic success has proved to be a major driving force in most regions of the world, surpassing the psychological barriers that inhibit cooperation. The economic dynamism and entrepreneurial spirit of India and Pakistan need to be harnessed not only for economic growth, but also for regional cooperation.

NOTES

1. Dr. Mubashir Hasan, former federal finance minister of Pakistan and chairman, Independent Planning Commission of Pakistan, is currently undertaking a project to compile the Indo-Pakistani unofficial dialogues. He currently estimates a total of thirty-two such dialogues.
2. Both were established during the seventh SAARC summit in Dhaka in April 1993. An abundance of detailed information is available on SAARC and SAPTA published by such organizations as the SAARC Secretariat (Kathmandu), SAARC Chambers of Commerce and Industry (Karachi), and Federation of Indian Chambers of Commerce and Industry (New Delhi).
3. The "unofficial trade" between India and Pakistan consists of direct smuggling of goods across the border from both countries as well as indirect trade via "third countries" such as Dubai, Singapore, and Hong Kong. Although there are no "official" estimates of the "unofficial trade" between India and Pakistan, the Independent Planning Commission of Pakistan has estimated it to be in "several millions of dollars."
4. Rauf A. Azhar and Asad Amin, "Pak-India Trade Prospects: A Preliminary Assessment," Research Paper #9411, The Lahore Chamber of Commerce and Industry.
5. "Economic Cooperation in the SAARC Region: Potential Constraints and Policies," Research and Information System for the Non-Aligned and Other Developing Countries, Interest Publication, New Delhi, 1990.
6. Pakistan's trade policy during 1987-90 had linked tea imports with countertrade of engineering goods. The policy made Indian exports of tea to Pakistan difficult because India already has a good domestic production base of engineering goods. The govern-

ment of Pakistan has recently placed tea on the freely importable list of commodities from India, which has improved prospects for increasing import of tea from India.

7. In the absence of trade in finished textiles between India and Pakistan, Indian silks are currently being bought by Pakistanis via Dubai.
8. These projects could also benefit from export-oriented units established under "export processing zones." The Karachi Export Processing Zone (KEPZ) is the first export processing zone to be established in Pakistan. It provides land, electricity, water, gas, telephone, and telex to the investors within two weeks and issues import permits and export authorizations to set up in the zone. The zone is fully operational and all infrastructure facilities are available.
9. For an overview of Pakistan's liberalization policies, see Aurangzeb Z. Khan, "South Asia: A Review and Appraisal of Current Regional Economic Trends," *Strategic Perspectives* 2 (Summer 1994), The Institute of Strategic Studies, Islamabad.
10. Controversy has overshadowed the privatization program of Pakistan. Accusations were leveled against the Privatization Commission of disinvesting public-sector enterprises at throw-away prices to individuals and business concerns closely affiliated with the former Nawaz Sharif government and also against some newly privatized enterprises of rescinding on worker compensatory agreements given prior to denationalization. The government was accused of misappropriating the privatization proceeds, and the proposed privatization of some larger public-sector enterprises generated considerable public and political opposition. For further details on Pakistan's privatization programs, see A.A. Khan, "Problems of Non-Performing Loans and Advance of Banks and Development Finance Institutions," *The News*, November 6, 1993. Also see *Proceedings of the National Workshop on the Privatization Policy of Government and Its Impact on Employment and Productivity*, (August 31-September 2, 1992), published by the Friedrich Ebert Foundation, Islamabad.
11. For details on India's economic reforms program, see "Economic Survey of India," 1993 and 1994, Ministry of Finance, New Delhi.
12. For details on SAPTA, see "Agreement on SAARC Preferential Trading Arrangement (SAPTA)," South Asian Association for Regional Cooperation, Kathmandu (1994) and "SAARC in Brief," South Asian Association for Regional Cooperation, Kathmandu (March 1994).
13. See Rauf A. Azhar and Asad Amin, "Pak-India Trade Prospects: A Preliminary Assessment," Research Paper #9411, Lahore Chamber of Commerce and Industry.
14. India's engineering industry (i.e., its capital goods sector) is more advanced than Pakistan's, which reflects India's greater emphasis on development of indigenous capital good industry. As a result, India has succeeded in establishing a strong foothold in the international market for engineering goods. In 1990-91, Indian exports of engineering goods were registered at Rs. 39 billion, and were the second largest foreign exchange earner for India.

    Pakistan's imports of "machinery and transportation" equipment from India has been steadily increasing over the past several years. From Rs. 3.31 million in 1986-87, the figure has reached Rs. 127 million in 1991-92—a thirty-eight-fold increase over a period of five years. While these figures, in terms of absolute values, are somewhat deceptive due to inflationary effects, the picture after adjustment for inflation is not much different. During the period under consideration, the price level has risen by roughly 58 percent—based on the GDP deflator data—and therefore these imports register a whopping twenty-four-fold increase in real terms. Relatively speaking, in

1986-87, the import of machinery and transport equipment accounted for 2 percent of Pakistan's total imports from India. This figure went up to 10 percent in 1991- 1992, representing a five-fold increase. This trend is likely to continue in the foreseeable future.

15. Christian Wagner, "Regional Cooperation in Comparison: Can the European Community Serve as a Model for the SAARC?" in *The European Community and the South Asian Association for Regional Cooperation,* proceedings of an international seminar held in Brussels, June 6-12, 1993, Friedrich Naumann Stiftung.
16. Discussions with professional business groups in India and Pakistan are found in Poonam S. Barua, "Economic Confidence-building between India and Pakistan: A Report," prepared for the Friedrich Naumann Stiftung, New Delhi (January 1995).
17. Ibid.
18. The founding members of this forum consist of five female entrepreneurs, including one Indian and one Pakistani, who are engaged in such business activities as jewelry and surgical instruments. The forum is financed entirely by these women from private funds. There has not been much progress in the activities of the forum since September 1994.
19. The India-Pakistan Neemrana Dialogue was initiated by the United States Information Service (USIS) in October 1991 in New Delhi and Islamabad. USIS fully funded the Neemrana dialogue until its fourth round. Since then, the Ford Foundation in New Delhi has funded the dialogue, although USIS still plays an active role in facilitating the meetings. During the initial meetings, seven Indians and seven Pakistanis—including academics, senior journalists, former ambassadors, social commentators and retired senior military officers—were present. Although some of the original participants have changed during the successive rounds, most of the members have been present through virtually all of the dialogue's rounds. During the eighth round of the dialogue held in New Delhi, some industrialists from India and Pakistan were invited to address the members on economic issues. Apart from brief discussions, there appears to be no follow-up action on recommendations for economic confidence-building measures. The author has been present through the first six Neemrana meetings as chief program adviser for USIS, New Delhi.
20. See "News From the Indo-Pak Desk," PHD (Punjab, Haryana, and Delhi) Chamber of Commerce and Industry, New Delhi.
21. The IMF and the World Bank have recently offered an assistance package that could provide Pakistan $1.5 billion in concessional loans over the next three years. As part of this package, the IMF approved $377 million in short-term emergency assistance in the form of standby facilities in September 1993. A medium term structural adjustment loan under the Fund's Enhanced Structural Adjustment Facility (ESAF) has also been proposed for approval by the IMF board.
22. See Q.K. Ahmed et al., *Converting Water into Wealth: Regional Cooperation in Harnessing the Eastern Himalayan Rivers,* Bangladesh Unnayan Parishad (BUP).

9

ENEMY IMAGES: THE MEDIA AND INDO-PAKISTANI TENSIONS

Navnita Chadha

When discussing the concept of confidence-building measures (CBMs), one normally thinks about the military steps undertaken by the adversaries to avoid an armed confrontation by accident or miscalculation. This chapter takes a broader view of confidence building, focusing on human interactions between India and Pakistan. With countries so closely tied by the links of history and culture, CBMs have to evolve naturally. Restricting CBMs to the military sphere is likely to yield only limited dividends because confidence building on the Subcontinent cannot succeed in a political vacuum; it must be part of the larger political process designed to stabilize and improve relations. Opinion-making elites, the media, and public opinion have an important role to play in this respect.

Enemy images often prove to be crucial in shaping public opinion and the agenda of policymakers. All images, and especially enemy images, oversimplify reality. Enemies in this context are "those who are defined as such and if one acts upon that definition, it is more than likely that the original definition will be confirmed."[1] Enemy images can easily be self-perpetuating, for the model itself denies the existence of data that could counter it. Once policymakers have developed an image of the other side, especially a hostile one, ambiguous and even discrepant information tends to be assimilated in their pre-existing beliefs and images.[2] New evidence is made to fit the decision makers' predispositions and initial hypotheses. In this way, leaders become prisoners of their own images. The same logic may be applied to public opinion trends. Once enemy images have taken root in the public's mind, they tend to be intractable and self-reinforcing.

Enemy Images in India and Pakistan

Enemy images are embedded in the history and politics of the Subcontinent. The unprecedented communal carnage at the birth of India and Pakistan in 1947 left bitter mental imprints that shape much of today's media coverage. Subsequently, the two countries became locked in a war over Kashmir in 1947-48, and since then have fought wars in 1965 and 1971. They were believed to have come close to a fourth round in the winter of 1986-87 and the spring of 1990.

The most fundamental aspect of Pakistan's enemy image of India is that New Delhi is unreconciled to Pakistan's independent existence. In the early years after independence, the refusal of the Indian Congress Party leadership to concede legitimacy of the two-nation theory and its public statements about the nonviability of the Pakistani state convinced many Pakistanis that India posed an ideological as well as a military threat to the country's survival. A belief developed among Pakistanis that India was trying constantly to impose its hegemony over its South Asian neighbors. India's role in East Pakistan's secession in 1971 confirmed Pakistan's worst fears that India would leave no stone unturned in its drive to humble Pakistan. Indian occupation of the Siachen glacier in the mid-1980s is cited as another case in point.

India's military might is viewed in pursuance of its expansionist objectives. Most Pakistanis find Indian threat perceptions of a military attack from Pakistan to be unwarranted, if not absurd. Thus, in their minds, India's quest for military power lies in its hegemonic designs in South Asia, a perception reinforced by military interventions in Sri Lanka in 1987 and in the Maldives in 1988. The enemy image extends to economic and sociocultural interactions between the two countries. In the economic sphere, India is perceived as an "economic Leviathan"; Pakistan fears that increased trade would swamp its markets with Indian goods, adversely affecting local industries. In a similar vein, many Pakistanis argue that by opening the doors of cultural interaction with India, Pakistan will lose its religious identity.

India views Pakistan as a recalcitrant neighbor that has refused consistently to accept regional power realities. Pakistan's bids to seek diplomatic and military succor from abroad in order to counterbalance India are invariably viewed in New Delhi as a contravention of the "natural" balance of power in the region. It is argued that Pakistan has repeatedly attempted to change the status quo by forcibly annexing Kashmir. A large majority of Indians share the belief that, since the 1980s, Pakistan has supported terrorism and stoked the fires of secession in India's two important border states—Punjab and Jammu and Kashmir—by giving armed support and training to Sikh and Muslim militants. Last, Indians argue that Pakistan's constant emphasis on Islamic ideology and Islamabad's proclivity to assume a guardianship for all Muslims in the Subcontinent impede Muslim integration into the Indian mainstream and encourages a countervailing Hindu nationalism.

Role of Mass Media

The mass media's role in generating and disseminating images assumes special importance in the Subcontinent. Bernard Cohen put it aptly: "... [the press] may not be successful much of the time in telling people what to think, but it is stunningly successful in telling people what to think about."[3] In the absence of direct personal contact between Indians and Pakistanis, images will be heavily and unavoidably media dependent.[4] In fact, mass media over the past four decades has reinforced enemy images in the Subcontinent.

Print Media. The fourth estate in both countries largely conforms and echoes government thinking on foreign policy, the news provided remains narrow and highly selective, and journalists on both sides of the border tend to focus on the "bad news" and shrug off the "good news." In reporting political events, for instance, the national press in either country seems to be guided more by the passions and prejudices of its own elite than by the objective standards of journalism.[5]

To be sure, there are differences between the English-language and vernacular press. The English press plays a more balanced role, is critical of some governmental policies, and is more fair-minded. It has a limited circulation, but holds enormous clout since it is read by the ruling and opinion-making elites. In Pakistan, the vernacular dailies' circulations are almost twice the size of English-language newspapers. The *Jang,* for instance, has the largest circulation in Pakistan, but is generally hostile towards India. What follows is a limited and selective survey of coverage between 1990-92 in the leading English-language dailies.

The Pakistani press portrays India as the enemy threatening Pakistan's existence. A *Frontier Post* article describes India's "expansionist aims [which] still entertain the belief that continued existence of Pakistan is something that should not be prolonged." No substantive evidence is presented to corroborate this view except that "one hears and reads lots of [unspecified] statements by important [Indian] public figures reflecting such desires."[6] India is presented not only as Pakistan's enemy but the "common enemy" of all smaller South Asian states with "the Big Brother [always] dealing with some small neighbor in a harsh manner." The onus of all South Asian tensions lies solely with India's "overbearing and imperial attitude."[7]

The Indian press depicts Pakistan as a renegade country that will do unlawful and seditious things to support terrorism across its borders. An article in the *Hindustan Times* states, "for Pakistan, hatred of India is a creed, destabilisation of India is her policy and fomenting trouble in Kashmir and Punjab is her strategy."[8] Pakistan's "irredentism" is described as the "root cause of the South Asian confrontation."[9] Another article in the *Times of India* states:

> Starting in the early 1980s, Pakistan commenced supporting separatism and terrorism in Punjab as well as building up the foundations of its policy of subversion in the state of Jammu and Kashmir. The primary objective of the policy was to undermine the very basis of the Indian nation-state and territorial expansion beyond the limits mutually accepted at Simla in 1972.[10]

Mirror imaging is prevalent in the press portrayal of the other side. On the Kashmir issue, for example, an Indian report states that "Pakistan continues to see in the current situation in Kashmir a 'historic opportunity' to wrest from India the valley it has coveted for so long."[11] Likewise, a Pakistani journalist quotes a report that India may seize a "last opportunity" to smash Pakistan's military machine, the principal obstacle to fulfilling India's hegemonic ambitions in South Asia and beyond.[12] Further, if Indian writers contemptibly depict Pakistan's Islamic policies as fundamentalist in nature, Pakistani reporters frequently refer to India's "bogus" or "so-called" secularism. Pakistani press commentators regard Indian Muslims as second-class citizens; Indian commentators like to point out the plight of the Mohajirs in Sindh who joined Pakistan at the time of partition. Indian writers dwell on the dictatorial nature of the military regimes in Pakistan; Pakistani authors dwell on the limitations of Indian democracy.

Press coverage focuses on political and social tensions and conflicts in each country, largely ignoring positive developments and changes across the border. "Soft news" such as the process of social change and development which each society is experiencing today goes virtually unnoticed.[13] Pakistani dailies, for instance, rarely comment on the positive aspects of Indian democracy or success stories of any kind. Similarly, Indian newspapers provide little insight into the inner dynamics of Pakistani politics and seldom write about human interest stories other than those concerned with violence, national disasters, and accidents. Little appears in the press that would humanize the adversarial image of the other country.

Press Negativity Toward the CBM Process. Years of negative and prejudiced ways of thinking have left the fourth estate in India and Pakistan more inclined to develop a skeptical if not dismissive attitude toward the ongoing bilateral confidence-building dialogue. A cursory review of the editorial headlines of some leading English-language dailies in the two countries illustrates this point. Editorial titles in the Pakistani press, for instance, include, "A Foredoomed Dialogue," "Misplaced Optimism," "A Counterproductive Exercise," "Inconclusive or Non-Starter," "Whose Success," and "No Cause for Applause." The Indian press reacted in a similar way: "Calling the Pakistani Bluff," "Ritual Talks with Pakistan," "Talking at Cross-Purposes," "Limited Outcome," and "Why Miscalculate." On the Indian package of CBMs proposed in June 1990, *The News,* for instance, commented, "What Delhi depicts as a comprehensive package seems to be a series of disembodied measures which have not been placed in any political context."[14] Before a round of foreign secretary-level talks on CBMs in 1990, a *Frontier Post* journalist wrote, "it develops that there is nothing to discuss. . . . [The foreign secretaries] are scheduled to start talking in New Delhi after the deadlock they will achieve so studiously in Islamabad."[15]

Another article in *The News* commented, "There are grounds to argue that such a dialogue—shorn of substantive content—enables New Delhi to derive both propaganda and real advantage."[16] A Muslim editorial stated,

> The continuation of dialogue with India in the present set of circumstances . . . would not only be useless, it would also be counterproductive by potentially undermining our principled national position on basic issues.[17]

Countless other examples would be found. Many Pakistani journalists appear to share the government's opinion that talking about CBMs only helps India to deflect attention away from the Kashmir issue, which, in their viewpoint, continues to be the heart of the matter.

Such views are echoed in large sections of the Indian print media, which dismisses CBMs as a cosmetic device that avoids the core issues of Pakistan's support of terrorism in India. The *Tribune* wrote,

> How can CBMs become a practical proposition as long as we in India go on saying on our side that the issue is not negotiable since Pakistan has no locus standi in the matter and Pakistan continues to wage a proxy war against us by training and arming Kashmiri insurgents? . . . The whole confidence-building exercise seems ridiculous in such circumstances.[18]

Likewise, a *Hindustan Times* editorial stated,

> Time is not opportune for any more discussions or bridge-building. Pakistan has imposed upon us a slow fuse war in the Punjab and Kashmir. Let us keep our powder dry but meanwhile confidence-building, bridge-building etc. should be suspended and [we should] . . . wait patiently until they are in a mood to behave as responsible members of [the] international community.[19]

In this way, the media tends to view the Indo-Pakistan confidence-building process through an enemy image lens, suspecting the other side's motivations and condemning the entire confidence-building dialogue as an unproductive venture. The process is damaged when such a negative attitude on the part of the media is used as an excuse by policymakers for not making any concessions. Bold initiatives are not pursued for fear of a public outcry.

Electronic Media. Electronic media is the most popular means of mass communication in the Subcontinent. With the advent of satellite technology, the role of television as a source of information and entertainment has undergone a revolutionary change. Until recently, electronic media had been under strict government control in both India and Pakistan, serving to reinforce government viewpoints by filtering out dissenting voices.

The use of television networks as a medium of conflict was amply demonstrated by Suneet Vir Singh, who analyzed the broadcasts of Doordarshan and Pakistan television during *Operation Bluestar* in June 1984.[20] Several programs on Doordarshan referred to Pakistani support for Sikh extremists. On the other side, Pakistan's television gave extensive coverage to the "Sikh agitation" by showing various clips of Khalistani protests in Indian cities, especially Amritsar, and some Western countries. One program—a thirty-minute documentary on June 19—dealt exclusively with refuting Indian allegations of Pakistani support for Sikh extremists. Pakistani television reports were watched by millions in Indian Punjab, creating much animosity over Pakistan's "TV interventions" in the Punjab crisis and nearly stalling ongoing political negotiations between the two countries.[21]

The advent of satellite television in the Subcontinent has drastically challenged the government stranglehold on information and news. With the successful launching of the Asiasat I communications satellite—a commercial satellite owned by a Hong Kong consortium—coupled with a profusion of cable networks on the ground, satellite TV has not only threatened national television monopolies but perhaps rendered them obsolete along with the notion that sovereignty includes the power to control television within a nation's borders. With bans on satellite dishes becoming increasingly difficult to enforce, governments in New Delhi and Islamabad are losing control over what people watch on television. Currently, nearly fourty-seven million TV sets are bringing "desi" and foreign satellite fare to viewers in India.

Viewers in India and Pakistan now get a varied picture of their external and internal affairs from both third sources, such as BBC and CNN, and domestically generated programs from private producers, like Zee TV and ATN.[22] There is no dearth of current affairs and news programs which often project a certain candor on bilateral issues and themes that official media do not. Although this programming is desirable and welcome, one must note that satellite television has also introduced an element of imbalance in information flows between India and Pakistan. In general, there is a much greater information flow from India to Pakistan. However, no formal studies have been done to study the impact of satellite television and its potential for peacemaking between India and Pakistan.

Radio. As a means of communication in the Subcontinent, radio has a larger reach than television. The Indian broadcasting agency, All India Radio, has beamed special transmissions for its Pakistani listeners since 1967: the External Services Division has been transmitting daily an Urdu-language service lasting 12 hours and 15 minutes and Punjabi and Sindhi services for 2 hours each. The Urdu-language service incorporates 9 hours of music and 3 hours of other programs, including news broadcasts and current affairs, catering to Pakistani listeners' interests in Indian music while simultaneously publicizing the Indian point of view.[23] Thus, the Urdu service fails to make a determined effort to foster cooperation based on a better understanding of each other's problems. On the Pakistani side, Radio Pakistan is received in most parts of North India. Its broadcasts include mostly music and cultural programs in Hindi for two hours and other daily broadcasts in Gujarati, Tamil, and Bengali for one hour each. Very few of the broadcasts, however, deal with news and current affairs programs and stories of human interest.

It may not be long before radio listeners also benefit from the cable revolution. The research department of All India Radio and Doordarshan have already developed a technology that enables cable operators to offer twenty Sky Radio channels along with Doordarshan's five satellite television channels through an additional expenditure of India Rs. 5000 ($170). The new technology will make it possible to receive the FM channel in the language of one's choice anywhere in the country. Because Doordarshan is not in a position to generate enough software to run the channels, it is likely to commission programs from private producers or lease some of the channels.

The dimensions of this prospective revolution are uncertain, however. The radio in India has long been the only source of entertainment for the lower classes, and the availability of inexpensive radio sets has popularized All India Radio. FM channels may not attain such popularity because of their cost, and the program content may not appeal to lower classes as, at present, they seem to be geared mainly to English-speaking elites.

In the final analysis, two processes seem to be going on with regard to technological developments in the electronic media: communication technologies have been improving tremendously while, simultaneously, the state has been losing control over the electronic media. In the coming years, economics will determine communication policy. Consequently, a dilution in the political content of programs may follow.

History Textbooks

The history textbooks taught in the schools of India and Pakistan are another forceful medium for shaping the beliefs of future generations, for nation-building, and for use as a propaganda tool. Of particular importance are the ways in which Indian and Pakistani history textbooks illustrate Hindu and Muslim communities in ancient and medieval history, the rationale for partition, and foreign relations since independence.

Two sets of Pakistani textbooks are used: one was written and taught in the 1947-77 period; the other is a modern Pakistan studies textbook in which the "Ideology of Pakistan" occupies a central position. There is a qualitative difference in their orientation. The post-1947 textbooks begin the history of the Subcontinent with the ancient Indus Valley civilization of the Ashoka and Mauraya empires. The modern textbooks (post 1977) all but obliterate the "Hindu" past of the Subcontinent, starting their history with the conquest of India by the first Muslim invader, Mohammad

Bin Qasim, in 712. The pre-1977 textbooks present the movement for Pakistani independence as a defense against Hindu domination; the post-1977 textbooks portray it as a movement for religious revival.[24]

The task of rewriting history started in earnest in 1981 under General Mohammad Zia ul-Haq. Pakistan's University Grants Commission issued a directive to prospective authors to center their texts around the theme of the "Ideology of Pakistan." Pakistan is described not as a geographical entity, but as an ideology reflecting a unique civilization and culture. The term, "Ideology of Pakistan" is not limited to the geographical boundaries of Pakistan, but to all Muslim majority areas of the Subcontinent. The phrase permeates all discussion, serves as a reference point for all debate, and makes its appearance at the very outset in all textbooks.[25]

Zia's textbooks depict Mohammad Ali Jinnah as a man of orthodox religious views who sought the creation of a theocratic state. The religious parties, especially the *ulema*, are portrayed as the genuine heroes of the movement for Pakistan. Further, "an emphasis on ritualistic Islam is accompanied by a conscious promotion of sentiments against non-Muslim communities, particularly Hindus and Qadianis."[26]

The Hindu is portrayed as cunning and treacherous, obsessively seeking to settle scores with his erstwhile masters. Justice Shameem Hussain Kadri, former chief justice of the Lahore High Court, writes of the "diabolical Hindus" and "Hindu conspiracies" in his officially circulated book.[27] Phrases like "oppression," "domination," "subjugation," "being crushed," "physical extermination," and "extinction" are used to describe the policies of Hindu rulers and subsequent views of the Congress Party leaders toward Muslims. The Congress Party is described as a pure Hindu body, and its goal of a united India is depicted as resulting from the extermination of Muslims from Indian society.[28] These textbooks discuss Pakistan's foreign relations solely with other Muslim states. No reference is made to India or any other South Asian neighbor except Bangladesh—a Muslim state.

In India, the history textbooks are written and taught at the national and state levels. At the national level, history is divided into ancient, medieval, and modern periods. The medieval history deals mainly with Muslim rule in India and depicts no ideological divide between Hindu and Muslim culture. Alliances between Muslim and Hindu kings, and the wars waged against each other, are explained in political rather than religious terms.

Turning to the modern period, Indian national textbooks paint the Muslim League and Jinnah in a poor light. They describe the Jinnah-led

Muslim League as a communal organization. The demand for an independent Muslim state is illustrated not as a religious movement, but one arising out of Muslims' fear of Hindu political domination. Textbooks emphasize that orthodox Muslims, represented by Majlis-i-Ahrar, Jamaat-Ulema-i-Hind, and Jamaat-i-Islami, did not support the League, maintaining that its leadership was not sufficiently Islamic.[29] The Muslim League's two-nation theory is described as "unscientific and unhistorical."[30] These textbooks argue that nationalist leaders accept partition not because there was a Hindu nation and a Muslim nation, but because the historical development of communalism created a situation in which the alternative to partition was mass killings. On the whole, national textbooks in India do not malign Muslims as villains, partly because of Indian secular values and partly because India continues to be the home of ninety million Muslims.

At the state level, however, some Indian history textbooks depict a different story. Khushwant Singh has cited Har Prasad Shastri's book, in which Shastri writes, "3,000 brahmins committed suicide as Tippu wanted to convert them forcibly into the one fold of Islam."[31] Although Shastri could not provide any authentic source of his information, his book was approved reading for high schools in Bengal, Assam, Bihar, Orissa, and Madhya Pradesh. Recently Bharatiya Janata Party (BJP) governments in Uttar Pradesh (UP) and Madhya Pradesh (MP) initiated a drive to rewrite history textbooks at the state level that present a communal view of Indian history and consciously nourish an anti-Muslim bias. The entire period of medieval Indian history, for instance, is presented basically as one of antagonism between Hindus and Muslims living in two communities that are like "two armed camps in which the atmosphere of mutual conflict was always present."[32] Most Muslim rulers are portrayed as Hindu-baiters, idol-smashers and converters by the sword.[33] State-level, modern history books describe these Muslim traitors as responsible for dividing modern India. The books also legitimize and glorify their role of Hindu communal organizations such as the Rashtriya Swayamsevak Sangh (RSS) and its leader, Keshavrao Hedgewar.[34]

Although Pakistan and India (at the state level) promote prejudicial views and enemy images through their school textbooks, other attempts have been made to improve sociocultural relations between India and Pakistan through people-to-people contacts, travel and tourism, and wider cultural exchanges. Furthermore, the sociocultural sphere does not remain a hostage to politics in New Delhi and Islamabad when contacts are at a non-official level.

Evaluation of Prior Attempts at Confidence Building

The various measures undertaken by India and Pakistan in the 1970s and 1980s to enhance people-to-people contacts, ease travel restrictions, and increase cultural exchanges have been, on the whole, implemented poorly.[35] Many of the agreements have never been implemented; others have been beset by bureaucratic delays, particularly in Pakistan. For example, Pakistani authorities have often taken as long as six to eight months to grant visas to Indian journalists wishing to visit Pakistan.[36] S.K. Singh pointed out that it took two years for two correspondents of the *Hindu* and *Hindustan Times,* to visit Pakistan. Despite protracted negotiations to ease travel restrictions, delays remain in issuing visas. Only a limited number of cities can be visited, and the annoying practice of police-reporting remains intact. The protocol facilitating group tourism, for instance, has met with serious drawbacks. Tours have to be arranged by tourist development corporations of both countries, which discourages individual sight-seeing tours. Groups must comprise between 30 and 100 members, foreclosing smaller groups. Individuals on foreign travel continue to encounter difficulties, and groups can travel only by air, discouraging tourists on tight budgets.[37] An important part of a comprehensive cultural agreement, signed by prime ministers Rajiv Gandhi and Benazir Bhutto in December 1988, pertaining to the revision of textbooks has also not been implemented during the past three years.

Bureaucratic delays are not the principal obstacle for implementation. Indian and Pakistani approaches toward enhancing sociocultural links have been at variance. New Delhi has always stressed the importance of people-to-people contacts. As Rajiv Gandhi has said,

> Friendships between neighbors such as ourselves are not built by governments alone. Our friendship has to be built, most of all, by our peoples, among ourselves. Nothing is more important than removing the roadblocks that have been placed in the way of our peoples getting to know each other.[38]

Such enthusiasm has not been shared by most Pakistani governments. The Islamic lobby, in particular, is most vocal against any kind of cultural cooperation with India, fearing, as a prominent opposition leader, Ghulam

Hyder Wyne, asserted in the National Assembly, that such agreements would "ultimately bring Pakistan under complete hegemony of India." He said that the agreement promoted by Benazir Bhutto would "destroy all kinds of Islamic and Pakistani values and traditions." Its cancellation would be needed to save the new generation of Pakistan from "cultural aggression."[39] This line of thinking reflects General Zia's convictions:

> after creation its [Pakistan] existence depends only on one thing—that the state should remain an ideological Islamic state. If that ideology goes, then there is no longer any justification for Pakistan's existence. . . .[40]

Such views may be reinforced on the Indian side. A noted Indian journalist argued:

> by having too many cultural exchanges with India, Pakistan's raison d'être vanishes. They [the Pakistanis] have failed to create a Pakistani identity separate from an Islamic identity and perhaps lack the cultural confidence.[41]

Others argue that such fears are largely confined to the conservative religious lobby and that Pakistan has nothing to fear from cultural exchanges with India.[42] As Yaqub Khan put it:

> I do not think that it is a judicious statement to say that the Indian Government or any responsible Indian opinion demands that Pakistan should give up its Islamic character and should become a secular state. We must be mindful of feelings of insecurity and inferiority complex eating our identity. . . .[43]

Another member of the Majlis-e-Shoora argued,

> Let us not feel insecure about being swamped culturally, economically and politically by a larger neighbor. In extending our hand to India, we need to make sure that we respond to the aspirations of the people of Pakistan . . . let there be ease of travel and people-to-people contacts. . . .[44]

Such sentiments are especially true for the new generation of Pakistanis who did not go through the trauma of partition. This generation has its roots in an independent Pakistan.

The Islamic lobby in Pakistan has been able to influence its government's decision making on sociocultural CBMs. For example, although Benazir Bhutto's government did not renege on the cultural agreement under the

Islamic lobby's pressure, it did not implement the most important part regarding the revision of textbooks. New Delhi considers sociocultural links as the key to bridge-building, but these exchanges are the last item on Pakistan's list of priorities and the first casualty of increased tensions. As an eminent Indian official put it:

> One gets the impression that they want to "delink" their public from India because such links can have a deleterious effect on their ideology. So every time we want to expand the scope of these relations, they insist "let's go down the road bit by bit."[45]

In Pakistan, a senior official also conceded that "our public will not accept complete normalcy or relations [in the sociocultural field] with India . . . when Kashmir is on boil. . . ."[46] On the Indian side, the forces of Hindu nationalism also raise a hue and cry about sociocultural interactions with Pakistan, as evidenced by Shiv Sena's demands to ban films involving Pakistani actors or actresses and its attempts to disrupt an India-Pakistan cricket match.

Building Blocks for New Confidence-building Measures

Despite problems with implementation of prior CBM agreements, people of goodwill in India and Pakistan are building the foundation for improved measures based on sociocultural links. Perhaps the most significantly positive development in this respect has been the confidence-building discussions between important elements of the body politic in the two countries. Former diplomat Joseph V. Montville calls this process "track two" diplomacy. Others have called it "public diplomacy" or a supplemental dialogue.[47] Government-to-government, or track one dialogue, consists of rigid official interaction between instructed representatives of sovereign states. In contrast, track two diplomacy is "informal and unofficial."[48] The participants have more freedom to explore the deescalation and resolution of conflicts.

In India there are opposing schools of opinion about track two diplomacy. One group argues that some problems are not the result of lack of communication or understanding and that nonofficial dialogues designed after the U.S.-Soviet experience are largely irrelevant in the Indo-Pakistan context. Others argue that unless both sides talk to each other perceptions will remain antiquated. In this view, misperceptions have grown because, for the past two decades, people of the two countries have not talked openly or directly to each other. Thus, nonofficial dialogues are needed to break through the communication gap. As one advocate in Pakistan has said,

> The confidence-building measures between India and Pakistan should not be confined only to military and security fields. They must be comprehensive. They must be supplemented by confidence-building measures in non-military fields, in culture, in travel and people-to-people contacts. . . .[49]

The impetus for dialogue has come from external and local sources. The United States Information Service (USIS), American universities, and think-tanks supported by the Ford, W. Alton Jones, and Rockefeller foundations, among others, have played key roles in encouraging their South Asian counterparts to undertake track two activities. Japanese, German, and Australian institutions have also played a significant role in facilitating confidence-building exercises in South Asia.

USIS in Delhi and Islamabad, for example, held a series of WORLDNET dialogues between Indian and Pakistani intellectuals. In 1991, a number of South Asian experts visited various research institutions, think-tanks, and public interest groups involved in conflict resolution in the United States under the aegis of USIS's International Visitors Program. As a result, some participants formed the South Asian Network for Conflict Resolution.

In another USIS-sponsored initiative, former diplomat Harold Saunders conducted a series of workshops on conflict resolution in the region. Based on the Dartmouth group experience,[50] USIS launched the "Nimrana process" in South Asia. A group of experts from India and Pakistan were invited to meet at Nimrana, a fort in Rajasthan, India. The participants identified the following issues they thought should be discussed over a long period of time: the conventional arms race, nuclear proliferation, Kashmir, and economic relations. The group continued to hold meetings, which alternated between the two countries, despite a sharp decline in official relations between India and Pakistan. The ground rules of such meetings include no repetition of history, partly because both sides are presumably well aware of each other's public positions and partly for fear of getting bogged down with past differences. Press publicity is eschewed.

The first meeting, held in November 1991, emphasized that "the two countries must change their political language for each other."[51] India must not reject any proposal coming from Pakistan without serious consideration, and vice versa. Each must treat the other with respect and empathy and on the basis of equality. It was suggested that the two countries should use their present modest basket of confidence-building measures to build a joint fence against any accidental drift toward war, gradually constructing bridges of mutual trust and confidence. Without such positive steps, serious cooperation between the two countries is not possible.[52] The biggest gain of this dialogue, as one of the organizers stated, was that "stereotype images of India and Pakistan vis-à-vis each other were broken . . . everybody felt that this was different . . . unexpected and unanticipated . . . a new kind of psychology was emerging."[53] Equally important was that both governments supported the dialogue and eschewed creating any obstacles.

Other efforts to promote people-to-people exchanges have been proposed by the *Sunday Mail (Hindi)*, New Delhi, the Democratic Lawyers Forum of the Lahore High Court, and conferences on strategic issues sponsored by *Time* magazine and by the *Frontier Post*, Lahore.[54] Another noteworthy initiative was launched by O.P. Shah, a Calcutta-based chartered accountant who organized two sessions of an "India-Pakistan dialogue" in Islamabad and New Delhi. A distinguishing feature of this dialogue was that it received wide press coverage partly because it also involved mainstream politicians of the two countries. Several intellectuals in India have also taken the initiative of establishing an India-Pakistan Friendship Society, composed of eminent people from various walks of life. The Friendship Society organizes meetings between the elites of the two countries.

Several regional dialogues were also organized by external as well as local actors. The Centre for Policy Research (New Delhi), for instance, initiated a South Asian dialogue on the lines of the Pugwash experience for about fifty people from all five SAARC countries. Confidence-building measures between India and Pakistan were at the center of discussion. The first such forum in New Delhi has been followed by more rounds in Colombo and Lahore.

In another initiative, the Friedrich Ebert Foundation brought scholars from the region together to assess the costs of non-cooperation and benefits of cooperation. A series of small seminars were organized to culminate in a major conference in Kathmandu in May 1994. Two sets of regional dialogues were held in Tokyo with funding from the Japanese Foreign Ministry; one through a newly created Japan-South Asia Forum and the other through the Japan Institute of International Affairs. Similarly, the U.S. Institute of Peace in Washington D.C. and Saferworld, a nongovernmental organization based in Manchester, England, have held workshops on the Kashmir problem.

The human traffic between India and Pakistan since the late 1980s has increased markedly. In May 1990, for example, a group of eminent Pakistanis, including Miraj Khalid, speaker of the National Assembly; Abida Hussain, MNA; Iqbal Ahmed; Nisar Usmani, vice-president of the Human

Rights Commission of Pakistan; and Mubashir Hasan came to India on a privately organized peace mission.[55] The members of another Pakistani team, Mubashir Hasan, Eqbal Ahmed, Asma Jehangir and Naseem Zehra, visited India in June 1990 and held discussions with a variety of groups and organizations including the India-Pakistan Friendship Society, People's Forum for Peace and Democracy, the People's Union for Civil Liberties, Citizens for Democracy, the Radical Humanist Association, *Manav Ekta Abhiyan,* and the Indian Center for Democratic Socialism.[56] Similarly, a number of Indian intellectuals, journalists, and human rights activists such as Bhabani Sen Gupta, Pran Chopra, Satish Kumar, Kuldip Nayar, Shekhar Gupta, S.D. Muni, and K.R. Malkani have visited Pakistan more frequently and interacted with Pakistani associations and organizations since the late 1980s.

These dialogues—both bilateral and regional—largely bypassed the younger generation and the future policymakers of the region. This gap was filled in part by Steven P. Cohen of the University of Illinois with help from the Ford Foundation, George Perkovich of the W. Alton Jones Foundation, and Chris Smith of Kings College, London. They launched an initiative to hold summer workshops on arms control and conflict resolution for young regional strategists, scholars, and journalists, aiming to create a network of younger scholars that transcends regional borders.[57] Participants included Chinese, Nepalese, and Sri Lankans, although the group, as well as the faculty, is dominated by Indians and Pakistanis. The first summer workshop was held at Bhurban, Pakistan, in May 1983; the second took place in May 1994 at Nathiagali, Pakistan.[58] A salient feature of the summer workshops is the active participation of women scholars and journalists. Another program for the "Third Generation" was instituted by the Henry L. Stimson Center in Washington D.C. Under this program, funded primarily by the Rockefeller Foundation, Indian and Pakistani visiting fellows are invited to spend up to two months together at the Center to study CBMs.

One manifestation of the benefits of nonofficial dialogue was evident in 1990 when the two countries came very close to war. Fifty-four eminent people of both countries issued an unofficial joint statement pleading for peace at a time of heightened tensions. The joint statement urged India and Pakistan to take immediate steps to avert the risks of the war by miscalculation:

> Our people earnestly desire lasting peace, therefore both governments and responsible leaders on either side must avoid what can only be a mutually destructive conflict. . . . Each country must satisfy the other that it was not interfering in its

> internal affairs . . . the assurance of stable and secure boundaries was essential to the ongoing process of nation-building in all of South Asia and for regional cooperation.[59]

Earlier, Group 83, an organization comprising Pakistani intellectuals, writers, and academics, directly appealed to Indian intellectuals to help resolve the Kashmir issue and ward off the dangers of another Indo-Pakistan war.[60]

Dissent is growing in some sections of Indian and Pakistani societies with the state of official bilateral relations.[61] Human rights activists in the Subcontinent have introduced a new strain of criticism over the "self-righteousness" of official postures.[62] Dissenting voices are also present in the national press of the two countries, but are much stronger in India than in Pakistan, partly because the Indian media has enjoyed freedom since independence—with a brief exception of the emergency period—while the Pakistani press has been under government control since 1986.

Those who support the confidence-building process have put forward less rigid proposals to address the core issues in dispute. Pervaiz Iqbal Cheema in Pakistan, for example, suggests a partition of Kashmir, and Mubashir Hasan argues that Kashmiris on both sides of the Line of Actual Control (LAC) should have the freedom of social, commercial, and cultural relations with both India and Pakistan. Many Indians—Kuldip Nayar, Pran Chopra, and B.G. Verghese, for example—dispute South Block's stand that the Kashmir question is non-negotiable. Prime Minister Nawaz Sharif's proposal for five-nation talks on nuclear issues was welcomed widely in the Indian press, which had criticized the Indian government for rejecting it out of hand. A *Times of India* editor wrote: "New Delhi should welcome such an initiative and get down to a serious consideration of his [Nawaz Sharif's] ideas without an *a priori* assumption that there must be a catch somewhere."[63] A political analyst in the *Hindustan Times* commented: "It is palpably unfair on the part of Indians to dismiss Sharif's ideas as a 'ploy.'"[64] A number of defense analysts have also questioned defense budget expenditures while advocating cuts. Likewise, Pakistani journalists such as Khalid Ahmed, M.H. Askari, Sultan Ahmed and M.B. Naqvi have questioned governmental policies toward India, especially in the sociocultural context.[65]

Sociocultural confidence-building is possible because there is a reservoir of goodwill among the peoples of India and Pakistan. They share a chemistry born of the same language and reference points. In the words of Rajiv Gandhi,

> when an Indian and Pakistani meet as human beings in a human encounter . . . in places like Europe, North America . . . there is an instant mutual recognition, an affection that wells from an inner core of our existence, an embrace that transcends the passing passions of politics.[66]

Profound differences continue to exist between the two countries. but at a private level, there is no natural animosity. When families meet, there is no rancor. Khalid Ahmed makes the point lucidly. He identifies a dual-level dialogue between an Indian and a Pakistani who may be businessmen, traders or the family members across the border. When they talk about their business, trade, family matters they talk to each other positively. It is only when they get on the official dialogue that they feel obliged to subscribe to the policies of their government. Then some kind of conflict takes place. Despite the fact that they may not be well-acquainted with the problems, they argue. And one can see that when they are quarreling it is just the sense of backing up the government or responding to the nation-building activities or "indoctrination" that has happened on both sides for forty years. So they are responding to some kind of psychological state within themselves. Because, the moment they get off the dialogue, their points of view relate to each other, they are friendly with each other.[67]

Despite all the restrictions on visas, about a million people travel each year between the two countries and they come back with generally happy impressions. Not everyone in Pakistan is comfortable with governmental efforts to turn away from the Subcontinent.[68] An eminent official in Islamabad noted,

> After 1,000 years of cultural interaction [in the Subcontinent] . . . Pakistan's attempts to create a sense of identity away from India . . . looking towards West Asia . . . [is a] forced exercise . . . [which] creates an illusion as if you are a part of West Asia which you are not. . . .[69]

Although Indian films have been banned in Pakistan, millions of video-cassettes of Indian films exchange hands in Pakistan. Similarly, PTV's plays and their video cassettes have become very popular in India. An underground trade in Indian books flourishes in Pakistan as do Pakistani books in India, particularly those of Urdu poets. Singers of the two countries make private visits across the border. Despite his public aversion to Indian artists performing in Pakistan, General Zia invited Indian singers Jagjit Singh, Chitra Singh, and actor Shatrugun Sinha to the marriage of his children.[70]

Next Steps in Confidence Building

There are further steps that could function as sociocultural building blocks on which India and Pakistan may construct a more open and comprehensive regime of confidence-building measures. A variety of proposals by Indian and Pakistani intellectuals may eventually help their respective governments break the deadlock on the Kashmir conflict. The media plays an especially important role in promoting these confidence-building measures.

The example of the Hindi *Sunday Mail* in India merits attention. Beginning in 1990, this leading news weekly carried out a dialogue in its pages for approximately seventy-five weeks. Through signed articles and special interviews, more than 300 Pakistani and Indian participants expressed their views on the need for more open-mindedness. The momentum from this exercise in peace and friendship culminated in a seminar held by the *Sunday Mail,* bringing these people together. Future ventures of this kind by other leading newspaper establishments in the region could follow. Leading dailies in the English-language and vernacular press in Indian could introduce a weekly or biweekly "Pakistan page" to apprise their readers about political developments and publish stories of human interest. Likewise, Pakistani newspapers could publish an "Indian page."

A conscious effort must be made not to project writings that sustain the stereotyped images of the other country. If newspapers are exchanged and develop a circulation in the other country, there may be more of an effort to present the news in a sober and rational manner. As a Pakistani journalist noted, "When the newsroom is looking for headlines, statements like, 'India to Teach Pakistan a Lesson' or 'BJP demands the Indian Government to Attack the Training Camps in Pakistan' are the obvious choice."[71] Similarly, independent political analysts or journalists should consciously rephrase articles to avoid demonizing those on the other side of the border. It may also make good business sense—news from Pakistan continues to be of great interest in India and vice-versa.

The proposal for an exchange of newspapers, magazines, and books has now been under consideration by the two governments for more than a decade. It was initialed in 1984 under the aegis of the Indo-Pak Joint Commission and was later included in the bilateral cultural agreement signed in July 1989. It enjoys wide support in the journalistic community as well as in the academic circles of both India and Pakistan. Still, this agreement has run into the customary bureaucratic snags and has not been implemented in its true spirit. The current availability of the other country's newspapers is minimal and largely out of reach for the common people. Even academic institutions find it difficult to get newspapers and journals from the other side of the border. The two governments should make sincere efforts to put this agreement into practice.

There are other ways of disseminating news across borders. The Indian and Pakistani embassies could consider setting up reading rooms or libraries whenever possible.[72] Further, some enterprising institutions could publish a news digest service for the other country's news. In India, for example, the Public Opinion Trends and Analysis in New Delhi and the IDSA News Service of the Institute of Indian Defence and Strategic Studies and Analysis give a regular digest of news from the Pakistani press. In Pakistan, the Institute of Regional Studies in Islamabad brings out a regular digest of news from the Indian press in its *Selections from Regional Press*, and its *Spotlight on Regional Affairs* presents analytical views of these issues. Such digests could be published and circulated in all major cities of India and Pakistan. They should be available in academic institutions and public libraries.

The fourth estate in India and Pakistan could take the initiative by sending more correspondents across the border. In the past, the *Jang* has had a resident correspondent in New Delhi, and the *Hindu*, *Hindustan Times*, and *Indian Express* each had one in Pakistan. The *Times of India* has a very pro-Congress Party image in Pakistan, which, in the view of Pakistani journalists, colored its reporting during Indira Gandhi's rule. Similarly, the *Jang* correspondent in New Delhi reported events to suit Pakistan's anti-Indian lobby, according to many journalists in India. Thus, the placement of journalists could prove to be a counterproductive exercise if they serve mainly to reinforce stereotyped images. More progressive forces remain in the minority on both sides of the border and often do not have the means to support resident correspondents.

New Delhi and Islamabad could help reduce the formidable costs of maintaining resident correspondents—without, however, interfering with their professional activities. Heavy reliance by resident correspondents on government patronage could color their reporting. As Singh argues, owing mainly to close links with their respective embassies, a great deal of emphasis is placed on the official statements and government activities. Hence, in India and Pakistan, both PTI and API concentrate on topics like internal political tensions, arms acquisitions, each country's nuclear program, relationships with the superpowers, and communal riots.[73] Alternatively, newspapers could encourage the practice of appointing local stringers across the border. The *Muslim*, *Pakistan Times*, and the *Jang* currently appoint local stringers in New Delhi, and the *Times of India, Hindustan Times,* and *Hindu* have appointed stringers in Pakistan. Pakistani columnists, M.B. Naqvi and Mushahid Hussain, for instance, write regularly for Indian newspapers, while Bhabani Sen Gupta and Kuldip Nayar contribute to Pakistan newspapers. These practices ought to be encouraged. Journalists in India and Pakistan might develop a joint syndicate for the exchange of material. Newspapers in both countries also face difficulties in obtaining appropriate photographs to go with their stories. Freelance photographers in India and Pakistan could address the problem by developing a network to exchange photographs.

There is a need to institutionalize and widen the dialogue to include editors, chief executives of radio and television corporations, and publishers. For instance, the Council of Newspapers Editors of both countries should meet at least once a year. The two governments might employ the SAARC forum for this purpose. Prior steps in this regard include the 1988 summit agreement in Islamabad to allow the free exchange of news and the 1991 SAARC meeting on promoting regional cooperation through print media. Subsequently, the Asian Mass Communications Research and Information Center organized four-day workshops on this issue.[74] India and Pakistan could initiate a discussion under SAARC on how the South Asian media could improve press coverage. The Indian Institute for Mass Communications and Technology could also reserve seats and perhaps even fellowships for some Pakistani students, and vice-versa. The two countries could also use the SAARC umbrella to this end.

It is essential to have more telecommunications links connecting the major cities of the region.[75] At present, API and PTI have a direct twenty-four-hour link between New Delhi and Islamabad. These links, however, are ill-maintained and underutilized. Major cities of the region like Karachi, New Delhi, Bombay, and Lahore often have no direct links. In the short term, the two governments may, therefore, make efforts to ensure better maintenance and use of existing links and, in the long term, to establish additional links.

Communication tariffs, especially the telex and cable rates, are very high in the South Asian region. For this reason, correspondents often have to rely on postal services, which means a time lag of ten to twenty days between the dispatch and the arrival of the stringer's copy across the border. The two governments could address the problem by agreeing on special press rates for developing countries, as suggested by UNESCO.

To improve sociocultural ties, the Pakistani government could seriously consider lifting its ban on Indian movies. A government ban only propels the illegal trade in video cassettes. By legalizing their import, government revenues increase and the Pakistani public benefits. A major obstacle in lifting the ban has been Islamabad's concern that to do so would ruin the national film industry. The problem could be resolved by promoting coproductions by Indian and Pakistani film makers, which may have considerable profit-making potential, and could generate goodwill from the general public of both countries. As a further step in this direction, India and Pakistan should exchange films and hold film festivals. An understanding on this issue already exists, but it needs to be implemented in its true spirit. Some scholars suggest a commercial exchange of a fixed number of films each year and urge the Indian government to buy Pakistani films irrespective of the profitability aspect.

New Delhi and Islamabad should also take steps to increase the frequency with which radio and television broadcast programs are available across the border. At present, the reciprocal broadcast of programs is restricted to the SAARC-based system. Once a month, a program from a SAARC country is transmitted by the electronic media elsewhere in the region. Thus, the frequency of a program produced in Pakistan transmitted to India is very low—once in six months. Frequency should be increased to at least once a month as a starting point on a reciprocal basis. For example, a "Pakistan Magazine" program featuring some positive images could be shown on Indian television for fourty to fifty minutes at least once a month, and vice-versa.

The banning of books across borders has only encouraged trade in their pirated versions. Pakistan has currently banned the import of all Indian publications. Only books by Indian authors that have been published abroad are allowed to be sold in Pakistan. It is argued in Pakistan that allowing Indian literature into the country would invite a cultural invasion. Such fears are unfounded. Many Pakistani scholars have argued that the free import of books—children's literature, fiction, text books, and those dealing with philosophical and political subjects—has not caused a furor.

Pakistans's book industry, which publishes barely 500 titles in a year, fears its Indian counterpart, which produces 20,000 new titles every year at lower prices.[76] Nonetheless, Pakistan's publishing industry stands to benefit from book trade with India, opening a huge new market for Pakistan's Urdu publications. Exceptional English-language publications from Pakistani publishers can also expect to find a sizable readership in India given the similar historical, cultural, and social backgrounds. Further, the Pakistani side may propose such safeguards as fixing a ceiling for book exports and imports. To tackle the problem of pirated books, the two countries could sign a convention on copyright and intellectual property rights. Finally, India and Pakistan should strictly adhere to the provisions of the cultural agreement, signed in 1989, to examine afresh educational textbooks, particularly those relating to history and geography.

With regard to wider sociocultural interactions, New Delhi and Islamabad should make efforts to promote an exchange of artists. Although extremist elements, such as the Islamic lobby on the Pakistani side and Shiv Sena on the Indian side, oppose such contacts, they are widely welcomed and would generate much goodwill. Would the people of Karachi boycott a Lata Mangeskar or an Amitabh Bachhan performance to show solidarity with the Kashmiri Muslims? Would the people of New Delhi enjoy Mehdi Hasan's gazals any less because Pakistan is believed to be supporting terrorism in Punjab and Jammu and Kashmir? As noted earlier, Indian and Pakistani artists are already performing across the border on their own initiative. Government-sponsored initiatives would only facilitate this process further.

A distinguished Indian poet, Ali Sardar Jafri, has proposed holding a convention of writers in both India and Pakistan. As a starting point, the writers and poets of India and Pakistan could hold a *mushaira* or a symposium to be inaugurated in Lahore and concluded in New Delhi. Similar functions could be organized successfully in various cities.

India and Pakistan should promote exchanges of scholars between the two countries. At present, most Indian academics cannot visit Pakistan unless they have been invited by a Pakistani academic institution and have the permission of their Interior Ministry. Pakistani academics also find it difficult to obtain an Indian visa for purely research purposes. As a confidence-building measure, the universities of the two countries should be open to scholars for academic research in science, literature, culture, and history. The research institutes and think-tanks in New Delhi and Islamabad could initiate a visiting fellows program for foreign scholars. India and Pakistan could also introduce a bilateral exchange of students. India offers cheap and sometimes even better research facilities in fields that are much more relevant to the Pakistani economy than are available elsewhere. Similarly, Indian students of Urdu literature, in particular, could benefit immensely from Pakistani educational institutions.

New Delhi should also refrain from adopting a "tit for tat" policy if and when the Pakistani side decides to tighten travel restrictions. When Pakistan, for example, was reported not to be abiding by the agreement to give non-police reporting visas to Indians visiting Pakistan for fourteen days or less, India retaliated by refusing such visas, except in exceptional cases, to Pakistani visitors. India also discontinued issuing visas for paying homage at the

Muhinuddin Chisti shrine at Ajmer after Pakistan's refusal to send *jathas* there for annual Urs.[77] When Pakistan announced unilateral suspension of transit facilities for Indian nationals and tighter transit visa procedures on the grounds that India was infiltrating "trained terrorists into the country," India reviewed its own transit policy.[78] Although the Pakistani government's behavior on this account may not have been justified, India could have adopted a more generous attitude. On the Pakistani side, too, governmental policy leaves much to be desired. Pakistani citizens visiting India not only need Indian visas but also prior clearance from their own Interior Ministry for this purpose. Islamabad should seriously consider abolishing this practice.

India and Pakistan should take immediate steps to implement their existing understanding on the opening of the Khokhrapar-Munabao rail link for facilitating the travel of Pakistanis living in Sind Province. Because almost ninety percent of Indo-Pakistani traffic is generated from Karachi and Sind, it makes no sense to force people from this region to travel through the Lahore-Amritsar link, which entails at least three times as much expense and time.[79] The Khokhraper-Munabao rail link was closed during the 1965 war and its reopening has been under consideration for more than a decade. Both countries agreed to recommission the rail link in October 1986, and in September 1986 all physical arrangements to reopen the route had reportedly been completed. Then, because of the sudden illness of the leader of the Indian delegation, progress ceased on this matter. Concerns have been raised that the new facility would give impetus to illegal immigration from India into Pakistan. However, such traffic normally employs underground channels in any event. The other argument against reopening the link pertains to subversive activity from the Indian side. This concern, too, is based on an abstract apprehension rather than actual experience in Punjab, where the Lahore-Amritsar route has existed for the last four decades. If the interchange of visitors is acceptable through a circuitous route, it should be equally acceptable through the simplified one that the renewed link can provide. This matter deserves immediate consideration by the two governments.

Conclusion

The essence of confidence building lies in winning the hearts and minds of the adversary. Deep sociocultural bonds between the Indian and Pakistani people and the ongoing nonofficial dialogues among their elites provides an excellent foundation to achieve this objective. If the respective ruling regimes were to match their citizens' efforts with an earnest and resolute political will, the era of peace between the two largest countries of the Indian Subcontinent could be realized.

NOTES

1. Ole R. Holsti, "Cognitive Dynamics and Images of an Enemy," in John C. Farrell and Asa P. Smith, eds., *Image and Reality in World Politics* (New York: Columbia University Press, 1967), 16.
2. Robert Jervis, "Hypothesis on Misperception," *World Politics*, vol. 20 (1968): 457. Also see his book, *Perception and Misperception in International Politics* (Princeton: Princeton University Press, 1976).
3. Bernard C. Cohen, *The Press and Foreign Policy* (Princeton: Princeton University Press, 1963), 13.
4. Palmgreen P. Clark, "Agenda Setting-With Local and National Issues," *Communication Research* 4 (1977): 435-452; and Jarol B. Manheim and Robert B. Albritton, "Changing National Images: International Public Relations and Media Agenda Setting," *American Political Science Review* 78, no. 3 (September 1984): 641-658.
5. Giri Deshingkar argues, in a similar vein, that images based on historical memories are incapable of interpreting the present or creating fresh perceptions based on current realties. See Giri Deshingkar, "War, Can Pakistan Take Us On?" *Illustrated Weekly of India*, August 5, 1984.
6. *Frontier Post*, August 20, 1991.
7. *Dawn*, July 1, 1989.
8. *Hindustan Times*, January 18, 1991.
9. *Indian Express*, February 5, 1992.
10. *Times of India*, March 22, 1991.
11. *Times of India*, August 16, 1990.
12. *The News*, May 3, 1990.
13. Suneet Vir Singh, "Regional Communication Policy for South Asia," in Bhabani Sen Gupta, ed., *Regional Cooperation in South Asia* (New Delhi: South Asian Publishers, 1986), 79.
14. *The News*, June 5, 1990.
15. *Frontier Post*, July 19, 1990.
16. *The News*, December 28, 1990.
17. *Muslim*, December 23, 1990.
18. *The Tribune*, August 30, 1991.
19. *Hindustan Times*, June 15, 1992.
20. Vir Singh, "Regional Communication Policy," 93-94.
21. Ibid. Also, Satish Kumar. ed., *Yearbook of India's Foreign Policy 1984-85* (New Delhi: Sage Publishers, 1987), 21.
22. One may note that the list of collaborators sharing ATN's channel time includes Times TV, HTV, Business India TV, United TV, PTI-TV, NDTV, ITV, Observer TV, Infocom, Sicon, Communique and IUCEC. *Hindustan Times*, March 23, 1992.
23. Singh, for instance, argues that during General Zia's rule in Pakistan, All India Radio's Urdu service programs on political affairs were carefully designed to highlight the activities of Pakistani dissidents. Vir Singh, "Regional Communication Policy," 92-3.

24. See Pervez A. Hoodbhoy and Abdul Hameed Nayyar, "Rewriting the History of Pakistan," in M. Asghar Khan, *Islam, Politics and the State: The Pakistan Experience* (New Delhi: Selectbook, 1986), 165-175.
25. See Government of Pakistan, Federal Ministry of Education, Pakistan Studies (Compulsory). For intermediate classes by Safdar Mahmood et al., (Islamabad: Government of Pakistan). Approved for the Department of Education of the Punjab, Sind, NWFP, Baluchistan, Federal Areas and Liberated Kashmir vide notification no. F.11-16/81-HST, dated November 2, 1981—as the sole textbook for intermediate classes. Also see M.D. Zafar, *Pakistan Studies for Medical Students* (Lahore: Aziz Publishers, 1982), 20.
26. Hoodbhoy and Nayyar, "Rewriting the History of Pakistan," 165.
27. Justice Shameem Hussain Kadri, *The Creation of Pakistan* (Lahore: Army Book Club, 1983).
28. M. Ikram Rabbani and Mohawwar Ali Sayyid, A*n Introduction to Pakistan Studies* (Lahore: Caravan Books, 1991) 48.
29. Bipin Chandra, Amales Tripathi and Barun De, *Freedom Struggle* (New Delhi: National Book Trust, 1992), 210.
30. Bipin Chandra, *Modern India* (New Delhi: NCERT, 1990), 258.
31. *The Telegraph,* November 14, 1986.
32. High School Itihas, Bhag I (Hindi), History Textbook for Secondary Schools, Government of Uttar Pradesh, 1992, 290.
33. Ibid., 278-290; and Bhag II, 119-121. Also see N.R. Sharma (Ex-Principal, Senior Secondary School, New Delhi), A Text Book of High School History, Part I & II (Agra: H.M. Publications, First edition, 1991); Gaurav Gatha (A Ballad for Heroism), for Class IV (Lucknow: Saraswati Shishu Mandir Prakashan, 1992) and *Itihas Gaa Raha Hai* (History is Singing) for Class V (Lucknow: Saraswati Shishu Mandir Prakashan, 1991). For key excerpts and a critical review of these books, see S.K. Pande, "Saffron History," *Frontline,* April 9, 1993, 60-63.
34. See the report submitted by the National Steering Committee on Textbooks Evaluation, NCERT Campus, New Delhi, January 30-31, 1993, pp. 5-6, 10-11. It may be noted that this report also severely criticized several textbooks used by many Muslim schools in U.P., for example, in a textbook for Class VI, *Aina-i-Tarikh, Part I,* 30th edition (New Delhi: Afzal Hussain Markazi Maktaba Islami, 1986.) In the introduction, the author discusses the concept and methods of writing history and concludes that Muslims should study history with a truly Islamic mentality. Also see, Geetha Gangadharan, "Use and Abuse of History," *Economic and Political Weekly,* April 2, 1994, 776.
35. For a list of agreements signed between India and Pakistan, see Appendix.
36. An assessment based on author's interviews with Indian journalists conducted in December 1991.
37. Kumar, *Yearbook on India's Foreign Policy 1983-84,* 73.
38. The *Telegraph,* July 18, 1989.
39. For a satirical criticism of his views, see Sultan Ahmed, "This Uproar Over a Non-Issue," *Dawn,* February 9, 1989.
40. Zia's interview with Atul Dev in *President of Pakistan General Mohammad Zia-ul-Haq's Interviews to Foreign Media,* Vol.7, January-December 1984, (Islamabad: Directorate of Films and Publications, Ministry of Information and Broadcasting, Government of Pakistan), 64.

41. Author's interview in New Delhi, December, 1991.
42. Author's interview in Lahore in October 1991.
43. See Yaqub Khan's statement in *Senate of Pakistan Debates*, February 12, 1986, p.863.
44. See Begum Salima Ahmed's statement in *Majlis-e-Shoora Debates* 3, no.1 (December 24, 1985), 50-51.
45. Author's interview in New Delhi, January 1992.
46. Author's interview in Lahore, October 1991.
47. The term was used by Harold Saunders, director of international programs at the Kettering Foundation in the United States, who co-ordinated one of the first such "unofficial dialogues" on confidence building in South Asia on WORLDNET, January 1990. Also see Khalid Ahmed, "A Supplemental Dialogue With India," *Frontier Post*, June 5, 1991.
48. John W.C. McDonald, "Further Exploration of Track Two Diplomacy," in Louis Kriesberg and Stuart J. Thorson, eds., *Timing the De-escalation of International Conflicts* (Syracuse: Syracuse University Press, 1991), 202-203.
49. Nia[illegible]. Niak's statement in WORLDNET dialogue, held in June 1990.
50. Waslekar, 6. Saunders had been involved in the Camp David negotiations as the US assistant secretary of state for Near East and South Asia. Later, he helped conduct a series of dialogues between influential American and Soviet citizens. The meetings became known as the Dartmouth Group, named after Dartmouth College, New Hampshire, where they were initially held.
51. See "Indo-Pak Seminar Calls for Amity," *Frontier Post*, November 12, 1991.
52. Ibid.
53. Author's interview with a participant of the seminar conducted in New Delhi, January 1992.
54. *Muslim*, June 8, 1991.
55. *Muslim*, May 19, 1990.
56. *Dawn*, June 5, 1990.
57. Waslekar, 7.
58. There are plans to have a third session in India, followed by a meeting of participants of the first three summer schools in 1995.
59. "Fifty-four Indo-Pak Personalities Joint Appeal: Reaffirm Commitment to Peaceful Solution," *Pakistan Times*, June 27, 1990; "Indo-Pak Intellectuals for Avoiding War," *Nation*, June 28, 1990.
60. *Nation*, May 14, 1990.
61. In the WORLDNET dialogue, Bhabani Sen Gupta, on the Indian side, made the point that there are many problems with India's behavior with regard to its neighbors; the behavior had not always been friendly. He added that many Indians had criticized the government of India sharply for its attitude toward its neighbors. Maleeha Lodhi and Khalid Ahmed, on the Pakistani side, agreed with Sen Gupta on these points.
62. Khalid Ahmed, WORLDNET dialogue.
63. *Times of India*, August 23, 1991.
64. *Hindustan Times*, August 19, 1991.
65. For example, see Sultan Ahmed, "This Uproar Over a Non-issue," *Dawn*, February 9, 1989; Liaquat Adeel, "Cultural Isolation: Myth or Reality," *Frontier Post*, September 20, 1991; Khalid Akhtar, "Normalizing Ties With India," *Muslim*, January 29, 1989; and Iqbal Khan, "The Need to Transcend History," *Frontier Post*, December 28, 1991.

66. *The Telegraph,* July 18, 1989. Nikhil Chakravarthy makes the same point in his article, "Only the Ordinary Citizens Can Rescue Indo-Pak Ties," *Pioneer,* April 7, 1994.
67. Khalid Ahmed's comments in WORLDNET dialogue, telecast on June 3, 1991.
68. See Liaquat Adeel, "Cultural Isolation: Myth and Reality," *Muslim,* September 20, 1991; "Reaching Out to Our Neighbor," *Viewpoint,* October 10, 1991, 22; and *Dawn,* March 23, 1983.
69. Author's interview in Islamabad in October 1991.
70. Sultan Ahmad, "While Officials Differ, Artists Perform," *Muslim,* August 17, 1984.
71. Author's interview in Lahore in Winter 1991.
72. Vir Singh, "Regional Communication Policy," 98.
73. Vir Singh, "Regional Communication Policy," 93.
74. *Hindustan Times,* April 4, 1991.
75. Singh, "Regional Communication Policy," 98.
76. Ibid.
77. *Times of India,* July 9, 1991.
78. *The Telegraph,* July 7, 1991.
79. *Dawn,* July 3, 1989.

10

CONFIDENCE BUILDING BETWEEN INDIA AND CHINA

Kanti P. Bajpai and Bonnie L. Coe

The end of the Cold War is not just the end of the U.S.-Soviet rivalry; it is also a period of opportunities and instabilities in regional and transregional conflicts all over the globe. In the language of mathematics, international politics is poised on a "saddle point." Certain trends and actions may push world affairs towards disintegration; others augur for greater integration. In this situation, it is productive to think about what kinds of policies will contribute to the latter over the former—to integration over disintegration.

Along with the U.S.-Soviet engagement, the India-China conflict has been one of the most enduring international conflicts. Since the late 1950s, and more so since their war in 1962, the two Asian giants have been locked in a cold war of their own. In spite of periodic remissions in the Asian cold war and promises of improvement, the two sides have been unable and at times unwilling to settle their differences. With the end of the global Cold War, India-China relations are also poised on a saddle point.

Cooperation between longstanding rivals is difficult. Unilateral, bilateral, or multilateral strategies for cooperation, in a situation of deep-rooted mistrust, may well be misperceived. States may not be able to distinguish between strategies aimed at eliciting cooperation, on the one hand, and maneuvers for advantage, on the other.[1] Yet some minimally cooperative measures are possible as a starting point, if only to enhance the stability of a relationship. In Europe, particularly since 1975, a whole series of confidence-building measures (CBMs) were instituted. Drawing on the European experience, but customized for the India-China conflict, a set of CBMs might be fashioned that would at least stabilize, if not improve, this Asian relationship.

The basic conflict between China and India centers on disagreements about the border. Much of the literature on Sino-Indian relations has been written from the Indian perspective, and, indeed, this chapter weights the Indian perspective more than the Chinese, for an important reason: China won the 1962 war and, from its perspective, the status quo of the border is perfectly acceptable for an indefinite period. Chinese politicians and scholars are less likely to address the issue than their Indian counterparts because it is simply not a pressing issue for them. Since Indian Prime Minister Rajiv Gandhi's 1988 visit to China, many observers have wondered whether the two countries' relations would take a turn for better or worse. In the years since Chinese Premier Li Peng's 1991 visit to New Delhi, both governments cautiously circled the border question. Finally, during Indian Prime Minister Narasimha Rao's 1993 visit to Beijing a decisive step was taken on the CBM front. An agreement on the "Maintenance of Peace and Tranquility Along the Line of Actual Control in the India-China Border Areas" was signed which stated the intention of both sides to work toward a peaceful resolution of the border issue. It also outlined the two sides' intention to negotiate a number of CBMs.[2]

Precursors to Confidence-building Measures

Even as Sino-Indian relations deteriorated in the latter part of the 1950s over the demarcation of the border, a number of cooperative and tension-reducing measures were implemented or proposed right up to the outbreak of war in 1962. After the war, the unilateral cease-fire by the Chinese led to force disengagements. A group of African and Asian states proposed additional tension-reducing measures. The pages that follow present an overview of these events to set the stage for a discussion of contemporary possibilities.

The 1950s and 1960s. In 1950, barely a year after the Communist party came to power in China, the Chinese government forcefully integrated Tibet with the rest of the country. New Delhi protested but eventually recognized Tibet as an autonomous region of China. Four years later, India and China signed an agreement on "Trade and Intercourse Between the Tibet Region of China and India." The agreement dealt with a number of diplomatic and trade issues and its preamble contained the famous "Panchsheel" principles which were supposed to guide India-China relations. These "Five Principles of Peaceful Coexistence" are mutual respect for each other's territory and sovereignty, mutual non-aggression, mutual noninterference in each others domestic affairs, equality and mutual benefit, and peaceful coexistence.[3]

As relations deteriorated in 1959 and fighting broke out, on September 8 China once again proposed that the status quo be observed and provisional agreements be negotiated on specific isolated stretches of the borderland that were in dispute.[4] On September 26, Nehru replied with the suggestion that Chinese forces should be withdrawn from recently opened posts at Spanggur, Mandal, Longju, and "one or two other places in Ladakh."[5] On November 7, Zhou Enlai proposed that both armies move twenty kilometers back from the McMahon Line in the eastern sector and from the Line of Actual Control (LAC) in the western sector. Beijing also suggested that a summit be held.[6] India responded by suggesting that, to ease tensions, limits be instituted on the range of armed patrolling. Patrols were to be stopped in the eastern and middle sectors but to continue in the western sector. New Delhi agreed to an interim pullback of forces but disagreed on how far. It also conceded that Chinese civilian traffic could be permitted on the contested Aksai Chin road.[7] On December 17, while rejecting New Delhi's proposed pullback limits (primarily because of their implications for the western sector), Beijing continued to press for an interim pullback and agreed to stop forward patrolling though it asked for clarification on whether this included the entire border—a position it preferred. It also pressed for an immediate summit. India, in turn, rejected Chinese suggestions, including the idea of a summit.[8]

India soon changed its mind on the summit, however, and in January 1960 Zhou Enlai came to New Delhi. The only positive decision at the meeting arose from Zhou's suggestion that a joint border commission go to the frontier. India rejected this idea, contending that the frontier was already adequately delimited with only minor adjustments required. New Delhi proposed instead that officials meet to consider the documentary evidence. The Chinese agreed, though evidently they had something more ambitious in mind, namely, a joint-survey team. Little changed with Zhou's visit and the subsequent meetings of officials charged with resolving the boundary question.[9] In the key western sector, the Indians went on to implement what came to be called "the forward policy," namely, lightly armed patrols moving into disputed territory to reconnoitre and establish a presence but not to challenge Chinese positions; and the Chinese, according to the Indians, proceeded with "reconnaissance, probing, surveys, and road-building."[10]

Thereafter the relationship steadily worsened until war broke out in September 1962. Two months later, after a victorious campaign, China declared a unilateral cease-fire and withdrew its troops to a point twenty kilometers behind the line of actual control as it had existed on November 7, 1959. This action was consistent with its proposal of that date and with the terms enunciated in China's first cease-fire offer of October 24. Beijing expected India to reciprocate; if not, China reserved the right to take further military action.[11]

Six Asian and African states put forward a set of proposals for the easing of tensions, pending a final solution of the border conflict. The so-called Colombo Proposals combined elements of the Indian and Chinese suggestions surveyed above. In the eastern sector, the LAC was to become a cease-fire line. In the western sector, China was to withdraw to a point twenty kilometers from the LAC as it had existed on November 7, 1959, and the Indians were to stay where they were before the fighting had broken out. Pending a final solution of the border, the area that China vacated was to serve as a demilitarized zone without prejudice to either side's case. Civilian rather than military posts were to be established in the demilitarized zone. Both sides initially accepted the Colombo Proposals in principle, but China asked for certain modifications which caused India to insist on the original proposals.[12] That, in effect, was the end of the Colombo Proposals as a basis for solving the conflict.

The 1970s. The 1970s saw the first real thaw in Sino-Indian relations since the 1962 war. Five developments were significant: Chinese indications in 1970 and 1971 that they wanted to improve relations with India; the resumption of full diplomatic relations in 1976; the visit of Indian foreign minister A.B. Vajpayee to Beijing in 1979; Chinese signals that Beijing would no longer help secessionists and militants in India's northeast; and China's advice to India's neighbors to improve their relations with New Delhi.

In 1970, Mao signaled the beginning of a Chinese desire for better relations when he approached and greeted the Indian chargé d'affaires in a Beijing diplomatic reception line. Indian reaction was cautious: one response was to ask Beijing to restrain the Chinese news agency, Xinhua, in its reporting of the border issue. Following Mao's signal, Zhou Enlai congratulated Indira Gandhi on her landslide electoral victory in 1971.[13]

This rather modest start toward more normal diplomatic intercourse was interrupted by the Bangladesh crisis just weeks after Mrs. Gandhi's victory. New Delhi feared Chinese intervention in the crisis and signed a treaty of friendship and cooperation with the Soviet Union. Beijing warned New Delhi of the consequences of intervening in East Pakistan, but it was unable to prevent an Indian victory in the December war. Relations once again became glacial. New Delhi took the next step in the normalization process. In 1976, Mrs. Gandhi proposed upgrading diplomatic representation to the ambassadorial level. Later the same year, ambassadors went out to the two capitals.[14] By this time, China was taking a different view of South Asia, encouraging the smaller South Asian countries to settle their differences with New Delhi. China also stopped its encouragement and aid to various secessionist groups operating in India's northeast.

In 1977, Mrs. Gandhi was voted out of office. The new Janata government, eager to make changes not only domestically but also in foreign policy, attempted to normalize relations further and reopen the border issue. While Foreign Minister Vajpayee was in Beijing for talks in 1979, however, China opened its punitive military campaign against Vietnam. There was to be little action in India-China relations until 1980.

The 1980s and 1990s. The 1980s and 1990s were the most eventful period for India-China relations since the border war. In Belgrade in May 1980, Chinese Premier Hua Guo Feng raised the possibility of reopening border talks. A joint communiqué stressed the need to avoid border clashes. In June 1980, Deng Xiaoping repeated China's interest in improving relations. Despite further minor delays over the Vietnam question, Hua eventually came to New Delhi in June 1981 and both sides made concessions at the talks. China had originally proposed a "package deal," with minor adjustments along the LAC in the eastern and western sectors to settle the border conflict. Hua, however, now agreed to consider alternatives if this proposal was not acceptable to India. He also announced that China would open two ancient Hindu pilgrimage sites in Tibet—Mansarovar and Kailash. India moved away from its commitment not to discuss substantive issues until China withdrew from "Indian" territory.[15]

There followed numerous rounds of border talks between the two sides in spite of various tensions: Indian and Chinese differences over Afghanistan, the 1986 Sumdurong Chu incident, reported Chinese involvement in Pakistan's nuclear and missile programs, the conferral of full statehood to the Indian territory of Arunachal Pradesh (which China claims is disputed territory), and the massive 1986-87 Indian military exercise ("Operation Checkerboard"), among others.

Notwithstanding the roller-coaster quality of the talks, the two countries agreed to continue the process of normalization. Trade, cultural, scientific and other exchanges were to some extent delinked from the ups and downs of the talks and from the strategic and diplomatic disagreements listed above. Even as the talks continued in phases, the two sides held high-level meetings and reached various modest agreements. Thus, the foreign ministers met in New York before the sixth round of talks. Prime Minister Rajiv Gandhi and Premier Zhao Ziyang held a brief summit, also in New York, in October 1985. The foreign ministers conferred again after the seventh round of talks during which measures to avoid confrontation in Sumdurong were discussed; and Rajiv made a state visit to China in December 1988.[16]

In short, from 1980, the two sides entered a phase of relatively continuous communication and low-level agreements although disagreements and tensions persisted. This process of communications and agreements clearly had its limits. At the same time, both sides saw the process as part of a movement toward confidence building and stabilization leading up to dealing with the great outstanding issue, namely, resolution of the border dispute.

The 1990s have seen the institution of CBM talks. At the fourth meeting of the Joint Working Group, India and China agreed to hotline communications between local army commanders. They also agreed that their commanders would meet face-to-face at least twice a year—in June and October—at the Bumla Pass in the eastern sector and the Spanggar Gap area in the western sector. Additional meetings may be held if and when necessary. Both countries are now committed to prior notification of army exercises.[17] Details on how much notification is due have not been made public, nor have the size and type of notifiable exercises been publicly specified—within what range of the border, engaged in what kinds of maneuvers, and with what kinds of weapons.[18]

In addition to military-to-military CBMs, China and India may regularize other less formal measures. Indian security analysts from the Institute for Defence Studies and Analyses (IDSA) met with Chinese counterparts in 1991 and 1992.[19] In addition, a delegation of the Indian National Defence College visited Beijing in September 1992. Subsequent exchanges can be expected.[20] On a more political note, during the 1991 visit of Prime Minister Li Peng to India, New Delhi repeated its view that Tibet was a part of China. The Indian government also took strong measures to contain Tibetan protests during the prime minister's visit.[21] In the fall of 1992 it was rumored that joint naval exercises would be held between China and India, although it is not clear whether the planning for such a project took place.[22]

The September 1993 agreement stipulates a number of additional CBMs and cooperative measures that the two countries are to negotiate. These include the thinning of forces along the border (Article II) and prior notification of troop movements and exercises (Article III). They have also begun to discuss the possibility of force pullbacks from some forward positions (Article II). It was also agreed to constitute a joint committee of military and diplomatic experts to supervise implementation of the agreement and to advise on the alignment of the Line of Actual Control (Article VIII).

Indian Incentives and Impediments for New CBMs

In addition to their boundary dispute, India and China vie for continental and regional influence. Both states see themselves as major powers in mainland Asia. Over several hundred years, both have been influential in Southeast Asia, and they will likely compete in this region regardless of a border settlement.[23] A more extended zone of competition will be the Indian Ocean. India has seen this as its "lake," but China's naval presence has grown.[24] Published reports suggest that even as Beijing supplies Rangoon with weapons it is negotiating for port facilities in Burma, a move that has made New Delhi nervous.[25] New Delhi is also watching Beijing's approach to the Spratly Islands dispute for clues to Chinese naval behavior closer to Indian waters.[26]

From New Delhi's point of view, China poses a number of threats. First, China is seen as a conventional and nuclear threat to India. While the Indian arms modernization program of the 1970s and 1980s leaves it confident of handling a Chinese conventional attack, the People's Liberation Army (PLA) significantly outnumbers the Indian army. When they fought in 1962, China won convincingly. Since then China has added to its capabilities by developing a nuclear weapons force. India has accused the Chinese of deploying nuclear weapons in Tibet. Although Chinese deployments have not been verified and even though China has always stressed that it would not use nuclear weapons against a non-nuclear power, New Delhi's concerns have not been alleviated.

It is not altogether clear why Chinese nuclear weapons are viewed as a threat to India, since Beijing already has achieved most of its goals with respect to India. As a result of the 1962 war, China has controlled the tracts of territory it most sought (which have improved contact between Xinjiang and Tibet), and its military defeat of India has left little doubt as to who is the greater power in Asia. India's perception of a nuclear threat from China would therefore appear to be based on intent inferred from Chinese capability rather than from new Chinese aggressive designs. In any event, China's no-first-use pledge has not greatly reassured India. The leadership in New

Delhi feels that in the heat of a crisis nuclear scruples may well be set aside. Moreover, India's ambiguous stand on its own nuclearization make it unclear whether it falls under the "non-nuclear" category in Beijing's view.

Second, China has in the past exacerbated New Delhi's troubles in its turbulent northeastern states and could do so in the future. Beijing could even play a hand in the Kashmir dispute. New Delhi's secessionist problems in the northeast are by no means over, as the last rounds of violence in Assam and Manipur indicate. Meanwhile, Kashmir remains volatile.

Third, China has been a steadfast ally of Pakistan. As such, it has been Pakistan's diplomatic partner since the late 1950s, has threatened to intervene in Indo-Pakistani hostilities, and has been a major supplier of weapons and weapon technology. Since the 1970s, China has been widely suspected of having helped in the development of Pakistani nuclear and missile capabilities.

Fourth, Beijing is a weapons supplier to a number of extra-regional states which, in New Delhi's reckoning, bear careful watching. These include Saudi Arabia, Iran, Iraq, and Burma. The Chinese intermediate-range ballistic missiles sold to the Saudis caused New Delhi particular concern because the missiles could hit Indian territory from deployments in the Gulf. In addition, New Delhi fears that they could be transferred to Pakistan either during, or independent of, Indo-Pakistani hostilities. In August 1993, based on U.S. intelligence reports that China had transferred M-11 missile technology and components to Pakistan, the U.S. government imposed sanctions on both countries.[27] Those sanctions were lifted for China, but not Pakistan, in October 1994.

Despite these conflicts and threats, two opportunities in the Indian relationship with Beijing are worth noting. First, precisely because China has been such an influential ally of Pakistan, Beijing could help to restrain Islamabad.[28] China is not about to abandon Pakistan, but Beijing has shown an independence from Pakistani views in the past and since the mid-1970s has urged the smaller South Asian states, including Pakistan, to improve relations with India.

Second, with the disappearance of the Soviet Union and the relative elevation of the United States, China is a potential partner against Western pressures and positions. Both China and India face Western pressures on arms control, especially proliferation, internal and external economic practices, and domestic repression of dissidents and separatists. Both undoubtedly resent Western policies and pronouncements on these issues.[29]

Given this profile of conflicts, threats, and opportunities, what incentives and disincentives exist for new stabilizing measures?

India's Incentives for CBMs. Internationally, New Delhi faces at least two new realities that are incentives to further stabilize the relationship with China. First, the Cold War's quasi-alliance and counter-alliance structure—the United States and China versus the Soviet Union and India—is gone. Moscow no longer sees India as a factor in its relations with China. Thus, from New Delhi's point of view, Moscow is no longer either a constraint or a reassurance in India's relationship with China. For the first time since 1949, India cannot fall back on either Anglo-American or Soviet power.

Second, with the end of the Cold War, India faces the possibility of increased pressure to improve relations with adversaries, including China. The U.S. concern about nuclear proliferation is the primary reason that Washington can be expected to encourage New Delhi to enter into cooperative arrangements with China and Pakistan.[30] Furthermore, the secondary powers in the international system, especially Japan and Germany, are for the most part supportive of U.S. nonproliferation efforts. This "concert" of great powers could choose a more intrusive role in regional politics to India's disadvantage if New Delhi does not attempt to stabilize relationships with its neighbors. Faced with a gang-up of outside powers, New Delhi may even find it preferable to negotiate matters such as proliferation on a bilateral basis rather than multilaterally.

In addition to mounting international political pressure, India faces growing economic pressures. Multilateral economic institutions such as the International Monetary Fund (IMF) have warned that economic assistance may be tied to defense spending. Japan and Germany have signaled New Delhi that continued economic aid may be tied to Indian choices on nonproliferation and defense spending. Given the seriousness of Indian economic problems, New Delhi cannot afford to ignore these warnings. Some sort of beginning evidently must be made to improve and stabilize the relationship with both China and Pakistan.

While the United States, Japan, the European powers, and other actors are exerting direct and diffuse pressures on India to curb nuclear proliferation, defense spending, and tensions with its neighbors, it is not clear how consistently they will continue to do so. The West in particular, even as it worries about arms proliferation, is distracted by a host of international and domestic problems. The United States has a number of levers it can activate against India, but Washington must deal with a variety of more salient issues. Thus, foreign pressure alone is unlikely to be sufficient to push New Delhi toward serious negotiations.[31] Bilateral, regional, and domestic factors, however, point in the direction of additional Sino-Indian cooperation.

Bilaterally, relations with China have scarcely been better since the 1950s, symbolized by the efforts of the Joint Working Group. New Delhi does not exaggerate the significance of this process but does not want it derailed. The Indian leadership is also aware that backsliding can occur rapidly, as was the case in 1986-87. In 1986, Chinese units were found in the Sumdurong Chu area. Then, India's massive military exercise in the northeast, Operation Checkerboard, following close on the even more massive exercise on the border with Pakistan in December 1986, caused the Chinese to increase and shift their deployments. The motivation for the Sino-Indian agreements on prior notification of military exercises and on the institution of local, military commander hotlines and meetings dates back to the events of 1986-87 and the unease they generated. At the very moment that the relationship was heading for a certain degree of stability, misjudgments and the responses to them, as well as the unpredictability of local military dynamics, made for a dangerous slide in relations.

The questionable readiness of the Indian military provides a further compelling reason to negotiate CBMs. The Indian military is currently in a defensive and introspective phase for a variety of reasons: increasing numbers of "aid to civil" operations; the uncertain availability of military spare parts and equipment as a result of the disintegration of the Soviet Union; financial stringencies; and reductions in the size of the army. In sum, the Indian military is ill-prepared to deal with major military confrontations at a time when Chinese military spending is increasing and the PLA is improving and modernizing its forces.[32]

Another key incentive for stabilization vis-à-vis China is India's economy. In the 1980s, India moved from a low growth (1 to 2 percent per year) to a moderate growth path (4 to 5 percent per year). India remains among the poorest countries in the world, however, in terms of per capita income (roughly $300), the extent of poverty, and various indices of socioeconomic development. The relative advance of other Asian states and especially China, over the past ten years is particularly salient and, in the Chinese case, worrying to India because of its long-term strategic implications. To make matters worse, Indian economic liberalization in the 1980s landed New Delhi with a debt problem for the first time since independence. The combination of economic backwardness and indebtedness has made India much more sensitive to the possibility of unregulated military competition and, even more important, hostilities arising by accident, inadvertence, and misperception.

India's Constraints Against CBMs. While secessionism, the instabilities of electoral and party politics, social turbulence and violence, the introspection and diversion of the military, and economic problems are incentives to engage in some form of stabilization with China, internal factors also may work against stabilization.

First, certain domestic groups may actually favor external instability as opportunities for internal political advantage. In a period of austerity, for instance, the military may have an interest in having a Chinese enemy as a reminder to the government and public opinion that cut-backs are dangerous. The political right wing in India, with its traditional hostility to China and its growing political ambitions, may also be tempted to use instabilities to its advantage. It will be difficult for an Indian political leader to conclude any agreement on the border dispute that could possibly be perceived as a "concession" to the Chinese.

Up to a point, domestic concerns may drive the Indian government to seek CBMs: to limit external (including Chinese) intervention in internal politics and to maximize the attention and resources it can devote to domestic problems. But beyond a point, New Delhi's domestic preoccupations may so consume institutional time and capacity as to derogate from engagement in a consistent, continuous CBM process.

The Indian Balance Sheet. On balance, prospects are good within India for further CBMs with China, as demonstrated by the 1993 agreement. The Indian position can be summarized in the following terms: Internationally, with the end of the Cold War and with the disappearance of the logic of Cold War alliances and counter-alliances, India is no longer constrained from cutting a deal with China. At the same time, it cannot count on support from either Washington or Moscow against China. This means that India must work out bilateral agreements to stabilize the relationship—a process, moreover, that is likely to be backed by the United States and the secondary powers. Bilaterally, Sino-Indian relations have not been better since the early 1950s. At the same time, New Delhi is aware of the continuing fragility of interaction along the border and the potential for escalation.

In short, Sino-Indian relations are good enough for CBMs but not good enough to render CBMs irrelevant. India's regional problems are more immediate than its China problems, but they must be quarantined from extra-regional interference. India needs to stabilize the northern front with China in order to work on instabilities along the eastern, western, and southern fronts and to ensure China's abstinence from South Asia's quarrels. Domestically, while various interests might be tempted to embarrass the government over any cooperative process with China, the seriousness of India's economic and political problems will likely restrain them. In the end, the single most constraining—though not fatal—factor is the extent to which Indian governments, confronting a series of internal threats, will dispose of enough institutional capacity, time, and political capital to carry forward a CBM process. Overall, analysis suggests that India will seek to continue the CBM process even though there may be domestically generated impediments from time to time. These impediments may slow the pace and may constrain the types of CBMs sought, but they will not necessarily be fatal to Indian involvement.

Chinese Incentives and Impediments for New CBMs

Chinese policy toward India presents special problems. While relations with India are important, they are not currently at the forefront of China's foreign policy agenda. Relations with the United States, Russia, Taiwan, Japan, North and South Korea, and Cambodia all appear to be more important to Chinese leaders than relations with India. Indeed, many Sinologists agree that while regional issues are currently a top priority for Beijing, China's leaders would prefer to diminish India's regional influence.

Regionally, Beijing's primary focus is on North and East Asia, not South Asia. Many in and out of the region are especially concerned over China's recent arms buildup. Beijing may well see past animosities as a drag on regional and domestic economic development and political stability. If so, improved relations with India would naturally follow. But a note of caution is in order. China's military expenditures could fuel Asian arms buildups, since China has the most potentially threatening arsenal in the region. An Asian buildup, led by China, could well work at cross purposes with improved economic relationships in the region as a whole. Nevertheless, China's main goal appears to be economic expansion, and it has been attempting to improve relations with its neighbors as a means toward reaching that goal. Trade relations with Russia, Vietnam, and the Republic of China have improved dramatically in recent years.

Domestically, Beijing's primary goal is economic development. China was recently ranked as first among the "emerging markets" by the World Economic Forum.[33] Even some of those concerned with China's recent military buildup recognize that Chinese leaders today are primarily concerned with economics and with maintaining foreign relationships that contribute to, or at least do not hamper, continued economic development.[34]

As long as this remains Beijing's domestic strategy, China's foreign policy goals should be oriented toward creating an external environment that promotes and aids long-term economic development.[35] War is expensive, as is stationing and maintaining troops and equipment along the Sino-Indian border. Money saved by reducing forces here could be used in force modernization or other public sectors.

Peaceful relations and increased economic opportunities go hand-in-hand, as is clearly evident in China's improved relations with Russia. Russia, however, has more to offer China in terms of trade than India does, including the transfer of advanced military equipment. In contrast, Sino-Indian trade has increased only minimally in the 1990s.

Any policy decisions taken now, including CBMs, would have to be reaffirmed by new leadership. China will certainly continue to move slowly and cautiously on CBMs with India, in part due to lingering competition for status and power, in part due to the changeover in Chinese leadership. Yet the basic philosophy behind CBMs is that they can help to stabilize situations where fear and mistrust prevail. It would be in China's interest to implement CBMs that could facilitate economic relations with its neighbors, including India. On balance, China has little to fear from the region and much to gain from continued peaceful relations.

Bilateral or Trilateral CBMs

China, India, and Pakistan form a trilateral security complex: Pakistan has relied on China as a ballast against Indian power; China has used Pakistan to divide India's strategic attention; and India has seen in the Pakistan-China relationship the threat of a two-front strategic problem. Thus, the security choices of the three have been intertwined over the past four decades. This would suggest that a CBM process should include all three in a comprehensive trilateral structure.

Moreover, a purely bilateral CBM process between India and China might make Pakistan more insecure and this might not be a net gain for regional security whatever the localized and immediate gains for India and China. If CBMs mean a reduction in Sino-Indian tensions leading to the freeing of Indian resources to deal with Pakistan, or if CBMs mean that China would be less likely to help Pakistan during Indo-Pakistani crises, then Pakistan is likely to feel less secure.[36] Pakistan may come to feel isolated and make choices with respect to nuclearization, advanced weaponry, and force size that would not necessarily serve the cause of restraint and stability.

Although trilateral, rather than bilateral, CBMs would more fully meet the security problems of the region, they would also complicate CBM negotiations and implementation. Moreover, notwithstanding its "rationality," India will vigorously oppose trilateralization. New Delhi will see Pakistan as a disruptive factor. It will expect Pakistan to try to align with China, try simultaneously to undermine Indian deals with China, and raise bilateral issues such as Kashmir. New Delhi may also fear that China would use Pakistani objections to cover its own hesitations. Thus, all kinds of procedural difficulties might arise in trilateral CBM talks. India would seek assurances that the three-way process would not become a gang-up and that Pakistan would not turn it into a forum for "India-bashing."

In any case, India would probably prefer to deal one-on-one with China from the point of view of prestige and regional diplomacy. Status considerations apart, India has long favored bilateralism in its dealings with its South Asian neighbors, including Pakistan. Bilateralism was written into the Simla agreement (1972) with Pakistan and, for New Delhi, it is still the cornerstone of the relationship. India fears that any change in this norm would lead to increased diplomatic concerns.

Additional arguments for bilateral CBMs merit consideration. In the first place, one can argue that the Sino-Indian diplomatic track is effectively a "two-and-a-half" actor process, informally involving Pakistan, given the longstanding ties between Beijing and Islamabad. In the course of negotiations with New Delhi, one can expect Beijing to keep Islamabad periodically informed, to reassure it, even to leak information to it, and to take some account of Islamabad's concerns.[37] If so, then one might argue that there is no great need to broaden the CBM process formally to include Pakistan in view of the likely greater complexity of three-party interactions and strenuous Indian objections.

A second argument against trilateralization is that Pakistan may not necessarily oppose Sino-Indian CBMs. Bilateral CBMs that do not free Indian resources for redeployment against Pakistan pose little direct military risk. Moreover, if certain Sino-Indian agreements do lead to Indian force redeployments, Islamabad may choose CBMs with India rather than escalate the arms race. By 1991, India had relocated three of eleven divisions from the China border, at least two divisions of which went to Kashmir. Evidence suggests that New Delhi told Beijing of its relocation plans and was reassured that China would not take advantage of the move.[38] Clearly, this is the kind of effect Islamabad fears, yet Pakistani reactions have been muted. This may be because Pakistan sees no advantage in escalating tensions with its most dangerous neighbor while distancing itself from erstwhile friends and allies. It is worth noting that after the 1990 war scare over Kashmir and U.S. envoy Robert Gates' mission to the Subcontinent, Pakistan concluded a number of agreements with New Delhi while Sino-Indian relations were improving.

Finally, whatever Pakistan's preferences, it has little power either to "crash" or disrupt the Sino-Indian talks. Although Pakistan has some "tail-wagging-the-dog" power with China, this is probably at its lowest level ever, thanks to the end of the Cold War and the improvement in China's relations with the former Soviet Union. While Beijing still sees Pakistan as a useful ally—if only as a link to the Islamic countries and as a way to keep India off-balance—and while it feels a sense of obligation for an ally, China has gone its own way when necessary (e.g., during the 1965 and 1971 wars, in the mid 1970s on Kashmir, and the warming of relations with India in the 1990s). Thus, although Pakistani objections to a Sino-Indian CBM process are unlikely to stop Beijing from moving ahead, Pakistani concerns may help shape some of China's stances. In sum, whereas trilateralization may seem the most "rational" approach, given the history of regional security dynamics, it seems best to proceed with separate Sino-Indian and even Indian-Pakistani bilateral negotiations that could be merged if and when necessary.

The above discussion suggests that the two CBM tracks can and should proceed independently and that progress on one will probably not affect the other. This does not mean that if there is serious decay in either the Sino-Indian or Indian-Pakistani relationship, the other CBM track will be unaffected. Should there be a serious crisis between the two pairs, this could well entail a resurrection of the Sino-Pakistani entente against India. In this event, both CBM tracks would be affected adversely if only because domestic opinion, particularly in India and Pakistan, would intervene to stop any significant cooperative engagement including CBMs. The specifics of the two pairings will determine the paths and sequences of the CBM tracks. Similar military and political problems, as well as the demonstration effect of one CBM process on the other, may lead to similarities in the paths and sequences but, equally, they are likely to differ.[39]

Preconditions for Additional Sino-Indian CBMs

What preconditions must be met for India and China to engage in additional CBMs? Clearly, one condition is that both sides judge first-generation CBMs to have been "successful." An assessment of the impact of CBMs may not be altogether easy: if the relationship remains stable, should stability be attributed to CBMs or to other factors? Despite this analytical difficulty, if political leaders deem first-generation CBMs to be successful, what other preconditions would help both sides invest in more CBMs?

Periodic and private reminders of the utility of CBMs by outside powers, and their willingness to share experiences, ideas, and technical systems, may be a positive incentive to continue with the process. Interested outsiders could offer economic incentives as well, which might be more powerful. A continuation of the CBM process requires that both sides see overall improvement in relations, including a normalization process along the border.

Another precondition for more CBMs is the ability of both countries to insulate the process from sensitive relations with third parties. For instance, India has warned publicly that the sale of Chinese M-11 missiles to Pakistan could jeopardize the CBM process. Although it is unclear that this sort of behavior on either side would derail the process altogether, it could slow it down.[40] Chinese arms sales to Burma and the possibility of Chinese access to Burmese naval facilities have also agitated New Delhi. In the past, New Delhi's relations with Vietnam and stand on Cambodia have annoyed Beijing. For the CBM process to move forward, Indian and Chinese internal politics must show enough stability and continuity to enable both governments to negotiate a variety of cooperative measures and then implement them reliably, despite rough patches. Finally, especially because of India's open political system, relations with China and measures such as CBMs must not become hostage to larger domestic political battles.

Sino-Indian CBMs for the Future

The Sino-Indian security problem, first and foremost, is one of two huge land armies confronting each other. Instabilities between large armies arrayed over a long and poorly demarcated border could lead to costly preparations for fighting, if not actual fighting. CBMs might therefore be focused on the issues relating to each side's forces and weapons.

Transparency and Force Reductions Along the Border. India and China lack reliable information on the nature and disposition of the huge forces deployed along their common border. An initial CBM might involve an exchange of information on land forces to improve base-line knowledge of each other's capabilities against which reductions might eventually be carried out. These informational exchanges might include data on the size of typical Indian or Chinese units at various levels and the armored complement of these units and locations. Such exchanges would require some means of verification, possibly with the help of outside powers. The two countries could, for example, buy Western satellite imagery. Once an initial exchange of information has taken place and has been verified satisfactorily, a follow-up measure might be to institute regular information exchanges and to agree that any significant changes in numbers and dispositions would be notified prior to effecting changes.

At the present stage, a more direct (and possibly financially cheaper) option than satellite reconnaissance would be on-site inspections of military equipment and observations of force dispositions. Neither side has ever engaged in such intrusive measures, and, as a result, they are likely to be hesitant to do so. The exact nature of such inspections or observations would require considerable thought. For instance, should there be scheduled inspections, short-notice challenge inspections, or would a combination be more appropriate? Could India and China consider moving to a crude "Open Skies" regime? It may be too early to ask such questions, given the memory of past hostilities, domestic disorders, the lack of prior experience with intrusive CBMs, and the infancy of the CBMs that have thus far been instituted. If the practice of other regions is any guide, however, India and China may well feel the need to move down the road to greater transparency.

After the two sides establish reliable base-line knowledge regarding each other's forces, they could contemplate actual reductions in numbers. Doing so would not necessarily constitute an arms control measure; the aim would not be reduction in the overall size of the forces, but rather a theater or sectoral reduction from present deployments. Several different reduction measures might be used, but certain general characteristics of those measures deserve mention.

First of all, both sides could reduce their forces in phases, with relatively small numbers in each phase. An incremental approach is important because the two sides are suspicious of each other and fear the other might "cheat" in various ways. In the early phases of a confidence-building process, recoupable moves are essential to reassure both sides.

Second, both parties could thin out forces not only in phases but also according to location. Both armies could designate areas where hostile terrain and weather rule out, or limit, dramatic—and therefore destabilizing—military moves. In such areas, it could be possible to thin out forces with redeployments to reinforce more vulnerable points or, preferably, troops could be moved to nonforward stations. Precisely where the two armies will station their forces would vary by the access features in different areas. For instance, it is usually easier for Chinese forces to move up to the mountain crests from their stations on the high plateaus of Tibet.[41] China might therefore redeploy PLA units further in the interior.

Third, if thinning out forces all along the border over time or by locations is not feasible, the creation of demilitarized or buffer zones may serve to disengage the two forces. Both forces, adjusting for local conditions, might be able to pull back a designated distance from the LAC. Once again, a pullback might be done by location. Areas that have featured the highest rate of straying or incursions might be the most important locations for such a measure. To ask both sides to pull back from these strategically more sensitive areas may be difficult, but if both sides disengage, each might be reassured that they have not lost or conceded any advantage.[42] Verification structures would be important here.

CBMs Relating to Nuclear Forces. On the nuclear front, China's nuclear weapon arsenal includes intercontinental ballistic missiles (ICBMs), intermediate-range nuclear missiles (IRBMs), submarine-launched ballistic missiles (SLBMs), and nuclear capable bombers, all of which could be deployed against India. In addition, China reputedly possesses tactical nuclear weapons. For its part, India has not assembled and deployed nuclear weapons, but it conducted a nuclear test in 1974, and is developing a missile capability within the range to strike targets in China.

Cooperative measures regarding nuclear capabilities will be difficult to negotiate because China, as a matter of declared policy, claims that it will not use nuclear weapons against a non-nuclear state. India's ambiguous nuclear posture and its continuing missile and space programs further complicate this matter. From New Delhi's point of view, Chinese declarations of nonhostile intent are said not to be credible, just as Beijing is dubious of New Delhi's declaratory policies regarding nuclear weapons, missiles, and space launch vehicles. Both sides would be safer if they were reassured about each other's nuclear capabilities, intentions, and practices; but neither is willing to make their nuclear and missile programs more transparent.

In these murky circumstances, it is difficult to see what kind of CBMs might evolve. On the issue of nuclear capabilities, China might start with a declaration that no nuclear-tipped IRBMs were deployed in Tibet,[43] a source of public concern in India. This might be followed by Indian verification of the declaration through commercial satellite imagery which could be analyzed for missile sites. Beijing might resist such a gesture, however, regarding a declaration on Tibet to have implications for its overall nuclear posture against other nuclear states such as Russia or the United States. New Delhi might doubt whether commercial satellite images could definitively settle the issue of missile emplacement in Tibet and, even if conventional Chinese missiles were deployed in Tibet, whether satellite imagery could confirm if they were conventionally or nuclear armed. In the absence of verification, no Chinese declaration is likely to reassure New Delhi.

One way to pursue greater transparency in this field is to increase contact between the national armies and strategic institutes. Such contact has already begun, but should occur more often. Regular and expanded contact between the security communities would allow for greater information exchange and for a better understanding of each other's strategic doctrines and practices.

Naval CBMs. While land borders and CBMs related to land forces are important, the increasing size of both navies, their growing ability to project power, India's massive Exclusive Economic Zone (EEZ) in the Indian Ocean, and China's burgeoning presence in the Indian Ocean, all suggest that naval CBMs may be required. The U.S.-Soviet Agreement on Incidents at Sea (1972), notification and observation of naval exercises, and the Agreement on the Prevention of Dangerous Military Activities (1989) might be useful referents for the India-China context.[44]

Borderland CBMs: Patrols, Probes, and Military Exercises

The Sino-Indian border is long, ambiguous, contested and, therefore, prone to incursions. Due to the ambiguous nature of the border, patrolling troops sometimes stray off course and end up captured or in local firefights and artillery duels. To address these problems, China and India have already agreed to some CBMs, such as the February 1992 agreement to institute regular local commanders' meetings at a designated spot in the western and eastern sectors.

Existing measures do not address the use of ground probes. Probes are dangerous because they involve substantial numbers of troops and are designed precisely to violate borders in order to clarify the other side's readiness, dispositions, the salience of given areas, or reactions of third parties. In contrast, patrols usually involve small numbers of soldiers who are lightly armed and are supposed to be confined to their own territory. Most important, patrols can be conducted by local constabulary and not regular army troops.

One problem is how to distinguish probes from patrols. A probing force could simply be passed off as a wayward patrol. There seems to be no easy way to deal with this possibility, but certain measures might be contemplated.

Under an accord such as the 1989 U.S.-Soviet agreement on the "Prevention of Dangerous Military Practices," probes could be listed as a dangerous and proscribed military practice and could be distinguished from patrols on the basis of the size and armed complement of the latter.[45] Verification of the size and arming of patrols would be nearly impossible. Nonetheless, to the extent that CBMs presuppose mutual self-interest in stabilizing a military relationship and do not primarily rest on verification, both sides could be expected to abide by the agreement. At a minimum, agreement on the distinction between a patrol and a probe and on the proscription of the latter would constitute an advance. Any violation of the agreement, if and when detected, would diminish the prospects of negotiating further agreements and might provoke countermeasures. This possibility would exert a certain discipline on both sides.

A second possibility would be to ban forward patrolling by proscribing patrols within some areas or within a specified distance from the line of actual control. The U.S.-Soviet Dangerous Practices Agreement envisaged, for instance, the designation of Special Caution Areas, a sectoral concept, in which greater caution is to be exercised and better communication instituted and practiced. In the Sino-Indian context, a border-wide caution area or, more realistically, sectorally specific caution areas might also be negotiated with improved hotline communications and more regular commander meetings. The practicality of this may be doubted, but it is worth noting that in 1962 China proposed banning all forward patrolling. In addition, both sides have reportedly talked of force pullbacks in certain areas. The establishment of hotline communications and sector commander meetings has already begun.

A third possibility to address the problems posed by patrols and probes would be some form of joint-patrolling of the borderlands, especially in areas that, over the years, have been the site of militarized incidents.[46] Although this may seem a distant possibility, and although the technicalities of such a procedure would be complex, there are signs that the two sides might be moving toward arrangements such as a joint committee of military representatives to look into border transgressions. Joint-patrolling, as an outgrowth of the work of such a committee, might not be as far-fetched as it now appears.[47]

Roads and Rivalry in the Borderlands

The borderland is not only long, ambiguous, and contested, but remote for both sides. Access is difficult, and logistics are troublesome, which has led China and India to build bigger and better roads. Good roads are force multipliers, facilitating the mobility and maintenance of large and more heavily armed units. Despite improvements, Indian and Chinese roads remain susceptible to slides, bad weather, and military attack.

China has invested more heavily in road systems primarily because its supply lines are much longer, running from Xinjiang in the northwest, through Tibet, to Qinghai and Gansu provinces and beyond in the east. The Indian problem, particularly in the northeast, is altitude. While Chinese military units have to climb 5,000 feet from the Tibetan plateau to the mountain crests, Indian units must climb as high as 20,000 feet in some places. Moreover, Indian lateral mobility is limited because most of the roads run north-south along the great ridges.[48]

For both sides, road building and maintenance is essential for security as well as for development purposes. Mahnaz Ispahani notes in her study, *Roads and Rivals,* that although roads are essential in the region, they can be highly contentious as one side's developmental access may be the other side's military penetration.[49] The Sino-Indian war of 1962 may have had more to do with roads as sources of access and penetration than anything else. The Indian discovery in 1957 of the Chinese road through the Aksai Chin linking Xinjiang and Tibet was a turning point in the buildup toward war.

New road construction could be destabilizing especially if either side seeks to undertake construction clandestinely. A notification protocol regarding logistical innovations, such as additional roads or enhancement of road capability (widening or increasing load capacity), would at least avoid the kind of surprise the Indians got in 1957. Because China has invested in these roads at least in part for internal and external trade reasons, Beijing will be unlikely to agree to actual restrictions on road building. Given the primacy of economics in Chinese foreign policy, at this stage any CBMs that might hamper trade are likely to be rejected. For the present, then, notification of road building rather than restrictions on the numbers and types of roads built are stressed. Later, actual restrictions might be contemplated. Alternatively, China and India could agree to limit the military uses of roads leading to sensitive areas and to create joint patrols or aerial surveillance of the roads to insure that rapid concentrations of offensive—and therefore destabilizing—force cannot be assembled unnoticed. Once again, proper verification procedures for such a CBM would be critical.

Integration and Disintegration in the Borderlands

Both sides worry about the loyalties of borderland populations. Both also worry about each other's role in instigating and sustaining disaffection that could hamper their ability to deal with external threats. New Delhi has faced various internal rebellions and instabilities in the northeastern states. It also worries about the stability of Bhutan and Nepal, the two countries sandwiched between India and China. In the northwest, in Kashmir, New Delhi must confront militant and violent secessionists for the foreseeable future. Beijing's problems are also daunting. Tibet's size, its greater remoteness from central rule, its own imperial past, its unity under the Buddhist monkhood (despite the split between the Panchen and Dalai Lamas), the international stature and the spiritual and political authority of the India-based Dalai Lama, and the authoritarian structure of Chinese politics may make integration intractable.

Both sides have tried to reassure each other about their borderland policies. As noted earlier, since the mid-1970s China has refrained from helping Indian secessionists in the northeastern states. At about this time, too, Beijing's stand on Kashmir shifted toward a less partisan position.[50] Although the Chinese premier made no public reassurance regarding Kashmir on his visit to India in December 1991, he is reported to have told India privately that China is against the use of terrorism to solve the problem.[51] The premier also repeated Beijing's offer to meet the Dalai Lama to negotiate everything except the independence of Tibet. For its part, India accepted long ago that Tibet was a part of China. Although there have been signs of Indian aid to Tibetan rebels in the past, Indian action has largely consisted of giving refuge to the Dalai Lama and his followers and urging peace. Periodically, Indian spokesmen have reiterated the government's position on Tibet. Beyond continued abstinence from involvement in each others rebellions, it is unlikely that either side can do a great deal.

Third Parties and Sino-Indian CBMs

Can third parties, particularly the United States, do anything to help the Sino-Indian CBM process along? Both sides are wary of external powers, especially the United States, and do not want to be patronized. Outsiders must therefore move carefully. Outsiders at critical points could, however, volunteer either experience or technical expertise to help overcome hurdles to an ongoing CBM process.

Particularly on verification issues, outsiders could play a useful role. Remote verification devices such as satellites and high-resolution cameras might be required to help monitor force movements and dispositions. China has built and launched satellites. India has built them and for the most part had them launched by outsiders. These may not be adequate for the high resolution required to observe military forces and equipment. Moreover, the problem of image interpretation remains. The pictures taken must be analyzed and assessed correctly and in "real time" in order for decision makers to rely on them. Such analyses require a cadre of highly skilled interpreters as well as technical capabilities to enhance and "read" incoming data. Outsiders could play a role here, too. They might offer to share information and analyses that their own intelligence services possess.

Implementation might be difficult, however. Given the technical and interpretive load on American, European, and Russian services—which will grow even more onerous when the ambitious Open Skies Treaty enters into force—their involvement might be impossible or too expensive. Second, and more important, the Indian and Chinese governments could well balk at entrusting third parties with information-gathering operations and, even more crucially, interpretive responsibilities—no matter how neutral those parties might seem. A more plausible monitoring role for outsiders would be to offer to rent or sell reconnaissance capabilities and to help train personnel in monitoring tasks.

Conclusion

India and China are engaged in a low-level CBM process already. India has incentives to deepen the process, but China seems unlikely to give the process equal priority. This suggests that in the short term, New Delhi would have to provide the initiative. In any case, given mutual suspicions and internal, regional, and international conditions, progress is likely to be slow rather than dramatic. It is best to keep the Sino-Indian and Indian-Pakistani CBM dialogues moving along separate tracks. Movement along the India-Pakistan track will be slower and would, if anything, constitute a drag on the current momentum in the Sino-Indian track.

In addition to the September 1993 protocol, additional CBMs between India and China might be attempted at three levels. First, existing CBM agreements could be supplemented, deepened, and implemented more vigorously. The agreement to notify each other of army exercises in border regions could be supplemented by requiring observers to attend. The number of meetings between local force commanders could be increased and could be usefully supplemented by an energetic implementation of the September 1993 agreement to conduct regular meetings of security specialists and defense personnel to discuss overall strategic perceptions and policies.

Second, as Sino-Indian CBMs evolve, they could focus increasingly on conventional land forces. In particular, both sides could provide better information on the size, configuration, disposition, and movement of those forces to be used in their common border areas. Moreover, they could carry out phased, partial thin-outs and disengagements of forces in certain sectors along the LAC. Third, both sides could add to the CBM agenda measures that stabilize military and logistical practices and capabilities in the border-lands, with particular attention to the problems posed by patrols, probes, and road building. India and China could also usefully consider adding naval CBMs to the agenda of the Joint Working Group.

While the September 1993 agreement is heartening, very few details are publicly available. The agreement does not obligate either side to take any specific steps. The quality of implementation and the extent to which the two governments undertake the negotiations and processes outlined in the text will provide a clearer means of evaluating the future direction of the Sino-Indian CBM process.

This CBM agenda will require a high degree of political persistence as well as technical monitoring capabilities that both sides may lack. The significant and pragmatic measures agreed to in the September 1993 protocol have laid a valuable foundation. The quality of implementation and the pursuit of follow-on measures will be crucial to the success of the process. Third parties can play a cautious and supplementary role consisting primarily of occasional and subtle exhortations to keep the process alive and a willingness to share CBM experiences and technical expertise.

NOTES

1. For the argument that in an anarchic international system cooperative strategies and measures can be ambiguous, however benign their intentions, see Nancy Gallagher and Kanti Bajpai, "Building on Weak Foundations: Cooperation Under Anarchy and South Asian Nuclear Non-Proliferation," a paper delivered at the Annual Conference of the International Studies Association, Atlanta, Georgia, April 2-4, 1992.
2. Official citation of document from the government of India, "Agreement between the Government of India and the Government of the People's Republic of China on the Maintenance of Peace and Tranquility in the India-China Border Areas."
3. See Neville Maxwell, *India's China War* (London: Jonathan Cape, 1970), 79. The Panchsheel principles are still a theme in Sino-Indian relations. The preamble to the 1993 text refers to them as the basis for the agreement.
4. The Chinese had proposed something similar in Zhou Enlai's letter to Prime Minister Jawaharlal Nehru on January 23, 1959. Dorothy Woodman, *Himalayan Frontiers: A*

Political Review of British, Chinese, Indian, and Russian Rivalries (New York: Praeger, 1969), 236, 241 and Maxwell, *India's China War*, 122.

5. Woodman, *Himalayan Frontiers*, 248.
6. Maxwell, *India's China War*, 135.
7. Maxwell, *India's China War*, 137 and Woodman, *Himalayan Frontiers*, 251.
8. Woodman, *Himalayan Frontiers*, 251 and Maxwell, *India's China War*, 141-43.
9. Steven Hoffman, *India and the China Crisis* (Berkeley: University of California Press, 1990), 88-89.
10. Hoffman, *India and the China Crisis*, 92-114.
11. See Woodman, *Himalayan Frontiers*, 285-295 and Maxwell, *India's China War*, 417-420.
12. Maxwell, *India's China War*, 428-433 and Woodman, *Himalayan Frontiers*, 295-301 for an account of the Colombo conference and its proposals.
13. Sumit Ganguly, "The Sino-India Border Talks, 1981-1989," *Asian Survey* 29 (December 1989): 1124.
14. Ganguly, "The Sino-Indian Border Talks," 1125.
15. Ganguly, "The Sino-Indian Border," 1126.
16. For details on the various rounds of talks, see Ganguly, "The Sino-Indian Border Talks," 1126-32.
17. See the Joint Press Release issued at the end of the fourth meeting of the Joint Working Group, New Delhi, February 20-21, 1992. These measures are also reported in K.K. Katyal, "India, China Resolve to Keep Peace on the Border," *The Hindu International Edition*, February 29, 1991, 12.
18. While the two sides are working on greater transparency towards each other, they have evidently chosen not to be more transparent towards their own publics. If there are misconceptions, doubts, and fears about CBMs among certain domestic constituencies, the two governments have done little to assuage them.
19. Personal communication, C. Raja Mohan, March 31, 1993.
20. Batuk Vohra, "A Chance to Improve Relations," *India Abroad*, January 8, 1993, 15.
21. Sumit Ganguly, "Joint Beneficiaries," *Far Eastern Economic Review*, January 30, 1992, 24.
22. Rahul Bedi, "India/China Join Up," *Jane's Defense Weekly*, September 19, 1992, 24. For details on this episode, see Tai Ming Cheung, "Smoke Signals: China, India Tentatively Increase Military Ties," *Far Eastern Economic Review*, November 12, 1992.
23. On the historical influence and relationship between India and China and Southeast Asia, see G. Coedes, *The Making of Southeast Asia*, trans. H.M. Wright (Berkeley: University of California Press, 1966; paperback reissued, 1983).
24. For an Indian view of Chinese moves in the Indian Ocean (claiming to be based on a Chinese report), see the article by Ranjit Kumar of the *Navbharat Times*, reprinted as "Concern Expressed Over Chinese Plans in Indian Ocean," *FBIS Daily Report: Near East and South Asia*, March 8, 1993, 65.
25. See Cheung, "Smoke Signals." According to Cheung, who quotes Western intelligence sources, China recently supplied Burma with several patrol boats, is training Burmese sailors, and is helping build and refurbish naval port facilities at Hanggyi Island and at the Coco Islands near India's Andaman Islands. The latter facility is across the Bay of Bengal from India's rocket test site in Orissa. It remains unclear whether or not China has obtained basing rights for its warships. Western intelligence

reports speculate that China may be seeking to set up a signals station to monitor Indian missile tests conducted in the area.

26. "Concern Expressed Over Chinese Plans in Indian Ocean," mentions the Spratly Islands and ASEAN's nervousness in the light of recent Chinese pronouncements on the future of the islands. FBIS: NES, March 8, 1993, 65.
27. Patrick E. Tyler, "China Calls American Sanctions Unjustifiable," *New York Times*, August 27, 1993.
28. See Bhabhani Sen Gupta, "Nawaz Sharif's Visit to China," *India Abroad*, October 16, 1992.
29. For instance, the India-China Joint Communique at the end of Premier Li Peng's visit (December 11-16, 1991) takes aim at the (Western) notion that human rights can be restricted to political freedoms: "The principles of the UN Charter and the relevant international human rights should be respected, and the universal realization of human rights and fundamental freedoms for the whole of mankind should be safeguarded and protected. Human rights are indivisible. For the vast numbers of developing countries the right to subsistence and development is a basic human right."
30. Steve Coll, "India-China Talks Aim to Improve Ties, Defuse Regional Security Concerns," *Washington Post*, December 12, 1991, 46, notes that following U.S. Undersecretary of State Reginald Bartholomew's visit to India in 1991 Indian and Chinese officials were "expected to discuss U.S. proposals that could eventually lead to regional arms control talks."
31. During Chancellor Helmut Kohl's visit to New Delhi, Germany was relatively soft on these issues. Kohl encouraged India to come to an agreement with Pakistan on nuclear proliferation and to continue the confidence-building process, but did not explicitly tie Indian choices to German aid and investment. See the series of reprints in *FBIS: NES*, February 1993, 48-50.
32. See Shekhar Gupta, W.P.S. Sidhu, and Kanwar Sandhu, "A Middle-Aged Military Machine," *India Today*, April 30, 1993. It has been estimated that, over the past several years, up to 60 percent of the Indian army has been deployed in various internal operations. This point was made by General Gurbir Mansingh, formerly of the Indian army, in his talk, "South Asian Security in the Post Cold War Era," Program in Arms Control, Disarmament, and International Security, University of Illinois, October 2, 1992. On the army's excessive civil role, see also Brigadier H.S. Sodhi's article, "The Fire Brigades," reprinted as "Need to Reorganize Armed Forces Viewed," in *FBIS Daily Report: Near East and South Asia*, March 4, 1993, 40-44. On China, see Nicholas D. Kristof, "China Builds Its Military Muscle, Making Some Neighbors Nervous," *New York Times*, January 11, 1993.
33. Victor Ego Ducrot, "Trade: China Ranked First in World's Emerging Markets," *Inter Press Service*, March 25, 1993.
34. *Indian Express* (Delhi), November 4, 1992, 12, translated in "Sino-Indian Confidence-Building Measures," *FBIS-NES*, November 12, 1992.
35. Hwei-ling Huo, "Patterns of Behavior in China's Foreign Policy: The Gulf Crisis and Beyond," *Asian Survey*, (March 1992), 268.
36. Bhabhani Sen Gupta, "Nawaz Sharif's Visit to China," *India Abroad*, October 16, 1992.
37. In a personal communication, Moonis Ahmar, Department of International Relations, Karachi University, and Research Fellow, Program in Arms Control, Disarmament,

and International Security, University of Illinois, Urbana-Champaign, who has worked on India-Pakistan CBMs, bears out that there are those in Pakistan who fear isolation in the wake of an India-China detente. Ahmar also suggests that there have been China-Pakistan interactions over Beijing's talks with New Delhi. Among Ahmar's writings on CBMs and South Asian cooperation, see "Confidence-Building Measures in South Asia," *PSIS Occasional Paper*, No. 3 (Geneva: Program for Strategic and International Security Studies, The Graduate Institute of International Studies, 1991), "Security and Disarmament in Asia and the Pacific: Developments and Prospects—South Asian Perspectives," in United Nations Institute for Disarmament Research (UNIDIR), *Proceedings of the Beijing Conference: Conference of Research Institutes in Asia and the Pacific* (New York: United Nations, 1992), 65-77, and "Indo-Pak Relations: Confidence-Building Measures and the Normalization Process," *Globe*, February 1993, 47-59.

38. We thank Sumit Ganguly, Department of Political Science, Hunter College/CUNY, for bringing this to our attention and for sharing the information that China not only knew of the relocation, but reassured India on it. On the move, see Dilip Mukerjee, "Dealing With Beijing: Shared Interests in New Global Context," *Times of India*, September 20, 1991. Since then, China has told India that it has agreed in principle to reduce its forces along the border (though it has not provided specifics or indicated a timetable). Beijing has between 100,000 to 200,000 troops in Tibet. See "Frontier Wisdom," *Far Eastern Economic Review*, November 19, 1992, 8.
39. For instance, India and Pakistan have concluded an agreement not to violate each other's air space and, more positive, to allow aircraft to fly over and land in each other's territory through specified corridors. This arose out of a high rate of air incursions in 1989-1990. Nothing comparable has yet occurred along the India-China border. While air CBMs may be necessary between India and China, they are not a pressing area of concern. On the India-Pakistan air and other CBMs, see Ahmar, "Security and Disarmament in Asia and the Pacific," 75, and "Indo-Pakistan Relations," 57, cited in footnote 55. On the other hand, CBMs related to road building are relatively important in the Sino-Indian case, but less so in the Indian-Pakistani case.
40. "China Told Missiles for Pakistan Pose Threat," *FBIS: NES*, March 1, 1993, 62.
41. Mahnaz Ispahani, *Roads and Rivals: The Political Uses of Access in the Borderlands of Asia* (Ithaca: Cornell University Press, 1989), 173-74.
42. Straying and local firefights may also reflect the problems of terrain and the ambiguity of the LAC in certain areas.
43. This is only a start from the Indian point of view because of course there remains the question of Chinese ICBMs, which can hit Indian territory whatever the future of the IRBMs allegedly in Tibet.
44. For a more extended discussion of the possibilities and problems of naval CBMs, see Barry M. Blechman and Gunnar Gunnarsson, eds., *Arms Control and Confidence-Building in Northern Waters*, Reykjavik: University of Iceland University Press, 1990), a report on a conference that was jointly sponsored by the Henry L. Stimson Center, Washington, D.C. and The Center for International Studies, University of Iceland, Reykjavik, held in Akureyri, Iceland, August 14-16, 1990.
45. On the U.S.-Soviet accord, see Kurt M. Campbell, "The US-Soviet Agreement on the Prevention of Dangerous Military Activities," *Security Studies* 1 (Autumn 1991): 109-131.

46. If this seems an unlikely idea, it is worth noting that India proposed such a measure to Pakistan in June 1990. See Moonis Ahmar, "Confidence Building Measures in South Asia," *PSIS Occasional Paper,* no. 3, (1991): 33.
47. The idea of a joint border committee, to recall, has a precedent in Zhou Enlai's suggestion in 1960 to constitute a Sino-Indian survey team to delimit the border.
48. Ispahani, *Roads and Rivals,* 173-74.
49. See Ispahani, *Roads and Rivals,* 145-213, for a more extended discussion of India-China difficulties with roads and access.
50. Rosemary Foot, "The Sino-Soviet Complex and South Asia," in Barry Buzan et al., *South Asian Insecurity and the Great Powers,* London: Macmillan, 1986), 197.
51. See Ganguly, "Joint Beneficiaries," 25.

11

IMPROVING SINO-INDO RELATIONS

Zhao Weiwen and Giri Deshingkar

The first declaratory confidence-building measure taken by India and China was the famous 1954 Panchsheel agreement listing Five Principles of Peaceful Coexistence: respect for each other's territorial integrity and sovereignty; mutual non-aggression; noninterference in each other's internal affairs; equality and mutual benefit; and peaceful coexistence. To celebrate the signing of this agreement, Zhou Enlai and Jawaharlal Nehru exchanged messages of congratulations and paid visits to each other's country later that year.

The Five Principles of Peaceful Coexistence did not, however, alleviate Indian apprehensions about Chinese territorial claims or help resolve their border dispute. When sporadic border skirmishes escalated into a full-fledged war in October 1962, India's worst suspicions that China was an "expansionist" power seemed to be confirmed. Although China unilaterally withdrew its troops and thereby restored the status quo a month later, a militarily humiliated India remained convinced about Chinese "expansionism." The increased ties between China and Pakistan, India's major adversary on the Subcontinent, added fuel to the fire. In the mid-1960s, the reported Chinese support of the insurgency started by the Communist Party of India (Marxist-Leninist) and of the Naga and Mizo separatists in India's north-east further confirmed India's conviction about China's anti-India motives.

China, for its part, nurtured its own suspicions about Indian territorial aims. These suspicions acquired sharp edges when India began to firm up its military and administrative presence in what China considered to be disputed areas along their border. When attempts toward a negotiated solution failed, China concluded that India was taking an extremely rigid position because of "back-stage" support to New Delhi by the West, particularly by the United States. China also saw the hand of India and the West in the Tibetan revolt of 1959, exemplified by the Indian government's decision to give political asylum to the Dalai Lama after fleeing Tibet and allowing him to establish a Tibetan government-in-exile there. Chinese suspicions were also reconfirmed when, during the 1962 border war, India asked for U.S. military protection against China, notwithstanding India's policy of non-alignment. Soon thereafter, the Soviet Union became another "backstage" supporter of India, at a time when Moscow and Beijing had acute ideological differences and were becoming military adversaries. The Soviet Union's large-scale military support to India led China to believe that India had become an accomplice of the Soviet Union in its anti-China crusade.

Bitter memories of the 1962 war survived for three decades largely because India saw itself as having suffered a humiliating defeat at the hands of China. Ironically, improved relations can be traced to another period of border tensions, beginning around 1985. At the time, India accused China of having intruded into Sumdurong Chu, a small valley in the Thagla in the eastern sector of the disputed border. China, in return, accused India of having committed "new aggression" on the border.

The Sumdurong valley was not the scene of fighting during the 1962 India-China war. The Thagla area was, nonetheless, highly disputed. Since the end of the 1962 war, Indian and Chinese troops had constantly patrolled along the *de facto* Line of Actual Control (LAC) in close vicinity of, but not in, this particular valley. In 1986, the Indian army sent a patrol into Sumdurong Chu to "test both Chinese preparedness and the response of the Soviet Union." Chinese troops noticed their presence but probably were ordered not to intervene. At the end of autumn, when it began to snow in the valley, the Indian patrol withdrew with the intent of returning the following spring. When spring arrived, however, Indian troops discovered that a Chinese patrol had preceded them and had built a helipad there. Thereupon, the Indian troops were also ordered not to intervene for the time being, but to preempt the Chinese in the spring of the following year. To their surprise, the Chinese patrol did not withdraw, staying on during the winter months and giving the Indians no chance to reoccupy the valley the following spring. New Delhi publicized the dispute when it saw that the Chinese had come into the valley to stay. Accusations and counter-accusations were traded, but the episode disappeared from the Indian media within a few months. The incident never appeared in the Chinese media in any significant way. The Sumdurong Chu incident, however, seems to have persuaded Indian Prime Minister Rajiv Gandhi that the India-China border problem should not be handled through military means. Such thinking eventually led him to attempt a diplomatic breakthrough by visiting China in 1988.

Much has happened as a result of the changed atmosphere produced by Rajiv Gandhi's initiative. A series of visits between Indian and Chinese leaders have taken place which have been very well received. These visits have been followed by delegations led by parliamentarians, ministers, scientists, and military chiefs. A Festival of China has been held in India and a Festival of India held in China. The bitterness about the 1962 war is fading, and a whole range of confidence-building measures (CBMs) have been instituted.

During Indian Prime Minister P.V. Narasimha Rao's visit to China in September 1993, the two countries signed four bilateral agreements. The most important of these agreements called for both sides to cut their troops along the LAC in order to "maintain peace and tranquility." The other three agreements were for broadcast and television cooperation, environmental cooperation, and for opening up more border trade points. These fruitful results of Rao's visit have been enthusiastically welcomed in both countries. Chinese Premier Li Peng remarked that the visit marked a "new advance" in Sino-Indian relations, while Prime Minister Rao noted that his talks with Li signaled a "bright future" for bilateral relations.[1] The Indian media, somewhat surprisingly in the light of its previous stance, also reported quite favorably about Rao's visit, especially about the agreement on the LAC. The *Times of India* boldly stated that the agreements "mark[ed] the beginning of a new phase in bilateral relations based on mutual confidence and better political understanding."[2]

The most comprehensive set of CBMs ever reached between these two Asian neighbors has been instituted without mediation by third parties. Both countries will continue to reject such mediation. The time is ripe to build on the agreement to maintain peace and tranquility along the LAC. To strengthen this initial success, three broad categories of CBMs are proposed: security-related CBMs, economic and cultural CBMs, and CBMs dealing with Tibet and Pakistan.

Security-related CBMs Between India and China

In the 1950s, there were frequent visits between the Chinese and Indian leaders. From June 1954 to September 1957, for example, Chinese Premier Zhou Enlai visited India three times in an official capacity. Madame Song Qingling, vice-chairperson of the Standing Committee of the National People's

Congress, and He Long, Vice Premier, also led delegations to visit India. On the Indian side, Prime Minister Jawaharlal Nehru and Vice-President Sarvapalli Radhakrishnan made separate visits to China. During Nehru's visit in October 1954, he was accompanied by his daughter, Indira Gandhi. In those years, the slogan "Chini-Hindi bhai-bhai" (Chinese and Indians are brothers) was often heard. In April 1960, Premier Zhou also made what was to be his last trip to India in a bid to settle peacefully the border problem that had emerged the year before. After that, top-level visits between the two countries were suspended for a period of nearly twenty-eight years. Following this long interval, Indian Prime Minister Rajiv Gandhi, Chinese Premier Li Peng and Indian President Ramaswamy Venkataraman exchanged visits. Finally, there came the successful visit by Prime Minister Rao in 1993, mentioned earlier. Indian and Chinese leaders would be wise to continue frequent high-level meetings as a means to constructively engage each other on a variety of issues that can bring about further cooperative agreements.

After nearly three decades of virtually no interaction, the parliaments of China and India have recently resumed ties, with delegations making productive visits to each other's capital. Such visits can be useful in enhancing mutual understanding between the two countries' legislative bodies and political parties. An enhanced understanding between parliamentarians would not only further strengthen Sino-Indian cooperation but would also help overcome animosity created by the Indian parliament's resolution after the 1962 war pledging to "recover every inch of territory" allegedly usurped by China. Although the resolution was not constitutionally binding, it nevertheless stands as an obstacle toward final settlement of the border problem. Some Indian commentators have begun to question the resolution, suggesting that the 1962 parliament pledge was based on momentary excitement, rather than on rational decisionmaking.

China's "Security Threat." A number of Western assessments of Chinese military modernization programs and regional aspirations appear to be overstated. The old thesis that China and India are intrinsically rivals for hegemony over South Asia, Myanmar, Indochina, and Southeast Asia has also been revived by many Western analysts, especially as they express concern over increased Chinese military expenditure. In a variety of contexts, Westerners have spoken about an emerging military threat from China to its neighbors, including India.

The evidence suggests, however, that China, like India, is primarily preoccupied with economic development, not power projection. China's military modernization program is largely driven by the need to replace obsolescent equipment. China's military budget and annual *per capita* defense spending is quite low. Moreover, beginning in 1985, China unilaterally and voluntarily demobilized one million troops, a massive reduction that has not received much credit overseas.

Indian Nuclear Policies. Many in India justify that country's nuclear weapon option because of the potential nuclear threat from China. For example, Mr. K. Subrahmanyam, former director of the Indian Institute of Defence Studies and Analyses, New Delhi, argues that India must acquire nuclear weapons because of its "worries about China." He adds: "We say the [nuclear weapon] problem should be solved globally. When we say globally we do not mean the United States, we do not mean Britain and France. We mean China."[3]

In reality, the Indian nuclear option is maintained for a number of reasons, of which China is only one. As Ramesh Thakur observed,

> nuclear weapons would enhance India's international status, ensure its strategic autonomy, erode great power hegemony in the international system, reinforce New Delhi's leading role in the Non-Aligned Movement, expand its diplomatic choices in global affairs and stabilize relations with China and Pakistan.[4]

The Chinese sale to India of enriched uranium for the Tarapur nuclear power facility erodes further the rationalization of India's nuclear policies against a Chinese threat.[5]

Had India perceived a continuing and growing military threat from China, New Delhi's military budget would not have been effectively frozen in the early 1990s. Moreover, the Indian government would not have dared to withdraw some of its deployed mountain divisions along the India-China border. It would also have been difficult for India to have signed an agreement with China to withdraw troops along the LAC. A re-examination of Indian nuclear doctrine and a de-emphasis of the deterrent role vis-à-vis China might well be warranted and could help further in reducing tensions between the two countries.

Nuclear Disarmament. China and India have articulated common goals for nuclear disarmament, but have yet to cooperate closely to achieve these objectives. Both states stand for the complete prohibition and thorough destruction of nuclear weapons and have supported a comprehensive nuclear test ban as a step toward this goal. On the very day when China exploded its first nuclear weapon in October 1964, the Chinese government declared that "at no time and under no circumstances would it be the first to use or threaten to use nuclear weapons."[6] India has long articulated the need for strong security assurances by states with nuclear weapons. An Indian editorial commented: "In a sense, the Indian and Chinese positions are close. Both believe in the elimination and destruction of nuclear weapons, though the two may espouse varying ways of reaching the objective."[7] In light of the adoption of their common goal, it would be wise for China and India to work more closely toward their realization.

Military-to-Military Contacts. High-level military delegations have begun exchanging visits in the wake of Rajiv Gandhi's initiative. Beginning in February 1994, concrete discussions have been held in working groups, which include military officials, to delineate the LAC and determine the force levels to be maintained along that line. The explicit aim of these discussions is to eliminate all sources of military threats and to establish "peace and tranquility" not only along the LAC, but also in the border area as a whole. The more progress is made in these discussions, the more will political relations rapidly improve and lingering suspicions be removed. Many argue that confidence-building discussions between Indian and Pakistani civilian or diplomatic officials will only be effective if they are supported by similar talks between military officials. Frequent direct talks between the military officials of both sides are also absolutely essential to firm up the confidence-building process between India and China.

Economic and Cultural CBMs Between India and China

Due to historical, geographical, and economics reasons, Sino-Indian trade has never been significant. This was true even in the 1950s, when relations were rather warm. Because increased trade creates interdependence, it generally becomes an important guarantee for an enduring friendship between nations. With two great neighbors engaged simultaneously in a drive for development, it is even more imperative for China and India to strengthen their economic and trade relations. In the decade after India and China signed a new trade agreement in 1984—after the suspension of direct trade for almost three decades—their bilateral import and export trade increased tenfold, from $60 million to about $600 million. Still, this accounts for only 0.165 percent of the total foreign trade of the two countries. Clearly, there is much room for further trade between them.[8]

Economic Interaction. Political difficulties explain only why trade relations were terminated, not why trade fails to expand. The major reason why trade remains at low levels is that the Indian and Chinese economies did not develop in a complementary fashion. (This also helps explain why China-Pakistan trade remained at a low level despite very good political relations). With the implementation of market reforms and the opening up to the outside world in China, and the new policy of economic liberalization adopted by India, potential new areas of trade have emerged. India has begun to import steel-making and coal-mining technologies from China. Computer software is a highly developed field in India, while China is a lucrative market for Indian software. China is also offering highly competitive rates for launching Indian satellites. However, the decades-long suspension of trade has meant that no infrastructure exists for direct trade. There are no direct shipping lines or airline connections and no interstate banks. Postal communications are pitifully slow. Establishing a reliable infrastructure for direct trade is the first step in improving economic relations. Traders do not even know what the market in the other country is like. Like companies, these two governments might consider doing their own market research.[9]

Border Trade. Border trade is extremely important, despite its limited nature due to the rugged terrain separating both countries. Increased border trade would be highly beneficial for the people who live in these areas so remote from the main production centers in both India and China. Since 1988, two trading posts on the India-China border have been opened and are a great success. More such posts have not been opened because the issue of sovereignty of the passes at which additional trade can be carried out is still contested between the two governments. Pending the final settlement of the India-China border dispute, additional passes could be opened for trade along the LAC without prejudice to the claims of either side. The agreement over the LAC signed in September 1993 incorporates this principle, leaving specific actions up to both sides.

Cultural Exchanges. Cultural exchanges are an important mechanism for promoting mutual understanding between the Chinese and Indian peoples. The ancient pilgrimage of Chinese monk Tang Seng to India during the Tang Dynasty is well known throughout China and India. Many others have made similar pilgrimages to different parts of India. Zheng He's naval expeditions also touched many Indian ports. Rabindranath Tagore, the great Indian poet, is held in high esteem by Chinese intellectuals, and "Awara," an Indian film featuring Raj Kapoor, has been popular in parts of China. Similarly, in India, there is great interest in Lu Xun, the Chinese writer. In the future, the cultural departments of the two countries could formulate a program to translate contemporary literary masterpieces into each other's language, in order to cultivate cross-national artistic and literary interests. Academic, literary, and art circles in both countries are eagerly waiting to meet their counterparts.

Touching Upon Thorns: Relations with Pakistan and Tibet

The Pakistan factor has always loomed large in Sino-Indian relations, particularly in Indian eyes. As Sino-Indian relations worsened, Sino-Pakistani relations became correspondingly warmer. The axis between Beijing and Islamabad came to be seen by India in a sinister light, as it was assumed to be based on China's enduring hostility toward India. The assumption became entrenched by the China-Pakistan treaty of 1963 ceding the Aksai Chin part of Kashmir to China, Beijing's *gratis* military aid to Pakistan, Chinese statements around the Indo-Pakistan wars of 1965 and 1971, and alleged Chinese help to Pakistan's nuclear weapon program.[10]

In light of past allegations of Chinese support for Pakistan's nuclear program, mutual confidence building between India and China will remain seriously incomplete unless Sino-Pakistani relations are more transparent to India. Of course, so long as relations between India and Pakistan remain at a low ebb, Pakistan's relations with any major power will be suspiciously watched in India. Under the present circumstances, India and China should begin a frank dialogue on the Pakistan factor in their relations.

Dialogue on Tibet. During the British rule in India, Britain acquired several privileges in Tibet as a part of its imperial design. Britain wanted Tibet as a "buffer zone" between China and India as well as between India and Russia. After the independence of India, Prime Minister Jawaharlal Nehru described China's action to liberate Tibet as a "surprise onslaught" and instructed the Indian Government to address diplomatic notes to China conveying India's "regret" and "protest" at the Chinese action. On April 29, 1954, he reversed course, signing an "Agreement between China and India on trade and intercourse between the Tibet region of China and India." Later, in the Indian parliament on September 30, 1954, he explained that the government of India had no alternative but gracefully to give up the rights that the British had acquired by coercion in Tibet. By a simultaneous exchange of notes, India agreed to withdraw its military contingent stationed in Tibet and to hand over to China its posts and telegraphs installations in Tibet.

Since then, Nehru and succeeding Indian leaders never repudiated the status of Tibet as defined by both sides in 1954. During a visit to China in

December 1988, Prime Minister Rajiv Gandhi explicitly reaffirmed Tibet's status as an autonomous region of China. Subsequently, even during the 1989 riots in Lhasa, the Indian government adhered to this position.

Some in India, including politicians within the ruling and opposition parties, continue to support the demand for Tibetan independence. With the differing perceptions that still exist over Tibet, it would be wise for India and China to continue their dialogue on this region, perhaps even issuing a joint statement regarding their common understanding of Tibet's status.

Conditions Ripe for Reconciliation

The basis for stronger CBMs between India and China clearly exists. The authors are persuaded that measures can be implemented in the areas listed for several reasons.

First, the two countries have adopted similar positions on many key issues in the post-Cold War world. In his talks with Prime Minister Rao, Premier Li Peng noted that the international situation had become turbulent, with bloody conflicts occurring in the areas adjacent to Europe. In contrast, the political climate in Asia continues to turn for the better: regional disputes are in the process of settlement, the political situation in most Asian countries is relatively stable, and bilateral relations between countries in the region have improved. Areas of contention between China and India are in the process of being resolved.

Second, there is a new level of political maturity in Sino-Indian relations. As Prime Minister Rao observed during his visit, "The two sides do not allow differences between them to hamper their mutually beneficial cooperation."[11] Furthermore, Rao visited China before the United States and Russia, as is the custom. On the other side, China accorded Rao a top-level reception. Out of the seven members of the Standing Committee of the Politburo of the Chinese Communist Party, the Indian prime minister met five; the other two were abroad. This was the highest-level reception given to a visiting foreign dignitary by China in a decade. Moreover, these five Politburo members all accepted invitations to visit India, further indication of a high-level commitment to build confidence and improve bilateral relations.

Third, the Soviet Union is no longer a deterrent to improved Sino-Indian relations. In the past, the Kremlin tried repeatedly to drive a wedge between India and China. Thus, in 1976, when Indian Prime Minster Indira Gandhi decided to normalize relations with China and took the initiative to restore Sino-Indian diplomatic relations at the ambassadorial level, she made the decision before her visit to Moscow and without prior consultation with the Kremlin. In the three years from 1979 to 1982, top Soviet leaders visited India. Among those who paid visits were General Secretary L. Brezhnev, Prime Minister A. Kosygin, First Vice-President of the Supreme Soviet Presidium V. Kuznetsov, and Defense Minister D. Ustinov. During his stay in India, Kosygin made a speech highly critical of China. Kuznetsov asked India to guarantee that its exchanges with China "would not rebound to Moscow's disadvantage" and warned India of the "forces on the continent of Asia" that had "hegemonic designs and territorial claims on contiguous states." Ustinov, accompanied by the Soviet navy and air force chiefs, the deputy chief of the army and thirty other high-ranking officers, warned India of the "danger of taking Beijing's protestations of friendship at face value" and asked India to cooperate with the Soviet Union militarily in order to cope with "militarism" and "expansionism."

During Rao's visit to the Soviet Union in 1981 as Indian foreign minister—following Chinese Foreign Minister Huang Hua's visit to India three weeks earlier—pressure was brought to bear upon Rao to inform Moscow about his talks with Huang Hua and to guarantee that any change in Sino-Indian relations would not be at the Soviet Union's expense. Again, when Prime Minister Indira Gandhi revisited Moscow in September 1982, Soviet leaders warned her that "China's ultimate aim is to dominate all of Asia" and expressed to her their "concern" over her inclination to "play the China card."

The clear purpose behind these Soviet moves was to impede improved Sino-Indian relations. It was only when Mikhail Gorbachev assumed the leadership of the Soviet Union that Moscow began to change its policy toward Sino-Indian relations. The Russian government of Boris Yeltsin, to all appearances, seems to have decided to continue Gorbachev's policy. Hence, a formidable obstacle to friendly relations and mutual trust between China and India has now been removed.

Fourth, China and India are both engaged in economic reform efforts that can yield significant mutual benefit. The summit meetings between Prime Minister Rao and Premier Li Peng were particularly devoted to increased economic and trade cooperation. In January 1993, during a meeting of the Sino-Indian Joint Group on Economic Relations, Trade, Science and Technology, Li Lanqing, leader of the Chinese delegation, drew particular attention to the potential for Sino-Indian cooperation in the fields of aviation, electronics, railways, machine-building, mining, and construction. Lanqing said also that he was optimistic that the trade figure could jump ten times, to $3 billion, in the near future. China and India are two of the biggest potential markets in the world. They have unlimited prospects for developing stronger economic relations to their mutual benefit. In 1983, China purchased only about 100,000 tons of iron ore from India. One decade later, the figure reached 4 million tons.

Fifth, a consensus within India exists today on improving relations with China, constituting a firm foundation for the establishment and implementation of CBMs. When Indira Gandhi began to think in terms of fully normalizing India's relations with China during her last years in office, she was inclined to settle the border problem with China on the basis of mutual concessions. But strenuous political opposition shelved her initiative. Sensing that public opinion in India was in favor of a settlement with China, she decided to resume negotiations on a new footing after the general elections of 1984. Her assassination pushed this issue to the back-burner. Rajiv Gandhi's visit to China in December 1988 was made after clearing away a number of obstacles and overcoming resistance within the government. After his visit, a consensus in favor of friendship with China became visible in India, becoming even more visible after Prime Minister Rao's visit in September 1993. Before his departure for China, Rao discussed the issue with leaders of the opposition parties, including the Bharatiya Janata Party, the Janata Dal and the CPI(M), and received their approval.[12]

Conclusion

The possibility of improved Sino-Indian relations has great significance, both in economic and strategic terms. The resolution of the border dispute can set an example, especially for the developing countries, that peaceful resolution of seemingly intractable disputes is possible between nations. Confidence-building measures can also provide experience and insights for the peaceful settlement of other disputes in the region. The authors are persuaded that the establishment and implementation of CBMs between China and India will pave the way to the ultimate resolution of their boundary problem, while encouraging more countries in the region to engage in similar activities.

NOTES

1. *Xin Hua* News Agency, Beijing, September 7, 1993.
2. *Times of India,* September 8, 1993.
3. K. Subrahmanyam, "Path to Nuclear Disarmament," *USI Journal,* New Delhi, No. 4-6, (1993), 205-215.
4. Ramesh, Thakur, *International Herald Tribune,* February 1, 1993.
5. *Associated Press,* January 6, 1995.
6. E. Ted Gladue Jr., *China's Perception of Global Politics* (Washington: University Press of America, 1982).
7. *The Hindu* (Madras), October 6, 1994.
8. See speeches from the Confederation of India Industry Seminar on India-China Trade, October, 27, 1994.
9. Shri Prakash, "Economic Dimensions of Sino-Indian Relations," *China Report,* (April/June 1994): 248-250.
10. Raj Chengappa, "India-China Relations: Issues and Implications," *Strategic Analysis,* (April 1993): 41.
11. *Economic Times,* September 7, 1993.
12. *Indian Express,* January 6, 1993.

APPENDIX:
TEXT OF AGREEMENTS TO REDUCE TENSIONS IN SOUTH ASIA

Partial list, arranged chronologically.

I. AGREEMENTS BETWEEN INDIA AND PAKISTAN

The Karachi Agreement

July 27, 1949 (Karachi)

A. Considering:

1. That the United Nations Commission for India and Pakistan, in its letter dated 2 July 1949, invited the Governments of India and Pakistan to send fully authorized military representatives to meet jointly in Karachi under auspices of the Commission's Truce Sub-Committee to establish a cease-fire line in the State of Jammu and Kashmir, mutually agreed upon by the Governments of India and Pakistan;
2. That the United Nations Commission for India and Pakistan in its letter stated that "the meetings will be for military purposes; political issues will not be considered," and that "they will be conducted without prejudice to negotiations concerning the truce agreement;"
3. That in the same letter the United Nations Commission on India and Pakistan further stated that: "The cease-fire is a complement of the suspension of hostilities, which falls within the provisions of part I of the resolution of 13 August 1948, and can be considered separately from the question relating to part II, of the same resolution;"
4. That the Governments of India and Pakistan, in their letters dated 7 July 1949 to the Chairman of the Commission, accepted the Commission's invitation to the military conference in Karachi;

B. The delegations of India and Pakistan, duly authorized, have reached the following agreement:

1. Under provisions of part I of the resolution of 13 August 1948, and as a complement of the suspension of hostilities in the State of Jammu and Kashmir on 1 January 1949, a cease-fire line is established.
2. The cease-fire line runs from Manawar in the south, north to Keran, and from Keran east to the glacier area, as follows:
   (a) The line from Manawar to the south bank of the Jhelum River at Urusa (inclusive to India) is the line now defined by factual positions about which there is agreement between both parties. Where there has hitherto not been agreement, the line shall be as follows:
      (i) In the Patrana area: Kohel (inclusive to Pakistan) north along the Khuwala Kas Nullah up to Point 2276 (inclusive to India), thence to Kirni (inclusive to India).
      (ii) Khamba, Pir Satwan, Point 3150 and Point 3606 are inclusive to India, thence the line runs to the factual position at Bagla Gala, thence to the factual position at point 3300.
      (iii) In the area south of Uri the positions of Pir Kanthi and Leda Gali are inclusive to Pakistan.

(b) From the north bank of the Jhelum River the line runs from a point opposite the village of Urusa (NL 972109), thence north following the Ballaseth Da Nar Nullah (inclusive to Pakistan), up to NL 973140, thence north-east to Chhota Qazinag (Point 10657, inclusive to India), thence to NM010180, thence to NM037210, thence to Point 11825 (NM 025354, inclusive to Pakistan), thence to Tumari Gali (to be shared by both sides, posts to be established 500 yards on either side of the Gali),thence to the north-west through the first "R" of the Burji Nar to north of Gadori, thence straight west to just north of Point 9870, thence along the black line north of Bijidhar to north of Batarasi, thence to just south of Sudpura, thence due north to the Kathaqazinag Nullah thence along the Nullah to its junction with the Grangar Nullah, thence along the latter Nullah of Kajnwala Pathra (inclusive to India), thence across the Danna ridge (following the factual positions) to Richmar Gali (inclusive to India), thence north to Thanda Katha Nullah, thence north to the Kishanganga River. The line then follows the Kishanganga River up to a point situated between Jargi and Tarban, thence (all inclusive to Pakistan), to Bankoran thence north-east to Khori, thence to the hill feature 8930 (in Square 9053), thence straight north to Point 10164 (in Square 9057), thence to Point 10323 (in Square 9161), thence north-east straight to Guthur, thence to Bhutpathra, thence to NL980707, thence following the Bugina Nullah to the junction with the Kishanganga River at Point 4739. Thereafter the line follows the Kishanganga River to Keran and onwards to Point 4996 (NL 975818).

(c) From Point 4996 the line follows (all inclusive to Pakistan) the Jamgar Nulla eastward to Point 12124, to Katware, to Point 6678, then north-east to Sarian (Point 11279) to Point 11837, to Point 13090, to Point 12641, thence east again to Point 11142, thence to Dhakki, thence to Point 11415, thence to point 10301, thence to Point 7507, thence to Point 10685, thence to Point 8388, thence south-east to Point 11812. Thence the line runs (all inclusive to India) to Point 13220, thence across the river to the east to Point 13449 (Durmat), thence to Point 14586 (Anzbari), thence to Point 13554, thence to Milestone 45 on the Burzil Nullah, thence to the east to Ziankal (Point 12909), thence to the south-east to Point 1114, thence to Point 12216, thence to Point 12867, thence to the east to Point 11264, thence to Karo (Point 14985), thence to Point 14014, thence to Point 12089, thence following the track to Point 12879. From there the line runs to Point 13647 (Karobal Gali, to be shared by both sides). The cease-fire line runs thence throughout Retagah Chhish (Point 15316), thence through Point 15889, thence through Point 17392, thence through Point 16458, thence to Marpo La (to be shared by both sides), thence to Point 17561, thence through Point 17352, thence through Point 18400, thence through Point 16760, thence to (inclusive to India) Dalunang.

(d) From Dalunang eastwards the cease-fire line will follow the general line Point 15495, Ishmam, Manus, Gangam, Gunderman, Point 13620, Junkar (Point 17628), Marmak, Natsara, Shangruti (Point 17531), Chorbat La (Point 16700), Chalunka (on the Shyok River), Khor, thence north to the glaciers. This portion of the cease-fire line shall be demarcated in detail on the basis of the factual position as of 27 July 1949 by the local commanders, assisted by the United Nations Military Observers.

C. The cease-fire line described above shall be drawn on a one-inch map (where available) and then be verified mutually on the ground by local commanders on each side with the assistance of the United Nations Military Observers, so as to eliminate any no-man's land. In the event that the local commanders are unable to reach agreement, the matter shall be referred to the Commission's Military Adviser, whose decision shall be final. After this verification, the Military Adviser will issue to each High Command a map on which will be marked the definitive cease-fire line.

D. No troops shall be stationed or operate in the areas of the Burzil Nullah from south of Minimarg to the cease-fire line. This area is bounded on the west by the ridge leading north-east from Dudgaikal to Point 13071, to Point 9447, to Point 13466, to Point 13463, and on the east by the ridge running from Point 12470, to Point 11608, to Point 13004, to Point 13976, to Point 13450. Pakistan may, however, post troops on the Western [*sic*] of the above ridges to cover the approaches to Kamri Bal Pass.

E. In any dispositions that may be adopted in consequence of the present agreement troops will remain at least 500 yards from the cease-fire line except where the Kishanganga River constitutes the line. Points which have been shown as inclusive to party may be occupied by that party, but the troops of the other party shall remain at a distance of 500 yards.

F. Both sides shall be free to adjust their defensive positions behind the cease-fire line as determined in parargraphs A through E, inclusive, subject to no wire or mines being used when new bunkers and defences are constructed. There shall be no increase of forces or strengthening of defences in area where no major adjustments are involved by the determination of the cease-fire line.

G. The action permitted by paragraph F above shall not be accompanied or accomplished by the introduction of additional military potential by either side into the State of Jammu and Kashmir.

H. Except as modified by paragraphs A to G, inclusive, above, the military agreements between the two High Commands relating to the cease-fire of 1 January 1949 shall continue to remain operative.

I. The United Nations Commission for India and Pakistan will station observers where it deems necessary.

J. The delegations shall refer this agreement to their respective Governments for ratification. The documents of ratification shall be deposited with the United Nations Commission for India and Pakistan not later than 31 July 1949.

K. A period of thirty days from the date of ratification shall be allowed to each side to vacate the areas at present occupied by them beyond the cease-fire line as now determined. Before the expiration of this thirty day period there shall be no forward movement into areas to be taken over by either side pursuant to this agreement, except by mutual agreement between local commanders.

In faith whereof the undersigned sign this document in three original copies.
Done in Karachi on 27 July 1949.

[Signed:]

S.M. Shrinagesh
Republic of India

J. Cawthorn
Islamic Republic of Pakistan

Hernando Samper
M. Delvoie
United Nations Commission for India and Pakistan

The Liaquat-Nehru Agreement

April 8, 1950 (New Delhi)

A. The Governments of India and Pakistan solemnly agree that each shall ensure to the minorities throughout its territory, complete equality of citizenship, irrespective of religion, a full sense of security in respect of life, culture, property and personal honour, freedom of movement within each country and freedom of occupation, speech and worship, subject to law and morality. Members of the minorities shall have equal opportunity with members of the majority community to participate in the public life of their country, to hold political or other office, and to serve in their country's civil and armed forces. Both Governments declare these rights to be fundamental and undertake to enforce them effectively. The Prime Minister of India has drawn attention to the fact that these rights are guaranteed to all minorities in India by its Constitution. The Prime Minister of Pakistan has pointed out that similar provision exists in the Objectives Resolution adopted by the Constituent Assembly of Pakistan. It is the policy of both Governments that the enjoyment of these democratic rights shall be assured to all their nationals without distinction.

Both Governments wish to emphasize that the allegiance and loyalty of the minorities is to the State of which they are citizens, and that it is to the Government of their own State that they should look for the redress of their grievances.

B. In the respect of migrants from East Bengal, West Bengal, Assam and Tripura, where communal disturbances have recently occured, it is agreed between the two Governments:

(i) That there shall be freedom of movement and protection in transit;

(ii) That there shall be freedom to remove as much of his movable personal effects and household goods as a migrant may wish to take with him. Movable property shall include personal jewellery. The maximum cash allowed to each adult migrant will be Rs. 150 and to each migrant child Rs. 75;

(iii) That a migrant may deposit such of his personal jewellery or cash as he does not wish to take with him with a bank. A proper receipt shall be furnished to him by the bank for cash or jewellery thus deposited and facilities shall be provided, as and when required, for the transfer to him, subject as regards cash to the exchange regulations of the Government concerned;

(iv) That there shall be no harassment by the Customs authorities. At each Customs post agreed upon by the Governments concerned, liaison officers of the other Government shall be posted to ensure this in practice;

(v) Rights of ownership in or occupancy of the immovable property of a migrant shall not be disturbed. If, during his absence, such property is occupied by another person, it shall be returned to him provided that he comes back by the 31st March 1951. In exceptional cases, if a Government considers that a migrant's immovable property cannot be returned to him, the matter shall be referred to the appropriate Minority Commission for advice. Where restoration of immovable property to the migrant who returns within the specified period is found not possible the Government concerned shall take steps to rehabilitate him.

(vi) That in the case of a migrant who decides not to return, ownership of all his immovable property shall continue to vest in him and he shall have unrestricted right to dispose of it by sale, by evacuee in the other country, or otherwise. A Committee consisting of three representatives of the minority and presided over by a representative of Government shall act as trustees of the owner. The Committee shall be empowered to recover rent for such immovable property according to the law.

The Government of East Bengal, West Bengal, Assam and Tripura shall enact the necessary legislation to set up these Committees.

The Provincial or State Government as the case may be, will instruct the District or other appropriate authority to give all possible assistance for the discharge of the Committee's functions.

The provisions of this sub-paragraph shall also apply to migrants who may have left East Bengal for any part of India, or West Bengal, Assam or Tripura for any part of Pakistan, prior to the recent disturbances but after the 15th August, 1947. The agreement in this sub-paragraph will apply also to migrants who have left Bihar for East Bengal owing to communal disturbances or fear thereof.

C. As regards the Province of East Bengal and each of the States of West Bengal, Assam and Tripura respectively the two Governments further agree that they shall:

(1) Continue their efforts to restore normal conditions and shall take suitable measures to prevent recurrence of disorder.

(2) Punish all those who are found guilty of offences against persons and property and of other criminal offences. In view of their deterrent effect, collective fines shall be imposed where necessary. Special Courts will, where necessary, be appointed to ensure that wrongdoers are promptly punished.

(3) Make every possible effort to recover looted property.

(4) Set up immediately an agency with which representatives of the minority shall be associated, to assist in the recovery of abducted women.

(5) Not to recognise forced conversions. Any conversion effected during a period of communal disturbance shall be deemed to be a forced conversion. Those found guilty of converting people forcibly shall be punished.

(6) Set up a Commission of Enquiry at once to enquire into and report on the causes and extent of the recent disturbances and to make recommendations with a view to preventing recrudescence of similar trouble in future. The personnel of the Commission, which shall be presided over by a Judge of the High Court, shall be such as to inspire confidence among the minority.

(7) Take prompt and effective steps to prevent the dissemination of news and mischievous opinion calculated to rouse communal passions by press or radio or by any individual or organization. Those guilty of such activity shall be vigorously dealt with.

(8) Not permit propoganda in either country directed against the territorial integrity of the other or purporting to incite war between them and shall take prompt and effective action against any individual or organization guilty of such propoganda.

D. Sub-paragraphs(1),(2),(3),(4),(5),(7) and (8) of C of the Agreement are of general scope and applicable according to exigency to any part of India or Pakistan.

E. In order to help restore confidence, so that refugees may return to their homes, the two Governments have decided:

(i) to depute two Ministers, one from each Government to remain in the affected areas for such period as may be necessary;

(ii) to include in the Cabinets of East Bengal, West Bengal and Assam a representative of the minority community. In Assam the minority community is already represented in the cabinet. Appointments to the cabinets of East Bengal and West Bengal shall be made immediately.

F. In order to assist in the implementation of this Agreement, the two Governments have decided, apart from the deputation of their Ministers referred to in E, to set up Minority Commissions one for East Bengal, one for West Bengal and one for Assam. These Commissions will be constituted and will have the functions described below.

(i) Each Commission will consist of one Minister of the Provincial or State Governments concerned, who will be Chairman, and one representative each of the majority and minority communities from East Bengal, West Bengal and Assam chosen by and from among their respective representatives in the Provincial or State Legislatures, as the case may be.

(ii) Two Ministers of the Governments of India and Pakistan may attend and participate in any meeting of any Commission. A minority Commission or any two Minority Commissions jointly shall meet when so required by either Central Minister for the satisfactory implementation of this agreement.

(iii) Each Commission shall appoint such staff as it deems necessary for the proper discharge of its functions and shall determine its own procedure.

(iv) Each Commission shall maintain contact with the minorities in Districts and small administrative headquarters through Minority Boards formed in accordance with the Inter-Dominion Agreement of December, 1948.

(v) The Minority Commissions in East Bengal and West Bengal shall replace the Provincial Minorities Boards set up under the Inter-Dominion Agreement of December, 1948.

(vi) The two Ministers of the Central Governments will from time to time consult such persons or organizations as they may consider necessary.

(vii) The functions of the Minority Commission shall be:

(a) To observe and to report on the implementation of this agreement and for this purpose, to take cognizance of breaches or neglect.

(b) To advise on action to be taken on their,recommendations.

(vii) Each Commission shall submit reports, as and when necessary, to the provincial and State Governments concerned. Copies of such reports will be submitted simultaneously to the two Central Ministers during the period referred to in E.

(ix) The Governments of India and Pakistan and the State and Provincial Governments, will normally give effect to recommendations that concern them when such recommendations are supported by both the Central Ministers. In the event of disagreement between the two Central Ministers, the matter shall be referred to the Prime Ministers of India and Pakistan who shall either resolve it themselves or determine the agency and procedure by which it will be resolved.

(x) In respect of Tripura, the two Central Ministers shall constitute a Commission and shall discharge the functions that are assigned under the Agreement to the Minority Commissions for East Bengal, West Bengal and Assam. Before the expiration of the period referred to in E, the two Central Ministers shall make recommendations for the establishment in Tripura of appropriate machinery to discharge the functions of the Minority Commissions envisaged in respect of East Bengal, West Bengal and Assam.

G. Except where modified by this Agreement, the Inter-Dominion Agreement of December 1948 shall remain in force.

[Signed:]

Jawaharlal Nehru
Prime Minister of India

Liaquat Ali Khan
Prime Minister of Pakistan

The Indus Waters Treaty (Abridged)
September 19, 1960 (Karachi)

The Government of India and the Government of Pakistan, being equally desirous of attaining the most complete and satisfactory utilisation of the waters of the Indus system of rivers and recognising the need, therefore, of fixing and delineating, in a spirit of goodwill and friendship, the rights and obligations of each in relation to the other concerning the use of these waters and of making provision for the settlement, in a cooperative spirit, of all such questions as may hereafter arise in regard to the interpretation or application of the provisions agreed upon herein, have resolved to conclude a Treaty in furtherance of these objectives, and for this purpose have named as their plenipotentiaries:

The Government of India: Shri Jawaharlal Nehru, Prime Minister of India, and The Government of Pakistan: Field Marshal Mohammad Ayub Khan, H.P., H.J., President of Pakistan, who, having communicated to each other their respective Full Powers and having found them in good and due form, have agreed upon the following Articles and Annexures:

Provisions Regarding Eastern Rivers

All the waters of the Eastern Rivers shall be available for the unrestricted use of Inida, except as otherwise expressly provided in this Article.

Except for Domestic Use and Non-Consumptive Use, Pakistan shall be under an obligation to let flow, and shall not permit any interference with, the waters of the Sutlej Main and the Ravi Main in the reaches where these rivers flow in Pakistan and have not yet finally crossed into Pakistan. The points of final crossing are the following: (a) near the new Hasta Bund upstream of Suleimanke in the case of the Sutlej Main, and (b) about one and a half miles upstream of the syphon for the B-D Link in the case of the Ravi Main.

Except for Domestic Use, Non-Consumptive Use and Agricultural Use, Pakistan shall be under an obligation to let flow, and shall not permit any interference with, the waters (while flowing in Pakistan) of any Tributary which in its natural course joins the Sutlej Main or the Ravi Main before these rivers have finally crossed into Pakistan.

All the waters, while flowing in Pakistan, of any Tributary which, in its natural course, joins the Sutlej Main or the Ravi Main after these rivers have finally crossed into Pakistan shall be available for the unrestricted use of Pakistan: Provided however that this provision shall not be construed as giving Pakistan any claim or right to any releases by India in any such Tributary.

There shall be a Transition Period during which India shall (i) limit its withdrawals for Agricultural Use, (ii) limit abstractions for storages, and (iii) make deliveries to Pakistan from the Eastern Rivers.

The Transition Period shall begin on 1st April 1960 and it shall end on 31st March 1970, or, if extended under the provisions of Part 8 of Annexure H, on the date up to which it has been extended. In any event, whether the Transition Period shall end not later than 31st March 1973.

During the Transition Period, Pakistan shall receive for unrestricted use the waters of the Eastern Rivers which are to be released by India in accordance with the provisions of Annexure H. After the end of the Transition Period, Pakistan shall have no claim or right to releases by India of any of the waters of the Eastern Rivers. In case there are any releases, Pakistan shall enjoy the unrestricted use of the waters so released after they have finally crossed into Pakistan: Provided that in the event that Pakistan makes any use of these waters, Pakistan shall not acquire any right whatsover, by prescription or otherwise, to a continuance of such releases or such use.

Provision Regarding Western Rivers

Pakistan shall receive for unrestricted use all those waters of the Western Rivers which India is under obligation to let flow under the provisions of Paragraph (2).

India shall be under an obligation to let flow all the waters of the Western Rivers, and shall not permit any interference with these waters, except for the following uses, restricted in the case of each of the rivers, The Indus, The Jhelum and The Chenab, to the drainage basin thereof: (a) Domestic Use; (b) Non-Consumptive Use; (c) Agricultural Use, as set out in Annexure C; and (d) Generation of hydro-electric power, as set out in Annexure D.

Pakistan shall have the unrestricted use of all waters originating from sources other than the Eastern Rivers which are delivered by Pakistan into The Ravi or The Sutlej, and India shall not make use of these waters.

Except as provided in Annexures D and E, India shall not store any water of, or construct any storage works on, the Western Rivers.

Provisions Regarding Eastern Rivers and Western Rivers

Pakistan shall use its best endeavors to construct and bring into operation with due regard to expedition and economy, that part of a system of work which will accomplish the replacement, from the Western Rivers and other sources, of water supplies for irrigation canals in Pakistan which, on 15th August 1947, were dependent on water supplies from the Eastern Rivers.

Each Party agrees that any Non-Consumptive Use made by it shall be made as not to materially change, on account of such use, the flow in any channel to the prejudice of the uses on that channel by the other Party under the provisions of this Treaty.

Nothing in this Treaty shall be construed as having the effect of preventing either Party from undertaking schemes of drainage, river training, conservation of soil against erosion and dredging, or from removal of stones, gravel or sand from the beds of the Rivers: Provided that in executing any of the schemes mentioned above, each Party will avoid, as far as practicable, any material damage to the other Party.

Pakistan shall maintain in good order its portions of the drainages mentioned below with capacities not less than the capacities as on the Effective Date: (i) Hudiara Drain, (ii) Kasur Nala, (iii) Salimshah Drain, (iv) Fazilka Drain.

If Inida finds it necessary that any of the drainages mentioned in Paragraph (4) should be deepened or widened in Pakistan, Pakistan agrees to undertake to do so as a work of public interest, provided India agrees to pay the cost of the deepening or widening.

Each Party will use its best endeavors to maintain the natural channels of the Rivers, as on the Effective Date, in such condition as will avoid, as far as practicable, any obstruction to the flow in these channels likely to cause material damage to the other Party.

Neither Party will take any action which would have the effect of diverting the Ravi Main between Madhopur and Lahore, or the Sutlej Main between Harike and Suleimanke, from its natural channel between high banks.

The use of the natural channels of the Rivers for the discharge of flood or other excess waters shall be free and not subject to limitation by either Party, and neither Party shall have any claim against the other in respect of any damage caused by such use. Each Party agrees to communicate to the other Party, as far in advance as practicable, any information it may have in regard to such extraordinary discharges of water from reservoirs and flood flows as may affect the other Party.

Each Party declares its intention to operate its storage dams, barrages and irrigation canals in such manner, consistent with the normal operations of its hydraulic systems, as to avoid, as far as feasible, material damage to the other Party.

Each Party declares its intention to prevent, as far as practicable, undue pollution of the waters of the Rivers which might affect adversely uses similar in nature to those to which the waters were put on the Effective Date, and agrees to take all reasonable measures to ensure that, before any sewage or industrial waste is allowed to flow into the Rivers, it will be treated, where necessary, in such manner as not materially to affect those uses: Provided that the criterion of reasonableness shall be the customary practice in similar situations on the Rivers.

The Parties agree to adopt, as far as feasible, appropriate measures for recovery, and restoration to owners, of timber and other property floated or floating down the Rivers, subject to appropriate charges being paid by the owners.

Except as otherwise required by the express provisions of this Treaty, nothing in this Treaty shall be construed as affecting existing territorial rights over the waters of any of the Rivers or the beds or banks thereof, or as affecting existing property rights under municipal law over such waters or beds or banks.

Financial Provisions

In consideration of the fact that the purpose of part of the system of works referred to in Article IV (1) is the replacement, from the Western Rivers and other sources, of water supplies for irrigation canals in Pakistan which on 15th August 1947 were dependent on water supplies from the Eastern Rivers, India agrees to make a fixed contribution of Pounds Sterling 62,060,000 towards the costs of these works.

The sum of Pounds Sterling 62,060,000 shall be paid in ten equal installments on the 1st of November of each year.

Each of the instalments shall be paid to the Bank for the credit of the Indus Basin Development Fund to be established and administered by the Bank.

These financial provisions shall not be construed as conferring upon India any right to participate in the decisions as to the system of works which Pakistan constructs or as constituting an assumption of any responsibility by India or as an agreement by India in regard to such works.

Except for such payments as are specifically provided for in this Treaty, neither Party shall be entitled to claim any payment for observance of the provisions of this Treaty or to make any charge for water received from it by the other Party.

Exchange of Data

The following data with respect to the flow in, and utilisation of the waters of, the Rivers shall be exchanged regularly between the Parties: (a) Daily guage and discharge data relating to flow of the Rivers at all observation sites. (b) Daily extractions for or releases from reservoirs. (c) Daily withdrawals at the heads of all canals operated by government or by a government agency, including link canals. (d) Daily escapages from all canals, including link canals. (e) Daily deliveries from link canals.

Future Co-operation

The two Parties recognize that they have a common interest in the optimum development of the Rivers, and, to that end, they declare their intention to co-operate, by mutual agreement, to the fullest possible extent.

Permanent Indus Commission

India and Pakistan shall each create a permanent post of Commissioner for Indus Waters, and shall appoint to this post, as often as a vacancy occurs, a person who should ordinarily be a high-ranking engineer competent in the field of hydrology and water-use. Unless either Government should decide to take up any particular question directly with the other Government, each Commissioner will be the representative of his Government for all matters arising out of this Treaty, and will serve as the regular channel of communication on all matters relating to the implementation of the Treaty, and, in particular, with respect to (a) the furnishing or exchange of information or data provided for in the Treaty; and (b) the giving of any notice or response to any notice provided for in the Treaty.

The status of each Commissioner and his duties and responsibilities towards his Government will be determined by that Government.

The two Commissioners shall together form the Permanent Indus Commission.

The purpose and functions of the Commission shall be to establish and maintain co-operative arrangements for the implementation of this Treaty and to promote co-operation between the Parties in the development of the waters of the Rivers.

The Commission shall determine its own procedures.

Settlement of Differences and Disputes

Any question which arises between the Parties concerning the interpretation or application of this Treaty or the existence of any fact which, if established, might constitute a breach of this Treaty shall first be examined by the Commission, which will endeavor to resolve the question by agreement.

If the Commission does not reach agreement on any of the questions mentioned in the Paragraph (1), then a difference will be deemed to have arisen, which shall be dealt with by a Neutral Expert. If the Neutral Expert has informed the Commission that, in his opinion, the difference should be treated as a dispute, then a dispute will be deemed to have arisen.

As soon as a dispute to be settled has arisen, the Commission shall, at the request of either Commissioner, report the fact to the two Governments, as early as practicable, stating in its report the points on which the Commisssion is in agreement and the issues in dispute, the views of each Commissioner on these issues and his reasons therefor.

Either Government may, following receipt of the report, or if it comes to the conclusion that this report is being unduly delayed in the Commission, invite the other Government to resolve the dispute by agreement.

A court of Arbitration shall be established to resolve the dispute.

Emergency Provisions

If, at any time prior to 31st March 1965, Pakistan should represent to the Bank that, because of the outbreak of large-scale international hostilities arising out of causes beyond the control of Pakistan, it is unable to obtain from abroad the materials and equipment necessary for the completion, by 31st March 1973, of that part of the system of works referred to in Article IV (1) which related to the replacement referred to therein, (hereinafter referred to as the "replacement element") and if, after consideration of this representation in consultation with India, the Bank is of the opinion that (a) these hostilities are on a scale of which the consequence is that Pakistan is unable to obtain in time such materials and equipment as must be procured from abroad for the completion, by 31st March 1973, of the replacement element, and (b) since the Effective Date, Pakistan has taken all reasonable steps to obtain the said materials and equipment and has carried forward the construction of the replacement element with due dilligence and all reasonable expedition, the Bank shall immediately notify each of the Parties accordingly. The Parties undertake that in being so notified, they will forthwith consult together and enlist the good offices of the Bank in their consultation, with a view to reaching mutual agreement as to whether or not, in light of all circumstances prevailing, any modifications of the provisions of this Treaty are appropriate and advisable and, if so, the nature and the extent of the modifications.

Final Provisions

This Treaty consists of the Preamble, the Articles hereof and Annexures A to H hereto, and may be cited as "The Indus Waters Treaty 1960."

This Treaty shall be ratified and the ratifications therof shall be exchanged in New Delhi. It shall enter into force upon the exchange of ratifications, and will then take effect retrospectively form the first of April 1960.

The provisions of this Treaty may from time to time be modified by a duly ratified treaty concluded for that purpose between the two Governments.

The provisions of this Treaty, or the provisions of this Treaty as modified under the provisions of Paragraph (3), shall continue in force until terminated by a duly ratified treaty concluded for that purpose between the two Governments.

In witness whereof the respective Plenipotentiaries have signed this Treaty and have hereunto affixed their seals.

Done in triplicate in English at Karachi on this Nineteenth day of September 1960.

[Signed:]

For the Government of India:
Jawaharlal Nehru

For the Government of Pakistan:
Mohammad Ayub Khan
Field Marshal, H.P., H.J.

For the International Bank for Reconstruction and Development:
W. A. B. Iliff

The Tashkent Declaration

January 10 1966 (Tashkent)

The Prime Minister of India and the President of Pakistan having met at Tashkent and having discussed the existing relations between India and Pakistan, hereby declare their firm resolve to restore normal and peaceful relations between their countries and to promote understanding and friendly relations between their peoples. They consider the attainment of these objectives of vital importance for the welfare of the 600 million people of India and Pakistan.

1. The Prime Minister of India and President of Pakistan agree that both sides will exert all efforts to create good neighbourly relations between India and Pakistan in accordance with the United Nations Charter. They reaffirm their obligation under the Charter not to have recourse to force and to settle their disputes through peaceful means. They considered that the interests of peace in the region and particularly in the Indo-Pakistan subcontinent and, indeed, the interests of the people of India and Pakistan were not served by the continuance of tension between the two countries. It is against this background that Jammu and Kashmir was discussed, and each of the sides put forth its respective position.
2. The Prime Minister of India and the President of Pakistan have agreed that all armed personnel of the two countries shall be withdrawn not later than 25 February 1966 to the positions they held prior of 5 August 1965 and both sides shall observe the cease-fire terms on the cease-fire line.
3. The Prime Minister of India and the President of Pakistan have agreed that relations between India and Pakistan shall be based on the principle of non-interference in the internal affairs of each other.
4. The Prime Minister of India and the President of Pakistan have agreed that both sides will discourage any propoganda directed against the other country, and will encourage propoganda which promotes the development of friendly relations between the two countries.
5. The Prime Minister of India and President of Pakistan have agreed that the High Commissioner of India to Pakistan and the High Commissioner of Pakistan to India will return to their posts and that the normal functioning of diplomatic missions of both countries will be restored. Both Governments shall observe the Vienna Convention of 1961 on diplomatic intercourse.
6. The Prime Minister of India and the President of Pakistan have agreed to consider measures towards the restoration of economic and trade relations, communications as

well as cultural exchanges between India and Pakistan, and to take measures to implement the existing agreements between India and Pakistan.

7. The Prime Minister of India and the President of Pakistan have agreed that they give instructions to their respective authorities to carry out the repatriation of the prisoners of war.
8. The Prime Minister of India and the President of Pakistan have agreed that the sides will continue the discussion of questions relating to the problems of refugees, evictions and illegal immigrations. They also agreed that both sides will create conditions which will prevent the exodus of people. They further agreed to discuss the return of the property and assets taken over by either side in connection with the conflict.
9. The Prime Minister of India and the President of Pakistan have agreed that both sides will continue meetings both at the highest and at other levels on matters of direct concern to both countries. Both sides have recognized the need to set up joint Indian-Pakistani bodies which will report to their Governments in order to decide what further steps should be taken.

The Prime Minister of India and the President of Pakistan record their feelings of deep appreciation and gratitude to the leaders of the Soviet Union, the Soviet Government and personally to the Chairman of the Council of Ministers of the USSR for their constructive, friendly and noble part in bringing about the present meeting which has resulted in mutually satisfactory results. They also express to the Government and friendly people of Uzbekistan their sincere thankfulness for their overwhelming reception and generous hospitality.

They invite the Chairman of the Council of Ministers of the USSR to witness this declaration.

[Signed:]

Lal Bahadur
Prime Minister of India

M. A. Khan, F.M.
President of Pakistan

The Simla Agreement

July 2, 1972 (Simla)

1. The Government of Pakistan and the Government of India are resolved that the two countries put an end to the conflict and confrontation that have hitherto marred their relations and work for the promotion of a friendly and harmonious relationship and the establishment of durable peace in the sub-continent, so that both countries may henceforth devote their resources and energies to the pressing task of advancing the welfare of their peoples.

   In order to achieve this objective, the Government of Pakistan and the Government of India have agreed as follows:

   (i) That the principles and purposes of the Charter of the United Nations shall govern the relations between the two countries;

(ii) That the two countries are resolved to settle their differences by peaceful means through bilateral negotiations or by any other peaceful means mutually agreed upon between them. Pending the final settlement of any of the problems between the two countries, neither side shall unilaterally alter the situation and both shall prevent the organization, assistance or encouragement of any acts detrimental to the maintenance of peaceful and harmonious relations;

(iii) That the pre-requisite for reconciliation, good neighborliness and durable peace between them is a commitment by both the countries to peaceful co-existence, respect for each other's territorial integrity and sovereignty and non-interference in each other's internal affairs, on the basis of equality and mutual benefit;

(iv) That the basic issues and causes of conflict which have bedeviled the relations between the two countries for the last 25 years shall be resolved by peaceful means;

(v) That they shall always respect each other's national unity, territorial integrity, political independence and sovereign equality;

(vi) That in accordance with the Charter of the United Nations they will refrain from the threat or use of force against the territorial integrity or political independence of each other.

2. Both Governments will take all steps within their power to prevent hostile propaganda directed against each other. Both countries will encourage the dissemination of such information as would promote the development of friendly relations between them.

3. In order progressively to restore and normalise relations between the two countries step by step, it was agreed that:

(i) Steps shall be taken to resume communications, postal, telegraphic, sea, land including border posts, and air links including overflights.

(ii) Appropriate steps shall be taken to promote travel facilities for the nationals of the other country.

(iii) Trade and co-operation in economic and other agreed fields will be resumed as far as possible.

(iv) Exchange in the fields of science and culture will be promoted.

In this connection delegations from the two countries will meet from time to time to work out the necessary details.4 In order to initiate the process of the establishment of durable peace, both the Governments agree that:

(i) Pakistan and Indian forces shall be withdrawn to their side of the international border.

(ii) In Jammu and Kashmir, the line of control resulting from the cease-fire of December 17, 1971, shall be respected by both sides without prejudice to the recognised position of either side. Neither side shall seek to alter it unilaterally, irrespective of mutual differences and legal interpretations. Both sides further undertake to refrain from the threat or the use of force in violation of this Line.

(iii) The withdrawals shall commence upon entry into force of this Agreement and shall be completed within a period of 30 days thereof.

5. This Agreement will be subject to ratification by both countries in accordance with their respective constitutional procedures, and will come into force with effect from the date on which the Instruments of Ratification are exchanged.

6. Both Governments agree that their respective Heads will meet again at a mutually convenient time in the future and that, in the meanwhile, the representatives of the two

sides will meet to discuss further the modalities and arrangements for the establishment of durable peace and normalisation of relations, including the questions of repatriation of prisoners of war and civilian internees, a final settlement of Jammu and Kashmir and the resumption of diplomatic relations.

[Signed:]

Indira Gandhi
Prime Minister
Republic of India

Zulfikar Ali Bhutto
President
Islamic Republic of Pakistan

Agreement on the Salal Hydro-Electric Plant

April 14, 1978 (New Delhi)

The Government of the Islamic Republic of Pakistan and the Government of the Republic of India, being desirous of promoting and strengthening friendly relations between them on the basis of sovereignty, equality and mutual benefit taking into consideration the provisions of the Indus Waters Treaty, 1960, to which both the Governments are parties, having discussed the differences that had arisen between the two Governments regarding the design of the Salal hydro-electric plant on the Chenab main, and;

Without prejudice to the provisions of the Indus Waters Treaty 1960 (herein-after referred to as the Treaty), or to the rights and obligations of the parties thereunder, have agreed as follows:

1. The sailent features of the Salal hydro-electric plant shall conform to the following:
   - (i) Location at Salal; Longitude: 74 degree 50 Ft. east; Latitude: 33 degrees 08 Ft. north not higher than 1,600 feet.
   - (ii) Full pondage level.
   - (iii) Dead storage level same as the full pondage level.
   - (iv) Operating pool nil.
   - (v) Dead storage capacity not exceeding 230,303 acre-feet.
   - (vi) Immovable crest level of the spillway not more than 30 feet below the full pondage level.
   - (vii) Spillway gates 12 numbers, 50 feet wide and 30 feet high. The design shall provide for water to spill over the top of the spillway gates if the gates are not opened in time.
   - (viii) Level of Power intakes the centreline of the penstocks at the intake to be not lower than 27.5 feet below the full pondage level.
   - (ix) Outlet works six numbers with cnl level not below el 1,365 feet.

These shall be permanently closed with concrete plugs within one year of the date of the first filing of the reservoir upto the full pondage level or within three years of the date of the first filing of the reservoir upto the crest of the spillway, whichever is earlier. The dead shortage shall not be depleted except in an unforseen emergency endangering the saftey of the earth or the concrete dams. In that event, India shall give immediate information to the

Government of Pakistan of the nature of the emergency and may simultaneously undertake such action as may be necessary. In case the removal of concrete plugs becomes necessary, India shall hold immediate consultations with the representatives of the Pakistan Government including site inspection of the plant.

2. India shall not make any further alterations in the features of the design of the plant specified in Article 1 above except by mutual agreement.
3. Any question which arises between the parties concerning the interpretation or application of this agreement or the existence of any fact which, if established, might constitute a breach of this agreement shall be dealt with under the provisions or Article (ix) of the treaty.
4. Matters not expressly provided for in this agreement shall be governed by the provisions of the treaty.
5. The terms used in this agreement shall have the same meanings as in the treaty.
6. This agreement shall come into force upon signature.

Done in duplicate in Urdu, Hindi, English languages at New Delhi on this fourteenth day of April 1978. All the texts will be equally authentic, however in the case of doubt, the English text shall prevail.

[Signed:]

Agha Shahi
Adviser on Foreign Affairs
Islamic Republic of Pakistan

Atal Behari Vajpayee
Minister of External Affairs
Republic of India

Agreement on the Prohibition of Attack Against Nuclear Installations and Facilities

December 31, 1988 (Islamabad)

The Government of the Islamic Republic of Pakistan and the Government of the Republic of India, hereinafter referred to as the Contracting Parties, reaffirming their commitment to durable peace and the development of friendly and harmonious bilateral relations; conscious of the role of confidence building measures in promoting such bilateral relations based on mutual trust and goodwill; have agreed as follows:

1. (1) Each party shall refrain from undertaking, encouraging or participating in, directly or indirectly, any action aimed at causing the destruction of, or damage to, any nuclear installation or facility in the other country. (2) The term "nuclear installation or facility" includes nuclear power and research reactors, fuel fabrication, uranium enrichment, isotopes separation and reprocessing facilities as well as any other installations with fresh or irradiated nuclear fuel and materials in any form and establishments storing significant quantities of radio-active materials.
2. Each Contracting Party shall inform the other on 1st January of each calendar year of the latitude and longitude of its nuclear installations and facilities and whenever there is any change.

3. This Agreement is subject to ratification. It shall come into force with effect from the date on which the Instruments of Ratification are exchanged.

Done at Islamabad on this Thirty-first day of December 1988, in two copies each in Urdu, Hindi and English, the English text being authentic in case of any difference or dispute of interpretation.

[Signed:]

Humayun Khan
Foreign Secretary
Islamic Republic of Pakistan

K.P.S. Menon
Foreign Secretary
Republic of India

Agreement on Advance Notice on Military Exercises, Manoeuvres and Troop Movements

April 6, 1991 (New Delhi)

Whereas Pakistan and India recognise the need to jointly formulate an agreement at the Government level on giving advance notice on exercises, manoeuvres and troop movements in order to prevent any crisis situation arising due to misreading of the other side's intentions. Therefore, the Governments of Pakistan and India jointly decide that:

1. Their Land, Naval, and Air Forces will avoid holding major military manoeuvres and exercises in close proximity to each other. However, if such exercises are held within distances as prescribed in this Agreement, the strategic direction of the main force being exercised will not be towards the other side, nor will any logistics build up be carried out close to it. The following will constitute a major military manoeuvres/exercise for the purpose of this Agreement:
   a. Land Forces:
      (1) India-Pakistan International Border: Concentrations of Corps level (comprising two or more divisions) and above.
      (2) Line of Control and the area between the Manawar Tawi and Ravi Rivers: Division level and above.
   b. Naval Forces: Any exercise involving six or more ships of destroyer/frigate size and above, exercising in company and crossing into the other's Exclusive Economic Zone (EEZ).
   c. Air Force: Regional Command level and above.
2. Both sides may not conduct exercises of Land Forces at Divisional level and above within five kilometres (kms) of the areas specified at paragraph 1. a (1) and (2).
3. Both sides will provide notice regarding exercises of Land Forces as follow:
   a. All exercises/concentrations at Divisional level in areas specified at Paragraph 1. a (2).
   b. All exercises/concentrations at Corps level within a distance of seventy five kms in areas specified at Paragraph 1. a. (1) and (2).
   c. All exercises above Corps level irrespective of the distance.

4. Both sides will give fifteen days prior notice when formations with defensive roles are moved to their operational locations for periodic maintenance of defences.
5. The schedule of major exercises with troops will be transmitted in writing to the other side through diplomatic channels in advance as follows:
    a. Air exercises at Regional Command level and above: Fifteen days.
    b. Divisional level exercises, and major Naval exercises involving six or more ships of destroyer/frigate size and above, exercising in company and crossing into the other's EEZ: Thirty days.
    c. Corps level exercise: Sixty days.
    d. Army level exercises: Ninety days.

    Provided that the above provisions relate to the commencement of moves of formations and units from their permanent locations for the proposed exercises.
6. Information on the following aspects of major exercises will be intimated:
    a. Type and level of exercises.
    b. General area of the exercise on land, air and sea. In respect of air and sea exercises, these will be defined in latitude and longitude.
    c. Planned duration of the activity.
    d. Number and type of formations participating.
    e. Any shifting of forces from other Commands/Corps Strategic formations envisaged.
    f. The move of strategic formations, particularly armoured divisions, mechanised divisions, air assault divisions/reserve infantry formations and artillery divisions/air defence artillery divisions.

    Provided that in respect of major Air and Naval exercises, only the information at Paragraph (a) to (c) need be intimated.
7. In case some change in exercise area/grouping of participating formations from the previously notified composition is necessitated, the country carrying out the exercises will intimate the details of changes so as to reach the other country at least thirty days in advance in respect of Corps level exercises and above, and fifteen days in advance in respect of divisional level exercises and Naval exercises. In respect of Air exercises, if minor changes to the previously notified details are necessitated, an advance notice of seven days will be provided.
8. Any induction/concentration of additional troops of a division size force and above, within one hundred and fifty kms of areas specified at Paragraph 1. a. (1) and (2), for internal security duties and/or in aid of civil power will be notified to the other side at least two days before the start of their movements, whenever possible. In case of immediate movements, information may be passed on Hot Line to the Army Headquarters of the other country. The force so employed will not move forward their logistic bases/installations and armour/artillery.
9. Each country will be entitled to obtain timely clarification from the country undertaking military manoeuvres/exercises concerning the assembly of formations, the extent, direction of the exercise and the duration.
10. The Naval ships and submarines belonging to the other Country are not to close less than three Nautical Miles (NMs) from each other so as to avoid any accident while operating in international waters.

11. Combat aircraft including fighter, bomber, reconnaissance, jet military trainer and armed helicopter aircraft will not fly within ten kms of each other's airspace, including the Air Defence Identification Zones (ADIZ), except when such aircraft are operating from Jammu, Pathankot, Amritsar and Suratgarh air bases on the Indian side, as well as Pasrur, Lahore, Vehari and Rahimyar Khan air bases on the Pakistan side, in which case they will maintain a distance of five kms from each other's airspace. Unarmed transport and logistics aircraft including unarmed helicopters and Air Observation Post (AOP) aircraft will be permitted to operate up to 1000 metres from each other's airspace including the ADIZ.
12. Aircraft of either country will refrain from buzzing surface units and platforms of the other country in international waters.
13. This Agreement supersedes all previous understandings in so far as the above points are concerned.
14. This Agreement is subject to ratification. It shall come into force with effect from the date on which the Instruments of Ratification are exchanged.
15. Done at New Delhi on this Sixth day of April, 1991.

[Signed:]

Shaharyar M. Khan
Foreign Secretary
Islamic Republic of Pakistan

Muchkund Dubey
Foreign Secretary
Republic of India

Agreement on Prevention of Airspace Violations and for Permitting Overflights and Landings by Military Aircraft

April 6, 1991 (New Delhi)

States parties to the present Air Agreement; recognising the fact that both the Pakistan Air Force (PAF) and the Indian Air Force (IAF) aircraft operate near each other's airspace; aware that despite best efforts by both sides, violations of each other's airspace have occurred for time to time; desirous of promoting good neighbourly relations between the two countries; conscious of the fact that renewed efforts should be made to avoid unnecessary alarm; have agreed to enter into the following Air Agreement:

1. Henceforth, both sides will take adequate measures to ensure, that air violations of each other's airspace do not take place. However, if any inadvertent violation does take place, the incident will be promptly investigated and the Headquarter (HQ) of the other Air Force informed of the results without delay, through diplomatic channels.
2. Subject to Articles 3, 4 and 6, the following restrictions are to be observed by the aircraft of both the forces:
   a. Combat aircraft (to include fighter, bomber, reconnaissance, jet military trainer and armed helicopter aircraft) will not fly within 10 kms of each other's airspace including ADIZ. No aircraft of any size will enter the airspace over the territorial waters of the other country, except by prior permission.

b. Unarmed transport and logistics aircraft including unarmed helicopters and Air Observation post (AOP) aircraft, will be permitted up to 1000 metres from each other's airspace including ADIZ.

3. In the event of a country having to undertake flights less than 1000 metres from the other's airspace including ADIZ, for purposes such as aerial survey, supply dropping for mercy and aerial rescue missions, the country concerned will give the following information in advance to their own Air Advisors for notification to the Air HQ for the other country:
   a. Type of aircraft/helicopter.
   b. Height of flight within Plus/Minus 100 ft.
   c. Block No of days (normally not to exceed seven days) when flights are proposed to be undertaken.
   d. Proposed timing of flight, where possible.
   e. Area involved (in latitude and longitude).

   No formal clearance would be required as the flights are being undertaken within own territory.
4. In order to avoid any tension being created, prior notice given with regard to air exercises, or any special air activity proposed to be undertaken close to each other's airspace including ADIZ, even though the limits as laid down in Article 2 are not likely to be infringed.
5. In matters of safety and any air operations in emergency situations, the authorities designated by the respective Governments should contact each other by the quickest means of communications available. The Air Advisor shall be kept informed of such contacts. Matters of flight safety and urgent air operations should be brought tot he notice of the other side through the authorities designated by using the telephone line established between the Army Headquarters of the two countries.
6. Combat aircraft (as defined in Article 2 a. above) operating from the air bases specified below will maintain a distance of 5 kms from each other's airspace:
   a. Indian Side: (1) Jammu, (2) Pathankot, (3) Amritsar, (4) Suratgarh
   b. Pakistan Side: (1) Pasrur, (2) Lahore, (3) Vehari, (4) Rahim Yar Khan
7. Military aircraft may fly through each other's airspace with the prior notification of the other country and subject to conditions specified in Appendix 'A' to this Agreement. [See below.] Notwithstanding paragraph 1 of the Article, each country has the sovereign right to specify further conditions, at short notice, for flights of military aircraft through its airspace.
8. This Agreement supersedes all previous understandings in so far as airspace violations and overflights and landings by military aircraft are concerned.
9. This Agreement is subject to Ratification. It shall come into force with effect from the date on which the Instruments of Ratification are exchanged.
10. Done at New Delhi on the Sixth day of April 1991.

Signed:

Shaharyar M. Khan
Foreign Secretary
Islamic Republic of Pakistan

Muchkund Dubey
Foreign Secretary
Republic of India

Appendix A: Conditions for Grant of Flight Clearance for Military Aircraft of Both Countries.

1. The side requesting permission for their military aircraft to fly through the airspace of the other country or for landing(s) by such aircraft at airfield(s) in the other country, will approach the respective Air HQ through their Air Advisor for clearance to undertake the flight, at least seven days before the scheduled date(s) of the flight(s). If, due to unforeseen circumstances, this notice is less than seven days, the other country would, as far as possible, make all efforts to accommodate the request. The following details of each flight will be intimated to the concerned Air Headquarters:
   a. Aircraft type.
   b. Aircraft registration number.
   c. Aircraft call sign.
   d. Name of the Captain of the Aircraft.
   e. Number of the crew.
   f. Cruising level.
   g. General nature of cargo carried and number of passengers who are on board the aircraft.
   h. Purpose of the flight.
   j. Standby aircraft number and call sign.
   k. Name of standby Captain and air crew.
   l. Flight plan for outbound and return legs including air route, Flight Information Region (FIR) entry/exit points and times, Expected Time of Arrival (ETAs)/Expected Time of Departure (ETDs) and flight levels etc.
   m. Type and quality of fuel required at various air fields landing.
2. All flights approved will be valid for 3 days within plus/minus 3 hours of the given schedule of each day provided flight details remain unchanged. Any subsequent changes of the flight plan will require fresh clearance from Air HQ, for which advance notice of 72 hours will be essential.
3. Routes to be followed by aircraft will be specified by respective countries at the time of requesting flight clearance. If the route proposed by the originator country is, for any reason, not acceptable to the other country, the latter would, if possible, suggest a viable alternative route at the earliest.
4. The aircraft will not fly below 8000 ft or over 40,000 ft Above Ground Level (AGL).
5. The concerned Flight Information Centre of the other country will be contacted by the transiting aircraft during the flight before entering the airspace of the other country.
6. Flights across each other's airspace will normally be completed between sunrise and sunset. Overflights by night may be permitted, on specific request, under special circumstances.
7. No war-like material e.g. arms, ammunition, explosives (except escape aid explosives), pyrotechnics (except emergency very light pistol signal cartridges), nuclear/fissionable material, Nuclear Biological and Chemical (NBC) material, photographic material

(whether or not installed), electronic devices other than required for the normal operation of the aircraft, may be carried in the aircraft.

8. Non-professional cameras belonging to the passengers and which are not capable of aerial photography, may however, be carried but photography at Airports or of defence installations, bridges and industries etc. is not permitted.
9. Normally, both countries shall permit overflights to transit across the other's airspace along approved international Air Traffic Services (ATS) routes without the aircraft having to make a technical halt. However, each country has the sovereign right to insist on such a halt if the country being overflown so desires.
10. Special care is to be exercised by the transiting aircraft to stay within the ATS routes and not to stray outside the limits of the route.
11. Visas for the crew and passengers will be issued by the respective Embassy with utmost promptness.

Joint Declaration on the Complete Prohibition of Chemical Weapons

August 19, 1992 (New Delhi)

The Government of the Islamic Republic of Pakistan and the Government of the Republic of India, reaffirming their commitment to durable peace and the development of friendly and harmonious relations; conscious of the role of confidence building measures in promoting such bilateral relations based on mutual trust and goodwill; recognising that disarmament agreements constitute an important confidence building measure; reaffirming their respective unilateral declarations on non-possession of chemical weapons; convinced that a complete and effective prohibition of chemical weapons will contribute to the security of all States; reaffirming their respective commitment to the Protocol for Prohibition of the Use in War of Asphyxiating, Poisonous or Other Gases, and of Bacteriological Methods of Warfare, signed in Geneva on 17 June 1925 and recalling the relevant resolutions of the General Assembly upholding the validity of the 1925 Geneva Protocol; reiterating the need for the early conclusion within the framework of the Conference on Disarmament of a global convention for the complete and effective prohibition of the development, production, stockpiling and use of chemical weapons and their destruction. Hereby declare that:

1. They undertake never under any circumstances:
   a) to develop, produce or otherwise acquire chemical weapons;
   b) to use chemical weapons;
   c) to assist, encourage or induce, in any way, anyone to engage in development, production, acquisition, stockpiling or use of chemical weapons.
2. They would cooperate with each other, in finalisation and adoption of a comprehensive Chemical Weapons Convention which ensures the security of all states and encourages the full utilization of achievements in the field of chemistry for peaceful purposes, especially for economic development of the developing countries.
3. They reiterate their resolve to become original States party to the proposed Convention currently being drafted in the Conference on Disarmament.
4. They would exercise their right to develop their chemical industry and related applications and products only for peaceful purposes and for the welfare of their peoples.

In witness whereof, the duly authorised representatives of the two Governments have hereto signed this Declaration and affix thereto their seals. Done at New Delhi on this Nineteenth day of August of the year one thousand nine hundred and ninety two.

[Signed:]

Shaharyar M. Khan
Foreign Secretary
Islamic Republic of Pakistan

J.N. Dixit
Foreign Secretary
Republic of India

II. AGREEMENTS BETWEEN CHINA AND INDIA

Agreement on Trade and Intercourse between Tibet Region of China and India

April 29, 1954 (Peking)

The Government of the Republic of India and the Central People's Government of the People's Republic of China, being desirous of promoting trade and cultural intercourse between Tibet Region of China and India and of facilitating pilgrimage and travel by the peoples of China and India, have resolved to enter into the present Agreement based on the following principles:

(1) mutual respect for each other's territorial integrity and sovereignty,
(2) mutual non-aggression,
(3) mutual non-interference in each other's internal affairs,
(4) equality and mutual benefit, and
(5) peaceful co-existence,

And for this purpose have appointed as their respective Plenipotentiaries:

The Government of the Republic of India, H.E. Nedyam Raghavan, Ambassador Extraordinary and Plenipotentiary of India accredited to the People's Republic of China; the Central People's Government of the People's Republic of China, H.E. Chang Han-fu, Vice-Minister of Foreign Affairs of the Central People's Government, who, having examined each other's credentials and finding them in good and due form, have agreed upon the following:

1. The High Contracting Parties mutually agree to establish Trade Agencies:

(1) The Government of India agrees that the Government of China may establish Trade Agencies at New Delhi, Calcutta and Kalimpong.

(2) The Government of China agrees that the Government of India may establish Trade Agencies at Yatung, Gyantse and Gartok.

The Trade Agencies of both Parties shall be accorded the same status and same treatment. The Trade Agents of both Parties shall enjoy freedom from arrest while exercising their functions, and shall enjoy in respect of themselves, their wives and children who are dependent on them for livelihood freedom from search.

The Trade Agencies of both Parties shall enjoy the privileges and immunities for couriers, mail-bags and communications in code.

2. The High Contracting Parties agree that traders of both countries known to be customarily and specifically engaged in trade between Tibet Region of China and India may trade at the following places:

(1) The Government of China agrees to specify (1) Yatung, (2) Gyantse and (3) Phari as markets for trade. The Government of India agrees that trade may be carried on in India, including places like (1) Kalimpong, (2) Siliguri and (3) Calcutta, according to customary practice.

(2) The Government of China agrees to specify (1) Gartok, (2) Pulanchung (Taklakot), (3) Gyanima-Khargo, (4) Gyanima-Chakra, (5) Ramura, (6) Dongbra, (7) Puling-Sumdo, (8) Nabra, (9) Shangtse and (10) Tashigong as markets for trade; the Government of India agrees that in future, when in accordance with the development and need of trade between the Ari District of Tibet Region of China and India, it has become necessary to specify markets for trade in corresponding district in India adjacent to the Ari District of Tibet Region of China, it will be prepared to consider on the basis of equality and reciprocity to do so.

3. The High Contracting Parties agree that pilgrimage by religious believers of the two countries shall be carried on in accordance with the following provisions:

(1) Pilgrims from India of Lamaist, Hindu and Buddhist faiths may visit Kang Rimpoche (Kailas) and Mavam (Tso Manasarovar) in Tibet Region of China in accordance with custom.

(2) Pilgrims from Tibet Region of China of Lamaist and Buddhist faiths may visit Banaras, Sarnath, Gaya and Sanchi in India in accordance with custom.

(3) Pilgrims customarily visiting Lhasa may continue to do so in accordance with custom.

4. Traders and pilgrims of both countries may travel by the following passes and route:

(1) Shipki La pass, (2) Mana pass, (3) Niti pass, (4) Kungri Bingri pass, (5) Darma pass, and (6) Lipu Lekh pass.

Also, the customary route leading to Tashigong along the valley of the Shangatsangpu (Indus) River may continue to be traversed in accordance with custom.

5. For travelling across the border, the High Contracting Parties agree that diplomatic personnel, officials and nationals of the two countries shall hold passports issued by their own respective countries and visaed by the other Party except as provided in Paragraphs 1, 2, 3 and 4 of this Article.

(1) Traders of both countries known to be customarily and specifically engaged in trade between Tibet Region of China and India, their wives and children who are dependent on them for livelihood and their attendants will be allowed entry for purposes of trade into India or Tibet Region of China, as the case may be, in accordance with custom on the production of certificates duly issued by the local government of their own country or by its duly authorised agents and examined by the border checkposts of the other Party.

(2) Inhabitants of the border districts of the two countries who cross the border to carry on petty trade or to visit friends and relatives may proceed to the border districts of the other Party as they have customarily done heretofore and need not be restricted to the passes and route specified in Article IV above and shall not be required to hold passports, visas or permits.

(3) Porters and mule-team drivers of the two countries who cross the border to perform necessary transportation services need not hold passports issued by their own country, but shall only hold certificates good for a definite period of time (three months, half a year or one year) duly issued by the local government of their own country or by its duly authorised agents and produce them for registration at the border checkposts of the other Party.

(4) Pilgrims of both countries need not carry documents of certification but shall register at the border checkposts of the other Party and receive a permit for pilgrimage.

(5) Notwithstanding the provisions of the foregoing paragraphs of this Article, either Government may refuse entry to any particular person.

(6) Persons who enter the territory of the other Party in accordance with the foregoing paragraphs of this Article may stay within its territory only after complying with the procedures specified by the other Party.

6. The present Agreement shall come into effect upon ratification by both Governments and shall remain in force for eight (8) years. Extension of the present Agreement may be negotiated by the two Parties if either Party requests for it six (6) months prior to the expiry of the Agreement and the request is agreed to by the other Party.

Done in duplicate in Peking on the twenty-ninth of April, 1954, in the Hindi, Chinese and English languages, all texts being equally valid.

[Signed:]

Nedyam Raghavan
Plenipotentiary of the Government
of the Republic of India

Chang Han-fu
Plenipotentiary of the Central People's Government, People's Republic of China

Exchange of Notes

Your Excellency Mr. Vice-Foreign Minister,

In the course of our discussions regarding the Agreement on Trade and Intercourse Between the Tibet Region of China and India, which has been happily concluded today, the Delegation of the Government of the Republic of India and the Delegation of the Government of the People's Republic of China agreed that certain matters be regulated by an exchange of Notes. In pursuit of this understanding, it is hereby agreed between the two Governments as follows:

1. The Government of India will be pleased to withdraw completely within six (6) months from the date of exchange of the present notes the military escorts now stationed at Yatung and Gyantse in Tibet Region of China. The Government of China will render facilities and assistance in such a withdrawl.
2. The Government of India will be pleased to hand over to the Government of China at a reasonable price the postal, telegraph and public telephone services together with their equipment operated by the Government of India in Tibet Region of China. The concrete measures in this regard will be decided upon through further negotiations between the

Indian Embassy in China and the Foreign Ministry of China, which shall start immediately after the exchange of the present notes.

3. The Government of India will be pleased to hand over to the Government of China at a reasonable price the twelve (12) rest houses of the Government of India in Tibet Region of China. The concrete measures in this regard will be decided upon through further negotiations between the Indian Embassy in China and the Ministry of Foreign Affairs of China, which shall start immediately after the exchange of the present notes. The Government of China agrees that they shall continue as rest houses.
4. The Government of China agrees that all buildings within the compound walls of the Trade Agencies of the Government of India at Yatung and Gyantse in Tibet Region of China may be retained by the Government of India. The Government of India may continue to lease the land within its agency compund walls from the Chinese side. And the Government of India agrees that the Trade Agencies of the Government of China at Kalimpong and Calcutta may lease these lands from the Indian side for the use of the Agencies and construct buildings thereon. The Government of China will render every possible assistance for housing the Chinese Trade Agency at New Delhi.
5. The Government of India will be pleased to return to the Government of China all lands used or occupied by the Government of India other that the lands within its Trade Agency compund walls at Yatung. If there are godowns and buildings of the Government of India on the above-mentioned lands used or occupied and to be returned by the Government of India and if Indian traders have stores, godowns or buildings on the above mentioned lands so that there is need to continue leasing the lands, the Government of China agrees to sign contracts with the Government of India or Indian traders, as the case may be, for leasing to them those parts of the land occupied by the said godowns, buildings or stores and pertaining thereto.
6. The Trade Agents of both parties may, in accordance with the laws and regulations of the local governments, have access to their nationals involved in civil or criminal cases.
7. The Trade Agents and traders of both countries may hire employees in the locality.
8. The hospitals of the Indian Trade Agencies at Gyantse and Yatung will continue to serve personnel of the Indian Trade Agencies.
9. Each Government shall protect the person and property of the traders and pilgrims of the other country.
10. The Government of China agrees, so far as possible, to construct rest houses for the use of pilgrims along the route from Pulan-chung (Taklakot) to Kang Rimpoche (Kailas) and Mava Tso (Mansarovar); and the Government of India agrees to pline of actual controle all possible facilities in India at the disposal of pilgrims.
11. Traders and pilgrims of both countries shall have the facility of hiring means of transportation at normal and reasonable rates.
12. The three Trade Agencies of each Party may function throughout the year.
13. Traders of each company may rent buildings and godowns in accordance with local regulations in pline of actual controles under the jurisdiction of the other party.
14. Traders of both countries may carry out normal trade in accordance with local regulations at pline of actual controles provided in Article II of the Agreement.
15. Disputes between traders of both countries over debts and claims shall be handled in accordance with local laws and regulations.

On behalf of the Government of the Republic of India I hereby agree that the present Note along with your Excellency's reply shall become an agreement between our two Governments which shall come into force upon the exchange of present Notes. I avail myself of this opportunity to express to Your Excellency Mr. Vice-Foreign Minister the assurance of my highest consideration.

[Signed:]

N. Raghavan
Ambassador Extraordinary and Plenipotentiary
of the Republic of India

Your Excellency Mr. Ambassador:

I have the honour to receive your note dated April 29, 1954.

On behalf of the Central People's Government of the People's Republic of China, I hereby agree to Your Excellency's note and your note along with the present note in reply shall become an agreement between our two Governments, which shall come into force upon the exchange of the present notes.

I avail myself of this opportunity to express to your Excellency, Mr. Ambassador, the assurances of my highest consideration.

[Signed:]

Chang Han-Fu
Vice-Minister, Ministry of Foreign Affairs
People's Republic of China

Agreement on the Maintenance of Peace and Tranquility Along the Line of Actual Control in the India-China Border Areas

September 7, 1993 (Beijing)

The Government of the Repubic of India and the Government of the People's Republic of China (hereinafter referred to as the two sides), have entered into the present Agreement in accordance with the Five Principles of mutual respect for sovereignty and territorial integrity, mutual non-aggression, non-interference in each other's internal affairs, equality and mutual benefit and peaceful coexistence and with a view to maintaining peace and tranquility in areas along the line of actual control in the India-China border areas.

1. The two sides are of the view that the India-China boundary question shall be resolved through peaceful and friendly consultations. Neither side shall use or threaten to use force against the other by any means. Pending an ultimate solution to the boundary question between the two countries, the two sides shall strictly respect and observe the line of actual control between the two sides. No activities of either side shall overstep the line of actual control. In case personnel of one side cross the line of actual control, upon being cautioned by the other side, they shall immediately pull back to their own side of the line of actual control. When necessary, the two sides shall jointly check and

determine the segments of the line of actual control where they have different views as to its alignment.

2. Each side will keep its military forces in the areas along the line of actual control to a minimum level compatible with the friendly and good neighbourly relations between the two countries. The two sides agree to reduce their military forces along the line of actual control in conformity with the requirements of the principle of mutual and equal security to ceilings to be mutually agreed. The extent, depth, timing, and nature of reduction of military forces along the line of actual control shall be determined through mutual consultations between the two countries. The reduction of military forces shall be carried out by stages in mutually agreed geographical locations sector-wise within the areas along the line of actual control.
3. Both sides shall work out through consultations effective confidence building measures in the areas along the line of actual control. Neither side will undertake specified levels of military exercises in mutually identified zones. Each side shall give the other prior notification of military exercises of specified levels near the line of actual control permitted under this Agreement.
4. In case of contingencies or other problems arising in the areas along the line of actual control, the two sides shall deal with them through meetings and friendly consultations between border personnel of the two countries. The form of such meetings and channels of communications between the border personnel shall be mutually agreed upon by the two sides.
5. The two sides agree to take adequate measures to ensure that air intrusions across the line of actual control do not take place and shall undertake mutual consultations should intrusions occur. Both sides shall also consult on posible restrictions on air exercises in areas to be mutually agreed near the line of actual control.
6. The two sides agree that references to the line of actual control in this Agreement do not prejudice their respective positions on the boundary question.
7. The two sides shall agree through consultations on the form, method, scale and content of effective verification measures and supervision required for the reduction of military forces and the maintenance of peace and tranquility in the areas along the line of actual control under this Agreement.
8. Each side of the India-China Joint Working Group on the boundary question shall appoint diplomatic and military experts to formulate, through mutual consultations, implementation measures for the present Agreement. The experts shall advise the Joint Working Group on the resolution of differences between the two sides on the alignment of the line of actual control and address issues relating to redeployment with a view to reduction of military forces in the areas along the line of actual control. The experts shall also assist the Joint Working Group in supervision of the implementation of the Agreement, and settlement of differences that may arise in that process, based on the principle of good faith and mutual confidence.
9. The present Agreement shall come into effect as of the date of signature and is subject to amendment and addition by agreement of the two sides.

Signed in duplicate at Beijing on the Seventh day of September 1993 in the Hindi, Chinese and English languages, all three texts having equal validity.

[Signed:]

R.L. Bhatia
Minister of State for External Affairs
Republic of India

Tang Jiaxuan
Vice-Foreign Minister
People's Republic of China

Agreement on Environmental Cooperation

September 7, 1993 (Beijing)

The Government of the Republic of India and the Government of the People's Republic of China (hereinafter referred to as the Parties); recognizing that the achievement of sustainable development and enhancement of the quality of the environment are issues that affect economic growth and the well being of the people;
noting that scientific and technological exchanges and cooperative activities are being conducted between India and China in global environmental negotiations and in the field of mountain development; wishing to increase this cooperation in sectors related to the environment for mutual benefits; have agreed as follows:

1. The Ministry of the Environment and Forests of the Government of the Republic of India and the National Environmental Protection Agency of the People's Republic of China shall be the nodal agencies for the implementation of this Agreement.
2. The Parties shall maintain and enhance bilateral cooperation in all fields of environmental activities on the basis of equality and mutual benefits.
3. Cooperation under this Agreement shall be carried out inter alia, in the following high priority areas:
    1. Global environmental issues, including protection of bio-diversity, global climate change and the protection of the ozone layer;
    2. Waste management;
    3. Environmental pollution control with emphasis on clean technology, water quality protection, air quality protection, packaging, recycling of solid wastes, hazardous waste issues, and emergency response;
    4. Evironmental impact assessment procedures and experience;
    5. Quality control and management of environmental protection products;
    6. Public awareness and education on environmental issues;
    7. Wildlife conservation with specific focus on the prevention of trade in endangered species of wild fauna and flora;
    8. Environmental legislation and enforcement;
    9. Any other areas that may be agreed between the Parties.
4. Cooperation under this Agreement shall be carried out inter alia through the following means:
    1. Exchange of scientists, scholars, specialists and environmental management personnel;
    2. Exchange of the information in the areas listed in Article 3;

3. Cooperative research on subjects of mutual interest, in which the Parties will exchange and provide each other with samples, reagents, materials, data, instruments and components for testing, evaluation and other purposes in accordance with mutually agreed conditions;
4. Joint organization of symposia, seminars, lectures and training courses;
5. Other means of cooperation as are mutually agreed upon, including entering into protocols for effecting and implementing concrete programmes of cooperation in areas identified.

5. The Parties shall encourage and facilitate the development of contacts and cooperation between other levels of government or organisational entities, research institutions, private sector, academia, etc. and coordinate the implementation of these activities.
6. (1) Each Party shall determine within its own country the allocation of intellectual property rights arising from cooperative activities under this Agreement; (2) The Parties shall decide jointly on the allocation of intellectual rights in third countries unless otherwise provided under particular project arrangements.
7. (1) Unless otherwise arranged between the Parties, international travel expenses related to such exchanges and cooperative activities will be borne by the sending Party. In-country expenses will be borne by the receiving Party on a reciprocal basis; (2) In principle, the number of persons dispatched and the duration of stay (based on persons/months) will be on an equal and reciprocal basis. In case where the principle of reciprocity is difficult to implement, the two parties will discuss the matter to find a satisfactory solution.
8. The terms and conditions of such exchanges and cooperative activities provided for in this agreement will be subject to the laws and regulations of the Parties and will be established in writing between appropriate officials of the Parties.
9. The parties shall make biennial reports to the respective heads of their organizations summarising progress on cooperative projects as presented in the work programme, and identifying possible opportunities for additional projects.
10. This Agreement shall enter into force upon signature. It will remain in effect for an initial period of five years. It may be terminated by either party with six months written notice to the other. It may be renewed by mutual consent for an additional period of time agreed to by both the Parties. The termination of this agreement shall not affect the validity or duration of specific activities or arrangements initiated under it, but not yet completed at the time of termination.
11. This Agreement may be amended at any time by mutual agreement of the Parties in writing.

Done in duplicate at Beijing this Seventh day of September 1993, in the Hindi, Chinese and English languages, each version being equally authentic. In case of divergence, the English text shall prevail.

[Signed:]

C. Dasgupta
Ambassador of India to China
Republic of India

Xie Zhenhua
Director, State Bureau of Environment
People's Republic of China

Protocol for Extension of Border Trade Across Shipkila Pass
September 7, 1993 (Beijing)

The Government of the Republic of India and the Government of the People's Republic of China; with a view to promoting the development of friendly relations between the two countries and their people; pursuant to the Memorandum between the Government of the Republic of India and the Government of the People's Republic of China on the Resumption of Border Trade signed at New Delhi on 13 December 1991; and Protocol on Entry and Exit Procedures for Border Trade signed on 1 July 1992; being desirous of extension of border trade to an additional point on India-China border; have agreed as follows:

1. The Government of the Republic of India and the Government of the People's Republic of China shall establish border trade markets at the following locations:
   1. Namgya in Kinnaur District of the State of Himachal Pradesh of the Republic of India.
   2. Jiuba in Zada County in Tibet Autonomous Region of the People's Republic of China.
2. Shipkila shall be the pass for entry and exit of persons, commodities and means of transport engaged in border trade, exchange of commodities and means of transportation.
3. All the provisions of the Memorandum on the resumption of border trade and the Protocol on Entry and Exit Procedures signed under the Memorandum shall be applicable to the border trade across Shipkila pass also.
4. This Protocol may be amended or supplemented by agreement in writing between the Government of the Republic of India and the Government of the People's Republic of China.
5. This Protocol shall come into force as from the date of its signature and shall be valid during the validity of the Memorandum on Resumption of Border Trade between the Governments of the two countries signed at New Delhi on 13 December 1991.

Done at Beijing on this Seventh day of September 1993, in two originals each in Hindi, Chinese and English languages, the three texts being equally authentic.

[Signed:]

C. Dasgupta
Ambassador of India to China
Republic of India

Liu Shenzai
Vice Minister, Ministry of Foreign Trade and Economic Cooperation
People's Republic of China

Agreement on Radio and Television Cooperation

September 7, 1993 (Beijing)

The Ministry of Information and Broadcasting of the Republic of India and the Ministry of Radio, Film and Television of the People's Republic of China (hereinafter referred to as the parties); desirous of strengthening further the friendly relations and cooperation between the Republic of India and the People's Republic of China; the Ministry of Information and Broadcasting of the Republic of India and the Ministry of Radio, Film and Television of the People's Republic of China, have agreed as follows:

1. The two parties will exchange at least once every six months tape recordings of songs, music or radio programmes as well some TV programmes.
2. To celebrate the National Day (or Republic Day) of the two countries (China: 1 October; India: 26 January), the two parties will send relevant audio and video tape recordings of special programmes to each other. The tape recording should reach the radio and TV stations of the other party two months before the national (or Republic) day.
3. The exchange of programmes can be delivered through the Embassy of the other party. The exchange and use of the programmes will be free of charge. Explanatory notes or synopsis in English should be attached with the song, music, radio and TV programmes exchanged between the two parties.
4. The radio and TV programmes exchanged under the terms of this agreement can be used in accordance with the need of the receiving party, keeping reciprocity as an important criterion.
5. Both the parties may send radio and television delegations and radio and TV coverage teams to visit each other or take part in radio and TV festivals sponsored by the other party through mutual consultations.
6. On equal and reciprocal basis, the guest party shall be responsible for the international travel expenses and the host party shall pay the expenses of meals, accomodation and local transportation for the visiting delegation or team during their visit.
7. This Agreement shall enter into force on the date of its signing and shall remain valid for a period of two years and shall be renewed for subsequent period of two years unless either of the Contracting Parties give to the other a written notice three months in advance of its intention to terminate the Agreement before expiry.

Signed at Beijing on this Seventh day of September 1993,in two originals each in Hindi, English and Chinese languages. All the texts being equally authentic. In case of doubts, the English text shall prevail.

[Signed:]

C. Dasgupta
Ambassador of India to China
Republic of India

Liu Xilang
Vice Minister, Ministry of Radio, Film and Television
People's Republic of China

CONTRIBUTORS

MOONIS AHMAR is an Assistant Professor at the Department of International Relations at the University of Karachi, Pakistan. He is a Visiting Research Associate at the Program in Arms Control, Disarmament and International Security (ACDIS) at the University of Illinois at Urbana-Champaign, where he also taught in the Political Science Department. He completed his Ph.D. and M.Phil in International Relations from the University of Karachi, and his M.S. in International Relations from Quaid-i-Azam University.

KANTI BAJPAI is an Associate Professor, School of International Studies, Jawaharlal Nehru University, New Delhi. He was a Resident Fellow, Rajiv Ghandi Institute for Contemporary Studies, and has taught at the Maharaja Sayajirao University of Baroda, Wesleyan University, and the University of Illinois at Urbana-Champaign. He has recently edited *Interpreting World Politics* (Sage Publications, 1995) and is co-author of *Brasstacks and Beyond: Perception and Management of Crisis in South Asia* (Manohar Publishers).

POONAM BARUA is Director of Public Affairs Management, an independent consulting firm specializing in business and economic affairs, based in New Delhi. She has previously served as chief program advisor with the United States Information Service (USIS), consultant for the United States Agency for International Development (USAID), and at the Indian Institute of Public Administration.

NAVNITA CHADHA is an Assistant Research Professor at the Centre for Policy Research in New Delhi. She completed her M.Phil. at Jawaharlal Nehru University, New Delhi, and her Ph.D. at the University of Kent at Canterbury. She has published several articles on confidence-building measures and conflict resolution in South Asia and is currently writing a book on confidence-building measures between India and Pakistan.

BONNIE COE is a professional staff member of the U.S. Senate Committee on Foreign Relations. She received an M.A. in political science from the University of Illinois and has worked extensively on nonproliferation and East Asian issues. She is author of *Europe's Conventional Balance: 'Tanks' for the Memories*, and ACDIS Occasional Paper.

GIRI DESHINGKAR is Professor/Senior Fellow at the Centre for the Study of Developing Societies, New Delhi. His research focus has been on Chinese military and security issues. He studied modern Chinese at the University of London and East Asian Studies at Yale University.

ARUN ELHANCE is a Program Director for the Program on International Peace and Security at the Social Science Research Council in New York. He received his Ph.D. from Boston University. He is co-author of *Mitsubishi Motors in Illinois: Global Strategies, Local Impacts* (West Port, CT: Quorum Books, 1995). He has also written numerous book chapters, journals pieces, and op-eds on such subjects as water resources and arms production.

SUMIT GANGULY is Professor of Political Science at Hunter College, City College of New York. He is the author of *The Origins of War in South Asia* (Westview Press, 1986 and

1994). He has published in *many journals including Asian Survey, Foreign Affairs*, and *The Bulletin of the Atomic Scientists*. He is currently finishing a manuscript that traces the origins of the insurgency in Kashmir.

PERVEZ HOODBHOY is a Professor in the Department of Physics at Quaid-e-Azam University, Islamabad. He received his B.S., M.S. and Ph.D. from the Massachusetts Institute of Technology. His research interests are quantum chromodynamics, quark effects in nuclei, and nuclear phenomenology. He is the author of *Islam and Science: Religious Orthodoxy and the Battle for Rationality* (1991), and numerous articles and research publications.

MICHAEL KREPON is President of the Henry L. Stimson Center. He is the author or editor of *Strategic Stalemate: Nuclear Weapons and Arms Control in American Politics* (1984), *Verification and Compliance: A Problem-Solving Approach* (1988), *Arms Control in the Reagan Administration* (1989), *Commercial Observation Satellites and International Security* (1990), *The Politics of Arms Control Treaty Ratification* (1991), and *Open Skies. Arms Control and Cooperative Security* (1992).

PETER LAVOY is Assistant Professor of National Security Affairs at the Naval Postgraduate School, Monterey, California. His research is published in numerous journals and edited books. Before joining the Naval Postgraduate school, he was a Research Fellow at the Center for Security and Technology Studies at Lawrence Livermore National Laboratory and at the Center for International Security and Arms Control at Stanford University. He will receive his Ph.D. in Political Science from the University of California at Berkeley in 1995.

C. RAJA MOHAN obtained his Ph.D. in international relations from Jawaharlal Nehru University at New Delhi in India. From 1983 to 1992, he was Research Associate at the Institute for Defence Studies and Analyses in New Delhi. From 1992 to 1993, he was a Jennings Randolph Peace Fellow at the United States Institute of Peace, Washington D.C. He is currently the national security correspondent of *The Hindu*.

A.G. NOORANI is a lawyer and columnist based in Bombay. He writes on foreign affairs and constitutional matters for the newspaper *The Statesman*, *Frontline* magazine, and other Indian journals. He is also the author of several books including *The Brezhnev Plan for Asian Security*, *Ministers' Misconduct*, *Indian Political Trials*, and *The Kashmir Question*.

AMIT SEVAK is a lecturer at the Foreign Affairs College, Beijing, as the recipient of the 1995-96 Henry Luce Scholarship. In 1994-95, he was the coordinator of the Visiting Fellows Program at the Henry L. Stimson Center, where he also worked on confidence-building measures in Asia. He holds an M.A. with Honors in International Relations and a B.A. with Honors in Sociology and Economics from the University of Chicago.

RAJU G.C. THOMAS is professor of political science at Marquette University and co-Director of the University of Wisconsin-Milwaukee and Marquette University's joint Center for International Studies. He has been a visiting scholar at numerous universities and the author of many books on South Asian security including, *Indian Security Policy*, *South Asian Security in the 1990s*. *Democracy. Security and Development in India*. Thomas was educated at Bombay University, the London School of Economics and U.C.L.A., where he obtained his Ph.D.

ZHAO WEIWEN is a research professor at the China Institute of Contemporary International Relations, Beijing. For over forty years, she has been analyzing, researching and writing on South Asian countries, with a focus on Sino-Indian relations. Her writing has appeared in government reports and articles published in various Chinese magazines.

INDEX